D1200543

THE PARK SYNAGOGUE

3300 MAYFIELD ROAD | CLEVELAND HEIGHTS, OHIO 44118

Presented By [redacted]

In Memory Of [redacted]

KRAVITZ
MEMORIAL LIBRARY

Kravitz Memorial Library
of Park Synagogue

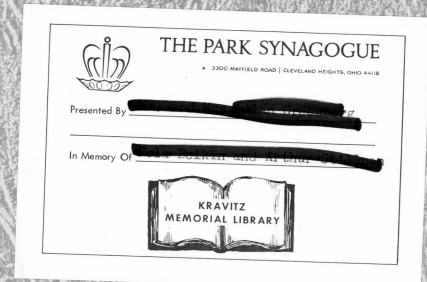

THE NEW ISRAEL ATLAS

THE NEW ISRAEL ATLAS

BIBLE TO PRESENT DAY

Zev Vilnay

Maps prepared by Carta, Jerusalem

McGraw-Hill Book Company
New York Toronto 1969

Co-published with:
ISRAEL UNIVERSITIES PRESS
(a publishing division of the
Israel Program for Scientific Translations, Ltd.
Kiryat Moshe, P.O. Box 7145, Jerusalem)

copyright © 1968, Israel Program for Scientific Translations Ltd., Jerusalem

All rights reserved. No part of this atlas may be reproduced, other than for the purpose of review, without the written permission of the Publisher.

Library of Congress Catalog Card Number: 69–19393

Translated by Moshe Aumann from the Hebrew original
Photographs by courtesy of: Government Press Office; Zionist Archives; Keren Kayemeth Leisrael; The Hebrew University, Jerusalem; Bar Ilan University, Ramat Gan; The Technion, Haifa

This atlas has been set by the Israel Program for Scientific Translations, Ltd., Jerusalem, and printed by United Artists, Tel Aviv, Israel.

956.910
Vi91

69-58

PUBLISHER'S FOREWORD

From the earliest period of civilization up to the present day the Land of Israel has played a central and unique role in the consciousness of the Western world. Geographically and geopolitically it is situated in the most strategic of positions—at the juncture of three continents. As army after army of foreign powers marched across its territory, its peoples must have wished on occasions that they could have been placed in the wings rather than on the center of the stage. But there is no escape from the fate of topography.

However, the central position of the Land of Israel was not due solely to an accident of geography. Human culture developed in this part of the world and this Land made its own especial contribution in inspiring spiritual and religious leaders, whose teachings became a universal heritage. For untold millions, Israel was the "Holy Land", revered by Jew, Christian and Moslem to whom–wherever they lived–the streets of Jerusalem seemed as familiar as those of their own towns. Indeed, medieval cartographers depicted Jerusalem as the very center of the world.

This atlas has been compiled to present in a graphic manner all these facets. Published on the 20th Anniversary of the establishment of the State of Israel, as part of the Israel Universities Press Anniversary Library, it charts the illustrious past, the checkered road to independence and the achievements of the Jewish people returning to their Land after 2,000 years of exile. It has been purposely designed as a comprehensive guide and the reader will find not only historical Biblical maps and campaign maps of the Six-Day War, but also maps showing flora and fauna, camping sites and sites of archaeological excavations.

During World War II, it was allegedly reported that vendors were selling "Map of Europe—midday edition". This atlas similarly is completely up-to-date and based on the most recent information and data available at the time of going to press.

The atlas tells the story of a thousand years of the First independent Jewish Commonwealth, fifty years of the First Exile, six hundred years of the Second Commonwealth, one thousand eight hundred seventy eight years of the Second Exile and twenty years more... Twenty years in time but many scores of years by the calculus of deeds.

It is our hope that the reader will find here both a reference book of readily understandable information and a source of subject matter for hours of study or leisure.

THE SYMBOLS IN THIS ATLAS

The problem of the transcription of place names has been dealt with simply: in modern Israel all names are given in transliteration from the Hebrew, unless they have passed into universal usage in another form, thus Jerusalem and Tiberias, and not Yerushalayim and Tveria; while in the historical maps anachronisms have been avoided: thus, the crusader town of St. Jean d'Acre is also modern 'Akko, Joppa is Yafo, Safed is Ẓefat, etc.

Ḥ is pronounced gutturally as in the Scottish *Loch*
Ẓ is pronounced ts as in *bits*

Where the 1949 Armistice lines coincide with British Mandatory boundaries they are marked ▬ ··· ▬ ···

Where they do not coincide, they are marked ....

Cease Fire Line, 1967

CONTENTS

Map No.		Page No.
	Introduction	5
	Table of Contents	6
	MODERN ISRAEL	
1	Israel in the World	9
2	Israel and the Diaspora	10
3	The Return of the Jews	11
4	Israel in the Middle East	12
5	Israel and its Neighbors	13
6	Geographical Regions	14
7	Climate : Summer	15
8	Climate : Winter	15
9	Geology	16
10	Soils	16
11	Natural Resources	17
12	Water Projects	18
13	Roads and Railroads	19
14	Ports : Sea and Air	19
15	Israel : North	20
16	Israel : South	21
17	Parks and Nature Reserves	22
18	Forests and Camping Sites	23
19	Fauna	24
20	Flora	25
21	Holy Places : Jews	26
22	Christians	26
23	Moslems	27
24	Others	27
25	Galilee	28
26	The Ḥula Valley	29
27	Lake Kinneret	29
28	Cities and Local Councils	30
29	Regional Councils	31
30	Samaria (Shomron)	32
31	The Jezreel Valley	33
32	Moshavim	34
33	The Kibbutz Movement	35
34	The Judean Hills	36
35	The Wilderness of Judea	37
36	The Population	38
37	Moslems and Christians	39
38	Druzes	39
39	The Negev	40
40	Rivers and Springs	41
41	Agriculture	42
42	Industrial Development	43
43	Universities	44
44	Yeshivot (Talmudic Academies)	45
45	Settlements Named after People : from the Bible	46
46	Settlements Named after People : Rabbis	46
47	Settlements Named after People : Christian Friends of Israel	46
48	Settlements Named after People : Zionists and Benefactors	47
49	Settlements Named after People : Pioneers and Soldiers	47
50	Sport	48
51	Tourism	49
52	From Tents to Houses	50
53	Naḥal Settlements	51
54	Israel in 1948	52
55	Israel in 1960	53
56	In the Twentieth Year . . .	54
	THE STRUGGLE FOR INDEPENDENCE	
57	The Nation Returns to its Land	57
58	Attacks on Jewish Settlements (1920, 1929, 1936-1938)	58
59	The Struggle against Restrictions (1939-1945)	59
60	The Struggle against British Policy (1945-1948)	60
61	The Vote at the United Nations	61
62	Invasion by Arab Armies	62
63	The War of Independence	63
64	Battles in the War of Independence : North	64
65	Battles in the War of Independence : South	65
66	Troubled Borders	66
67	The 1956 Sinai Campaign	67
68	The Arab Deployment for Attack 1967	68
69	Egyptian Preparations for Battle	68
70	The Six Day War : Sinai	69
71	The Six Day War : The West Bank	70
72	The Six Day War : Golan Heights	70
73	The Six Day War : The Battle for Jerusalem	71
74	War Memorials	72
	ROOTS IN THE PAST	73
75	New Settlements—Biblical names	75
76	The Ancient East	76
77	Joshua's Conquest	77
78	The Tribes of Israel	78
79	Saul's Kingdom	78
80	David and Solomon	79
81	Destruction and Exile	80
82	Return to Zion	81
83	The Hasmonaean Kingdom	82
84	Hasmonaean Campaigns	83
85	Roman Rule	84
86	Herod's Kingdom 37-4 BCE	84
87	Kingdom of Agrippa I 41-44 CE	84
88	The First Jewish Revolt	85
89	The Second Jewish Revolt	86
90	The Period of the Mishna and the Talmud	87
91	The Byzantine Period	88
92	The Persian Conquest	89
93	The Arab-Moslem Conquest	90
94	Jews under Arab-Moslem Rule	91
95	The Crusader Kingdom (1099-1291)	92
96	The Crusader Campaigns	93
97	Jews under the Crusaders and Mamelukes	94
98	Turkish Rule in the Middle East	95
99	The Jews of Palestine under the Ottoman Turks 1517-1840	96
100	Napoleon's Campaign (1799)	97
101	The Jews of Palestine under the Ottoman Turks 1840-1917	98
102	British Campaign, October 1917–September 1918	99
103	Archaeological Excavations	100
	PROPOSALS FOR A JEWISH STATE	
104	Proposals for a Jewish State	103
105	Sir Lawrence Oliphant's Proposal (1880)	103
106	Sykes-Picot Agreement 1915	104
107	Zionist Organization's Proposal	104
108	The British Mandate	105
109	The Peel Partition Plan	106
110	Partition Proposal 1938 (A)	106
111	Partition Proposal 1938 (B)	106
112	The Anglo-American Commission's Proposal	107
113	The Jewish Agency's Proposal	108
114	The U.N. Decision and the Borders of the Jewish State	108
	Gazetteer of Towns and Villages	109

modern israel

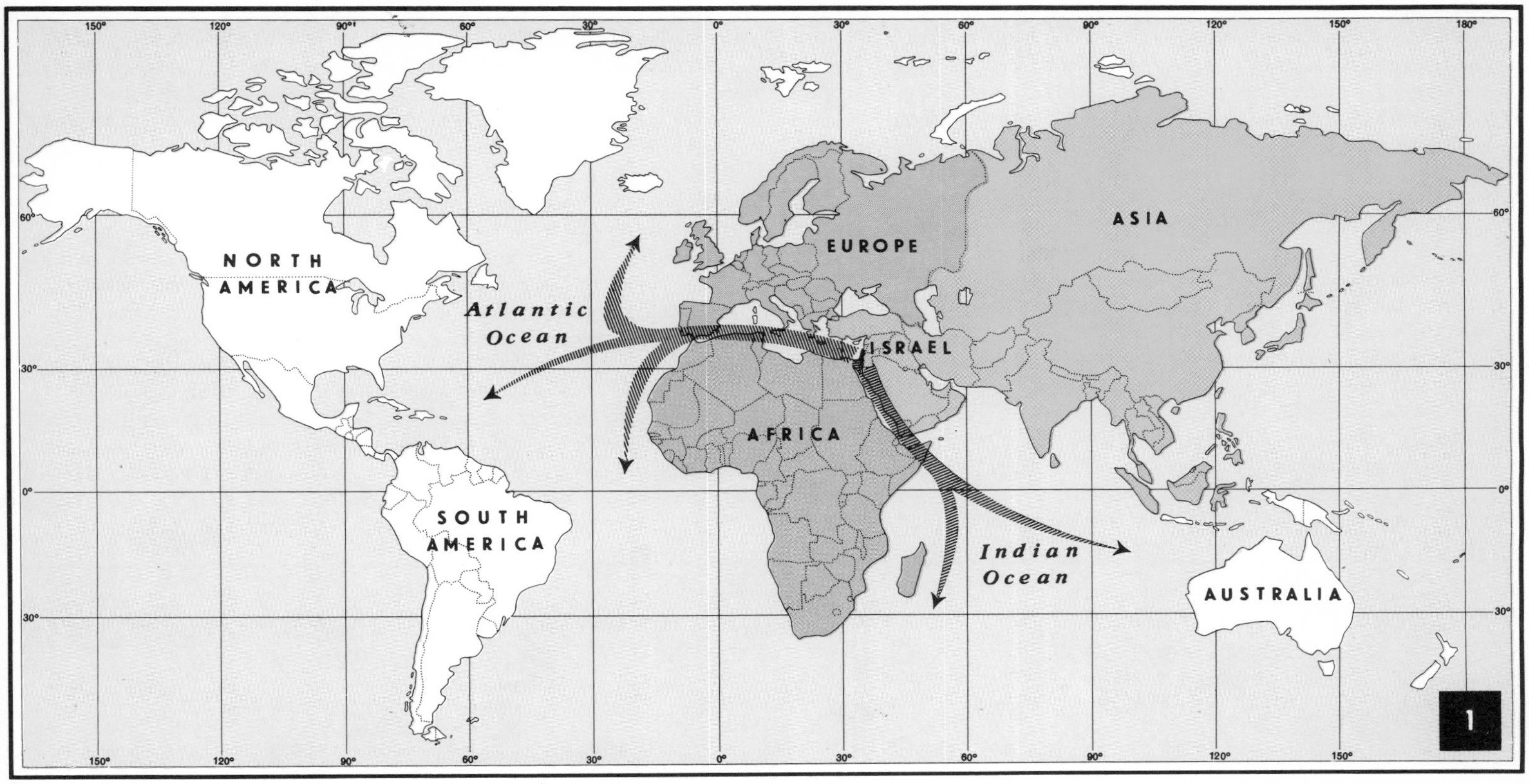

ISRAEL IN THE WORLD

LYING on the eastern shore of the Mediterranean Sea in the region known as the Near or Middle East, Israel is situated at the western extremity of Asia, close to Africa and Europe. As the cradle of human civilization and the birthplace of the monotheistic religions the country with its capital Jerusalem was regarded by the ancients as the center of the world, and appears as such in maps of the Middle Ages.

In olden times the two great powers in the region were Egypt and Assyria-Babylonia, the 'Fertile Crescent' where the earliest remains of human civilization have been uncovered. Between these two powers the Land of Israel served as a bridge, for the most important highway between them ran along the entire length of the country. This was the Biblical 'Way of the Sea,' later the Roman *'Via Maris,'* the history of which reflects the salient changes and significant events of antiquity, as for many generations merchant caravans passed over it in days of peace and armed forces in times of war.

During the course of its long history the Land of Israel was the arena in which great powers of the ancient world clashed. These events are referred to in the Bible in the exalted vision and message of the prophets of Israel. The Bible, the sublime creation of our forefathers in their homeland during many centuries, has been translated into most major languages and is known as the Book of Books by much of mankind.

In succeeding generations the Land of Israel played an important role in events of large significance. Here the conquests of Alexander the Great paved the way for the penetration into the east of Hellenistic culture, which exercised a profound influence on the people, the life and the history of the region.

The growing ascendancy of the Roman empire was accompanied by the conquest of the country, for long part of Rome's most easterly province. At the beginning of the seventh century, Arab-Moslem nomads, bursting out of the confines of the Arabian Desert, subjugated the country and the neighboring lands, but in the extraordinary extent of subsequent Moslem conquests, Palestine constituted no more than a small domain. It witnessed a clash of formidable proportions in the Middle Ages between Islam and Christianity as Crusaders from various European countries, making their way to the Holy Land, conquered it from the Moslems. For almost two hundred years the country continued to be the scene of bloody conflicts between the two sides, until the Moslems defeated the Christians and re-established their rule over Palestine. Thereafter, at the beginning of the sixteenth century, the Turks conquered the land, which was during four centuries a poverty-stricken province of the great Ottoman Empire.

The Holy Land in the center of the world, H. Bunting, 1580

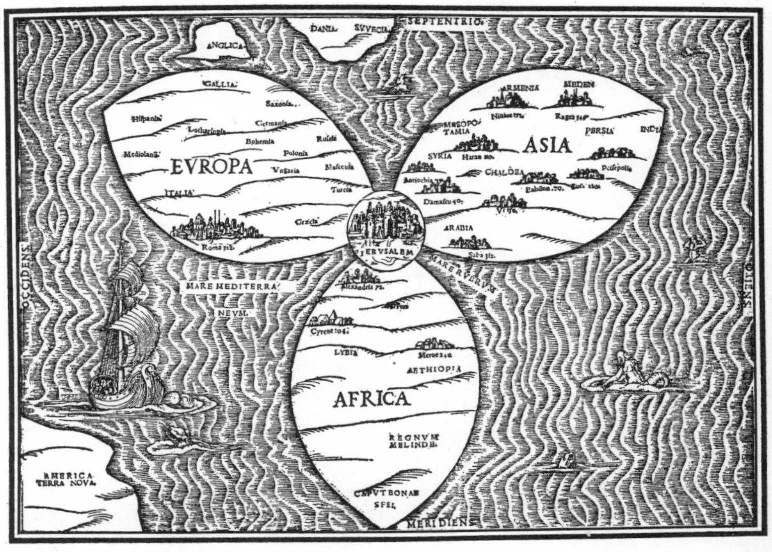

ISRAEL AND THE DIASPORA

IN BIBLICAL times, up to the destruction of the First Temple, the people of Israel lived in its own land. With the destruction of the Temple, many went into exile, and Jewish centers sprang up in neighboring countries: Egypt, Babylonia, Syria and Asia Minor. In the generations that followed, wars and oppressive decrees issued by foreign conquerors led to a dwindling of the Jewish population of Israel—which, under Roman rule, came to be known as 'Palestine'—and a corresponding expansion of the Diaspora throughout the Middle East and, during the Middle Ages, to much of Europe as well. In the course of time, the Jewish migrations also reached the distant shores of America, South Africa and Australia, where the foundations were laid for flourishing Jewish communities.

At the start of the twentieth century there were some 5,000,000 Jews in Czarist Russia and about 2,000,000 in the Austro-Hungarian Empire. Large concentrations of Jews were to be found in Germany (600,000), Britain (200,000), the Ottoman Empire, excluding Palestine (240,000), and America (about 1,000,000). In Palestine there were at this time about 65,000 Jews, nearly all of them living in the holy cities of Jerusalem, Hebron, Zefat and Tiberias.

War, revolution and vicious antisemitism contributed to more Jewish migration to the West, to the New World. But some turned their backs on the Diaspora and made their way to the Holy Land.

The monstrous campaign of the mass murder of European Jewry unleashed in 1941 by the Nazi German regime swept across Europe during the Second World War, eradicating not only individuals and families but entire communities from one end of the Continent to the other. Many of the remnants of that slaughter, after great trials and hardships, found a home in Israel, with the aid of their brothers and sisters there and in other parts of the world.

When Israel regained her independence in 1948, there were some 650,000 Jews in the country. That historic event was the signal for the influx of masses of Jews from all over the world, but particularly of refugees from the European holocaust and from the Moslem lands of North Africa and the Near East. Within a short period the population of Israel trebled; today it stands at two and a half million.

Beyond the borders of Israel, the largest Jewish community today is to be found in the United States, where it numbers over 5 million. In second place is the Soviet Union, with about $2\frac{1}{2}$ million. Communities of upwards of 100,000 are to be found in Britain, France, Romania, Canada, Argentina, Brazil; Morocco and South Africa.

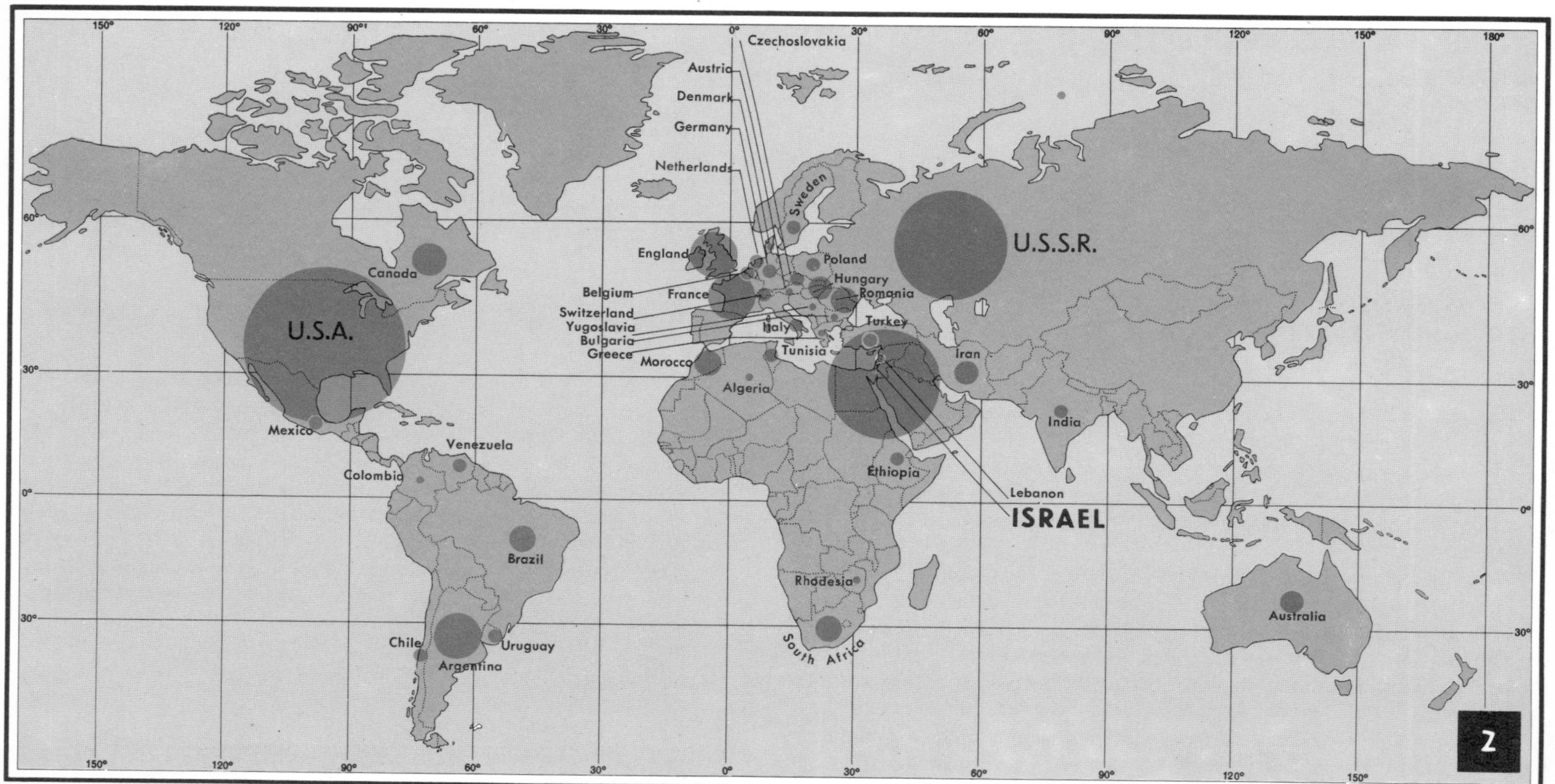

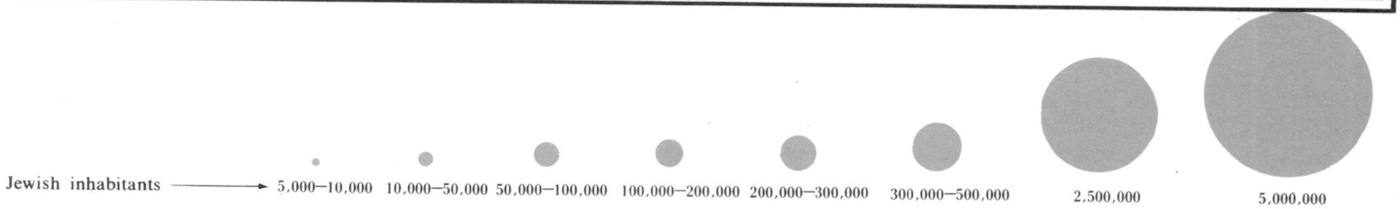

Jewish inhabitants
5,000—10,000
10,000—50,000
50,000—100,000
100,000—200,000
200,000—300,000
300,000—500,000
2,500,000
5,000,000

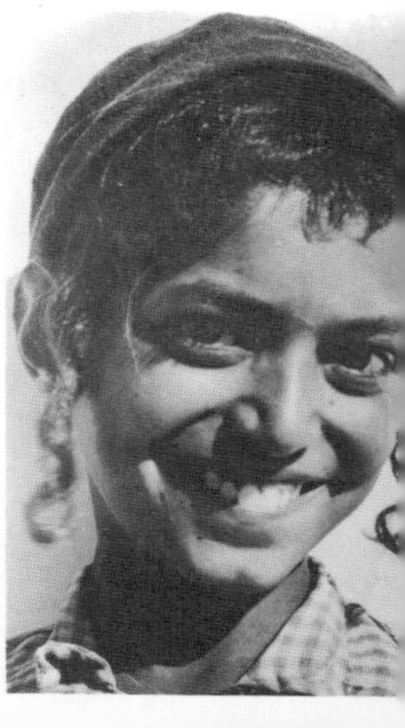

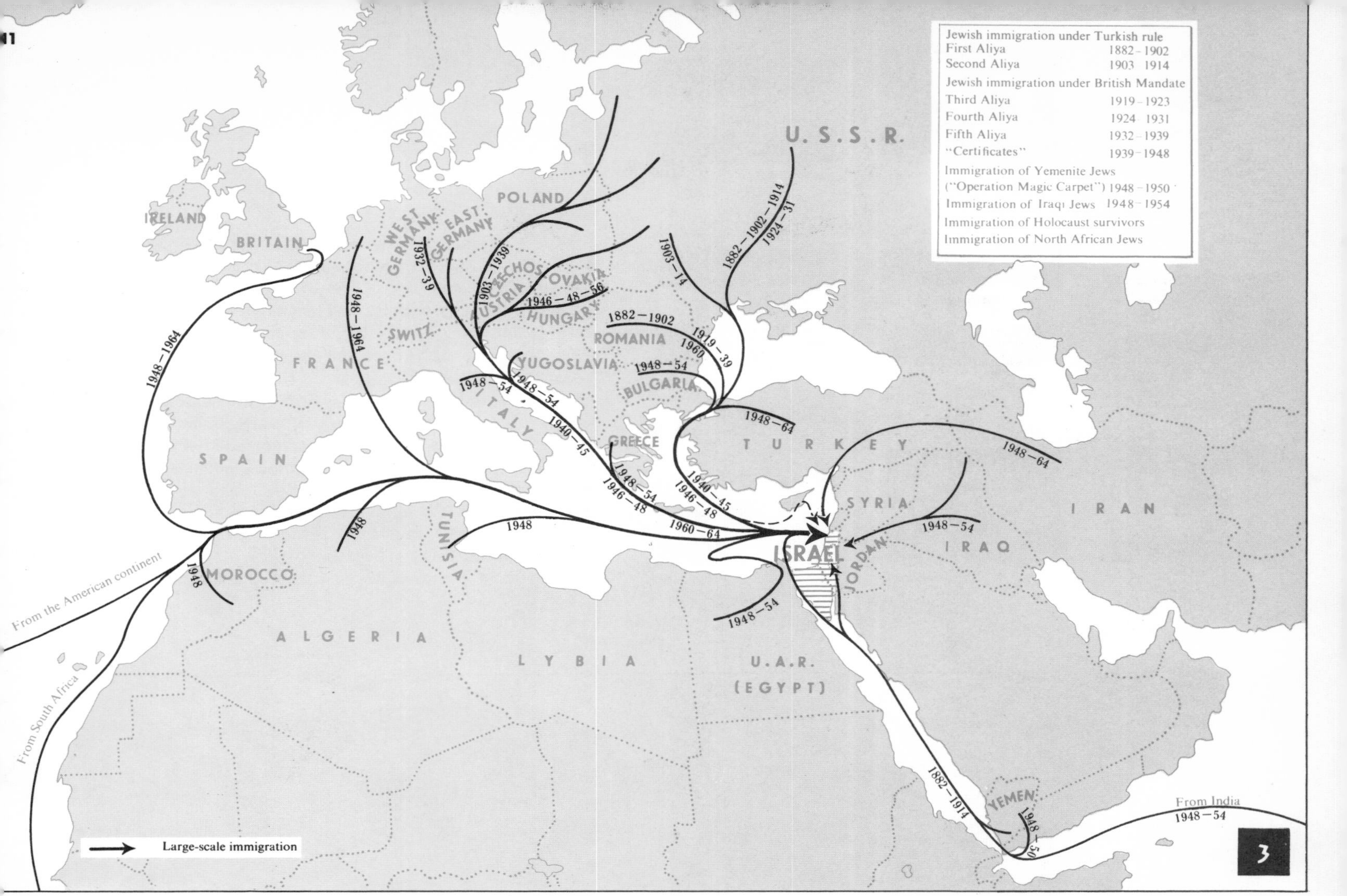

THE RETURN OF THE JEWS

JEWISH settlement of Israel after the destruction of the Second Temple may be traced back as far as the period following the defeat of Bar-Kochba, when Jews from the Diaspora came to settle in Israel, mainly in the holy cities. The immigrants came from Babylonia (Iraq of today) and from neighboring Egypt. In Israel they joined their brethren—Jews who had been living in the land for generations, who spoke Arabic and whose way of life was similar to that of their Arab neighbors.

With the expulsion of the Jews from Spain, at the end of the fifteenth century, many of the Spanish exiles boldly turned eastward and made their way to Israel. The Arabic-speaking Jewish population in the Holy Land thus was augmented by a Spanish-Jewish (or Sephardic) element, whose speech was the Judeo-Spanish dialect known as Ladino. They were followed, in subsequent generations, by Yiddish-speaking Ashkenazim (Jews from central and eastern Europe) who, as their numbers grew, began to set up synagogues and institutions of their own.

The birth and development of the *"Ḥovevei Ẓion"* (Lovers of Zion) movement in the nineteenth century witnessed the immigration to Israel—from Russia, Romania, Poland and Lithuania—of young men and women deeply imbued with nationalist feelings, who laid the foundations of new rural settlements in various parts of the country. The Hebrew tongue, which had been dormant for centuries, its use limited to liturgy and legal dissertations, was revived as the language of daily life among the people of Israel in their homeland.

In the wake of World War I, with the government of Palestine passing into the hands of the British under a mandate from the League of Nations, immigration, which had slackened off during the war years, increased once more, chiefly from the countries of eastern Europe. The Nazis' rise to power and the start of anti-Jewish persecution in Germany produced a wave of Jewish immigration from that country, and these immigrants, too, founded a number of new towns and settlements in Israel. In the years that followed, immigration continued, and the rural and urban development of the country made unprecedented strides forward. Even the British-imposed restrictions on Jewish immigration during and immediately after World War II failed to halt the influx of Jews to their homeland.

The rebirth of the State of Israel set in motion a stream of immigration from all over the world.

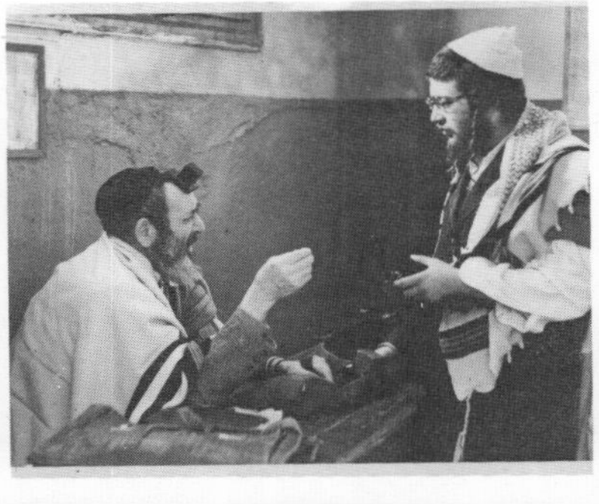

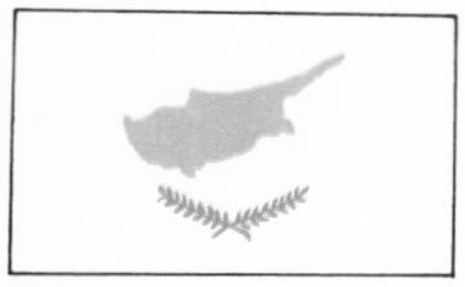
CYPRUS

TURKEY

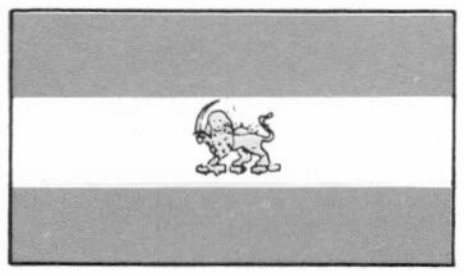
IRAN

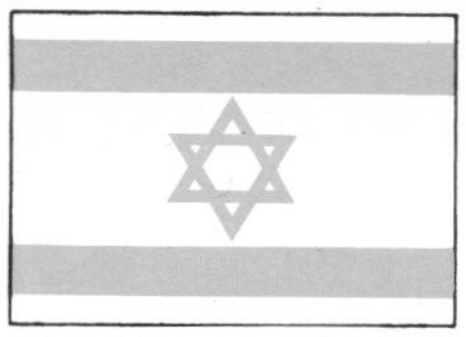
ISRAEL

ISRAEL IN THE MIDDLE EAST

JORDAN

EGYPT

SYRIA

LEBANON

SAUDI ARABIA

IRAQ

ISRAEL is situated in the Middle, or Near East, a region formerly known, among Europeans, as the Orient or the Levant.

Most of the countries of the Middle East—a region marked by a variety of peoples, cultures and languages—are part of the continent of Asia, and the majority of its inhabitants are Moslems, the rest being Christians of various denominations and members of other faiths.

Israel's central geographic position in the Middle East makes it a natural bridge between the countries and peoples of the region, and therein lies both its historic importance and its potential value to its neighbors. Current political enmities limit Israel's role in this capacity at the present time.

Down through the ages, large Jewish communities have lived in the Middle East, some of them tracing their ancestry in those lands back to Biblical times. These Jews often played an important role particularly in the commercial life of these countries.

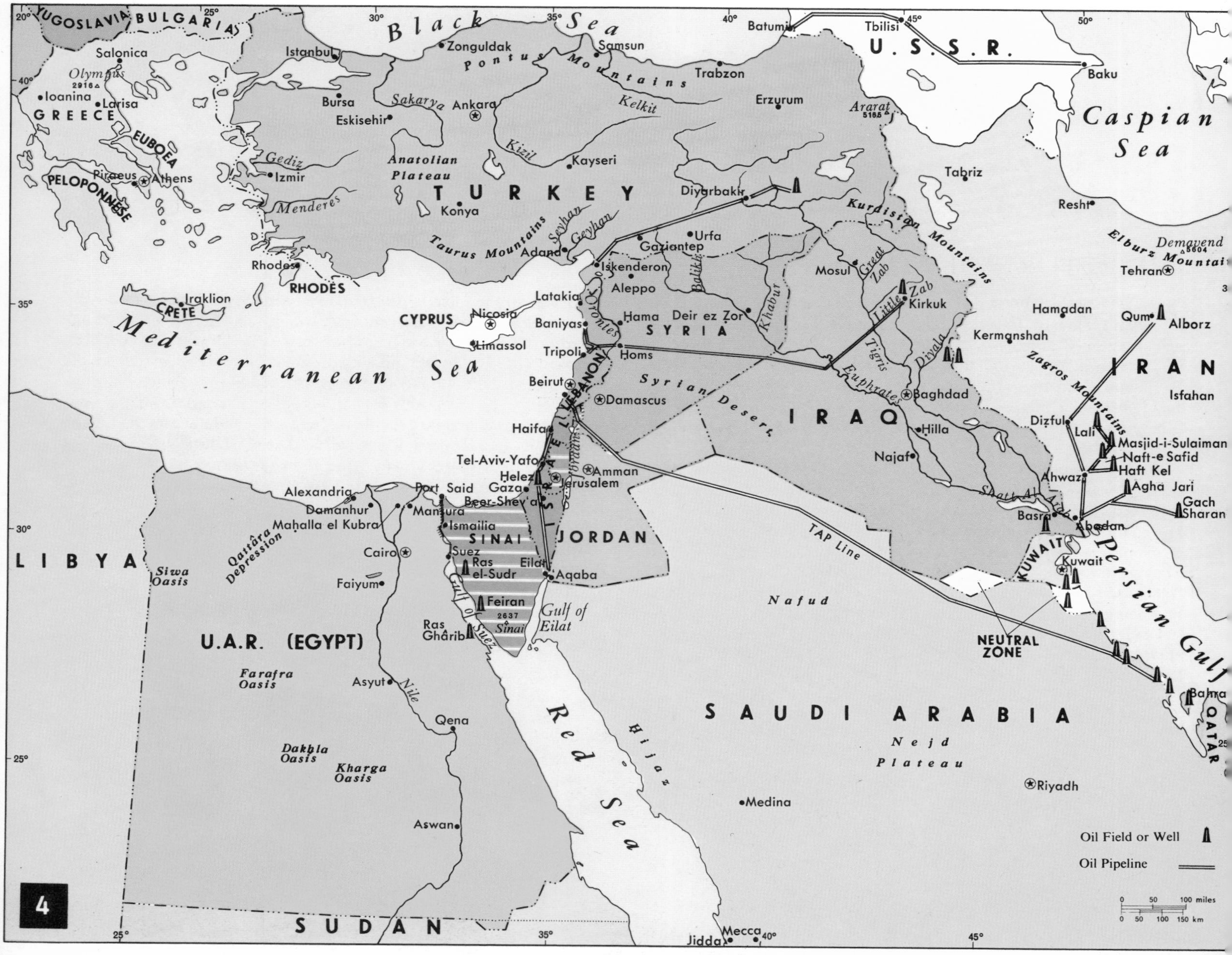

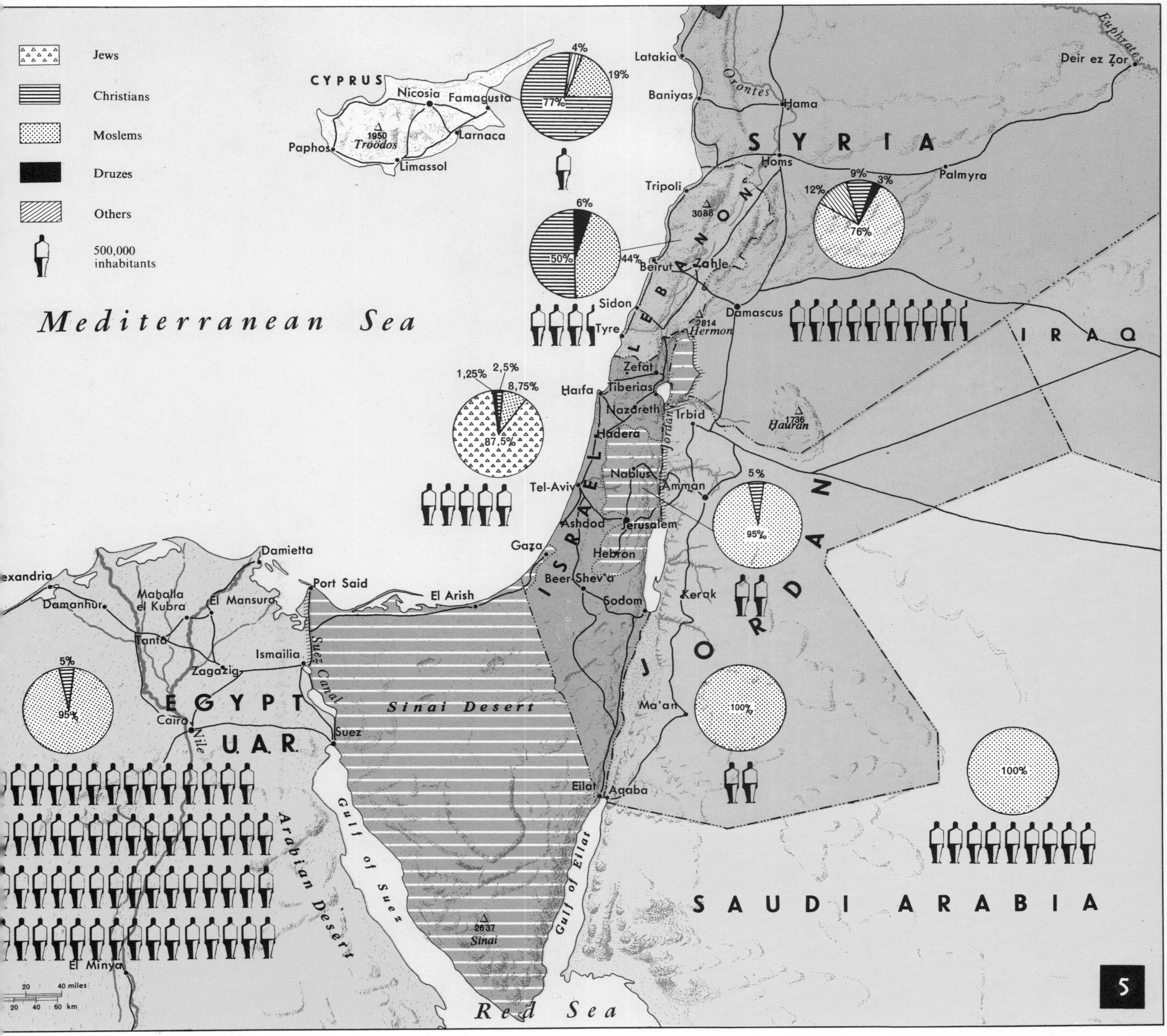

ISRAEL AND ITS NEIGHBORS

ISRAEL borders on four States: in the north—Lebanon; in the northeast—Syria; in the east—Jordan (officially: the Hashemite Kingdom of Jordan); and in the southwest—Egypt (officially: the United Arab Republic). Egypt is part of the African continent; the other countries mentioned, including Israel itself, are in Asia.

Most of the inhabitants of the neighboring countries are Moslems, and their language is Arabic. They belong, for the most part, to the Sunnite sect of Islam, whose members accept the Koran and orthodox Islamic tradition. In Syria and Lebanon are small communities of Shi'ite Moslems and large communities of Druzes. Lebanon is the birthplace of the Druze religion and Jebel Druze (Druze Mountain), in Syria, has the largest concentration of Druzes in the Near East.

Also to be found in the neighboring lands are Christians of various denominations, some of them of very early origin. A substantial percentage of the population in Lebanon are Christians, most of them Maronites, whose faith is very close to Catholicism. Egypt has a large community of Copts, who are in fact the oldest part of the Egyptian population; theirs is a separate Church in the Christian world.

Until recent years, large Jewish communities likewise played an important role particularly in the economic life of these countries, but Arab enmity towards Israel has had an adverse effect on their fortunes, and they have increasingly been subjected to degradation, discrimination, imprisonment and confiscation of property. Many have emigrated to Israel and to countries outside the Middle East.

GEOGRAPHICAL REGIONS

ISRAEL is a land of many contrasting geographical regions—formations of land and water exhibiting widely divergent and often highly distinctive characteristics. Many of the country's physical features carry historical associations going back to Biblical times.

The *Jordan Valley* runs the entire length of the land from north to south and includes the Dead Sea—the lowest spot on the earth's surface.

Galilee, in the north, constitutes the highest terrain in Israel, its loftiest elevation being Mt. Meron (3,692 ft.). Upper Galilee stretches from the Mediterranean coast in the west to the Ḥula Valley in the east. Lower Galilee extends from the Mediterranean to Lake Kinneret (the Sea of Galilee)—the lowest surface in the region (650 ft. below sea level).

The *Jezreel Valley*—popularly known as *Ha'emek* ('The Valley')—is the largest one in the country. At its eastern end it links up with the central Jordan Valley via the Beit Shean Valley, while in the west it meets the Zevulun Valley, running northward to the Mediterranean coast.

The hilly terrain of *Samaria* extends from the Jezreel Valley southward. Two extensions of the Samarian mountain chain are Mt. Gilbo'a in the east, and Mt. Carmel in the west.

The coastal strip between the Samarian foothills and the Mediterranean Sea is called the *Sharon Plain*. The Sharon Plain constitutes Israel's coastal link between Galilee in the north and the Judean Hills and the Negev to the south.

The *Shefela* is, in effect, the southern continuation of the Sharon Plain. Inhabited in ancient times by the Philistines of Bible fame, it is bordered on the west by the Mediterranean and on the east by the Hills of Judea and the northern Negev plateau.

The *Judean Hills* stretch southward from Jerusalem toward Beer-Shev'a.

In the south, covering the major part of the country, lies the wild, mountainous area known as the *Negev*. Some of its peaks reach altitudes approaching 3,400 feet. At its southwestern border it touches the Sinai desert.

Between the Negev plateau, to the west, and the Mountains of Edom (Jordan), to the east, we find the *'Arava*, the long, barren plain stretching southward from the Dead Sea to Eilat, Israel's Red Sea port.

Jordan entering Lake Kinneret

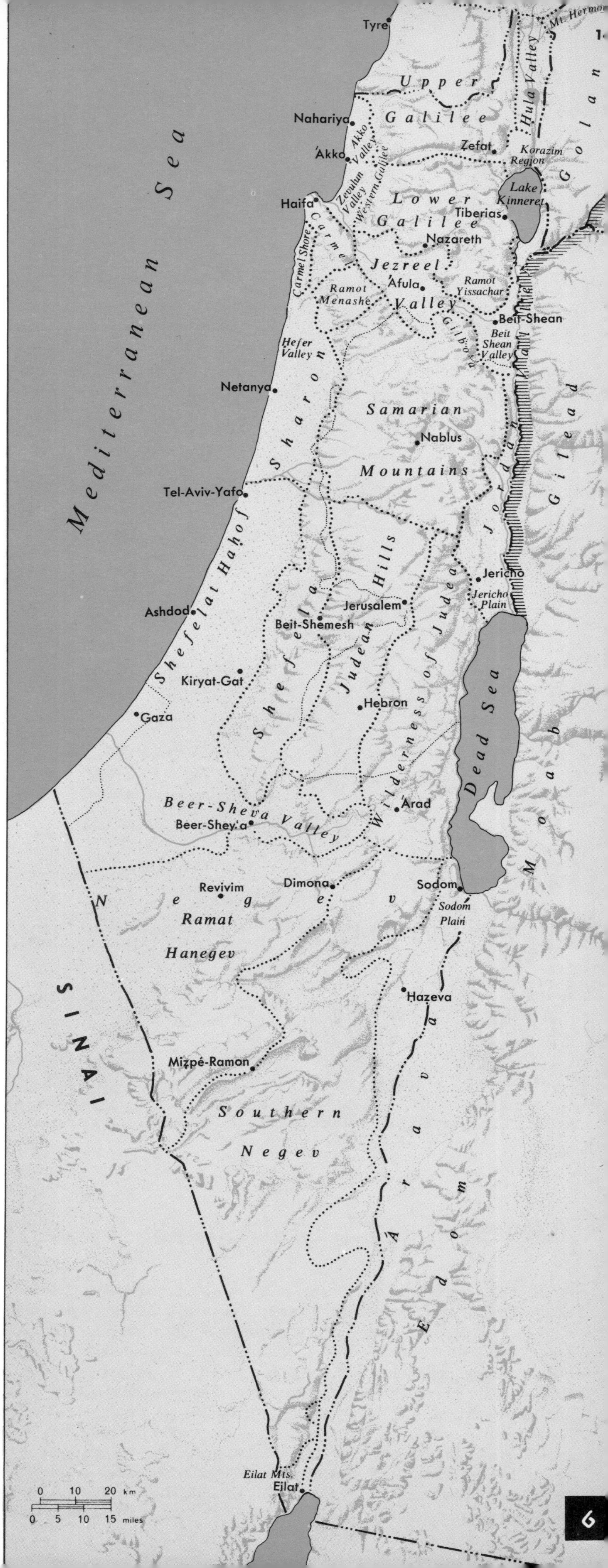

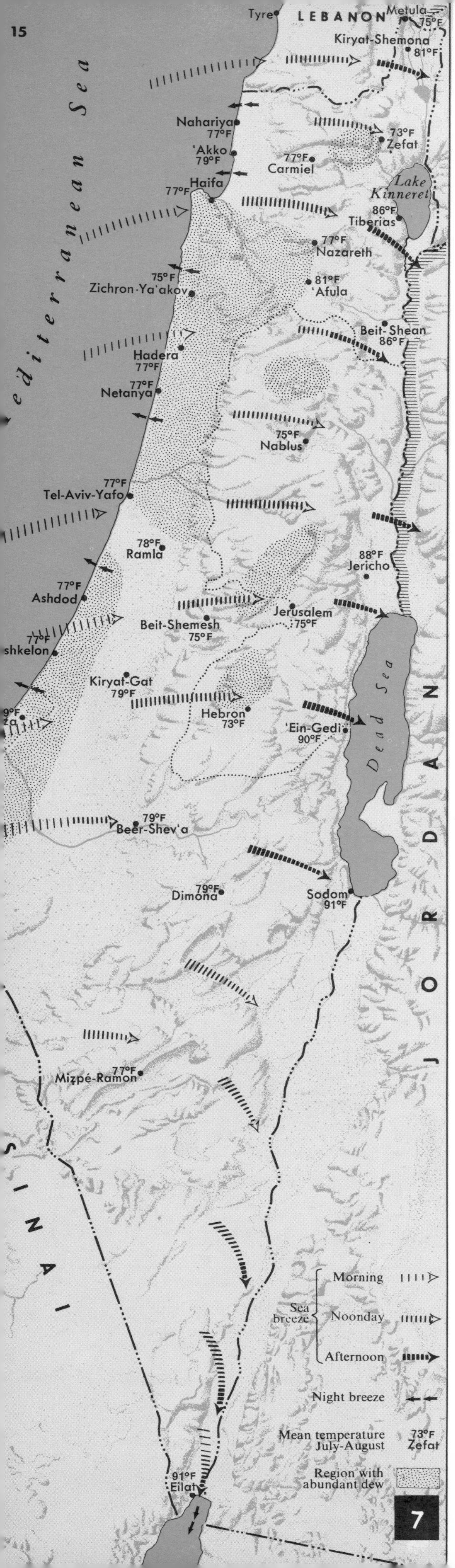

7

CLIMATE

THE YEAR is divided into two main seasons—a sunny summer and a rainy winter.

SUMMER

Generally, the *summer* begins in May and lasts until October. The air is dry, the skies clear, and in the coastal area the nights bring dew. Average minimum and maximum temperatures in August (usually the hottest month) range from 65°-85° F. in the hills of Jerusalem and Galilee to 80°-104° F. at the Red Sea port of Eilat. Sea breezes along the coast and mountain breezes in the hilly areas exercise a moderating influence on the summer temperatures in those areas. Occasionally, especially early and late in the season, a hot, dry desert wind—known by its Arabic name, *'hamsin'*—sweeps in from the east.

Aside from Eilat, the hottest areas in the country are the Dead Sea and the Jordan Valley. Temperature differences between day and night are greatest in the Negev, where differentials of more than 30° F. have been recorded in a single 24-hour period.

WINTER

The *winter* generally extends from November to April. Rain falls at intervals throughout this period, bringing much-needed moisture to the parched earth and new life to the country's vegetation. Heavy downpours are not unusual in winter, causing flooding and, where the soil is not adequately protected by trees or terracing, erosion. Nearly every year there is some snow in the mountain areas, especially in Upper Galilee.

Galilee is the coldest and wettest region, the mercury frequently dipping below freezing point and the annual rainfall averaging more than 40 inches. The driest region in Israel is the Negev, its southern part receiving only 1 to 2 inches of rain in most years. Again, Tel-Aviv and the Coastal Plain strike a happy medium: temperature range in January—47°-65° F.; rainfall—20-30 inches in most years.

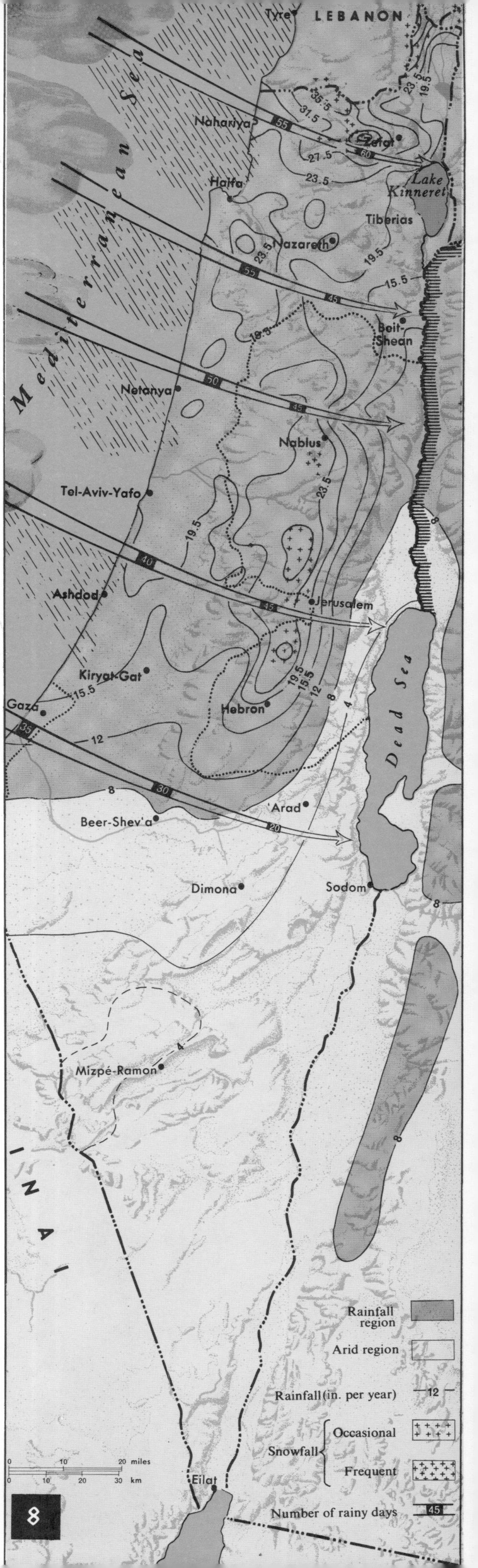

8

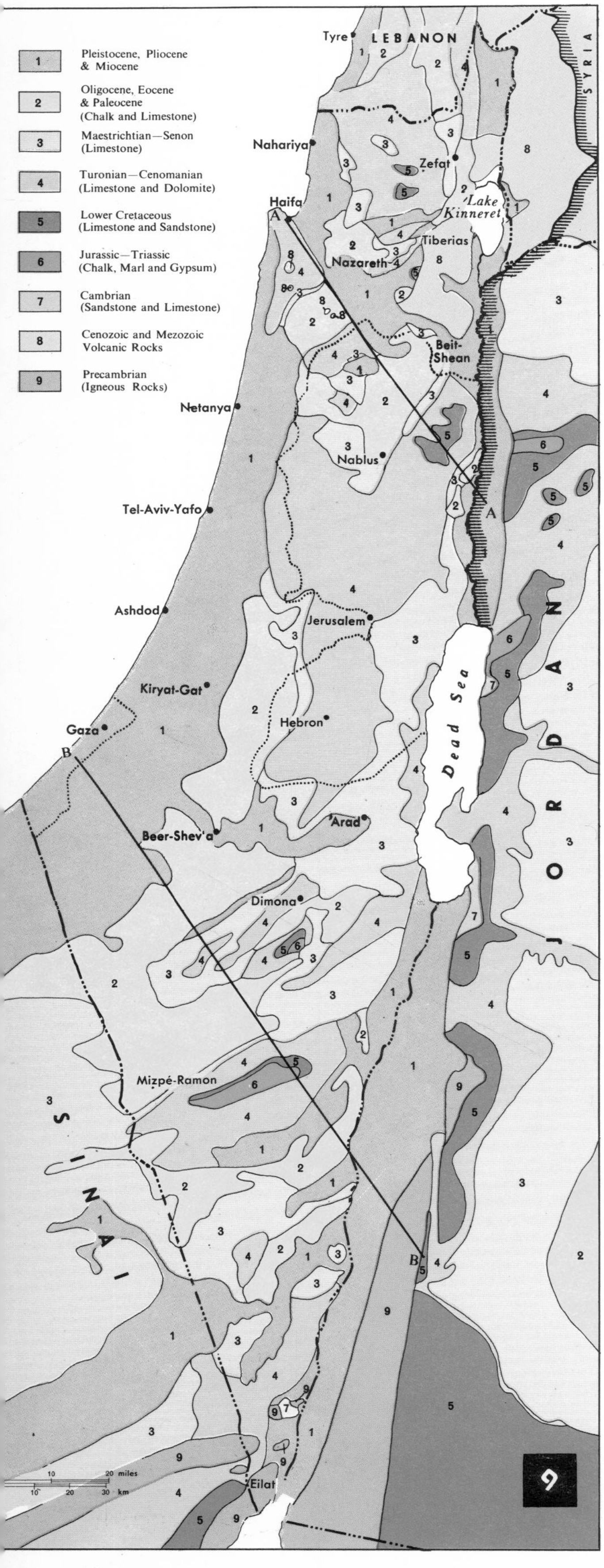

GEOLOGY

THIS geological map, which is drawn in the most general terms, shows that within the limited area of Israel, rock formations representing nearly every known geological period are to be found, going back as far as the Cambrian Period (in the Eilat area) more than 500 million years ago. Guided by the order of the appearance of these formations, their distribution and their characteristics, geologists are studying and piecing together not only the structure but also the history of the land. The two cross-sections—one along the breadth of the northern part of the country, the other across the Negev—illustrate the folds that are characteristic of these formations and the faults that run across them. As a result of the pre-historic upheavals indicated by these folds and faults, some of the mountains in the area settled, creating inner valleys such as the Jezreel Valley.

SOILS

GEOGRAPHICAL, geological and climatic factors account for the presence of different types of soil in various parts of the country. In the mountain area, a heavy, reddish earth—*Terra Rossa*—also known by its Arabic name *Hamra,* red earth, is found. The Coastal Plain is covered with a layer of soil brought down from the mountains by erosion, while adjacent to the seacoast itself, strips of sand and limestone may be found.

In Eastern Galilee there are substantial areas covered with basalt soils (black lava). Fertile loess soil is to be found in the northern part of the Negev, while further south are wide expanses of parched, arid soil, overlaid with dark flintstone called Ḥammada. Along the ‘Arava valley are substantial areas of sand swept down from the adjacent mountainsides. In the lower portions of this region—particularly in the Sodom (Dead Sea) and Eilat (Red Sea) areas—there are saline soils.

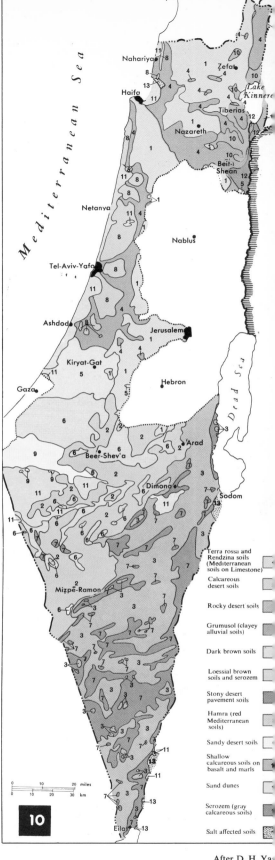

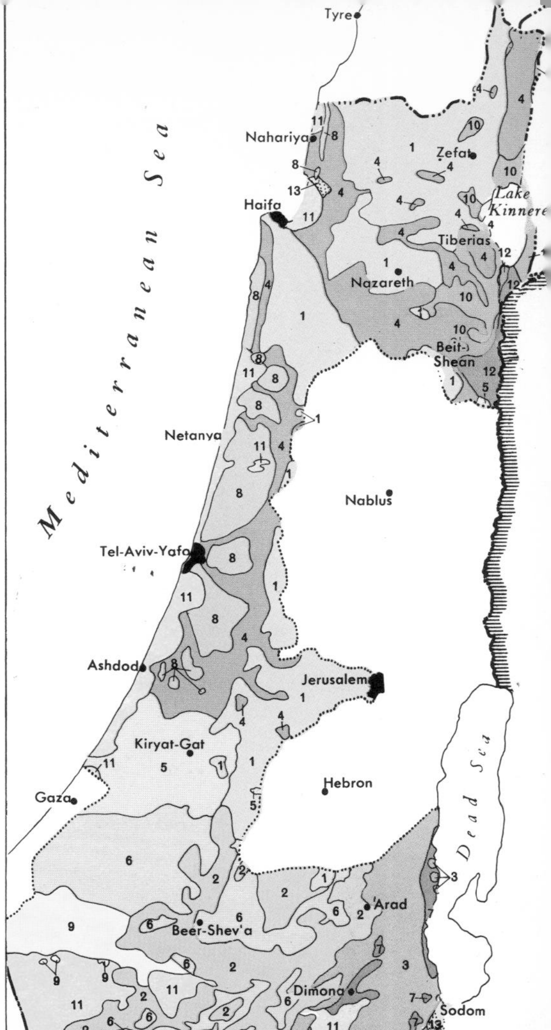

After D. H. Ya

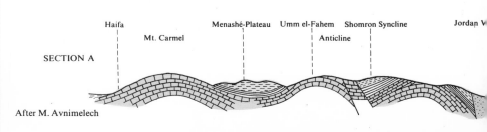

After M. Avnimelech

Mineral wealth of the Dead Sea

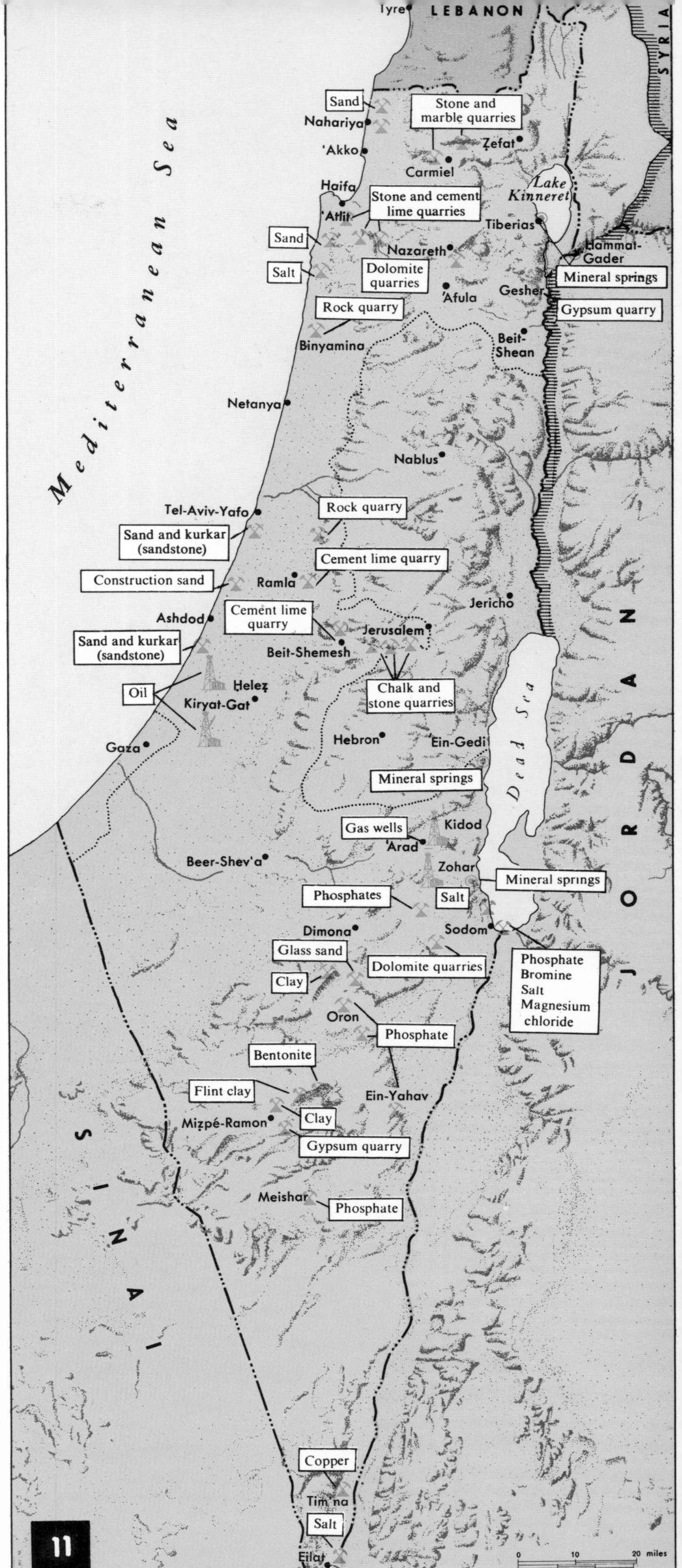

NATURAL RESOURCES

ISRAEL'S soil and waters yield natural resources of various kinds, which are exploited both for domestic use and for export.

Building stone of different types and grades (including marble) is found in the mountain areas. *Copper* is mined at Timn'a, in the far south, and, after processing, is exported via the nearby port of Eilat. *Iron* ores are found in Eastern Galilee and in the Negev; the method of exploitation has not been finally determined. *Phosphates*—in various parts of the Negev. At Oron, near Dimona, there are modern facilities for rapid and efficient quarrying and processing of this mineral, large quantities of which are shipped to the Chemicals and Fertilizers concern in Haifa for the production of super-phosphates for the domestic market and export. *Gypsum*—in large quantities in north and south, used chiefly in Israel's cement industry. *Glass-sand*—in the central Negev, used domestically in the glass industry. *Clay*—in the central Negev; an important element in the ceramics industry and in the manufacture of fireproof bricks. *Oil*—in the southern Coastal Plain, in the general vicinity of Ashkelon. *Natural Gas*—in the 'Arad region, serving the domestic requirements of 'Arad but used mainly as a source of energy for the Dead Sea Works, to which it is delivered by pipeline. *Potash* and *bromine*—in the Dead Sea. Exploitation began under the Mandatory regime, with plants being set up on the northern and southern shores of the sea. The events of 1948 and the resultant political division of the Dead Sea led to the abandonment of the northern plant and the gradual expansion of the southern one, in Israel territory, at Sodom. Most of the potash and bromine extracted by the Dead Sea Works is exported, mainly to Europe and the Far East. *Common Salt* is derived from two sources: the Mediterranean Sea (processed at 'Atlit) and the Dead Sea (processed at Sodom). Actually, the Dead Sea provides two sources—the briny waters of the sea itself and the salty rock of the mountains that line the shore.

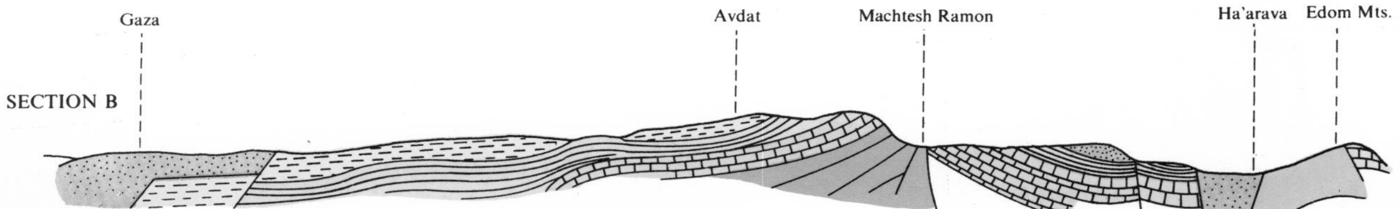

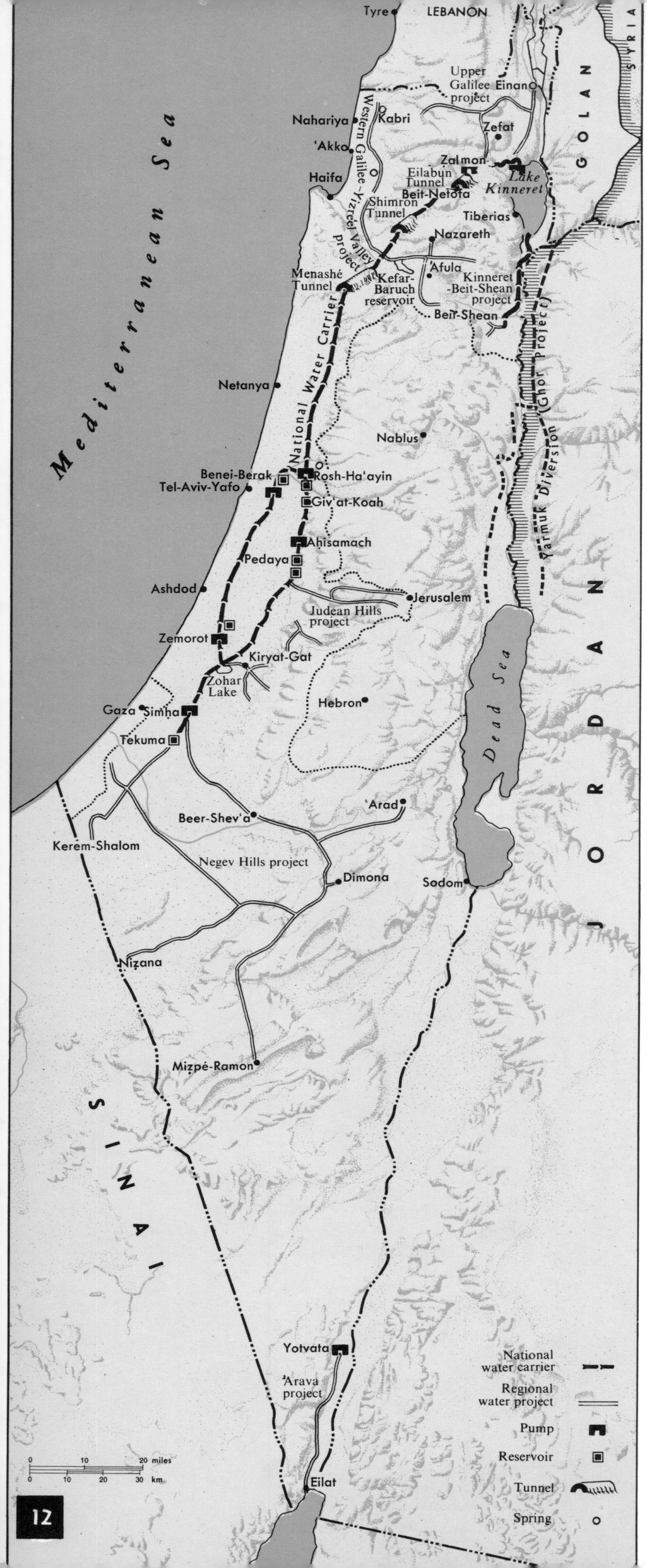
Tyre
LEBANON
SYRIA
GOLAN
Mediterranean Sea
Upper Galilee Einan project
Western Galilee–Yizre'el Valley project
Nahariya
Kabri
Zefat
'Akko
Zalmon
Haifa
Eilabun Tunnel
Lake Kinneret
Beit-Netofa
Shimron Tunnel
Tiberias
Nazareth
'Afula
Menashé Tunnel
Kefar-Baruch reservoir
Kinneret -Beit-Shean project
Beit-Shean
Yarmuk Diversion (Ghor project)
National Water Carrier
Netanya
Nablus
Benei-Berak
Rosh-Ha'ayin
Tel-Aviv-Yafo
Giv'at-Koah
Ahisamach
Pedaya
Ashdod
Jerusalem
Judean Hills project
Zemorot
Kiryat-Gat
Zohar Lake
Dead Sea
Gaza
Simha
Hebron
Tekuma
JORDAN
'Arad
Beer-Shev'a
Kerem-Shalom
Negev Hills project
Dimona
Sodom
Nizana
Mizpé-Ramon
SINAI
Yotvata
'Arava project
National water carrier
Regional water project
Pump
Reservoir
Tunnel
Spring
0 10 20 miles
0 10 20 30 km
Eilat

WATER PROJECTS

ISRAEL'S central water project starts at a point on the north western shore of Lake Kinneret (Sea of Galilee) and continues westward and southward more than half the length of the country, piping water from Lake Kinneret and the Yarkon River to the parched lands of the Negev.

The main pumping station is at Eshed-Kinnrot, on the Kinneret shore, nearly 700 feet below the level of the Mediterranean Sea. The subterranean pumps force the water up through a pipe concealed in the mountainside. Using the siphon principle, the pipes go down into a deep ravine (Naḥal 'Amud) and up the opposite side, and there deliver their waters into an open channel through which they flow, by force of gravity, westward to the Ẓelamon Reservoir. At this point, a second pumping station pumps the water up, through a pipeline, to the 2,600-foot-long 'Eilabun Tunnel (named after the near-by Arab village)—the highest point reached by the Carrier, nearly 1,200 feet above its starting point.

From the 'Eilabun Tunnel the water flows once more into an open channel built along the Beit-Netofa Valley in Lower Galilee, comes to a dam built across the Ẓippori riverbed and emerges from the valley near Kibbutz Hassolelim. After continuing through the foothills of Lower Galilee, the water passes through a second tunnel (Shimron), continues along an underground pipeline southward across the Jezreel Valley, through the Menashé 'A' Tunnel—longest (4 miles) in Israel—and then through Menashé 'B' Tunnel, at the northern end of the Samarian Mountains.

From this point, the water flows—again, by force of gravity—through a 108-inch underground pipeline down the length of the Sharon Plain for about 35 miles to Rosh-Ha'ayin, the sources of the Yarkon River. Here the waters of the Kinneret join the waters of the Yarkon and continue their way southward through two parallel subterranean pipes to the Zohar Reservoir, in the Lachish area, where they rejoin in a single pipeline for the last lap of the journey which ends in the Tekuma Reservoir, in the western Negev. From this point, the water is distributed to various parts of the Negev—to slake the thirst of man and beast and help fructify the soil.

Thanks to this project, a parched, water-starved wasteland is being transformed, over the years, into a fertile, closely settled region.

ROADS AND RAILROADS

ISRAEL has a well-developed road network; there is not a village or settlement that cannot be reached by car. The main traffic artery is a highway traversing the length of the country from north to south, passing, for most of the distance, along the famous coastal route of ancient times. Another important road is the highway going up to Jerusalem from Tel-Aviv and the Coastal Plain; this route is served also by several alternate roads running parallel to various segments of the main road.

Since Israel's independence in 1948, numerous new roads have been constructed—roads of considerable importance to the economy and security of the nation. Most of these are in the Negev, branching off from Beer-Shev'a. Two lead to Sodom—one via Dimona, the other, more recent road, via the new town of 'Arad—dropping more than 3,000 feet in altitude on their precipitous course to the Dead Sea shore. A road running through the heart of the Negev southward to Eilat opened up the country to maritime trade with East Africa and the Far East. Along this highway, and by way of the Red Sea port of Eilat, Israel trades with the East and Africa. The Sodom-'Arad-Beer-Shev'a link continues westward to the new Mediterranean port of Ashdod, through which the products of the Dead Sea Works are shipped to the West. *Railroad lines,* old and new, link Israel's three major cities—Jerusalem, Tel-Aviv and Haifa—as well as Beer-Shev'a, with Lod, in the center of the country, which is the central point of these lines. The Tel Aviv-Jerusalem line is the oldest, dating back to Turkish times. The British laid the groundwork for the Tel-Aviv-Haifa line in World War I, but the Israel Government added a set of tracks along the coast as an alternative to that segment of the old line that skirted the Jordanian border.

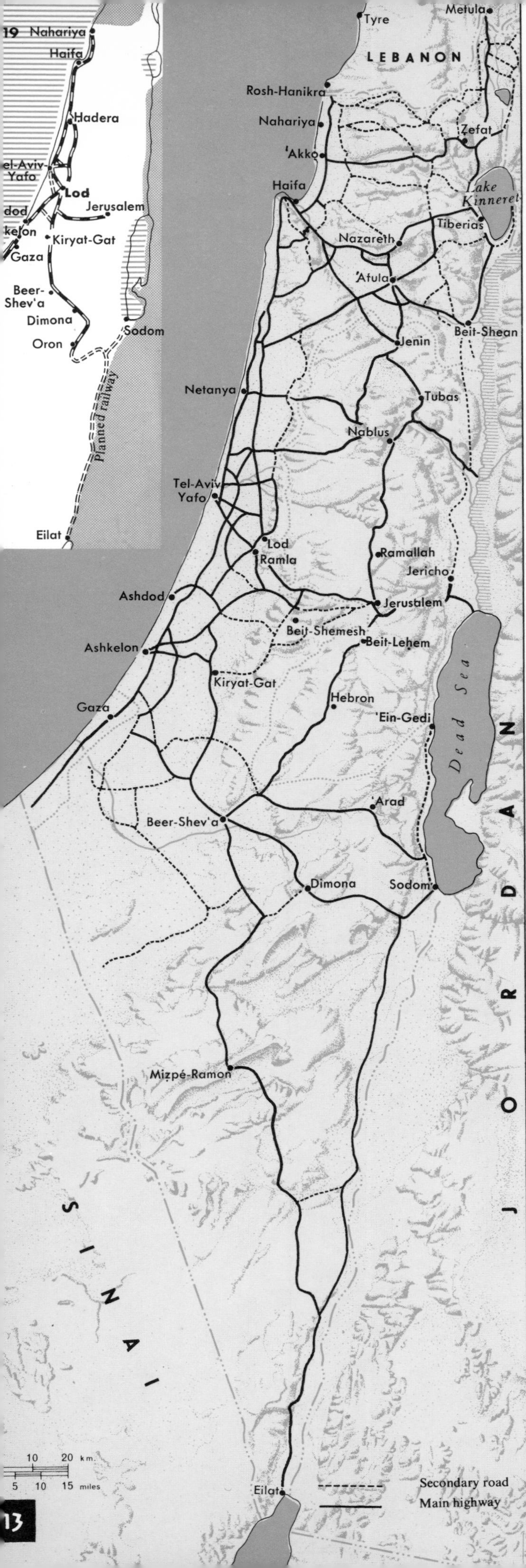

PORTS: SEA AND AIR

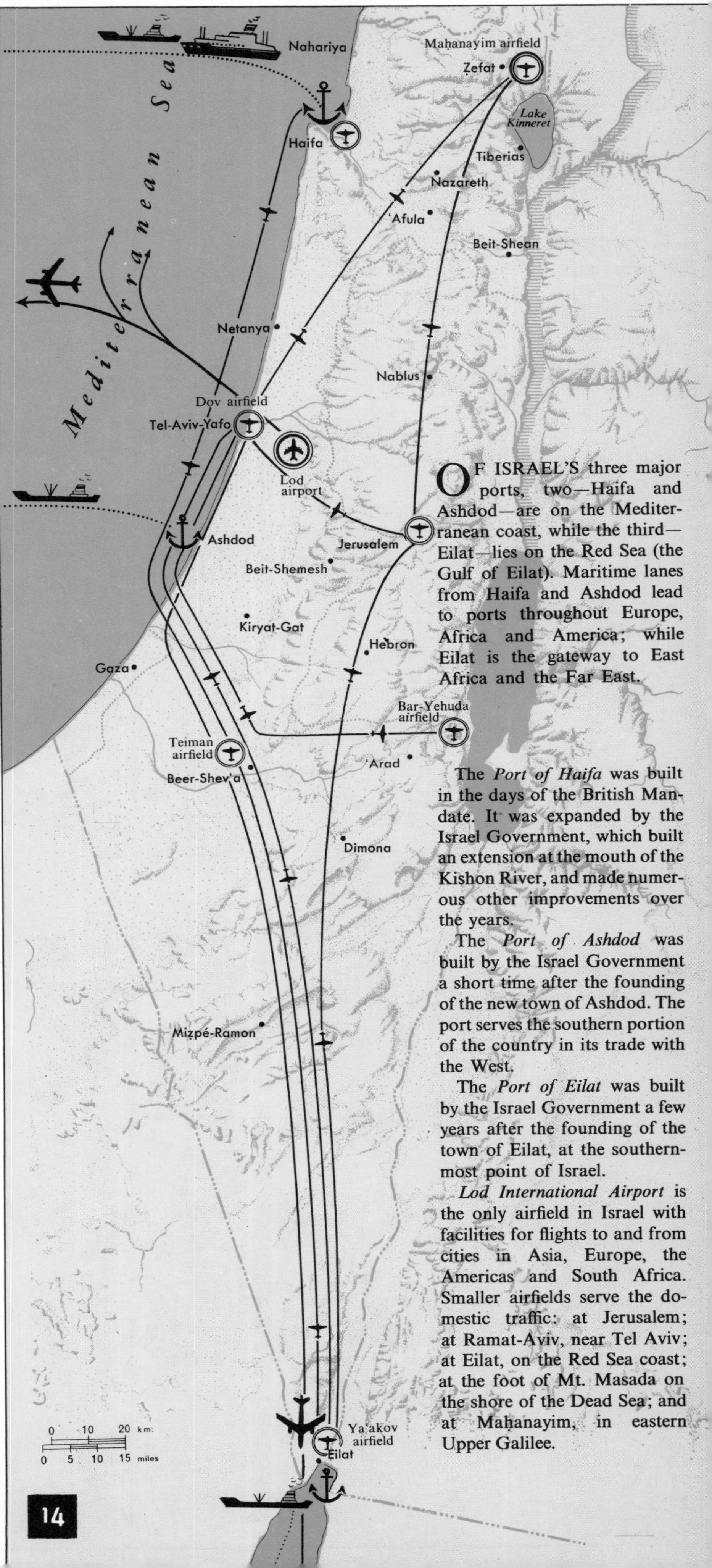

OF ISRAEL'S three major ports, two—Haifa and Ashdod—are on the Mediterranean coast, while the third—Eilat—lies on the Red Sea (the Gulf of Eilat). Maritime lanes from Haifa and Ashdod lead to ports throughout Europe, Africa and America; while Eilat is the gateway to East Africa and the Far East.

The *Port of Haifa* was built in the days of the British Mandate. It was expanded by the Israel Government, which built an extension at the mouth of the Kishon River, and made numerous other improvements over the years.

The *Port of Ashdod* was built by the Israel Government a short time after the founding of the new town of Ashdod. The port serves the southern portion of the country in its trade with the West.

The *Port of Eilat* was built by the Israel Government a few years after the founding of the town of Eilat, at the southernmost point of Israel.

Lod International Airport is the only airfield in Israel with facilities for flights to and from cities in Asia, Europe, the Americas and South Africa. Smaller airfields serve the domestic traffic: at Jerusalem; at Ramat-Aviv, near Tel Aviv; at Eilat, on the Red Sea coast; at the foot of Mt. Masada on the shore of the Dead Sea; and at Mahanayim, in eastern Upper Galilee.

ISRAEL: NORTH

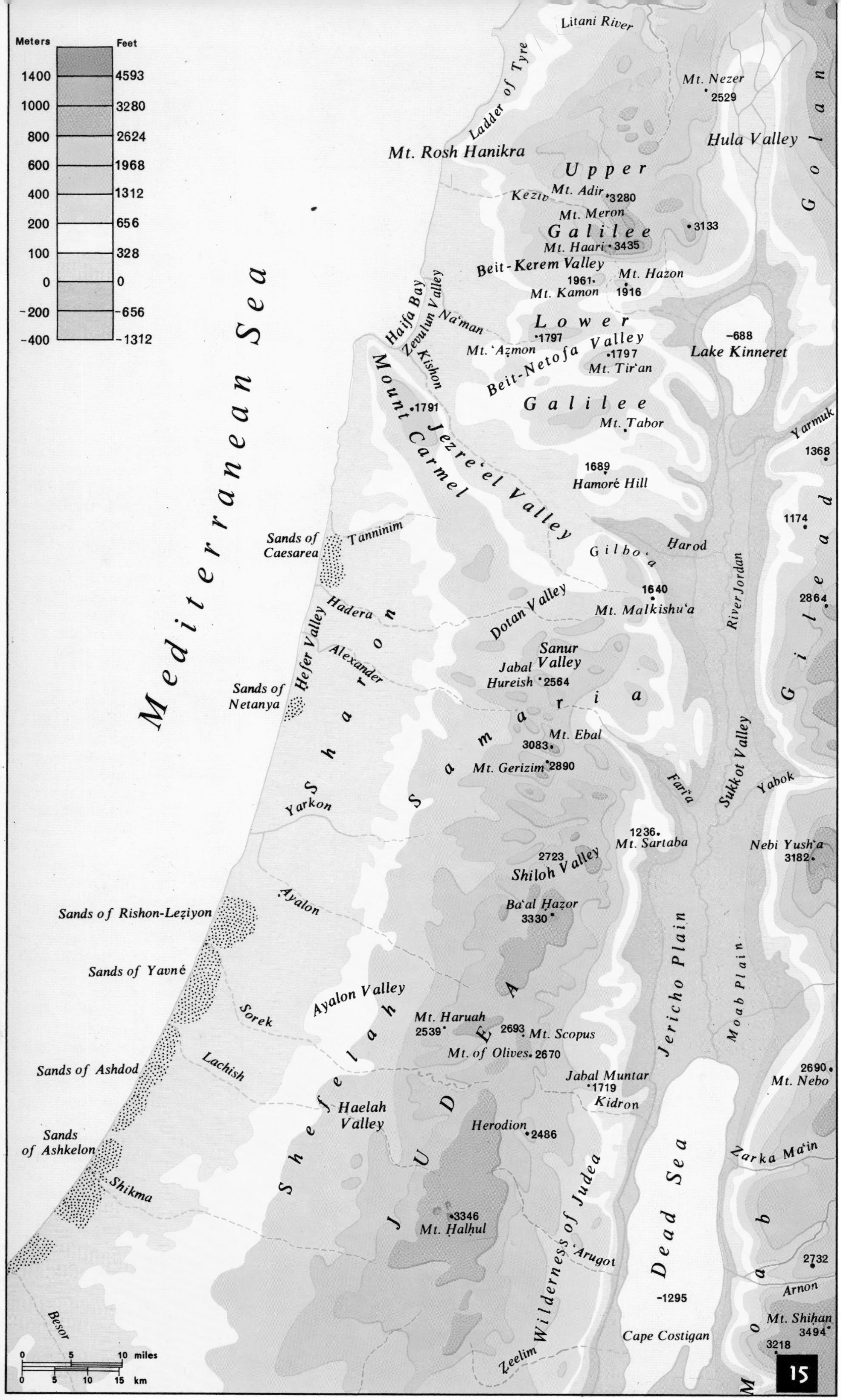
Meters
Feet
1400
4593
1000
3280
800
2624
600
1968
400
1312
200
656
100
328
0
0
-200
-656
-400
-1312
Litani River
Ladder of Tyre
Mt. Nezer
2529
Hula Valley
Golan
Mt. Rosh Hanikra
Upper
Keziv
Mt. Adir
3280
Mt. Meron
Galilee
3133
Mt. Haari
3435
Beit-Kerem Valley
Mt. Hazon
1961
1916
Mt. Kamon
Haifa Bay
Zevulun Valley
Na'man
Lower
1797
-688
Mt. 'Azmon
Beit-Netofa Valley
1797
Mt. Tir'an
Lake Kinneret
Kishon
Mount Carmel
1791
Galilee
Mt. Tabor
Yarmuk
1368
Jezre'el Valley
1689
Hamoré Hill
Mediterranean Sea
Sands of Caesarea
Tanninim
1174
Harod
Gilboa
River Jordan
Gilead
1640
Mt. Malkishu'a
2864
Hadera
Dotan Valley
Hefer Valley
Alexander
Sanur Valley
Jabal Hureish
2564
Sands of Netanya
Sharon
Samaria
Mt. Ebal
3083
Mt. Gerizim
2890
Far'a
Sukkot Valley
Yabok
Yarkon
1236
Mt. Sartaba
Nebi Yush'a
3182
2723
Shiloh Valley
Ayalon
Ba'al Hazor
3330
Sands of Rishon-Leziyon
Sands of Yavné
Jericho Plain
Moab Plain
Ayalon Valley
Sorek
Mt. Haruah
2539
2693
Mt. Scopus
Mt. of Olives
2670
Lachish
Sands of Ashdod
Jabal Muntar
1719
Kidron
2690
Mt. Nebo
Haelah Valley
Shefelah
Judea
Herodion
2486
Sands of Ashkelon
Zarka Ma'in
Dead Sea
Shikma
Wilderness of Judea
3346
Mt. Halhul
'Arugot
Moab
2732
-1295
Arnon
Besor
Mt. Shihan
3494
Cape Costigan
3218
Zeelim
0 5 10 miles
0 5 10 15 km
15

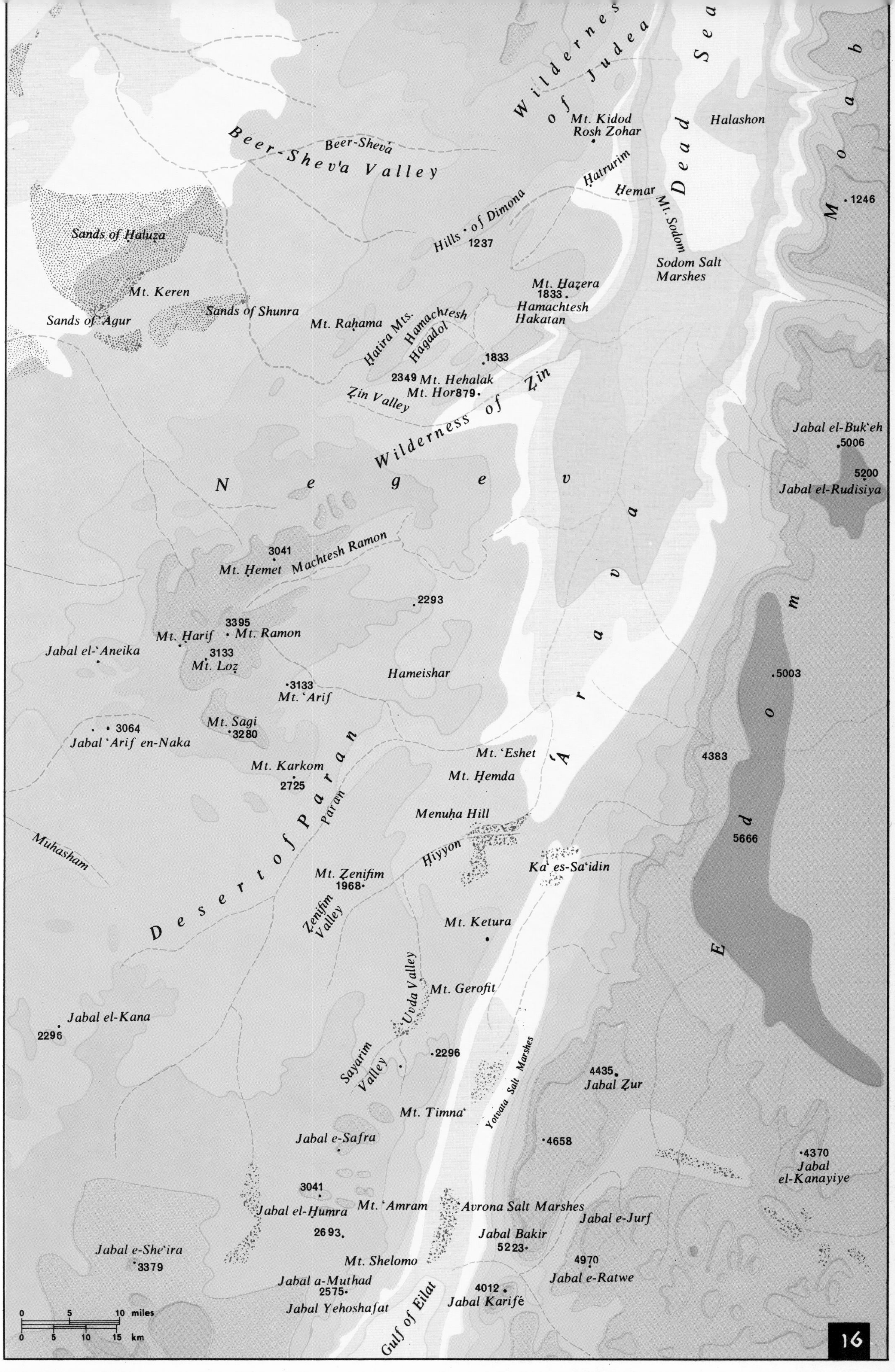
Wilderness of Judea
Dead Sea
Moab
Beer-Sheva
Beer-Sheva Valley
Mt. Kidod
Rosh Zohar
Halashon
Hatrurim
Hemar
Mt. Sodom
1246
Sands of Haluza
Hills of Dimona
1237
Sodom Salt Marshes
Mt. Hazera
1833
Mt. Keren
Hamachtesh Hakatan
Sands of Agur
Sands of Shunra
Mt. Rahama
Hatira Mts.
Hamachtesh Hagadol
1833
2349 Mt. Hehalak
Mt. Hor 879
Zin Valley
Wilderness of Zin
Jabal el-Buk'eh
5006
5200
Jabal el-Rudisiya
Negev
Arava
3041
Mt. Hemet
Machtesh Ramon
2293
Edom
3395
Mt. Harif
Mt. Ramon
3133
Jabal el-'Aneika
Mt. Loz
Hameishar
5003
3133
Mt. 'Arif
3064
Mt. Sagi
3280
Jabal 'Arif en-Naka
Mt. 'Eshet
4383
Mt. Karkom
2725
Mt. Hemda
Paran
Desert of Paran
Menuha Hill
5666
Muhasham
Hiyyon
Ka' es-Sa'idin
Mt. Zenifim
1968
Zenifim Valley
Mt. Ketura
Uvda Valley
Mt. Gerofit
Jabal el-Kana
2296
Sayarim Valley
2296
Yotvata Salt Marshes
4435
Jabal Zur
Mt. Timna'
Jabal e-Safra
4658
4370
Jabal el-Kanayiye
3041
Jabal el-Humra
Mt. 'Amram
Avrona Salt Marshes
Jabal e-Jurf
2693
Jabal Bakir
5223
Jabal e-She'ira
3379
Mt. Shelomo
4970
Jabal e-Ratwe
Jabal a-Muthad
2575
4012
Jabal Karifé
Jabal Yehoshafat
Gulf of Eilat
0 5 10 miles
0 5 10 15 km
16

ISRAEL: SOUTH

PARKS AND NATURE RESERVES

THE RAPID expansion of urban as well as rural settlement of the country and the steady conquest of formerly barren regions have placed in jeopardy areas distinguished for their natural beauty, for their special flora and fauna, or for their historical or archaeological importance. The Government of Israel has proclaimed, therefore, that areas designated as nature reserves or as national parks will enjoy the protection of the law, thus ensuring their integrity and special character, for the benefit of science and the general public. The care of these places is in the hands of the Society for the Protection of Nature.

Among the more well-known nature reserves of the country are those in the Ḥula Valley, in the northeastern corner of Israel; on the heights of Mount Meiron, in Upper Galilee; on the islands of Achziv and Dor, on the Mediterranean coast; at 'Ein-Gedi, on the shore of the Dead Sea; and at the Coral Coast, off Eilat, in the Red Sea.

Of the more important national parks in Israel, we may mention here the area around the ancient synagogue at Bar'am, the Crusader castle of Belvoir, and the antiquities at Beit-Shean and Megiddo, in the north, Ashkelon on the Mediterranean coast, Meẓada (Masada) in the Judean Desert, 'Avdat (Abda) and Shivta (Subeita) in the Negev.

'Ein-'Avdat, a spring in the Negev

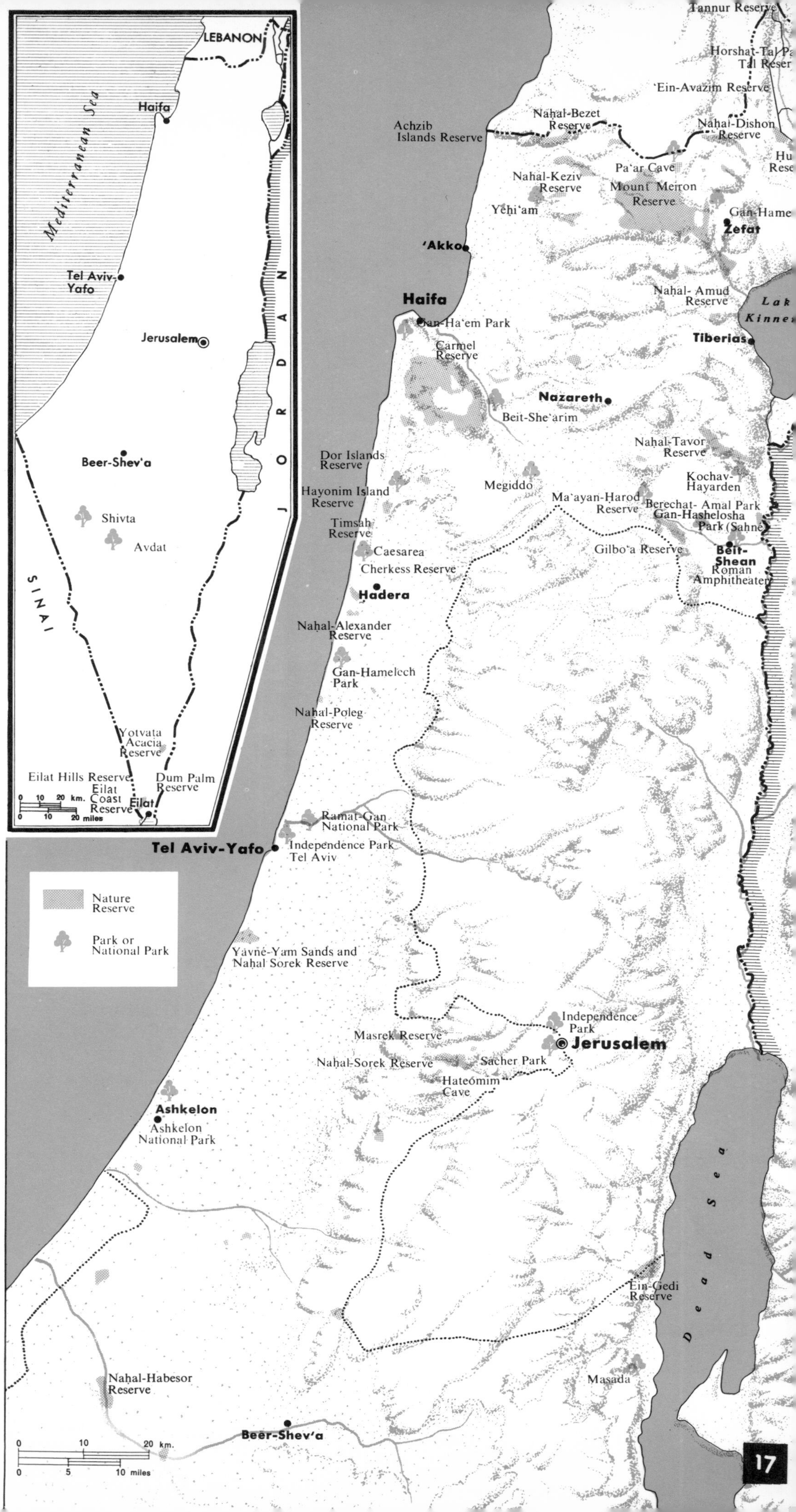

FORESTS AND CAMPING SITES

VARIOUS parts of the country are endowed with natural forests, mainly oaks, carobs, and pines: worthy of special mention are the woodlands on Mount Carmel, on the heights of Galilee and on Mount Tabor. In several places, isolated groves sanctified by historical associations have survived the ravages of war and general neglect through the centuries, such as Hamasrek (The Comb) in the Mounts of Jerusalem, Ḥorshat Haarba'im (The Grove of the Forty) on Mount Carmel, and Ḥorshat Tal Forest (Dew Grove) in the Ḥula Valley. A unique group of trees is the Palm Grove near 'Akko.

The neglect of past generations, and the frequent wars that ravaged the country, were responsible for the destruction of vast areas of woodlands, of which only a small remnant has been preserved.

Many acres have been reforested in recent decades, particularly with pine trees, most of them planted by the Jewish National Fund. At the approaches to the capital, there is the Jerusalem Forest and, just to the west of it, the President's Forest; then there is Herzl Forest, in the vicinity of Ben-Shemen and Ḥulda; Balfour Forest, at the edge of the Jezreel Valley; United States Forest, in the mountains of Lower Galilee; and the forests of Mishmar-Ha'emek and Yokne'am, on the Heights of Menashé and near the Jezreel Valley.

In recent years, camping grounds with parking and picnicking facilities have been built into many forests. Large numbers of Israelis make their way to these places, especially on holidays and special occasions.

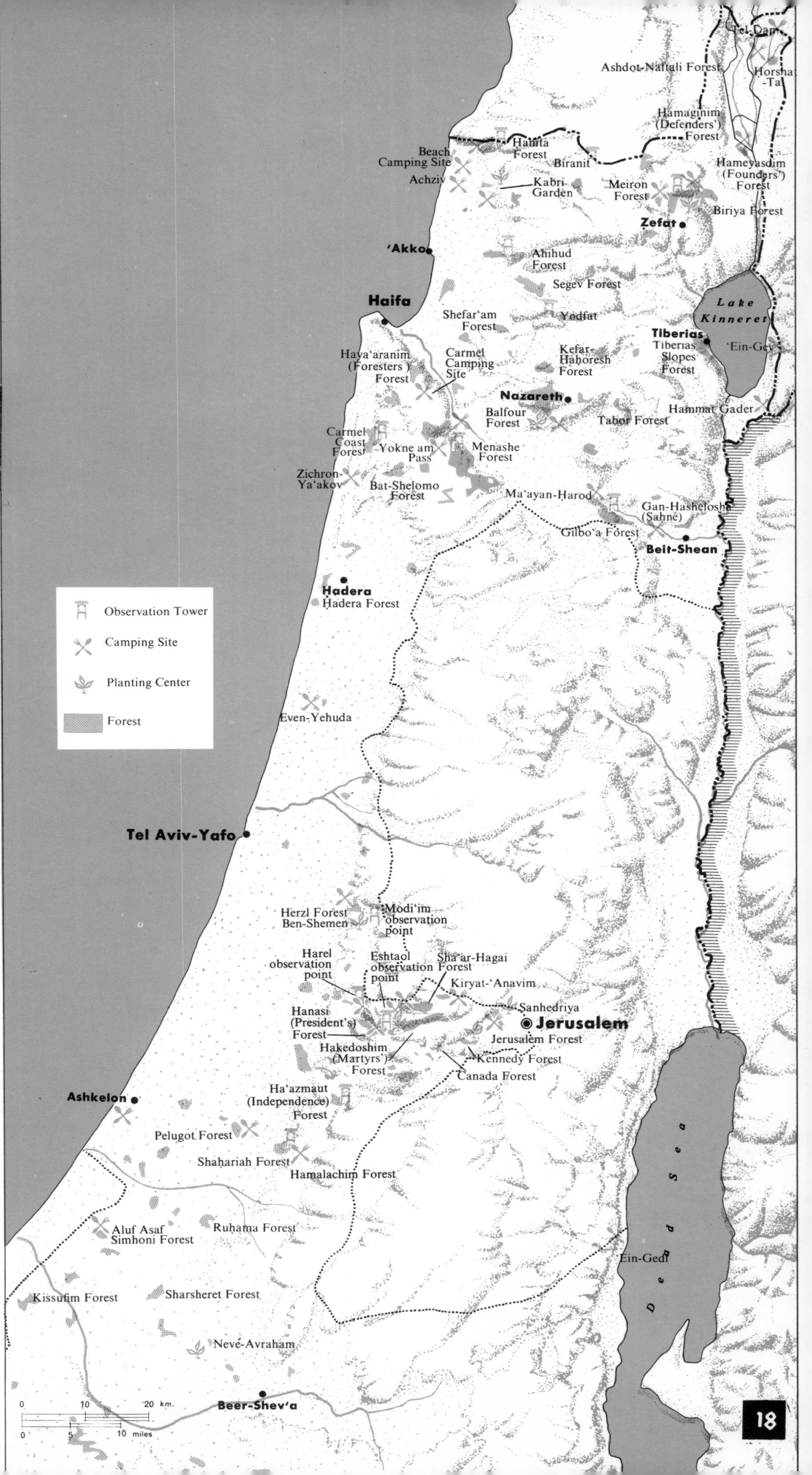
Observation Tower
Camping Site
Planting Center
Forest
Tel-Dan
Ashdot-Naftali Forest
Horshat-Tal
Hamaginim (Defenders') Forest
Beach Camping Site
Achziv
Hanita Forest
Biranit
Kabri Garden
Meiron Forest
Hameyasdim (Founders') Forest
Biriya Forest
Zefat
'Akko
Ahihud Forest
Segev Forest
Haifa
Shefar'am Forest
Yodfat
Lake Kinneret
Tiberias
Tiberias Slopes Forest
'Ein-Gev
Haya'aranim (Foresters) Forest
Carmel Camping Site
Kefar-Hahoresh Forest
Nazareth
Balfour Forest
Tabor Forest
Hammat Gader
Carmel Coast Forest
Yokne'am Pass
Menashe Forest
Zichron-Ya'akov
Bat-Shelomo Forest
Ma'ayan-Harod
Gan-Hasheloshah (Sahne)
Gilbo'a Forest
Beit-Shean
Hadera
Hadera Forest
Even-Yehuda
Tel Aviv-Yafo
Herzl Forest Ben-Shemen
Modi'im observation point
Harel observation point
Eshtaol observation point
Sha'ar-Hagai Forest
Kiryat-'Anavim
Sanhedriya
Jerusalem
Hanasi (President's) Forest
Jerusalem Forest
Hakedoshim (Martyrs') Forest
Kennedy Forest
Canada Forest
Ha'azmaut (Independence) Forest
Ashkelon
Pelugot Forest
Shahariah Forest
Hamalachim Forest
Aluf Asaf Simhoni Forest
Ruhama Forest
Ein-Gedi
Dead Sea
Kissufim Forest
Sharsheret Forest
Nevé-Avraham
Beer-Shev'a
0 10 20 km.
0 5 10 miles
18

FAUNA

EACH REGION in the Land of Israel has its characteristic wild life. The deer and the hind are to be found in some areas; indeed, 'Land of the Deer' (in the sense of "lovely country") is a name that has often been used, since Biblical times, to denote the Land of Israel. The ibex, or mountain-goat, lives in the wilderness of Judea and in the bare, rocky mountains around Eilat. The hyena lives in the bush and has been the subject of many a legend. Fox and jackal roam the country in large numbers. From time to time, wolves are seen and—very infrequently—an isolated leopard will be sighted. The habitat of the boar is in the swampy regions, and, as these are drained, their number dwindles.

There are also many snakes (some of them poisonous), lizards, mice and other rodents harmful to crops. Birds abound, particularly when they pass over in northward and southward migrations. An Israeli zoologist has identified a hitherto unknown species of owl. There are numerous kinds of insects and occasionally migratory locusts swarm across the borders with disastrous results. A variety of crab unknown anywhere else in the world is found in a small pond near Lake Kinneret.

As human habitation in the land and the cultivation of the soil expand, the country's wild life diminishes. From ancient literature and from archaeological finds we know that in days gone by the country was inhabited by creatures many of which have long since disappeared from its hills and valley: the lion, for example, which used to roam the Jordan Valley; the bear, in the mountains; the behemoth, or hippopotamus, in the rivers; and the crocodile in the swamps. In caves that once served as human dwellings the bones have been found of deer-like animals and other beasts now extinct.

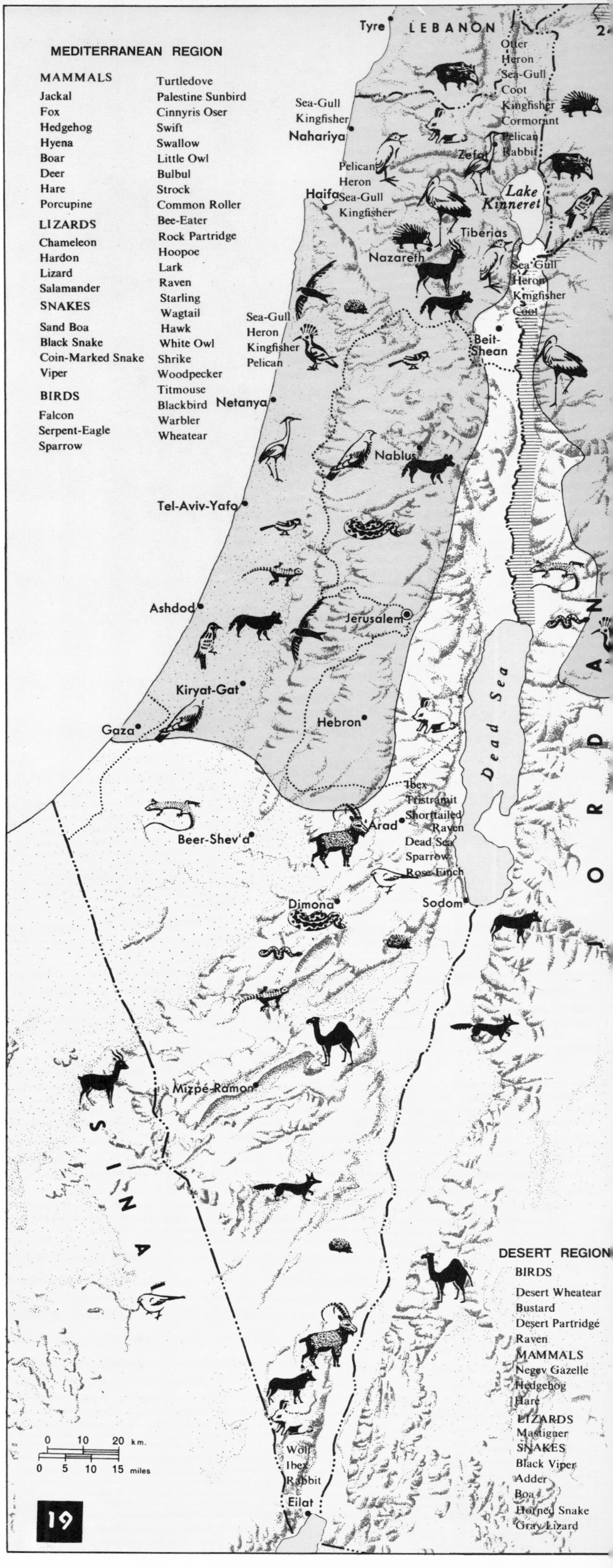

FLORA

THE GEOGRAPHIC position of the Land of Israel, the variegated structure of its soil, its changing climate, its proximity to the sea, on the one hand, and to the desert, on the other, the inclusion within its terrain of the lowest region on the face of the earth—all these have contributed to a vegetation rich in genera and species. The Land of Israel boasts more than 2,000 species of plants, some of them endemic, others typical of Mediterranean lands, still others to be found also in regions as distant as Iran, in the heart of Asia, and the Sahara Desert and Sudan, in Africa.

The first flower to bloom at the beginning of the rainy season is the white squill, famed in Hebrew folklore. Next to appear are the crocus, saffron, buttercup, narcissus, cyclamen, adonis and yellow-weed. With the onset of warm weather, fields are carpeted with poppies, anemone, wild mustard and other flowers.

Among the endemic plants there are altogether four genera, some 150 species and about 200 varieties. On the heights of Mount Gilbo'a there blooms, in the springtime, a special kind of iris named in Hebrew after the mountain; other local irises are the Negev iris, the Samarian iris and the Nazareth iris. One genus of Compositae is named after Aharon Aaronsohn, the Israeli botanist who discovered wild wheat here, and another local botanist, A. Faktorovsky. Another genus is called Warburgia, in memory of Otto Warburg, a well-known Zionist leader and a famous botanist. A genus of flora peculiar to Israel and found in Upper Galilee is known as the Galilean Mosheovit, after Gershon Mosheov, a young botanist and member of the Haganah who was killed in the line of duty in the riots of 1936.

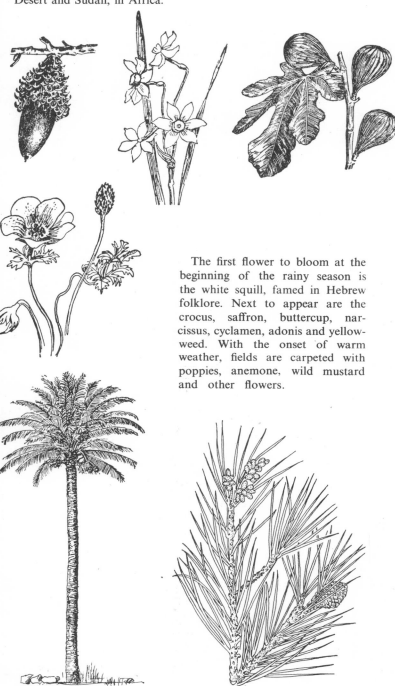

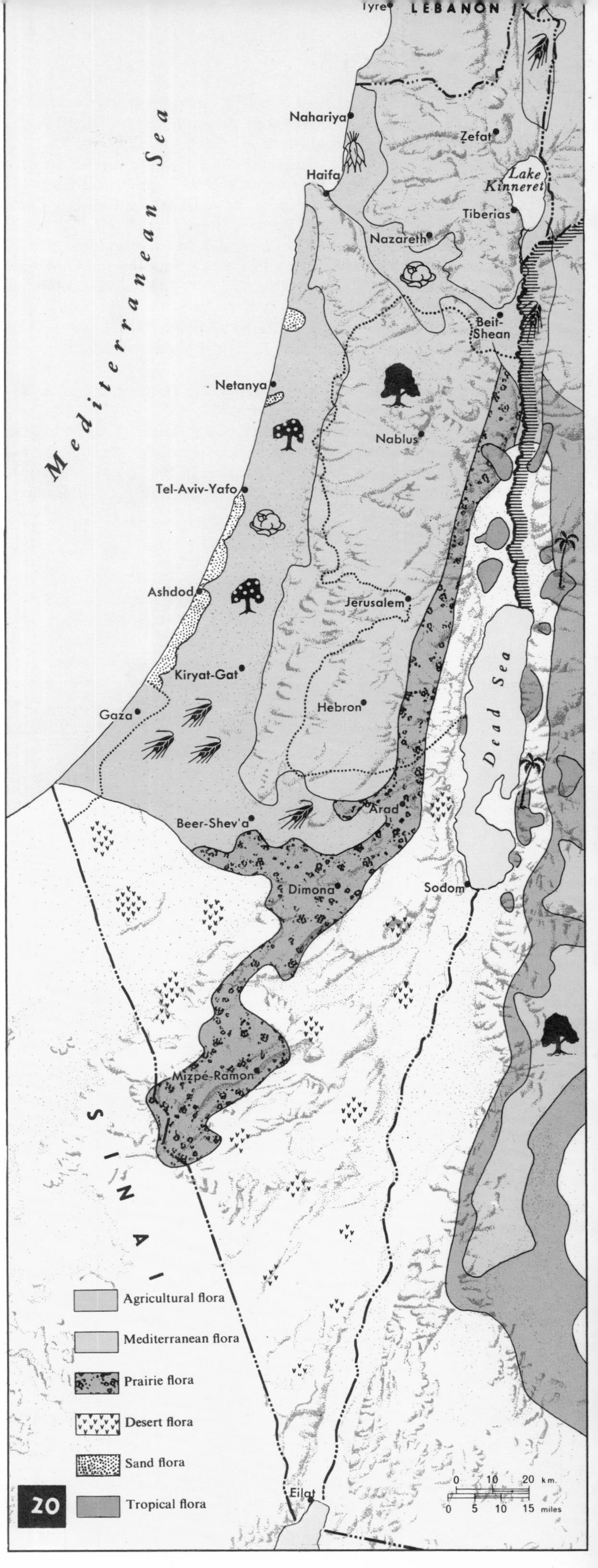

HOLY PLACES

THE SANCTITY of the Land of Israel derives from certain outstanding historical events and personalities connected with it; hence the name Holy Land (*terra sancta* in Latin).

For the Jewish people, the land is holy because it is its homeland —the cradle of its faith, its tongue and its culture and scene of its history during the golden age of its national independence. Here was written the Bible, Israel's Book of Books, which was later to serve as the foundation for the Christian and Moslem religions. In subsequent generations Jews living in Israel composed the Oral Law—the *Mishna* and the Palestinian (Yerushalmi) *Talmud*—two of the basic works of the Jewish faith.

Christianity originated in the Land of Israel. Its founder was born and worked there, and from it his faithful disciples went forth to spread the doctrine abroad.

There are places, in various parts of the country, sacred to Jews, Christians, Moslems, Druzes and Bahais.

Sacred to the *Jews* are the cities of Jerusalem, Hebron, Tiberias and Ẓefat. An object of particular veneration, down through the many centuries of exile, was the ancient remnant of the Temple, the Western Wall, known as the "Wailing Wall", in the Old City of Jerusalem. From 1948, when modern Israel proclaimed her independence, until 1967, the Old City was in the hands of the Kingdom of Jordan which persistently failed to comply with a clause in the Armistice Agreement guaranteeing free access to the Wall. When, in June 1967, King Hussein made a pact with Egypt's President Nasser and joined in what was proclaimed as a *jihad,* a "holy war" against Israel, the Old City was recaptured, and since that moment Jews have been able once more to worship at this most sacred of Jewish sites.

Among other places holy to the Jews are the tombs of King David and of the members of the Sanhedrin, in Jerusalem; of the Prophet Jonah, in Gath-Hefer (Mash-ḥad today), in Galilee; of Rabbi 'Akiva, Rabbi Meir ba'al Haness, Rabbi Yohanan ben Zakai and of Maimonides, in Tiberias; of Rabbi Shimon Bar Yohai and of Hillel and his followers, at Meiron; of the "Ari" spiritual leader of the Cabbalists, and of Rabbi Joseph Caro, in Ẓefat; and many others.

The *Christians* revere Bethlehem, the city where Jesus was born; Nazareth, residence of the Holy Family; Cana, where Christian tradition places the first miracle; Mount Tabor, where Jesus was transfigured before three of his disciples; Capernaum, where Jesus frequently preached; Tabgha, on the northern shores of the Sea of

Jews

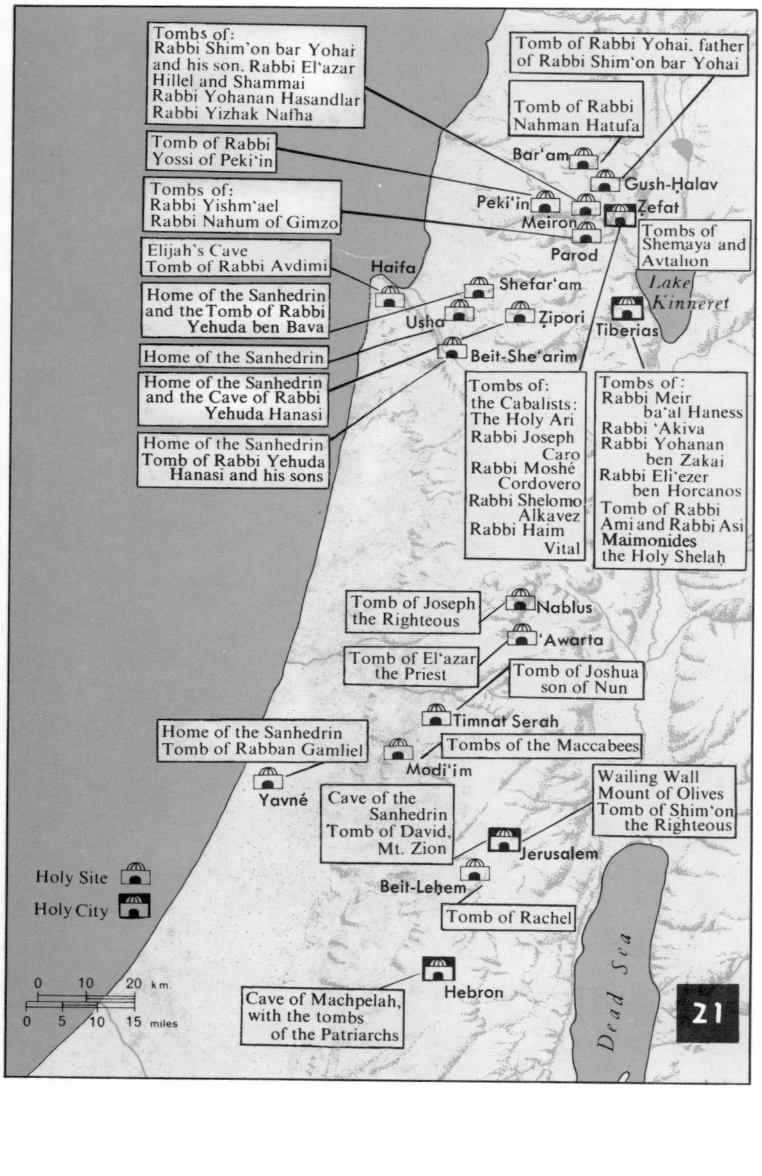

Christians

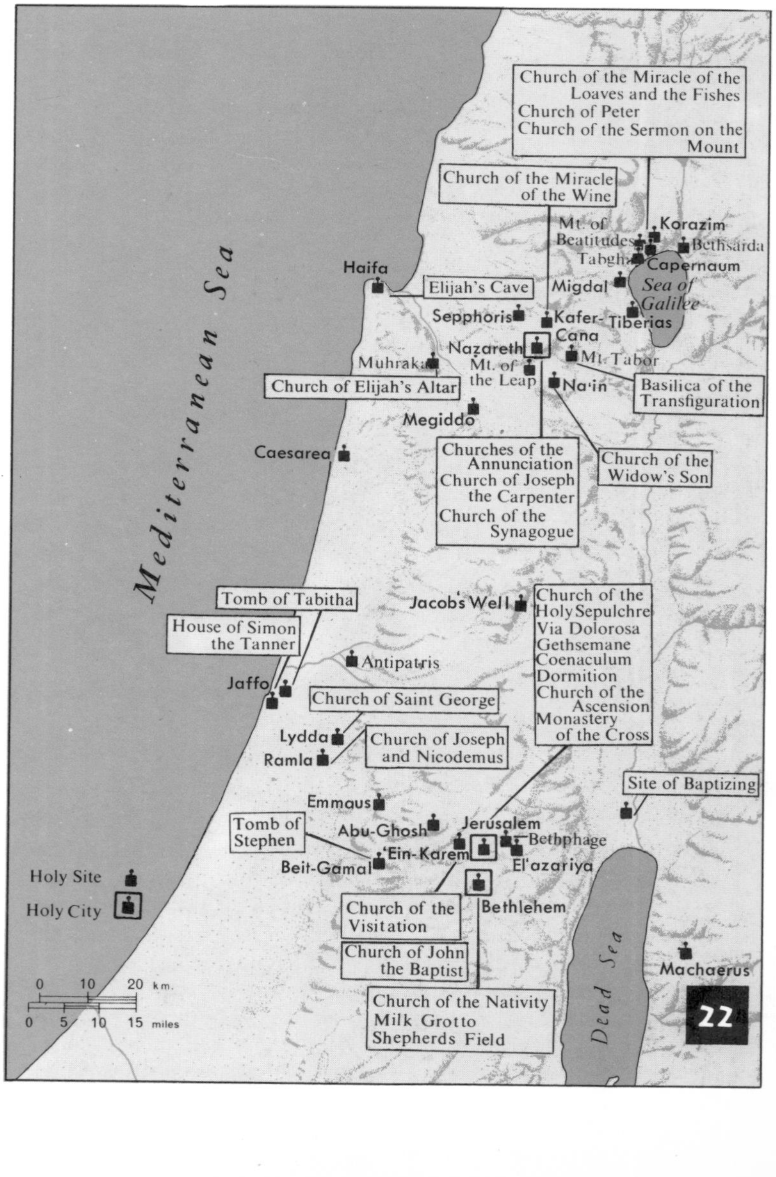

Galilee, site of the Church of the Loaves and the Fishes; Migdal, on the western shore, birthplace of Mary Magdalene; and the Sea of Galilee itself, in connection with which the New Testament relates a number of miracles. On the northwestern shore of the sea rises the Mount of Beatitudes, where Jesus preached the Sermon on the Mount and where he chose the Twelve Disciples.

On Mount Zion, in Jerusalem, is the Room of the Last Supper (Coenaculum) and, next to it, the Church of the Dormition. built on the spot where, according to Christian tradition, Mary, the mother of Jesus, died. The Monastery of the Cross, oldest structure in the New City of Jerusalem, was built in the valley from whose trees the wood was taken for the cross upon which Jesus was crucified. Several places in the Old City connected with the Crucifixion are also revered. Another sacred place for Christianity is the village of 'Ein-Karem, in the western outskirts of Jerusalem, the birthplace of John the Baptist and site of the Visitation of St. Mary.

Among *Moslem* holy places in Israel is the grave of Nebi (Prophet) Saleh, mentioned in the Koran as a predecessor of Mohammed, in Ramla; that of Nebi Rubin (said to be Reuben, the first-born son of Jacob) on the banks of the Sorek River, in central Israel; and that of Sidna 'Ali, a Moslem warrior who fell in the battle against the Crusaders in the 13th century, near Herzliya on the Mediterranean shore.

The Temple Mount, in the Old City of Jerusalem, at the base of which stands Jewry's holiest site, the Western Wall, is venerated by the Moslems as the place where, they believe, the Prophet Mohammed ascended to Heaven; the Mount is the site of two mosques—the Mosque of Omar (Dome of the Rock) and the Mosque of el-Aksa.

Revered by the *Druzes* is the tomb of Nebi Shu'eib, in Lower Galilee. According to Druze tradition, Shu'eib is Jethro, father-in-law of Moses. In the Middle Ages his grave was visited also by Jewish pilgrims.

The *Bahais* have a magnificent, gold-domed shrine on Mount Carmel, in Haifa. The shrine is the burying-place of the sect's founder, Firze Ali, also known as el-Bab—The Gate. In close proximity is the grave of 'Abbas Effendi ('Abd-el-Baha,' Slave of Glory). His father, the founder of the Bahai faith, Baha-Ullah, Glory of God, lies buried in a beautiful garden (el-Bahaja) near 'Akko.

Moslems

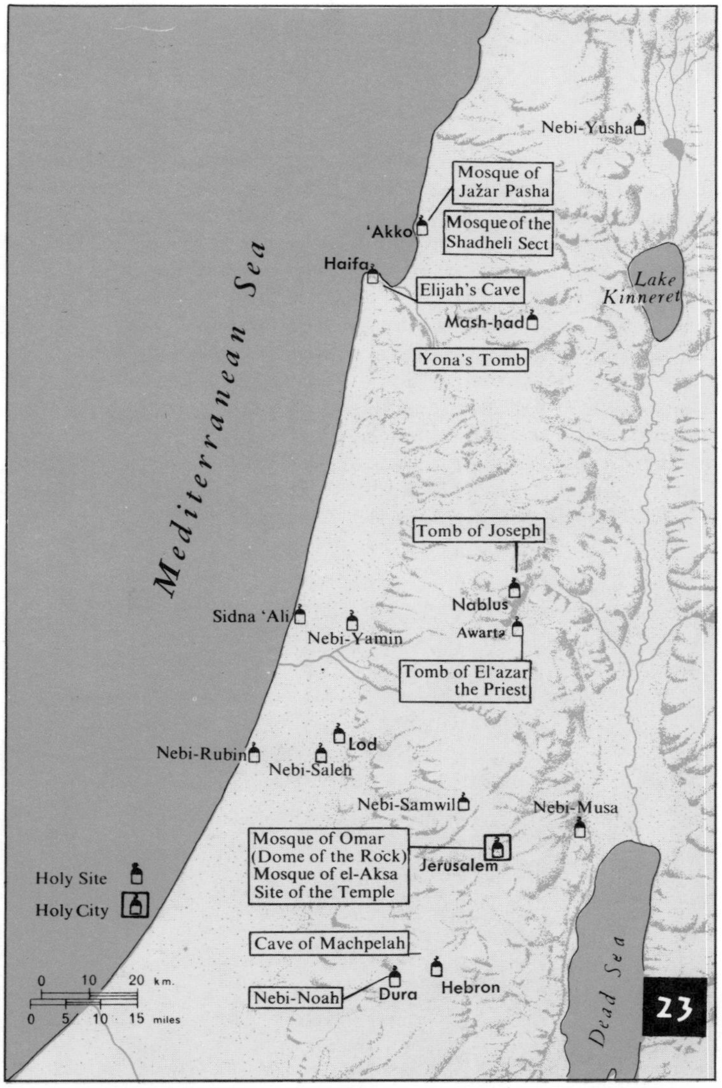

Others

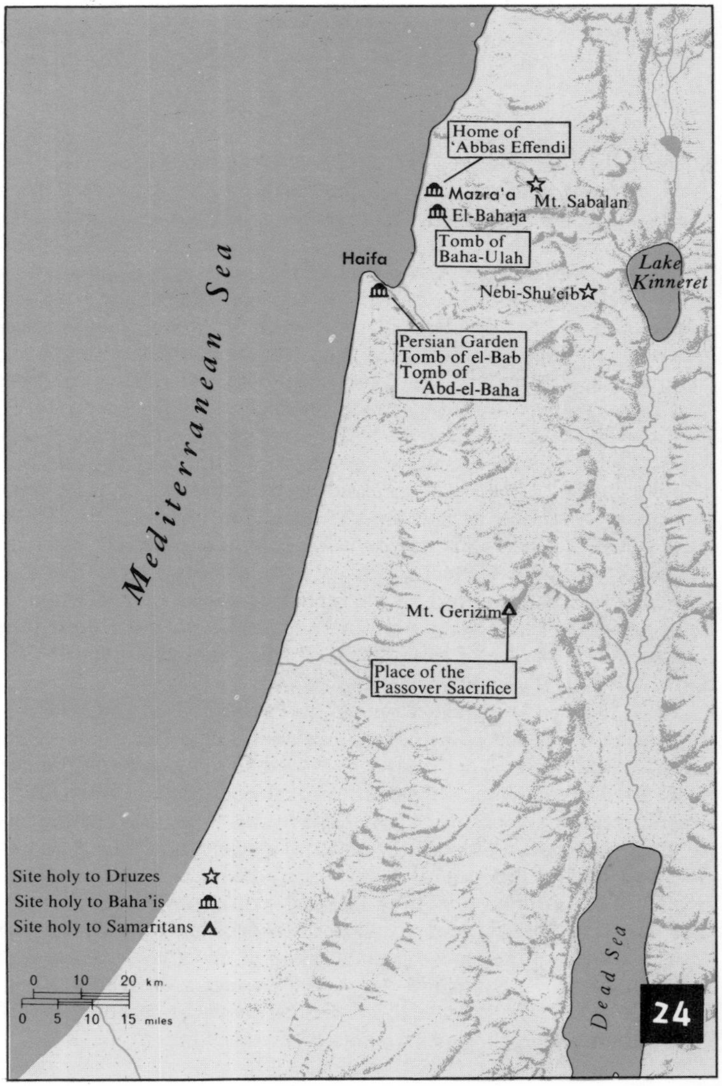

GALILEE

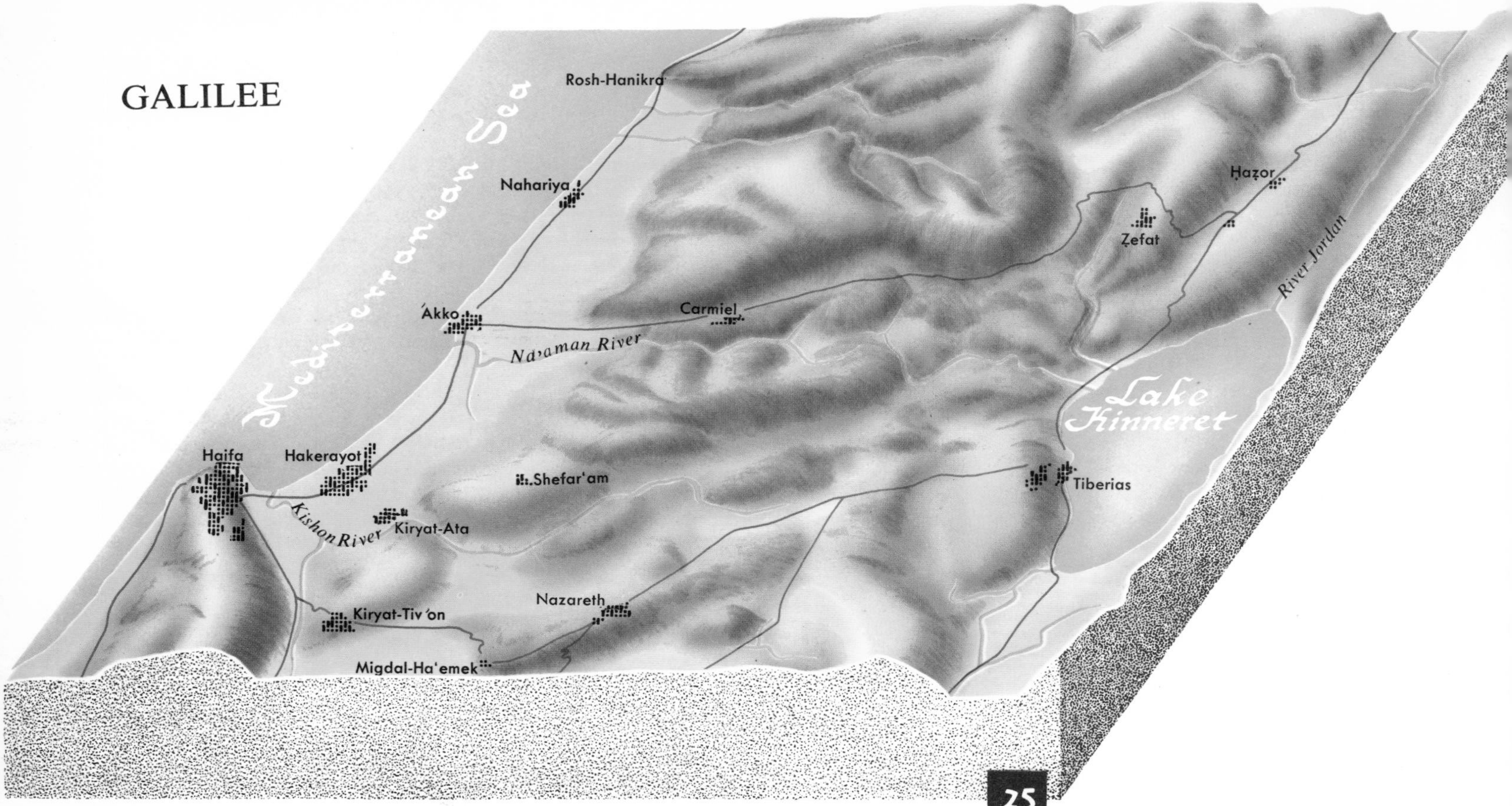

25

GALILEE is bounded by the Mediterranean Sea on the west, by the Lebanese border on the north, by the River Jordan on the east and by the Jezreel Valley on the south. Lower Galilee—the southern part of the region—reaches an elevation of about 1,500 feet above sea level; further north, the heights of Upper Galilee attain altitudes of 3–4,000 feet. The boundary between the two sub-regions follows a line extending from 'Akko, on the Mediterranean coast, eastward through the Valleys of Beit-Kerem and Ginnosar to the shores of the Sea of Galilee. The ancients differentiated between Upper and Lower Galilee according to the prevalence of the sycamore tree. "Whosoever does not raise the sycamore," the saying goes, "that is Upper Galilee; whosoever raises the sycamore—that is Lower Galilee." (Today, however, the sycamore is not to be found in Lower Galilee.)

Galilee is the coldest and the wettest region in Israel. Its climate is excellent, its soil fertile and its water resources plentiful; as might be expected, its settlement dates back to ancient times. The area abounds in natural caves, which served as places of habitation as far back as the Early Stone Age. In one of these caves was found the oldest human skull ever to be uncovered in Israel, giving rise to the appellation, "Galilee Man" *(Homo galilensis)*.

When the land was divided among the Twelve Tribes, under Joshua, four large tribes settled in Galilee: Zebulun and Asher in the west, Issachar and Naphtali in the east. Somewhat later, a number of families from the tribe of Dan in the south migrated northward, resettled in the northeastern corner of Upper Galilee and there founded the city of Dan—the northernmost city in Israel during the Biblical period. In the succeeding generations, Galilee continued to be a well-populated region. The historian Josephus Flavius, writing in the first century CE, gave the following account: "For the men of Galilee were warriors from a tender age and great in numbers at all times; their hearts were never ruled by fear, nor did this land ever lack men ready to bear arms. It is a very fertile land, containing areas for pasture as well as an abundance of trees and plants of various kinds."

It was in Galilee that the Oral Law, the *Mishna,* was completed at the close of the second century, and in the generations that followed its scholars composed the Palestinian (Yerushalmi) Talmud. There, too, various *Midrashim* (homiletical writings) were written, the Hebrew system of vowel points was invented, and much of the early Hebrew liturgy was composed.

With the start of modern Jewish settlement in Palestine, Galilee had its share of new agricultural settlements, the first of which (in 1882) was Rosh Pinna, in Upper Galilee. The first settlement in Lower Galilee was Sejera (now Ilania), founded in 1899. In the years that followed, numerous settlements were added to these, and their members transformed large areas of rock-strewn, long neglected soil into fruit-bearing, life-giving fields. There are also farms and villages inhabited by Moslem and Christian Arabs and by Druzes.

THE ḤULA VALLEY

THE NORTHERNMOST portion of the Jordan River basin is known as the Ḥula Valley. It is bounded by the mountains of Upper Galilee on the west, the Bashan-Golan Mountains on the east and Mount Hermon on the north. The three main headwaters of the Jordan River flow southward through the Ḥula Valley, joining there to form the Jordan. Until thirty years ago, the valley was covered with extensive swamps and papyrus thickets. The swamps were a serious focus of malaria and made human habitation and settlement impossible. After the area had been purchased by Jews during the British Mandate, the work of draining the swamps began, at the northern extremity of the valley.
With the establishment of the State of Israel, the work was intensified and extended in scale, until even the small lake that had been there all but disappeared, leaving only a small remnant as a nature reserve.

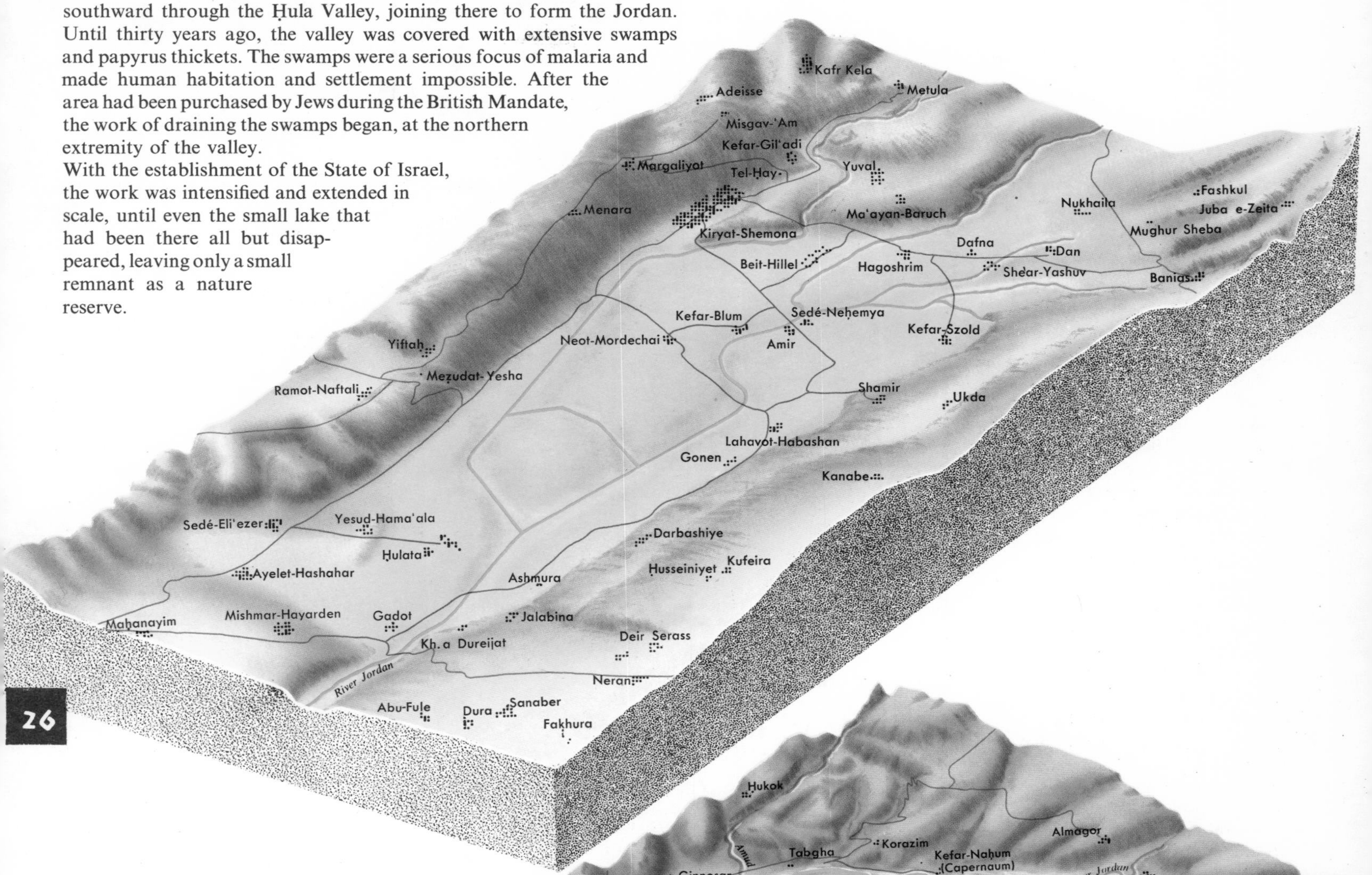

LAKE KINNERET

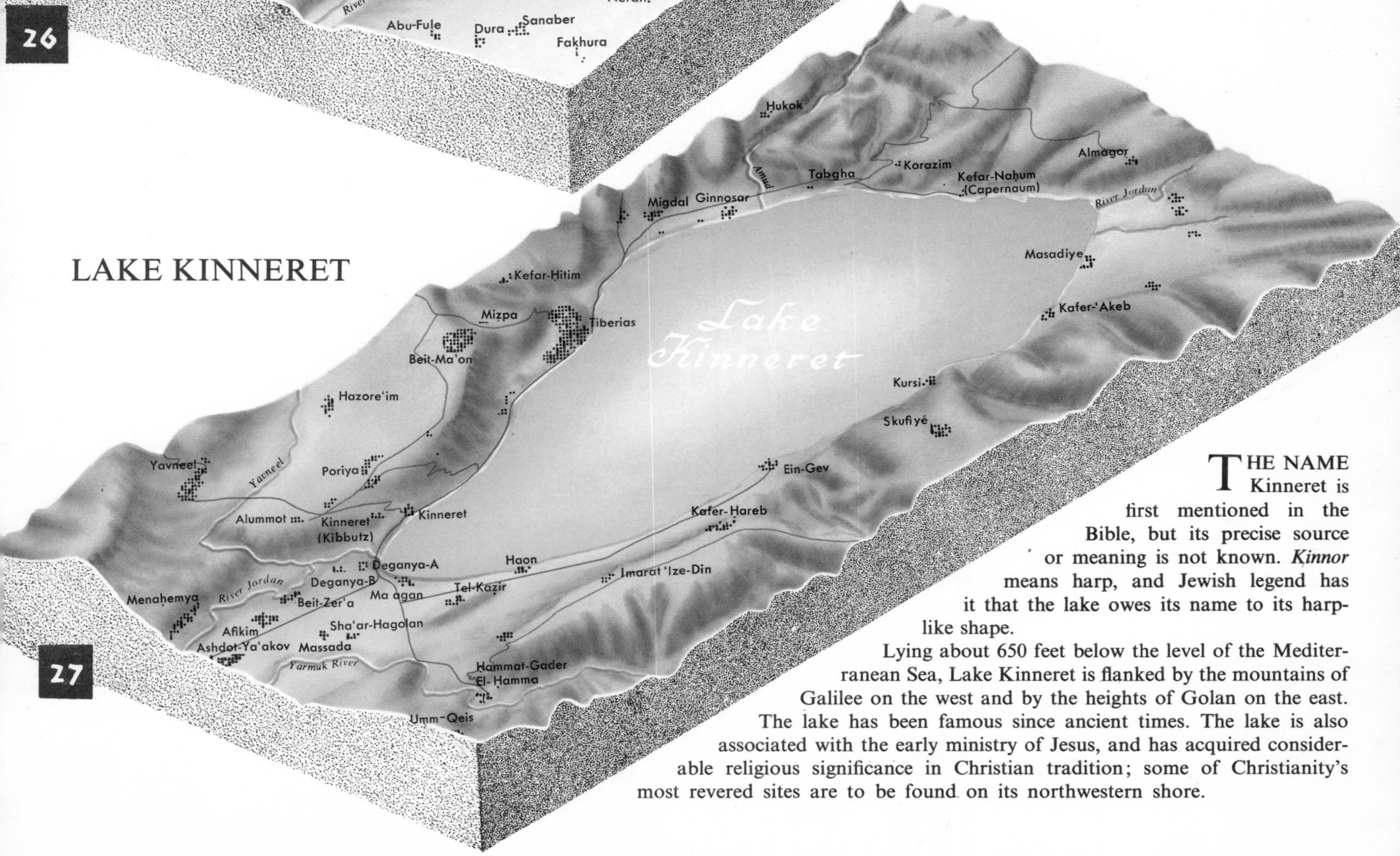

THE NAME Kinneret is first mentioned in the Bible, but its precise source or meaning is not known. *Kinnor* means harp, and Jewish legend has it that the lake owes its name to its harp-like shape.

Lying about 650 feet below the level of the Mediterranean Sea, Lake Kinneret is flanked by the mountains of Galilee on the west and by the heights of Golan on the east. The lake has been famous since ancient times. The lake is also associated with the early ministry of Jesus, and has acquired considerable religious significance in Christian tradition; some of Christianity's most revered sites are to be found on its northwestern shore.

CITIES AND LOCAL COUNCILS

THE CITIES and towns of Israel are of varied origin and character. Some are built on or near the sites of Biblical cities and are named after them, for example, Jerusalem, Yafo (Jaffa), Benei-Berak, Ashkelon, Ashdod, Lod (Lydda), Beer-She'va 'Akko (Acre) and Beit-Shean. Others are within the confines of cities that existed in the Second Temple era or during the period of the Mishna and the Talmud: Haifa, Tiberias, Nazareth, Shefar'am, Kefar-Sava and others. Ramla and Ẓefat (Safed) are towns that became famous in the Middle Ages. Ramla is the only town in Israel that was founded by the Arabs during their rule of the country.

Several of Israel's cities originated in modern times, being the product of the national Jewish rebirth. Among these are Tel-Aviv, Ramat Gan, Giv'atayim, Bat-Yam, Ḥolon and Netanya. Some grew out of agricultural settlements, e.g., Petaḥ-Tikva, Rishon-Leẓiyon, Reḥovot, Herẓliya, Ḥadera and Nahariya.

Jerusalem is the capital of the State of Israel. It comprises the Old City, including the Temple Mount and other sites sacred to Jews, Christians and Moslems, and the New City, where are located the Knesset (Parliament) as well as other Government buildings, the Residence of of the President, the Jewish Agency, the Chief Rabbinate, the Hebrew University and the National and University Library, the Hebrew Language Academy and the Israel Museum.

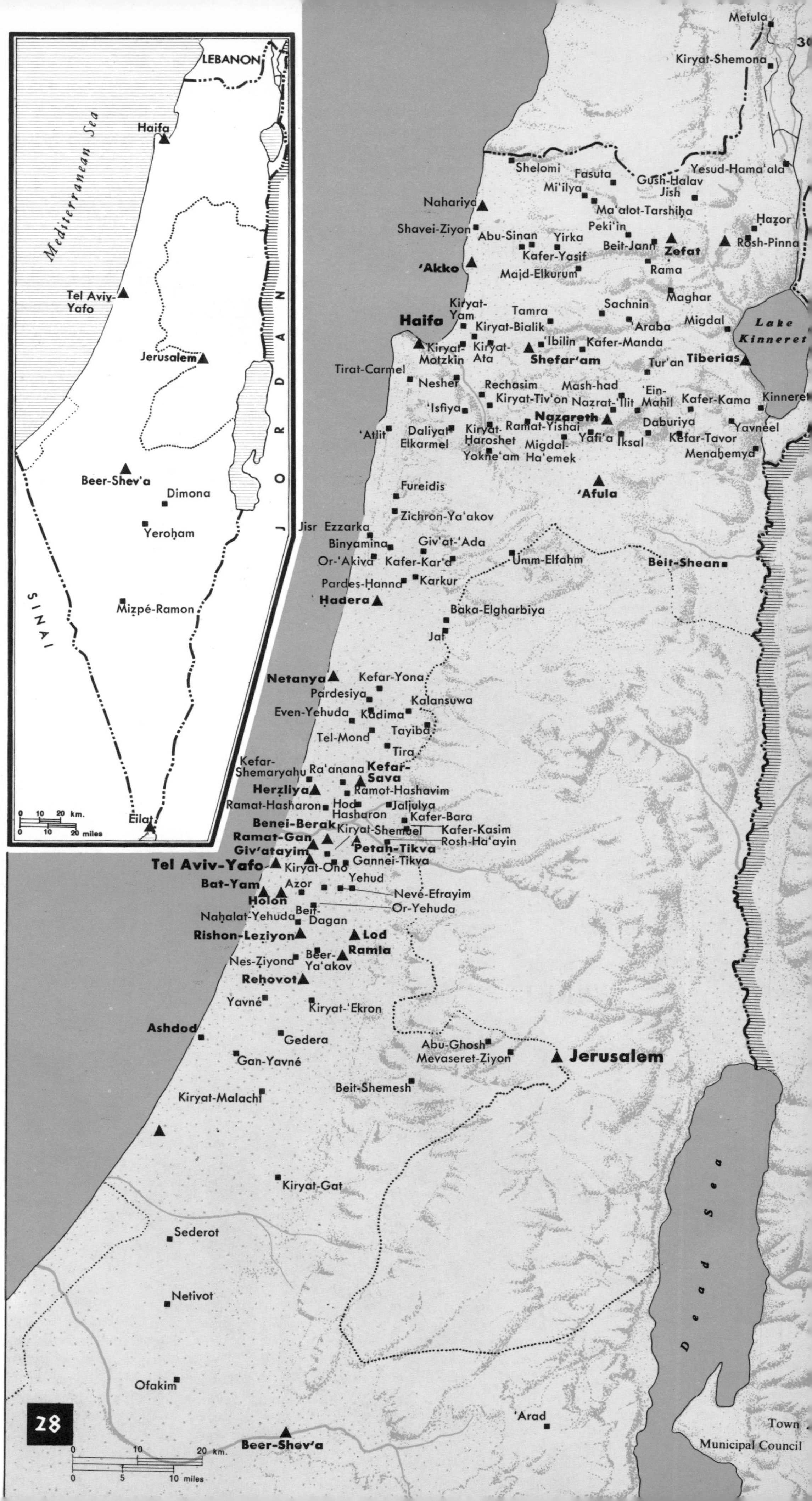

Tel-Aviv is the largest city in Israel. It was founded in 1909 by the Jewish inhabitants of neighboring Yafo. Today it is the center of the country's commerce and of its entertainment industry.

Haifa is the second-largest city and has the biggest port in Israel. It is the home of the Technion—Israel Institute of Technology.

Nazareth, the town where Jesus spent the early part of his life, is predominantly Arab in its population.

Local Councils govern the smaller towns. Their members are elected by the townspeople. As towns grow into cities, their status and form of government are duly revised by the Ministry of the Interior.

Jerusalem

Tel-Aviv-Yafo

Haifa

Beer-Shev'a

REGIONAL COUNCILS

THE AGRICULTURAL settlements or villages of a given area are linked together in an elected regional council. The council deals with common problems and projects such as the establishment of schools and other public institutions, road-building, water supply, security problems and the like.

Some regional councils are composed entirely of Jewish villages. In others, Jewish villages are linked with Arab villages in their vicinity. The councils, nearly all of which were founded after the establishment of the State in 1948, operate within the framework of the Ministry of the Interior.

Most of the regional councils in Israel are named after historical places located within their jurisdiction—for example, Jezreel, Kishon, Megiddo, Gilbo'a, Gezer, Lachish, Ga'aton, Tamar and so on. Others bear the names of the geographical regions in which they are located, such as Upper Galilee, Lower Galilee, Jordan Valley, Beit-Shean Valley, Ḥefer Valley, and Southern Sharon. The ancient tribes of Israel provide names for regional councils lying in their area: Maté-Yehuda (Tribe of Judah), Zevulun, Menashé and Benei-Shim'on (Sons of Simeon).

Each regional council has its own emblem.

'Emek Ḥefer

Lachish

Upper Galilee

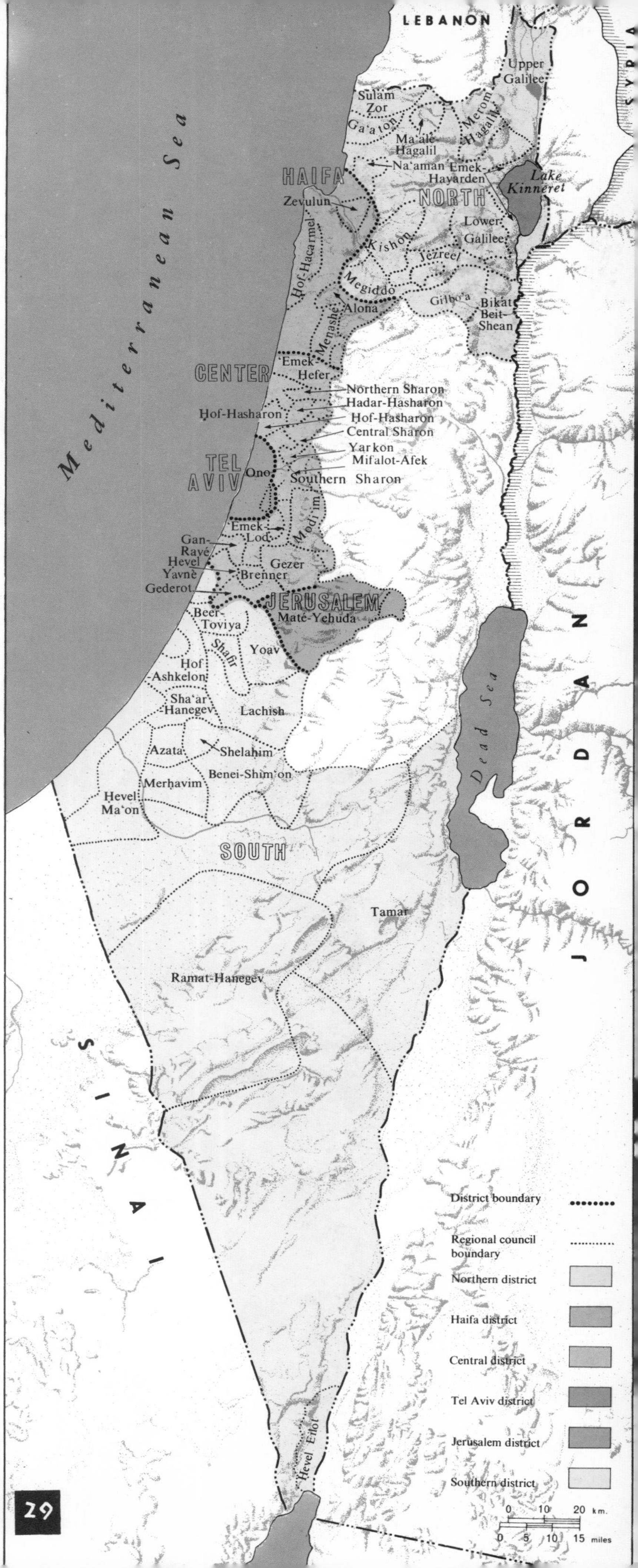

30

Beit-Shean
Gilbo'a
Jezreel Valley
Jenin
'Iron Valley
Umm-Elfahm
Dotan Valley
Zichron-Ya'akov
Sanur Valley
Tubas
Mt. Ebal
Nablus
Mt. Gerizim
Sabastiya
Binyamina
Pardes-Ḥanna
Mediterranean Sea
Ḥadera
Tul-Karm
Salfit
Netanya
'Azzun
Qalqiliya
Ra'anana
Kefar-Sava
Herẓliya
Petaḥ-Tikva
Tel-Aviv
Yafo
Ḥolon
Bat-Yam
Rishon-
Leẓiyon
Lod

Shechem (Nablus), capital of Samaria

SAMARIA (SHOMRON)

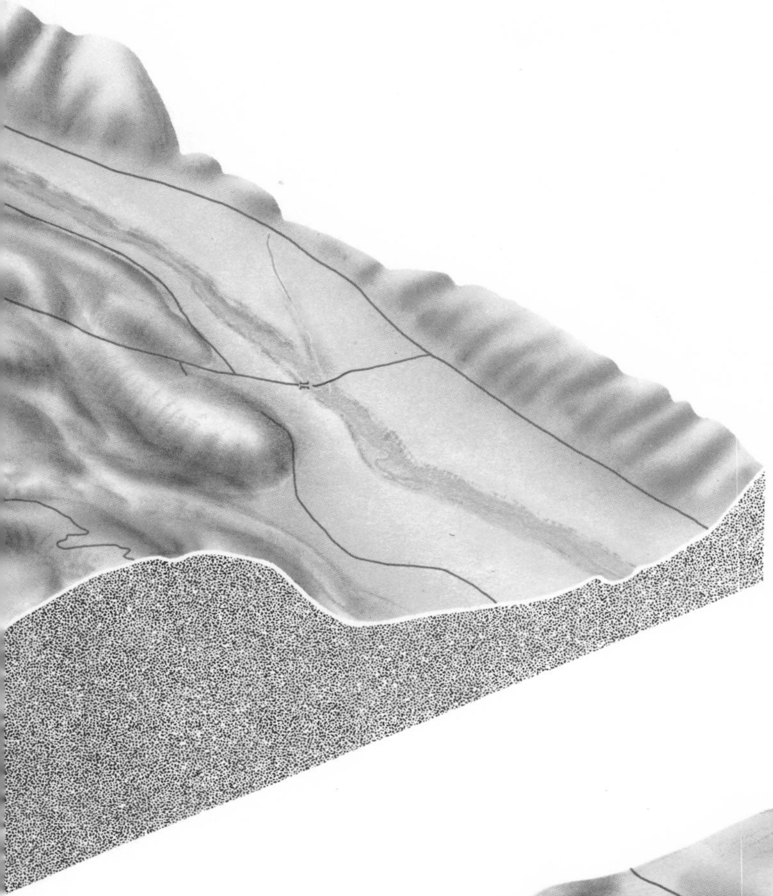

THE REGION of Samaria extends from the Judean Hills in the south to the Jezreel Valley in the north, and from the Jordan Valley in the east to the Sharon Plain in the west. The terrain is mountainous, the rolling hills divided by numerous fertile, water-blessed valleys; the climate is pleasant. The area, therefore, has been settled from earliest times. It was in Samaria that the tribes of Ephraim and Menasseh (descended from Joseph) made their home. The land that fell to their inheritance there, however, did not suffice for their needs, and so, upon the instructions of Joshua, they cleared much of the terrain of its forests in order to render it suitable for cultivation.[1]

At the division of the kingdom, after Solomon's death, the city of Samaria became the capital of the Northern Kingdom, called Israel. In 722 BCE, the king of Assyria, Shalmaneser, captured Samaria and exiled its inhabitants to distant lands; in their place he introduced a number of tribes from afar.[2] The descendants of these foreign tribes, which became assimilated with the remnants of the Israelites who had stayed behind, were Samaritans, or Cuthites, as they were referred to in early Jewish literature. A small Samaritan community remains in the area to this day.

Today, nearly all the inhabitants of the towns and villages in the Samarian Mountains are Arabs, the majority of them Moslems, the rest Christians. Samaria's major city is Shechem, also known by its Arabic name, Nablus; South of it is Ramallah, to the north, Jenin, and to the west, Tul-Karm. The entire region of Samaria was captured by the Israel Defence Forces in the Six-Day War of June 1967.

[1] Joshua 17:14ff. [2] II Kings 17:24

31

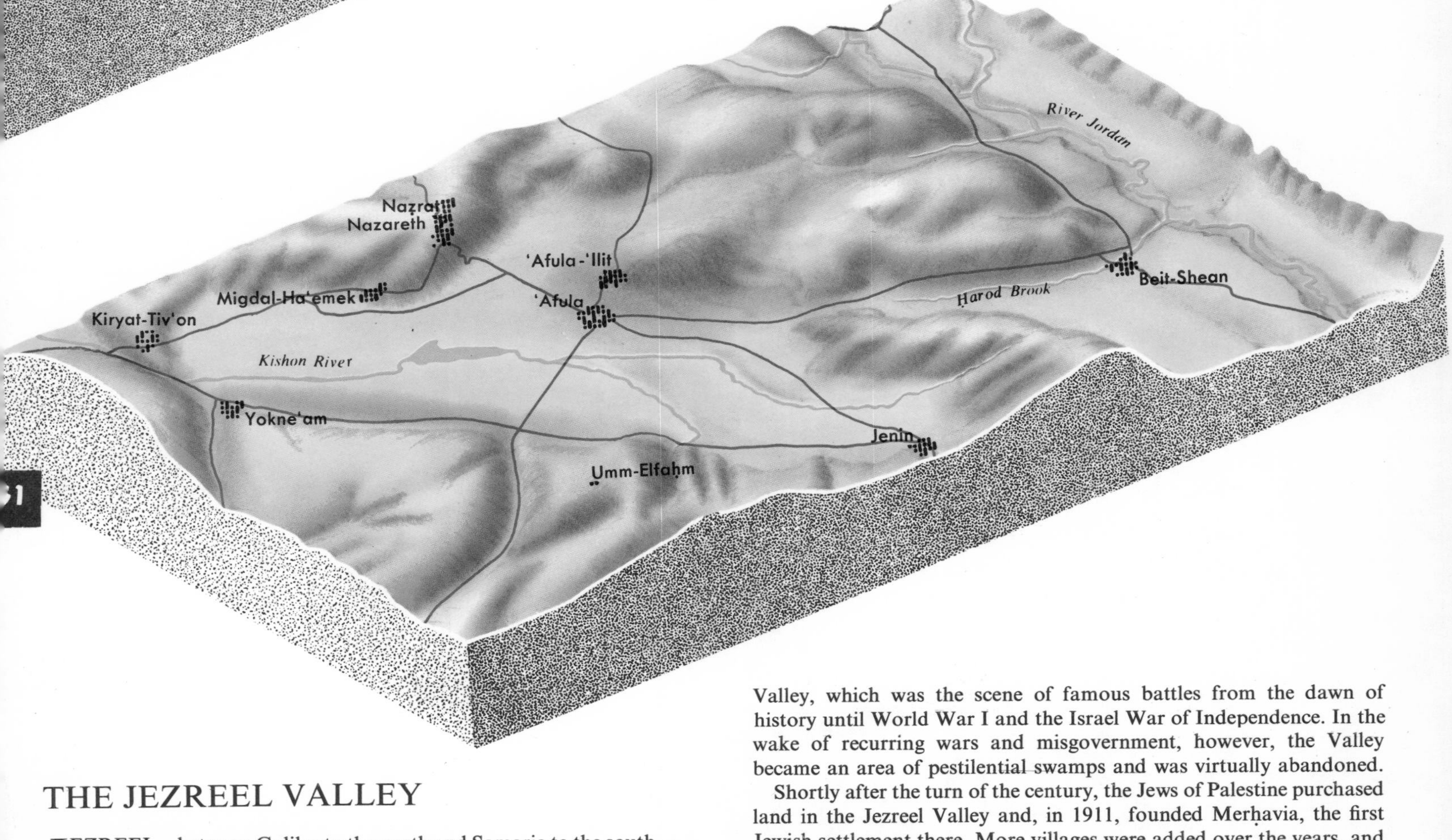

THE JEZREEL VALLEY

JEZREEL—between Galilee to the north and Samaria to the south—is the largest of Israel's valleys, and is often referred to simply as *Ha'emek* 'The Valley'. Because of its fertile soil, it has been densely settled since ancient times. The Via Maris, the old Coastal Route linking Egypt with Damascus and the east, traversed the Jezreel Valley, which was the scene of famous battles from the dawn of history until World War I and the Israel War of Independence. In the wake of recurring wars and misgovernment, however, the Valley became an area of pestilential swamps and was virtually abandoned.

Shortly after the turn of the century, the Jews of Palestine purchased land in the Jezreel Valley and, in 1911, founded Merḥavia, the first Jewish settlement there. More villages were added over the years, and the settlers undertook the dangerous and laborious task of draining the swamps and transforming that malaria-infested region into the fertile, fruit-bearing plain it once was. Their efforts proved an unqualified success.

This map shows the distribution of the moshavim of the different movements—names are listed in the Gazetteer.

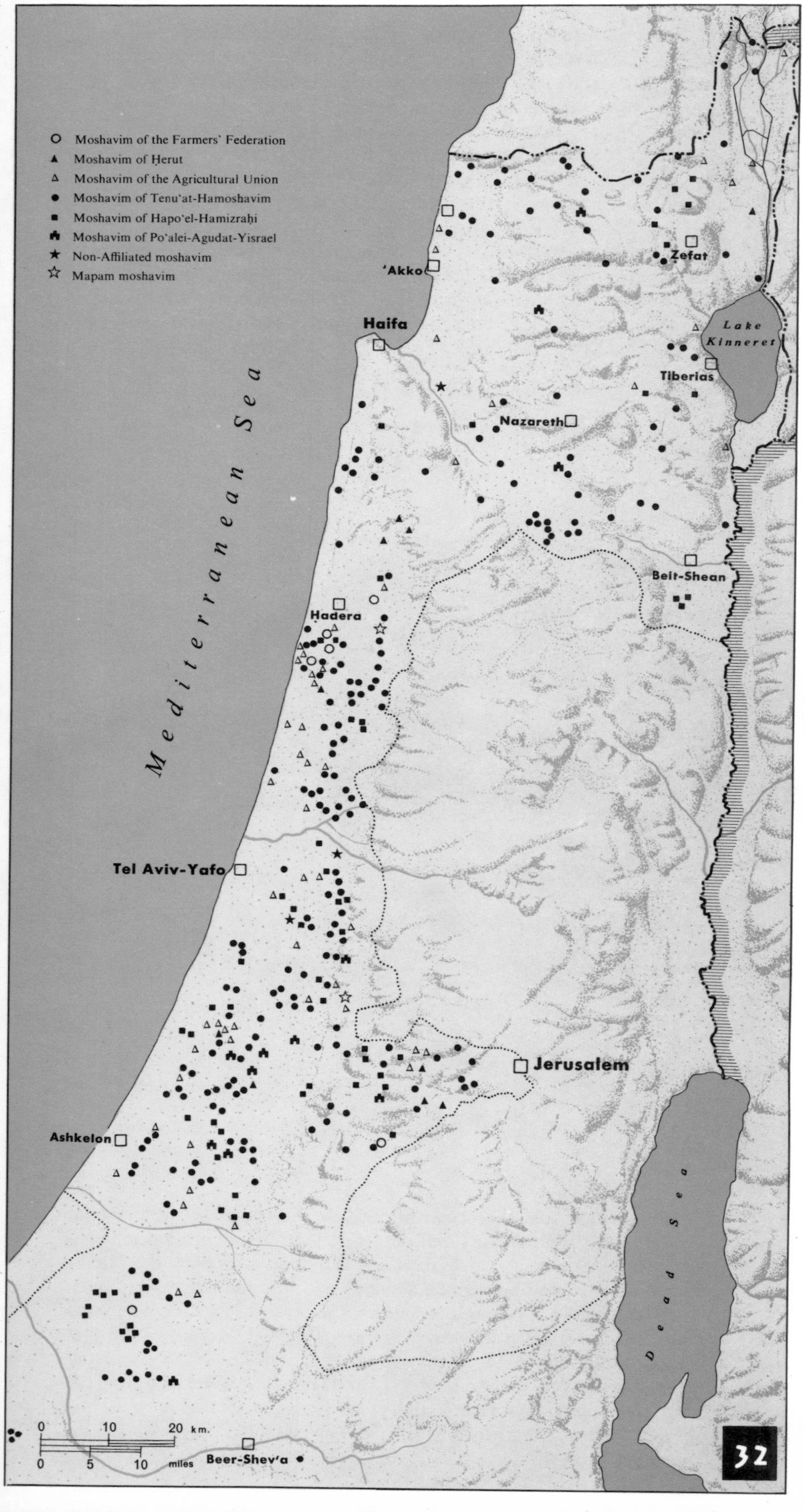

Sedé-Neḥemia, a kibbutz in Upper Galilee

MOSHAVIM

MOSHAVIM (sing.: moshav) are agricultural settlements, based on self-employment and mutual aid. Their products are sold by means of cooperative bodies owned jointly by the members. Built on national lands, the moshavim were founded with the help of the national funds of the World Zionist Organization. Most of the moshavim belong to the Tenu'at Hamoshavim Movement, organized within the framework of the Histadrut—General Federation of Labor. Religious moshavim are attached to the Hapoel Hamizraḥi and Po'alei Agudat Israel movements.

The idea of the moshav was born in the ranks of the pioneer farmers of the larger veteran settlements (*moshava*). The Jewish National Fund procured land near the moshava on which each new settler would receive a small plot and a small house of his own. At first the new settlers would work in the nearby moshava; little by little, they would set up and cultivate their own farmsteads.

The first such moshav was 'Ein-Ganim, established in 1908 near Petaḥ-Tikva. After World War I, Nahalal was founded (1921) in the Jezreel Valley, becoming the first moshav to be organized as an independent settlement. After the establishment of the State in 1948, immigrants from various countries set up additional moshavim, with the help of the Government and of world Jewry, acting through the Jewish Agency.

The *moshav shitufi* (pl.: moshavim shitufiim) combines certain features of the kibbutzim (in economic matters) with some of the moshav (concerning family life): purchasing and marketing and the work in the fields are all carried out cooperatively, while family life is separate and independent. The first moshav shitufi was Kefar-Ḥittim, founded in 1936, in Lower Galilee.

The pioneers of the moshavim were among the most daring and persevering in the conquest of the desert. They toiled hard and devotedly, for many years, to turn areas apparently unfit for cultivation into fertile fields. Together with the settlers of the kibbutzim, they stood fast against harassment and attacks from hostile elements, and they made a vital contribution to the country's security and economic consolidation.

THE KIBBUTZ MOVEMENT

Among the settlements of Israel there are many *kevuẓot* and *kibbutzim*—villages whose members live together communally, in equality; no property (with the exception of certain personal items) is privately owned. Founded mostly on lands of the Jewish National Fund, and financed initially by monies contributed by Jews all over the world, these settlements have constituted an important social, economic and security factor in the development of the country. It was their determination and their perseverance that turned Palestine's swamps and deserts into a fertile garden; and it was their steadfast courage that helped to decide the issue when Israel's fate was put to the military test.

The kibbutz movement is based on the principle of voluntary association, and all major decisions are taken by a majority of the members. The kibbutz is distinguished from the kevuẓa by its size, and generally also by differences in character. The early communal settlements, (the first of which was Degania), founded shortly after the turn of the century were all based on the cultivation of the soil. With the growth of immigration and the increasing complexity of the national economy, the kevuẓot grew in size, and many of them decided to diversify production and attract settlers by adding an industrial "sideline" to their agricultural activity: these villages came to be known as kibbutzim.

The first kibbutz was 'Ein-Ḥarod, in the Jezreel Valley. More kibbutzim sprang up as the years went by, in all parts of the land, their founders and members coming from the ranks of pioneering Jewish youth within the country and from abroad. In this cooperative movement, these young men and women saw the realization of the loftiest ideals of the Jew, and of mankind in general, in the old-new homeland.

Israel's cooperative villages are organized in several movements, according to the ideological outlook of their members. Various segments of the labor movement are represented in three networks: *Iḥud Hakevuẓot Vehakibbuẓim*, *Hakibbuẓ Hameuḥad*, and *Hakibbuẓ Haarẓi*. The religiously-oriented settlements are linked together either in *Hakibbuẓ Hadati* (affiliated with Hapoel Hamizraḥi) or in the smaller network of *Po'alei Agudat Israel*.

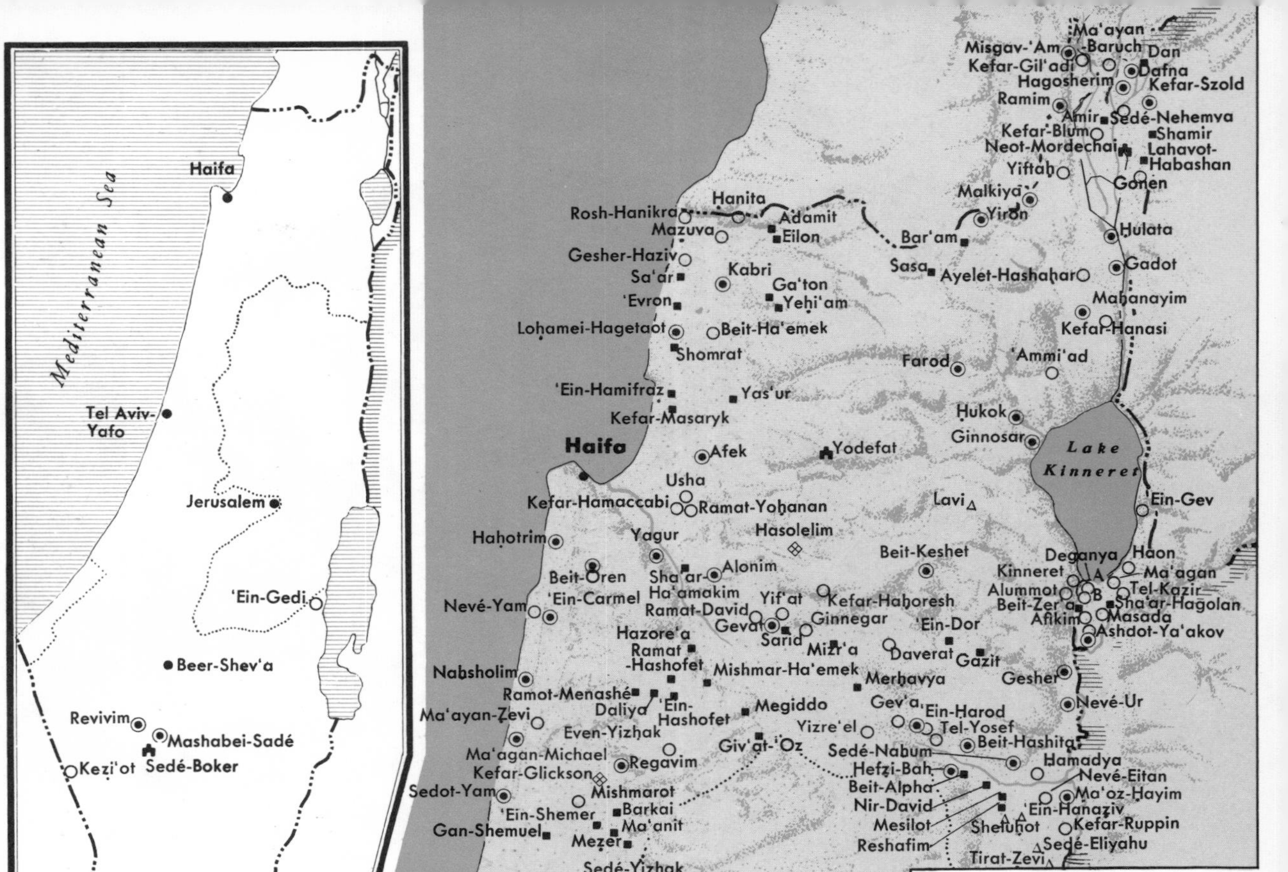

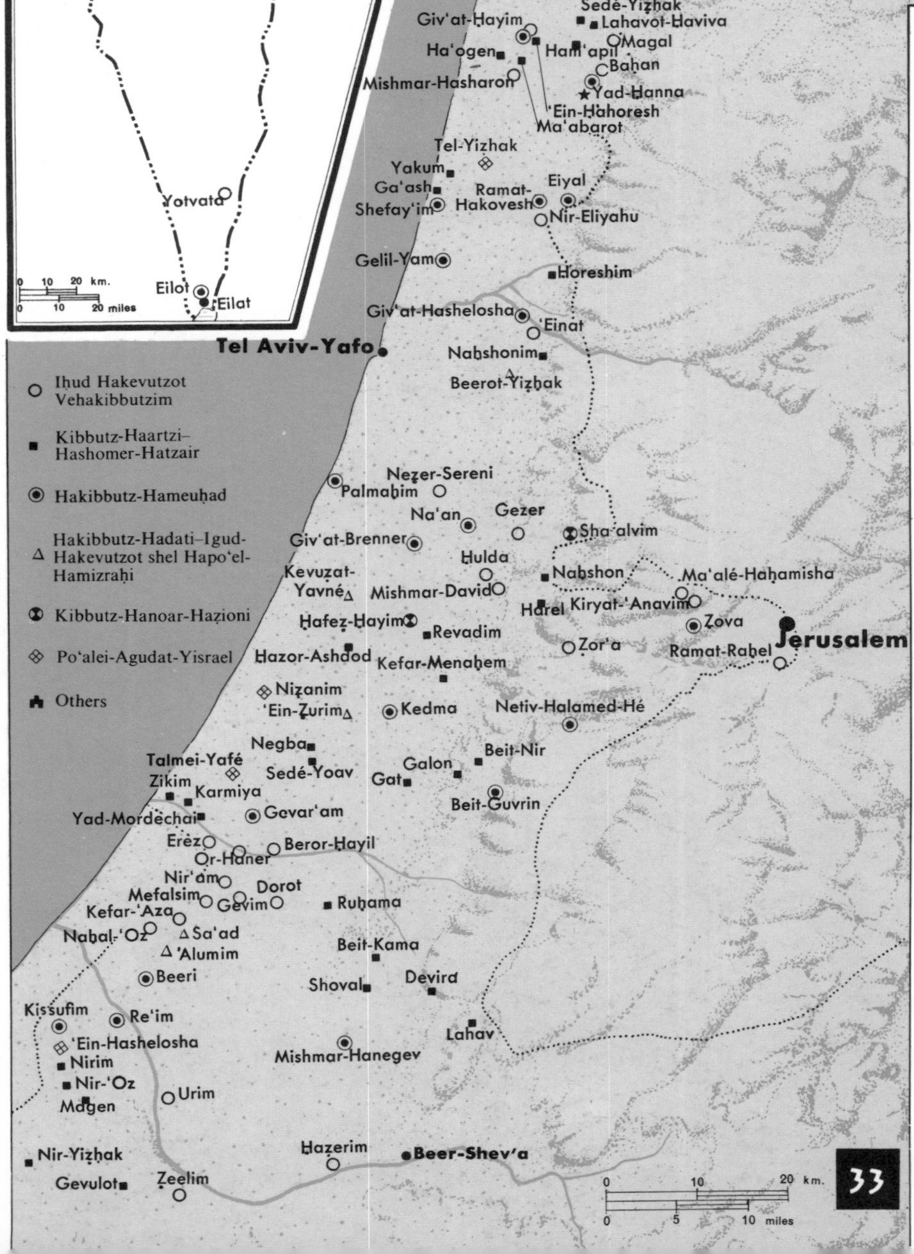

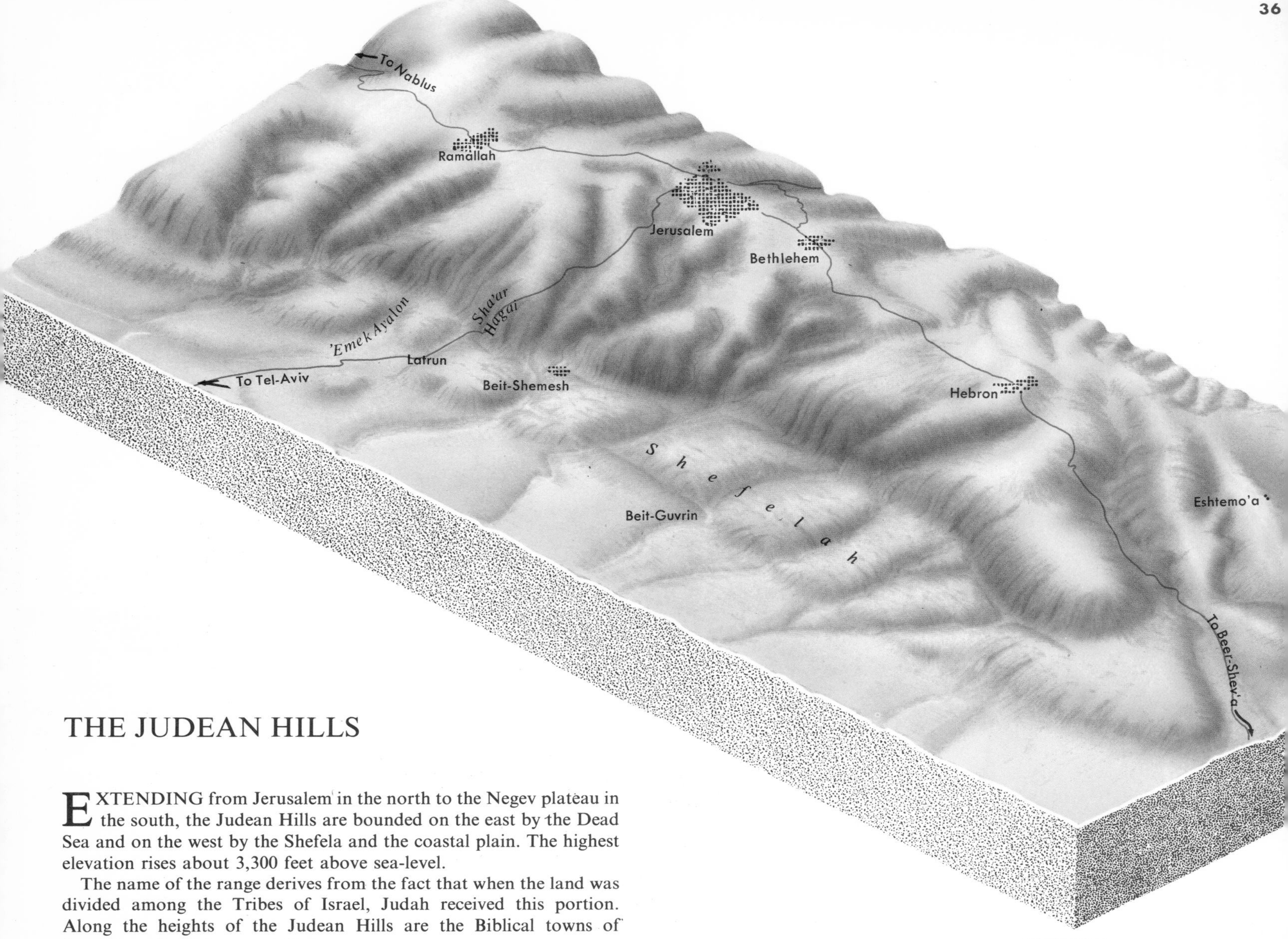

THE JUDEAN HILLS

EXTENDING from Jerusalem in the north to the Negev plateau in the south, the Judean Hills are bounded on the east by the Dead Sea and on the west by the Shefela and the coastal plain. The highest elevation rises about 3,300 feet above sea-level.

The name of the range derives from the fact that when the land was divided among the Tribes of Israel, Judah received this portion. Along the heights of the Judean Hills are the Biblical towns of Jerusalem, Bethlehem and Hebron.

THE WILDERNESS OF JUDEA

THE WILDERNESS of Judea extends along the western shore of the Dead Sea, as far as the heights of Jerusalem, Bethlehem and Hebron to the west. It is hilly, rocky country dissected by deep ravines and canyons running steeply down to the Dead Sea. Precipitation in this region is light, but in rainier years much of the ground is covered with vegetation and has therefore served as pasture-land since earliest times. King David, too, in his younger years grazed his herds in this region.

The southeastern portion of the wilderness is hot and arid. This is the desert (*yeshimon*) mentioned in the Bible, and is the area in which David concealed himself when he was constrained to flee from Saul. In succeeding centuries, this desert and its numerous natural caves served as a haven for monks and ascetic sects fleeing from the tumult of life. This, too, was the dwelling place of the Essenes, in the period of the Second Temple. During the Byzantine era, Christian monks found their way here, and to this day the area contains a number of impressive Greek-Orthodox monasteries.

In the southern part of the Judean Wilderness is the new town of 'Arad, which has a Biblical name.

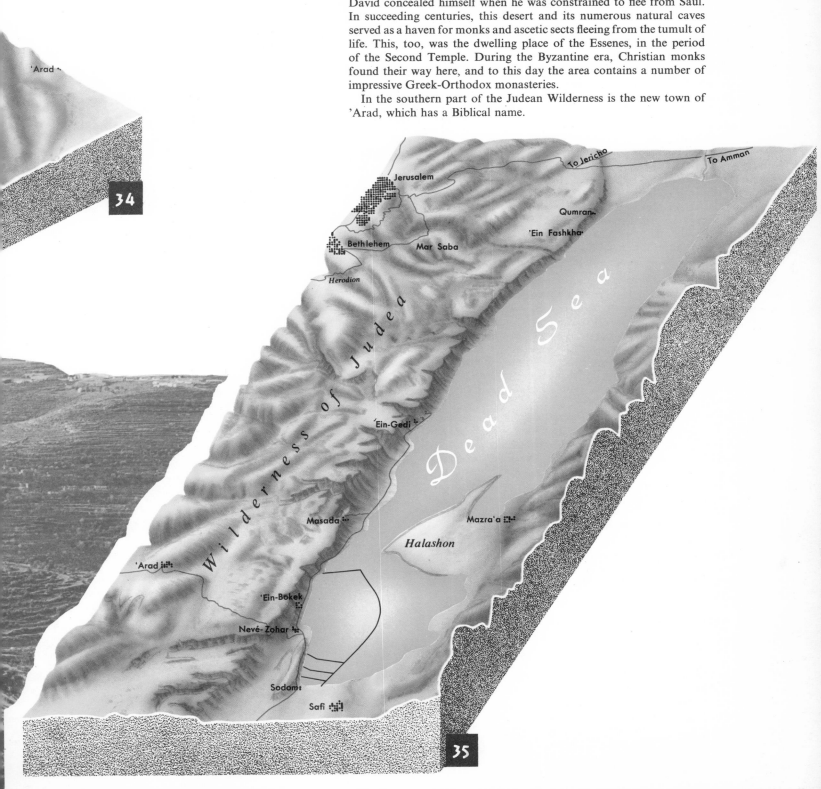

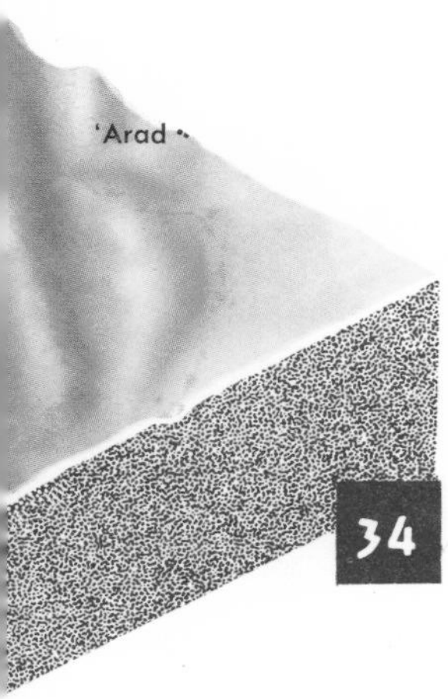

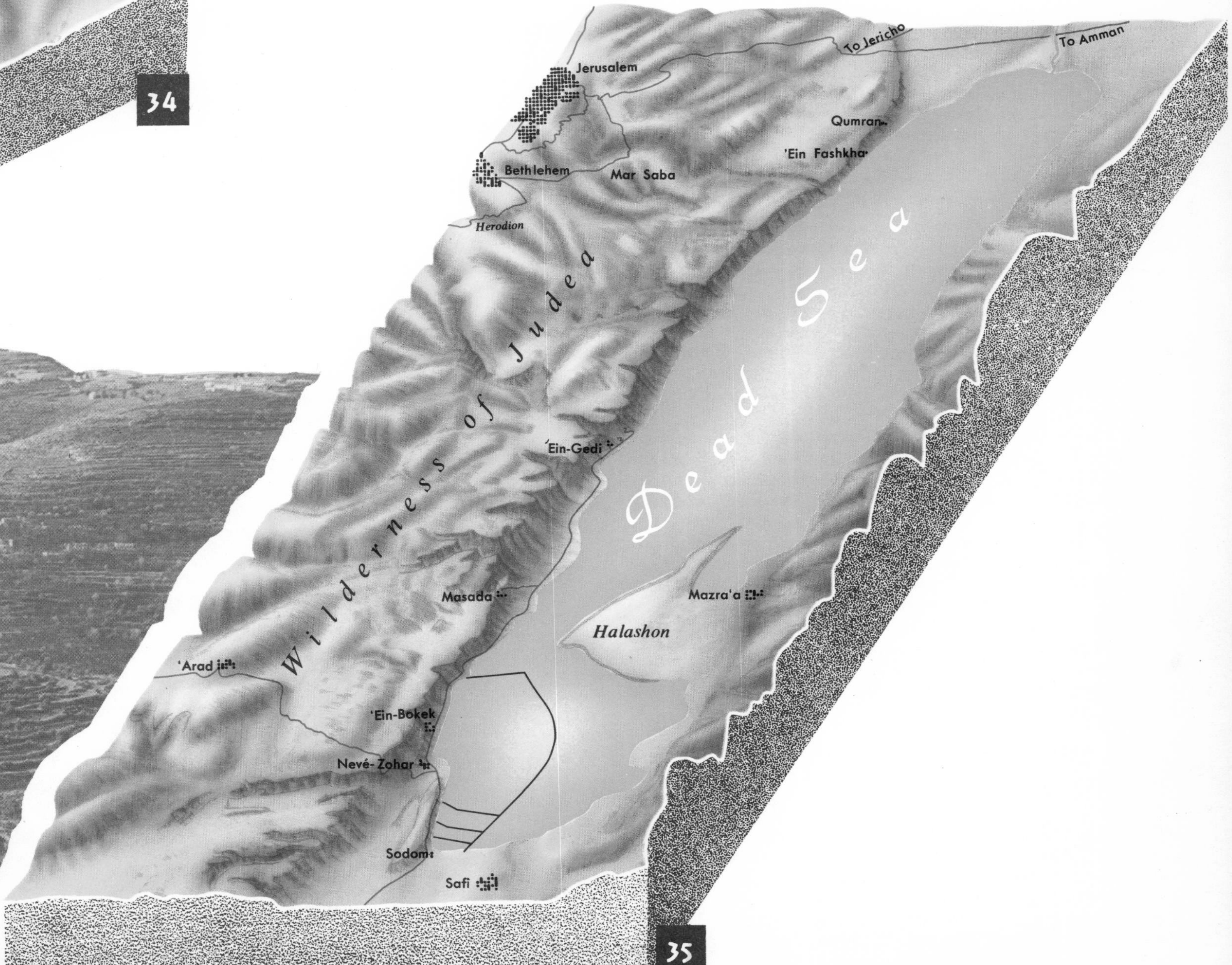

THE POPULATION

THE MAJORITY of Israel's inhabitants are Jews; the rest are Moslems, Christians of various denominations, Druzes and Bahais.

The *Jews* vary according to origin, history and time of arrival in the country. Some trace their ancestry back generations to men and women who had been drawn to the Holy Land by religious attachments and had settled in one of the big cities of those days, Jerusalem, Hebron, Tiberias or Ẓefat, which had been sanctified in Jewish tradition. Many of today's inhabitants of Israel are the sons of Zionist pioneers who left their homes in eastern Europe to hazard the journey to the Holy Land of Israel when it was still under Turkish rule, fired by the ambition to build and fructify its barren wastes and to live there as free men. Still others came during the period of the British Mandate, in one of the waves of immigration from many different countries, to join their brethren in the work of reconstruction and society-building in the land of their fathers. A bare majority of the population arrived after the proclamation of Israel's independence in 1948, most of them from the countries of North Africa and the Near East.

The non-Jewish population is made up mostly of Arabs, the majority of them Moslems, the rest Christians. Their language, Arabic, is one of the two official languages of the State. Most of them live in villages and the remainder in the towns and cities.

Most of the *Moslems* trace their ancestry in Palestine back generations. Some reside in urban centers such as Nazareth, Shefar'am, Haifa, Yafo, Ramla and Lod. The majority are farmers, fellahin, living in villages, others are nomadic or semi-nomadic Beduin in the Negev region in the south or Galilee in the north.

The *Christians* are of varied backgrounds and origins. Most of them are descendants of families that have lived in the country for many years. Their language is Arabic, their way of life similar to that of their Moslem neighbors. A small minority of the Christians are Europeans or Americans who came as monks or priests to live in the Holy Land. The Christians belong to various denominations. The oldest group in the country is the Greek Orthodox. Then there are Greek Catholics, (also known as Melchites), Roman Catholics (Latins), including Maronites, Protestants, Armenians, Ethiopians and Copts.

The Catholic monks belong to several Orders: Franciscans, Carmelites, Jesuits, Benedictines, Salesians and others. There are also Orders of Catholic nuns, among them the Sisters of Zion, Carmelites, St. Claire, St. Joseph, St. Vincent de Paul, St. Charles (Borromaeus) and others.

The *Druzes*, a separate ethnic group, have been living in the country since the twelfth century. Most of them are farmers living in villages on Mount Carmel and in Galilee. Their northernmost village is Hurfeish, in Upper Galilee; the southernmost is Daliyat Elkarmel, on Mount Carmel.

Most of the *Bahais* in Israel come from Europe or America; the rest are from Iran, the birthplace of their faith. They reside mainly in Haifa, where their beautiful shrine and the graves of two of their holy men are located.

POPULATION OF ISRAEL: 1948-1965

	1948	1950	1955	1960	1965
TOTAL	775,000	1,370,100	1,789,100	2,150,400	2,598,400
Jews	625,000	1,203,000	1,590,500	1,911,300	2,299,100
Non-Jews	150,000	167,100	198,600	239,100	299,300
Moslems		116,000	136,300	166,300	212,400
Christians		36,000	43,300	49,600	57,200
Druzes		15,000	18,800	23,100	29,600
Bahais			200	200	200

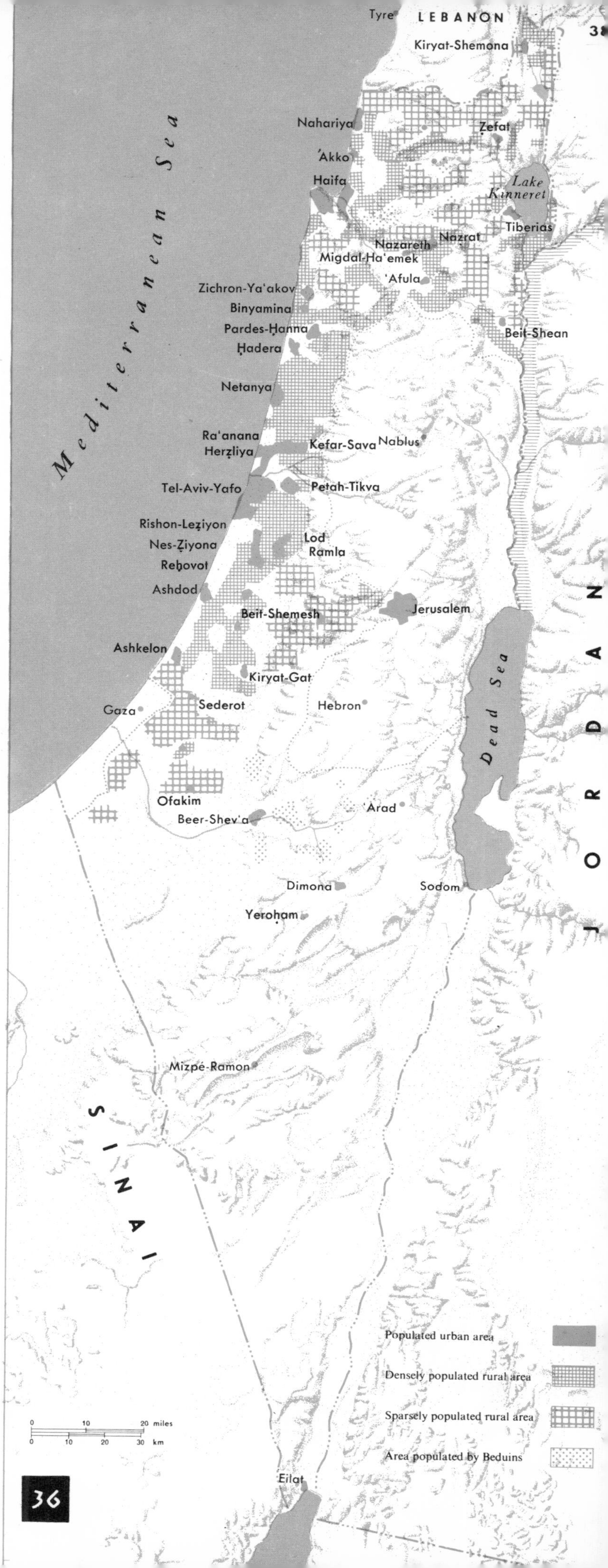

MOSLEMS AND CHRISTIANS

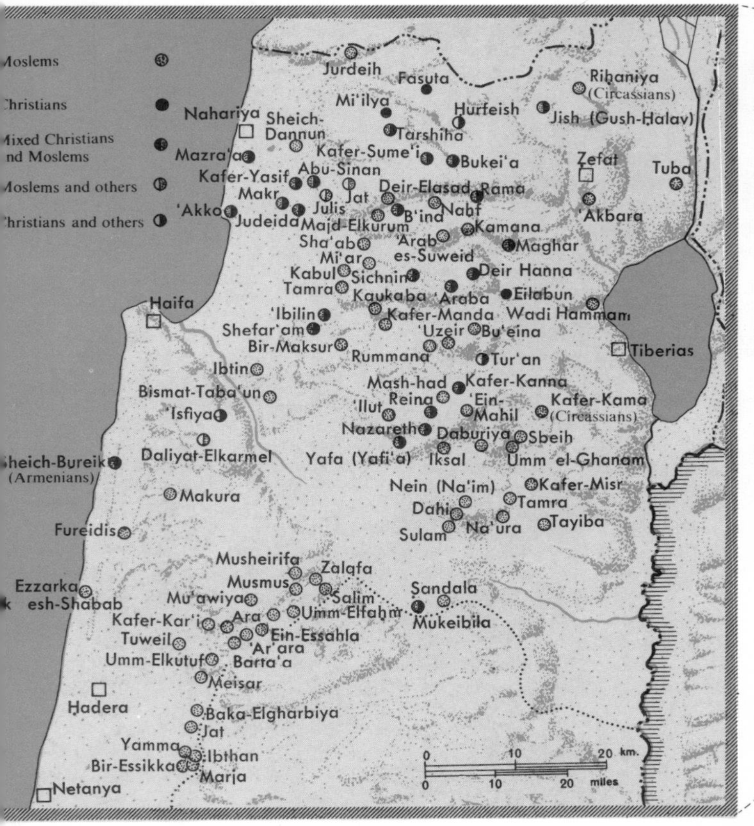

Moslems
Christians
Mixed Christians and Moslems
Moslems and others
Christians and others
Jurdeih
Fasuta
Rihaniya (Circassians)
Mi'ilya
Hurfeish
Jish (Gush-Halav)
Nahariya
Sheich-Dannun
Tarshiha
Kafer-Sume'i
Bukei'a
Zefat
Tuba
Mazra'a
Abu-Sinan
Kafer-Yasif
Deir-Elasad
Rama
Makr
Jat
Julis
B'ina
Nahf
'Akko
Judeida
Majd-Elkurum
'Akbara
Sha'ab
'Arab es-Suweid
Kamana
Mi'ar
Maghar
Kabul
Sichnin
Deir Hanna
Tamra
Kaukaba
'Araba
Eilabun
Haifa
'Ibilin
Kafer-Manda
Wadi Hammam
Shefar'am
'Uzeir
Bu'eina
Bir-Maksur
Rummana
Tiberias
Ibtin
Tur'an
Mash-had
Kafer-Kanna
Bismat-Taba'un
'Ilut
Reina
'Ein-Mahil
Kafer-Kama (Circassians)
'Isfiya
Nazareth
Daburiya
Sbeih
Daliyat-Elkarmel
Yafa (Yafi'a)
Iksal
Umm el-Ghanam
Sheich-Bureik (Armenians)
Nein (Na'im)
Kafer-Misr
Makura
Dahi
Tamra
Tayiba
Fureidis
Sulam
Na'ura
Musheirifa
Zalafa
Musmus
Ezzarka
Salim
Sandala
Mu'awiya
esh-Shabab
Ara
Umm-Elfahm
Mukeibila
Kafer-Kar'i
Tuweil
'Ar'ara
Ein-Essahla
Umm-Elkutuf
Barta'a
Meisar
Hadera
Baka-Elgharbiya
Jat
Yamma
Ibthan
Bir-Essikka
Marja
Netanya
0 10 20 km.
0 10 20 miles

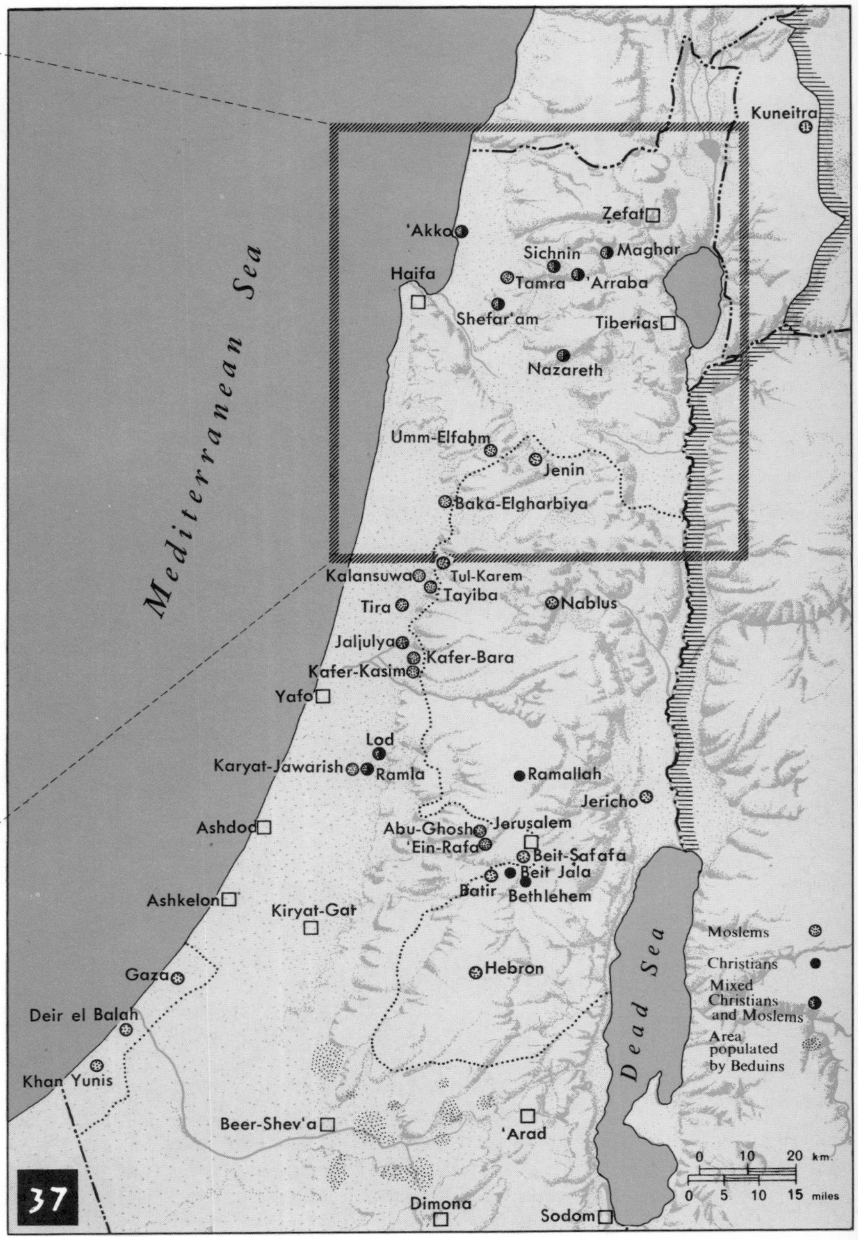

Kuneitra
Mediterranean Sea
Zefat
'Akko
Sichnin
Maghar
Haifa
Tamra
'Arraba
Shefar'am
Tiberias
Nazareth
Umm-Elfahm
Jenin
Baka-Elgharbiya
Kalansuwa
Tul-Karem
Tayiba
Tira
Nablus
Jaljulya
Kafer-Bara
Kafer-Kasim
Yafo
Lod
Karyat-Jawarish
Ramla
Ramallah
Jericho
Ashdod
Abu-Ghosh
Jerusalem
'Ein-Rafa
Beit-Safafa
Beit Jala
Batir
Bethlehem
Ashkelon
Kiryat-Gat
Moslems
Christians
Mixed Christians and Moslems
Area populated by Beduins
Gaza
Hebron
Dead Sea
Deir el Balah
Khan Yunis
Beer-Shev'a
'Arad
0 10 20 km.
0 5 10 15 miles
Dimona
Sodom
37

Beduins in the Negev

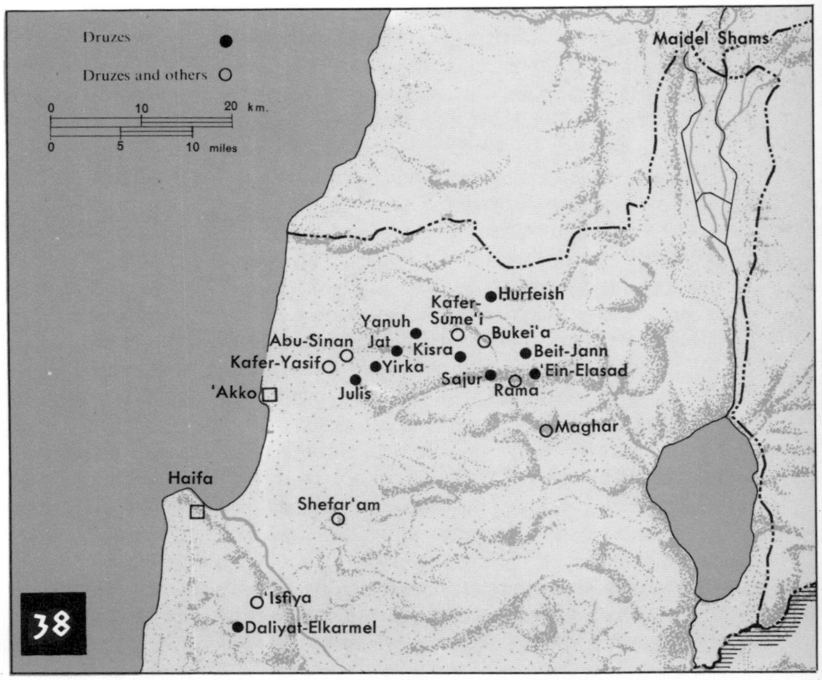

Druzes
Druzes and others
0 10 20 km.
0 5 10 miles
Majdel Shams
Hurfeish
Kafer-Sume'i
Yanuh
Bukei'a
Abu-Sinan
Jat
Kisra
Beit-Jann
Kafer-Yasif
Yirka
Sajur
'Ein-Elasad
'Akko
Julis
Rama
Maghar
Haifa
Shefar'am
'Isfiya
Daliyat-Elkarmel
38

DRUZES

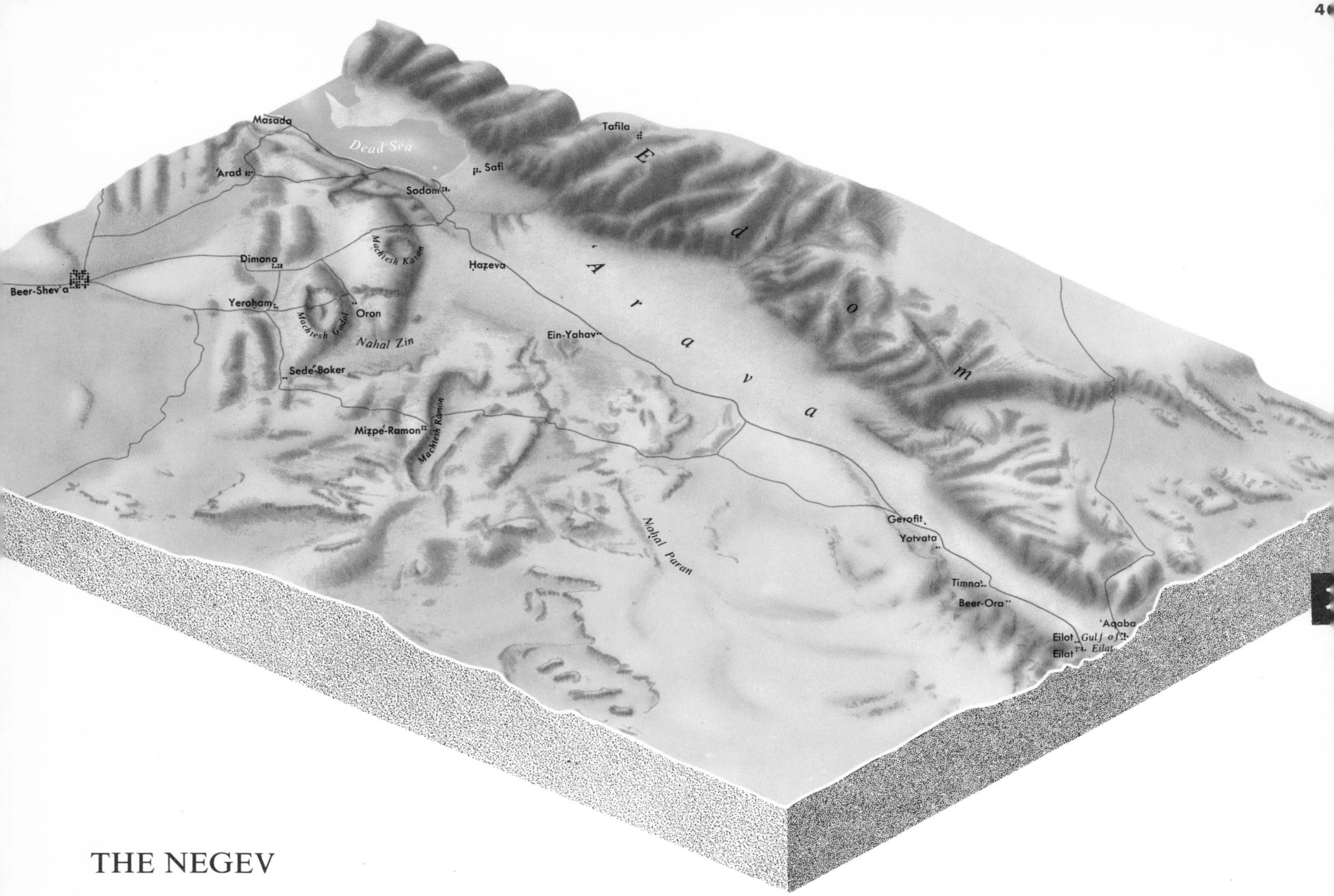

THE NEGEV

THE SOUTHERN portion of Israel, comprising more than 60 per cent of the country's total area, is known as the Negev. It is the driest region west of the Jordan River, hence its name, 'Negev'—"dryness." The Patriarchs made their home in the Negev, and many of the events described in the Bible took place there. After the Exodus from Egypt, Israelites made an abortive attempt to penetrate directly into the Promised Land by striking from Sinai into the Negev. Eventually, entry into the land was effected by a more circuitous route. In the distribution of the land among the twelve tribes, the Negev fell to the Tribe of Simeon; the northern part and its extension, known today as the Judean wilderness and the Judean Hills, went to the Tribe of Judah. After the division of Solomon's kingdom, the Negev comprised the bulk of the Southern Kingdom (Judah). A well-populated area, it contained both farms and pasture-land. King Solomon mined its copper and exported it via the Red Sea port of 'Ezion-Gever, at the extreme south of the Negev.

In the Roman Period, a line of fortifications for the defense of the Roman Empire traversed the Negev. The cities of the Negev reached new heights of growth and development under the Byzantines, only to be destroyed later in the Arab invasion. Their remnants constitute some of the most fascinating archaeological finds in Israel today. In the centuries that followed the Arab conquest, the Negev, abandoned by its settlers, its soil no longer cultivated, became a land of roaming Beduins.

After World War I, the Jewish National Fund began purchasing land in the Negev. During World War II, in 1943, Jews began to re-settle the region, although the settlers encountered difficulties from the British authorities. When the Egyptian army invaded Israel in the summer of 1948, most of the young Jewish settlements in the Negev came under siege. Israel's victory in that war was followed by a period of expansion in both the agricultural and the industrial development of the Negev, as additional towns and settlements were founded and steps were taken to exploit, in growing measure, the substantial mineral deposits to be found in the area. Two developments gave special impetus to this trend: the opening of the Red Sea port of Eilat in 1957, and the bringing of water to this arid region—first through the Yarkon-Negev pipeline (1955) and later with the completion of the National Water Carrier (1964), also known as the Kinneret-Negev Water Project.

Most populous city in the region is Beer-Shev'a of Biblical fame, often referred to as "Capital of the Negev."

RIVERS AND SPRINGS

OF ISRAEL'S many streams, some descend westward to the Mediterranean, while others run eastward into the Jordan Valley and its lakes—Lake Kinneret (Sea of Galilee) and the Dead Sea; streams originating in the Eilat area empty into the Red Sea. The watershed traverses the land from north to south; Jerusalem straddles the watershed.

Among the better-known of Israel's rivers are the *Jordan,* rising in the northeastern corner of the country, where its headwaters, the Dan, the Senir and the Hermon, meet, running and turning south, through Lake Kinneret, finally spilling its waters into the Dead Sea; the *Kishon,* flowing into Haifa Bay; the *Yarkon,* in the coastal plain, forming the dividing line between the Sharon (north) and Shefelah (south). The *Shikma,* southernmost of the Mediterranean-oriented streams, named after the ancient sycamores on its banks; the *Besor,* largest of the streams in the Negev, emptying into the Mediterranean; the *Zin* and the *Paran* and their numerous tributaries spread over the central Negev; and the *Shelomo,* the largest of the streams to be found in the Eilat area, flow only during the rainy season.

The northernmost and richest of Israel's springs is the *Dan,* one of the sources of the Jordan River. The spring of *Ḥarod* rises in the foothills of Mount Gilbo'a, feeding the stream of *Ḥarod,* which runs down into the Jordan. The springs of *Kabri,* emerging in the foothills of the Galilean Mountains near the Mediterranean coast, provide some of the finest water in the country; in the past it was brought to the town of 'Akko by an aqueduct, remains of which may be seen to this day.

From the mountains lining the western shore of the Dead Sea flow a number of springs, the principal one of which is *'Ein-Gedi,* cascading from its mountain top in a series of scenic waterfalls that have created a lovely oasis of verdure in the midst of the arid wilderness of Judea.

Israel also boasts a number of hot springs, over and around which bath-houses have been built for those who seek the healing powers of these waters. The most prominent of these are the Hot Springs of *Tiberias,* on Lake Kinneret, and the Hot Springs of *Zohar* and of *Mazor,* on the shores of the Dead Sea.

The Yarkon river

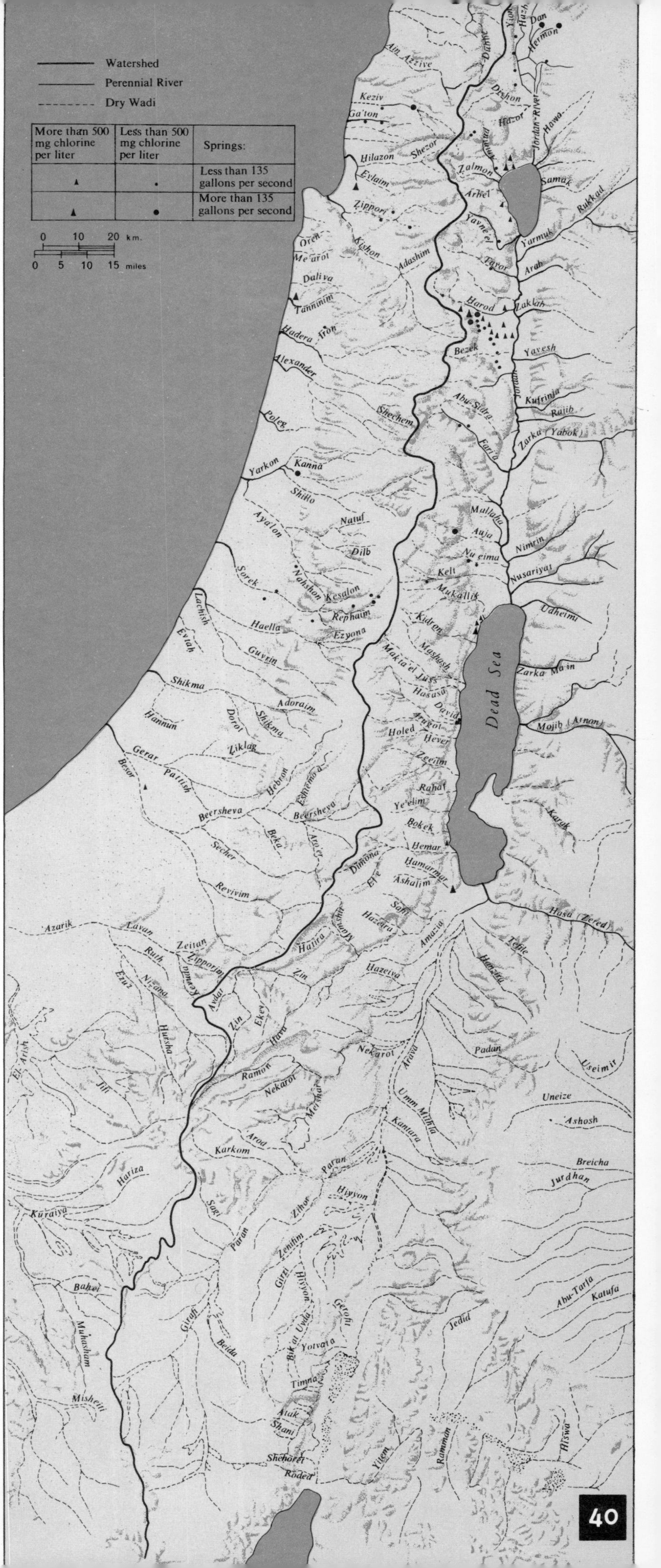

AGRICULTURE

FROM THE inception of the Jewish national revival in Palestine in the latter half of the 19th century, agriculture was the main occupation of the settlers. The early pioneers were keenly aware of the importance of re-establishing the link between people and soil if they were to strike root again in the ancient homeland and raise a generation whose attachment to the land would not be sentimental and spiritual alone.

The first Jewish farmers in Palestine cultivated field crops, vineyards and, in the coastal plain, fruit orchards. The eminent success of the citrus export led to an expansion of this branch of farming in the years that followed.

Over the years, considerable attention has been directed to agriculture by various scientific institutions and experimental stations, and the results of this research have been reflected in the development of more efficient methods of intensive farming, irrigation, crop rotation and the like, as well as in the introduction of new fruits and crops rarely or never before seen in Israel.

With the growth and development of farming settlements, agricultural production grew apace and underwent substantial improvement. Agriculture has become a major factor in Israel's economy: from a country that, in the early years of its statehood, had to import some seventy percent of its food requirements, Israel has become virtually self-sufficient agriculturally and even exports some products. The largest item of agricultural export is Israel's citrus fruit, particularly the Jaffa orange, which has made a name for itself in markets all over the world.

In recent years, the cultivation of flowers has taken on growing importance. Thanks to its warm climate, Israel is able to export its flowers to Europe even during the winter months.

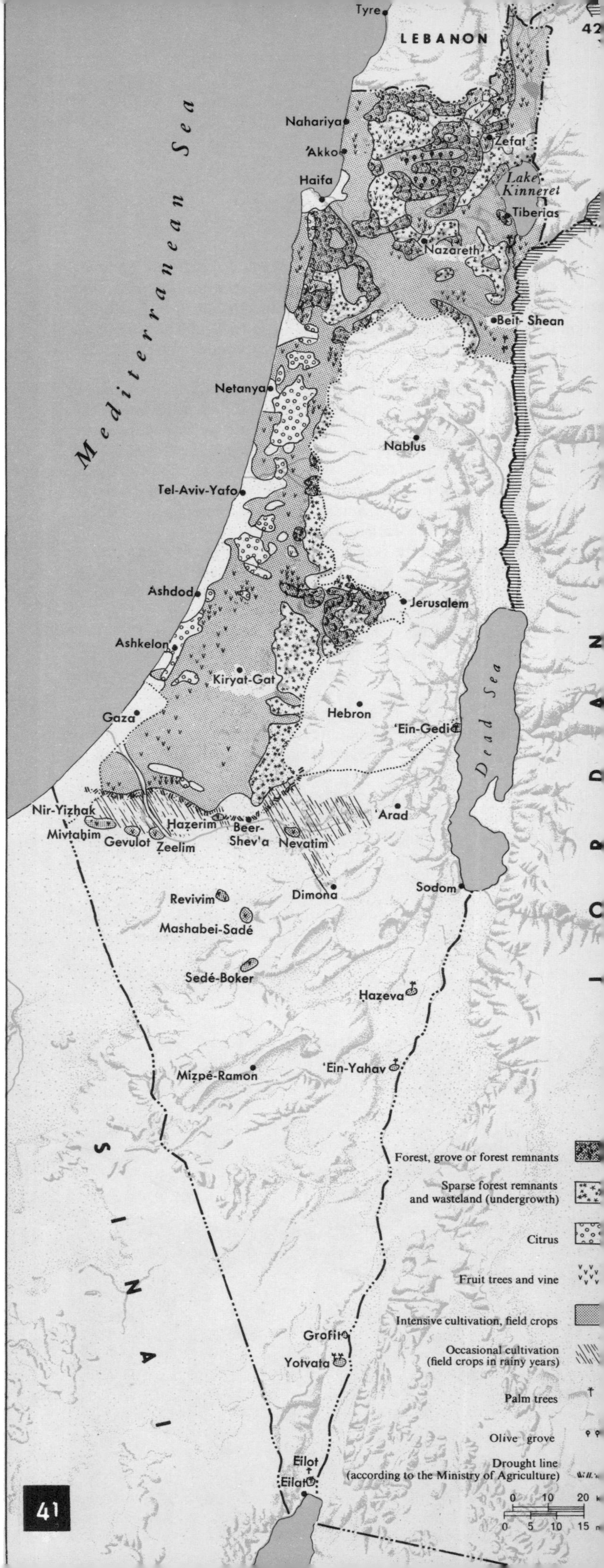

INDUSTRIAL DEVELOPMENT

THE EARLY pioneers who came to Palestine nearly a century ago worked on the land and there was in those days little in the way of industry. However, here and there industrial enterprises based on some agricultural product were established, such as the wine-cellars in Rishon-Leẓiyon and Zichron-Ya'akov, near the extensive local vineyards. The idea of using wines from the Holy Land for sacramental purposes has taken hold among growing numbers of Jews abroad, giving a boost to the wine industry in Israel.

The growth of immigration and the accelerated rate of building that has come in its wake led to the establishment of the 'Nesher' Cement Works near Haifa. Later, similar enterprises for the manufacture of building materials were founded elsewhere.

After World War I, a number of textile plants were built. Such a plant was the primary economic factor in the founding of the city of Ḥolon. Since the establishment of the State, numerous textile factories have been set up, frequently playing an important economic role in the life of the new towns—known as Development Towns—that have sprung up in various parts of the country.

The largest of Israel's glassworks is the Phoenicia plant on the Haifa coast, not far from the spot where, according to legend, glass was first made.

The beet-sugar grown in Israel is processed in two plants: one located at 'Afula, the other at Kiryat-Gat. Various industrial enterprises in the south exploit the mineral deposits located in the Dead Sea and the Negev region, some in substantial quantities. The Dead Sea minerals mined in the Negev include phosphates, petroleum, copper, gypsum, and quartz. Among Israel's leading industries today, mention should also be made of plywood, tires, plastics, paper, pharmaceuticals, trucks and automobiles and, of course, diamond-polishing—the country's major industrial export.

There has been a notable trend in recent years, among the kibbutzim, to add an industrial "sideline" to their main agricultural activity in order to supplement their income in what is becoming an increasingly industrial economy. In a number of instances, the industrial "sideline" has been so successful that over the years it has outstripped the farm in its economic importance to the kibbutz.

Tyre
LEBANON
Kiryat-Shemona
SYRIA
Nahariya
Ma'alot
Shipyard
Power station
Akko
Haifa
Carmiel
Zefat
Oil refineries
Lake Kinneret
Tiberias
Nesher
Nazareth
Afikim
Migdal-Ha'emek
Afula
Zichron-Ya'akov
Binyamina
Beit-Shean
Mishmarot
Pardes-Hanna
Hadera
Mediterranean Sea
Netanya
JORDAN
Nablus
Herzliya
Kefar-Sava
Power station
Tel-Aviv-Yafo
Petah-Tikva
Bat-Yam
Rishon-Leziyon
Nes-Ziyona
Lod
Ramla
Aeronautics industry
Rehovot
Power station
Jericho
Ashdod
Gedera
Jerusalem
Beit-Shemesh
Kiryat-Malachi
Ashkelon
Kiryat-Gat
Oil wells
Helez
Hebron
Gaza
Sederot
Netivot
Natural-gas wells
Integrated chemical industries
Phosphate and marble mines
Dead Sea
Ofakim
Beer-Shev'a
'Arad
Dimona
Sodom
Yeroham
Postash, Bromine and Magnesium production
Oron
Phosphates
Mizpé-Ramon
Flint clay and Gypsum mining
SINAI
Oil pipe line
Copper mining and refinery
Timn'a
Eilat
Desalination
0 10 20 km.
0 5 10 15 miles
Heavy industry
Light industry
Diamond polishing
Food processing
Textiles
Metal industry
Cement production
Mining
Atomic reactor
Chemical industry
Cosmetics industry
Electrical appliances
Wine cellars
Asbestos
Glass industry
Pharmaceutic industry
Motor construction
Sugar refinery
Electronics
Rubber and plastics
Plywood
Tyres
Furniture production
Paper making
Printing industry
Chemical fibers
Leather industry
Ceramics industry
Motor-car assembly
Bicycles
Packaging industry
Paints and varnishes
Building stone

UNIVERSITIES

ISRAEL'S two veteran institutions of higher learning are the Technion—Israel Institute of Technology, in Haifa, and the Hebrew University in Jerusalem—both founded long before Israel became an independent State. Two universities that have come on the scene since independence are Bar-Ilan, near Ramat-Gan, named after the Religious-Zionist leader, Rabbi Meir Bar-Ilan, and the University of Tel Aviv. The world-renowned Weizmann Institute of Science, at Reḥovot, primarily a research institution, opened more than thirty years ago.

The cornerstone of the first Hebrew University was laid on the heights of Mount Scopus in Jerusalem on July 24, 1918, shortly after the British army had captured the city, and while fighting could still be heard from the nearby front. The official opening was celebrated on April 1, 1925. The war that followed the Arabs' attack on Israel in 1948 left Mount Scopus and the University buildings located there cut off from the rest of Israel, and for nearly two decades—until Jerusalem was re-united in June 1967—the buildings were not in use. For a few years the University was housed in various buildings scattered throughout the New City of Jerusalem, until the completion of a beautiful new campus on one of the hilltops of western Jerusalem, which includes also the National and University Library, the largest in Israel.

Construction of the Technion—on the initiative of *'Ezra,* an association of German Jews—began in 1912. The building, in the heart of Haifa, was completed after the First World War and was officially opened in 1925. The steady growth of the institution necessitated removal to a new campus, which was built on the heights of Mount Carmel, commanding a majestic view of the Bay, the city of Haifa and the surrounding countryside.

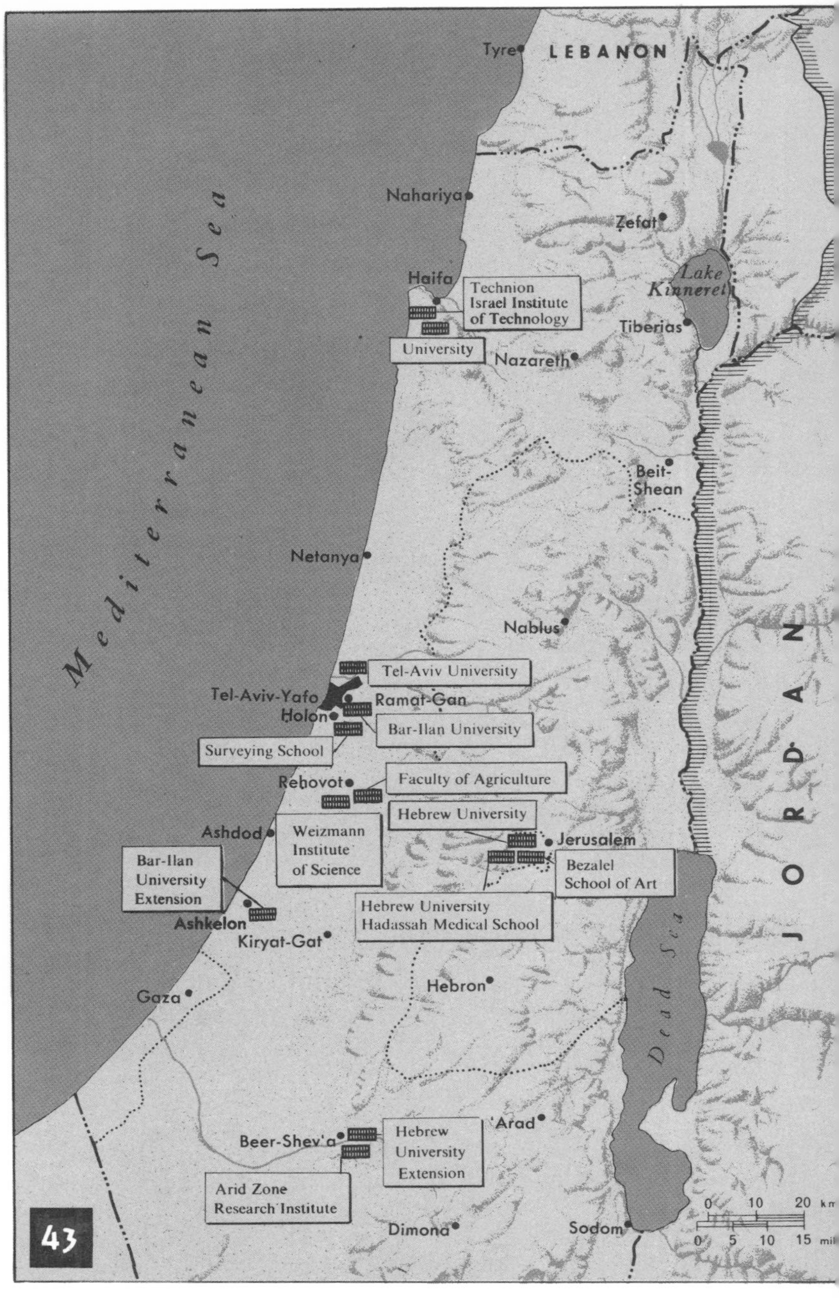

The Hebrew University of Jerusalem

YESHIVOT (TALMUDIC ACADEMIES)

THE TWO most prevalent types of Talmudic academy in Israel are the Great Yeshiva, providing full-time instruction in Talmud for young men from the age of 18 who study either towards ordination as rabbis or, not infrequently, for the sake of pure scholarship, and the Secondary Yeshiva, combining secular with religious studies at high school level.

Yeshivot, whose history in the Holy Land goes back to ancient times, have played an important role in molding the spiritual image of the Jewish people. The town of Yavne in the second century became known as the "Second Jerusalem" by dint of the yeshiva that had been founded there immediately following upon the destruction of Jerusalem at the hands of the Romans in the year 70. Many of the sages who contributed to the *Mishna* (Oral Law) studied and taught there. Further north, in the Galilean yeshivot of Caesarea, Tiberias and Ẓipori (Sepphoris), a later generation of rabbis and scholars created the Palestinian (*Yerushalmi*) Talmud, which was completed in the fourth century.

In the wake of oppression and persecution in the Middle Ages, the number of yeshivot in the Holy Land gradually dwindled, but the resumption of Jewish life in some of the cities (e.g., Jerusalem, Hebron, Ẓefat, Tiberias) led to the opening of new yeshivot—a process that was greatly accelerated with the advent of the major waves of Jewish immigration to the Land of Israel in the last century. In recent years, yeshivot have been established also in a number of agricultural settlements.

Most of the yeshivot are located in Jerusalem and Benei-Berak. Among the better-known academies are 'Eẓ-Ḥayim ("Tree of Life") and Hebron, in Jerusalem, and Ponevez, in Benei-Berak. 'Eẓ-Ḥayim was founded in the Old City; Hebron is named after the city of the Patriarchs, where it was located until the pogrom of 1929 forced it to move to Jerusalem. Among the rural yeshivot are Kerem Yavne, near the site of ancient Yavne, and the Yeshiva of Benei-'Akiva at Kefar-Haroé, in the northern coastal plain.

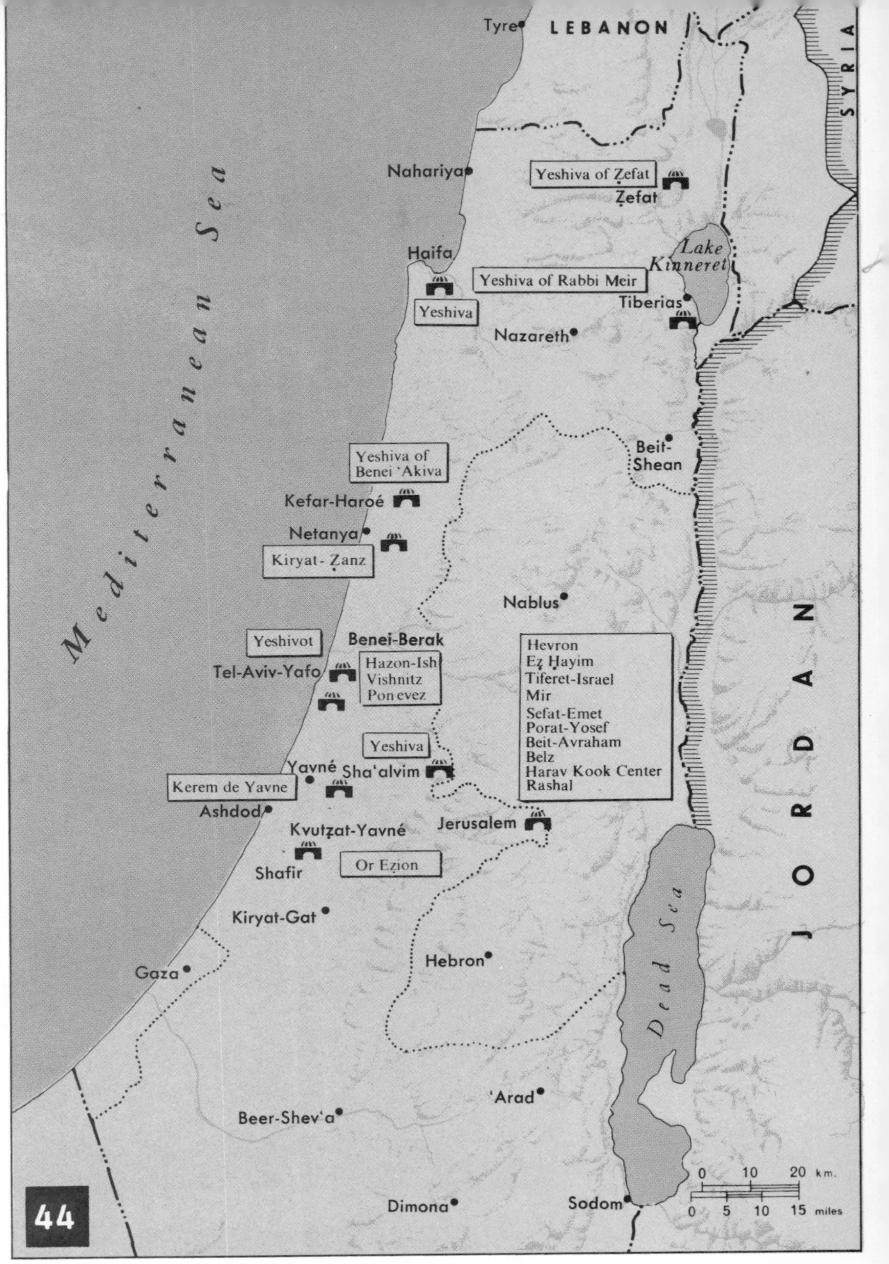

The Technion, Haifa

Bar-Ilan University, Ramat-Gan

SETTLEMENTS NAMED AFTER PEOPLE: FROM THE BIBLE

PERSONALITIES from the Bible, famous rabbis, Christian friends of Israel, Zionists, philanthropists, labor leaders, pioneers, and soldiers have all been honored in Modern Israel by having settlements named after them. Ramat-Raḥel, a kibbutz just south of Jerusalem, is named for the Matriarch Rachel, whose grave is nearby, in Bethlehem. Several settlements bear the names of the Tribes of Israel in whose territory they are located: Dan and Ramot-Naftali *(Naphtali)* in the North; the Regional Council of Zevulun *(Zebulun)* in Western Galilee; Ramot-Menashé, Sha'ar-Menashé (both from the tribe *Mannasseh)* and Sha'ar-Efrayim *(Ephraim)* at the edge of the Sharon Plain; and the Regional Council of Benei Shim'on *(Simeon)* in the South.

Joshua son of Nun is recalled in Kefar Bin-Nun in the Valley of Ayalon, where he won his greatest victory. The Judges are honored in Gid'ona, Kefar Gid'on *(Gideon),* Devora *(Deborah)* and Barak in the Jezreel Valley. Named after kings of Judah are Sede-'Uziyahu *(Uzziah)* in the coastal plain and Amaẓya *(Amasiah)* in Judea.

Various tribal leaders are commemorated in such places as Ḥaniel (*Haniel,* Manasseh) Elisham'a (*Elishamah,* Ephraim) in the Sharon; Aḥisamach and Aḥi'ezer (*Ahisamach* and *Ahiezer*, Dan) and Zeitan (Benjamin). Naḥshon and 'Amminadav (*Nahshon* and *Amminadab*) are villages in the Judean Hills, somewhat to the north of Shuval and Aḥuzam (*Shobal* and *Ahuzam*); all four of Judah. The Tribe of Simeon is represented by Yachini and Yoshivia (*Josibiah*).

RABBIS

CHRISTIAN FRIENDS OF ISRAEL

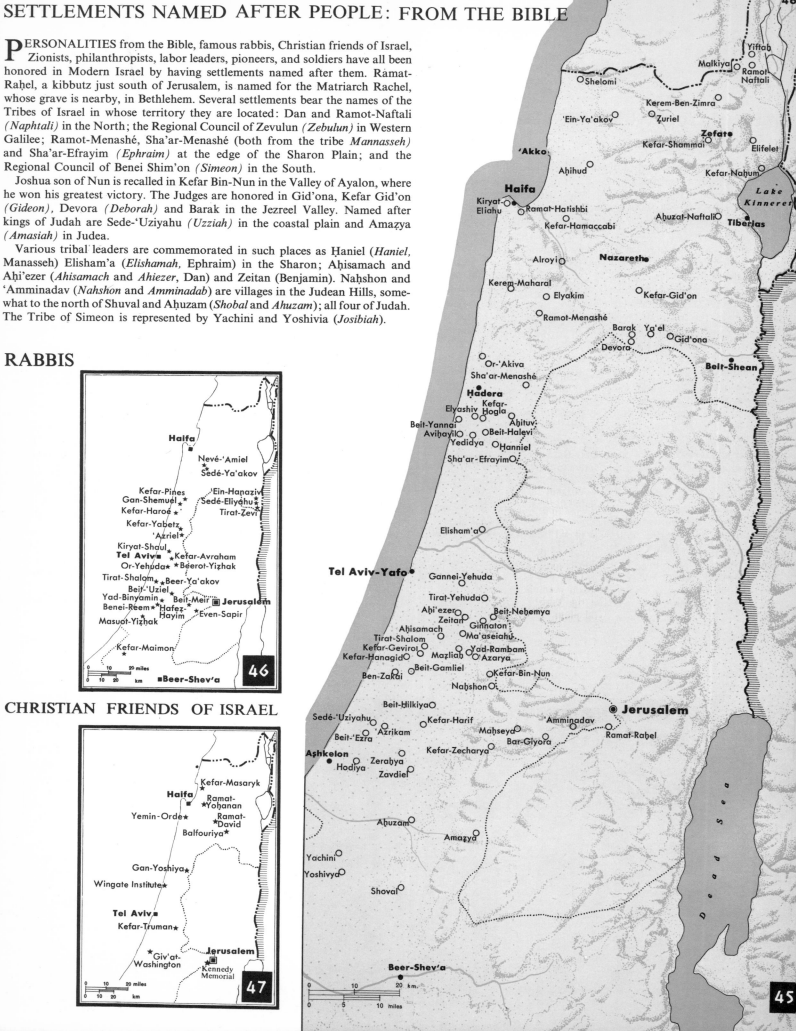

ZIONISTS AND BENEFACTORS

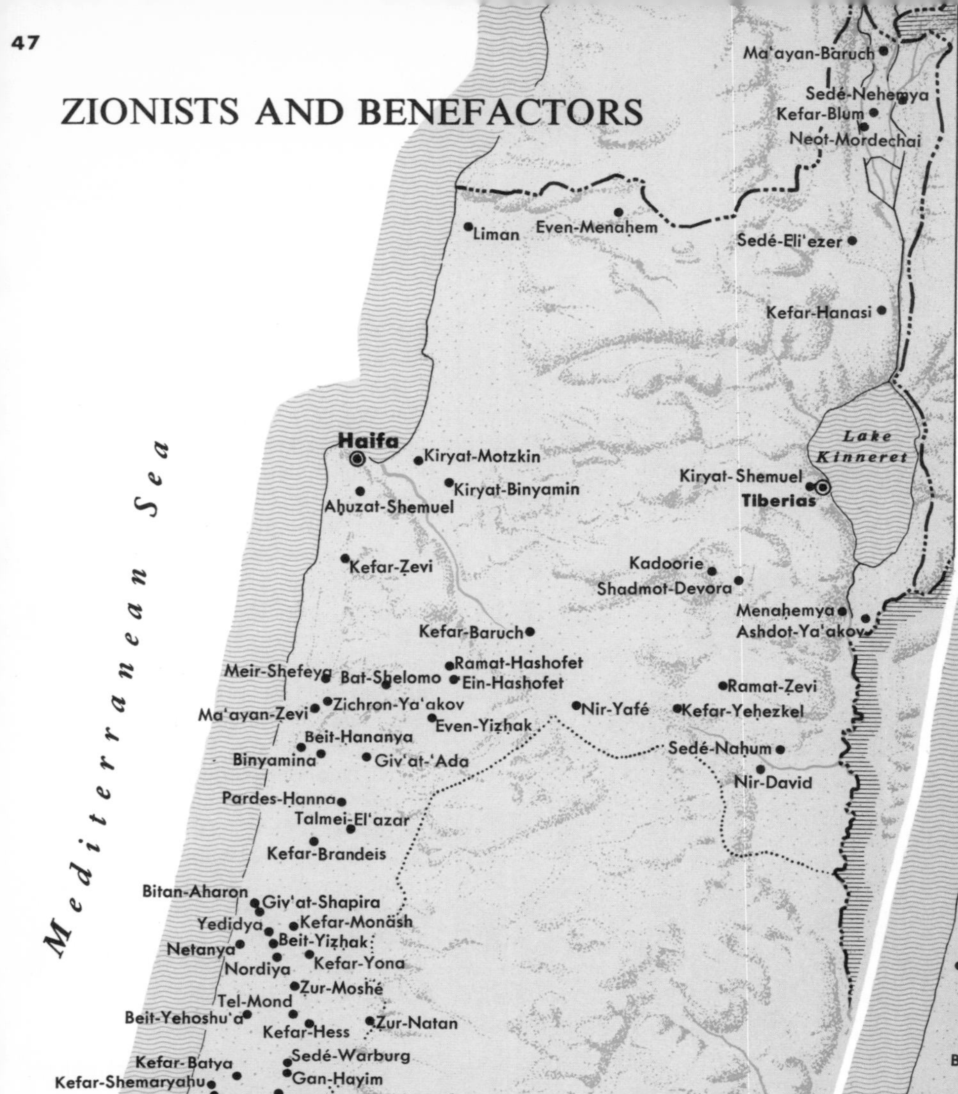
Ma'ayan-Baruch
Sedé-Nehemya
Kefar-Blum
Neot-Mordechai
Liman
Even-Menahem
Sedé-Eli'ezer
Kefar-Hanasi
Mediterranean Sea
Haifa
Kiryat-Motzkin
Kiryat-Binyamin
Ahuzat-Shemuel
Kiryat-Shemuel
Tiberias
Lake Kinneret
Kefar-Zevi
Kadoorie
Shadmot-Devora
Menahemya
Ashdot-Ya'akov
Kefar-Baruch
Meir-Shefeya
Bat-Shelomo
Ramat-Hashofet
Ein-Hashofet
Ramat-Zevi
Ma'ayan-Zevi
Zichron-Ya'akov
Even-Yizhak
Nir-Yafé
Kefar-Yehezkel
Beit-Hananya
Binyamina
Giv'at-'Ada
Sedé-Nahum
Nir-David
Pardes-Hanna
Talmei-El'azar
Kefar-Brandeis
Bitan-Aharon
Giv'at-Shapira
Yedidya
Kefar-Monäsh
Netanya
Beit-Yizhak
Nordiya
Kefar-Yona
Zur-Moshé
Tel-Mond
Beit-Yehoshu'a
Kefar-Hess
Zur-Natan
Kefar-Batya
Sedé-Warburg
Kefar-Shemaryahu
Gan-Hayim
Herzliya
Kefar-Malal
Tel-Baruch
Kefar-Sirkin
el Aviv-Yafo
Giv'at-Shemuel
Tel-Litvinski
Ramat-Pinkas
Nevé-Efrayim
Nahalat-Yehuda
Nir-Zevi
Kefar-Daniel
Kefar-Shemuel
Kefar-Hanagid
Gannei-Yohanan
Ramot-Meir
Mazkeret-Batya
Tal-Shahar
Jerusalem
Talmei-Yehiel
Sedot-Micha
Kefar-Warburg
Avigdor
Li-On
Avi'ezer
Abba-Hillel
Nevé-Michael
Yad-Natan
Beit-Nir
Kochav-Michael
Sedé-Moshé
Even-Shemuel
Eshel-Hanasi
Beer-Shev'a
0 10 20 km.
0 5 10 miles
48

PIONEERS AND SOLDIERS

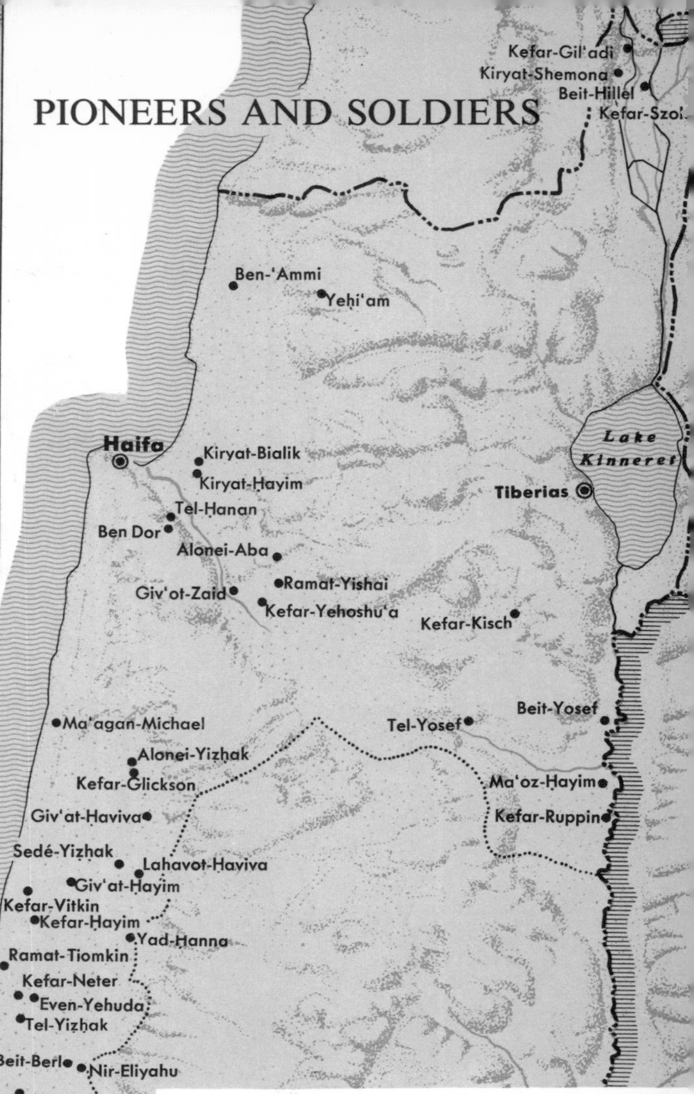
Kefar-Gil'adi
Kiryat-Shemona
Beit-Hillel
Kefar-Szol
Ben-'Ammi
Yehi'am
Haifa
Lake Kinneret
Kiryat-Bialik
Kiryat-Hayim
Tiberias
Tel-Hanan
Ben Dor
Alonei-Aba
Ramat-Yishai
Giv'ot-Zaid
Kefar-Yehoshu'a
Kefar-Kisch
Beit-Yosef
Tel-Yosef
Ma'agan-Michael
Alonei-Yizhak
Kefar-Glickson
Ma'oz-Hayim
Kefar-Ruppin
Giv'at-Haviva
Sedé-Yizhak
Lahavot-Haviva
Giv'at-Hayim
Kefar-Vitkin
Kefar-Hayim
Yad-Hanna
Ramat-Tiomkin
Kefar-Neter
Even-Yehuda
Tel-Yizhak
Beit-Berl
Nir-Eliyahu
Giv'at-Hen

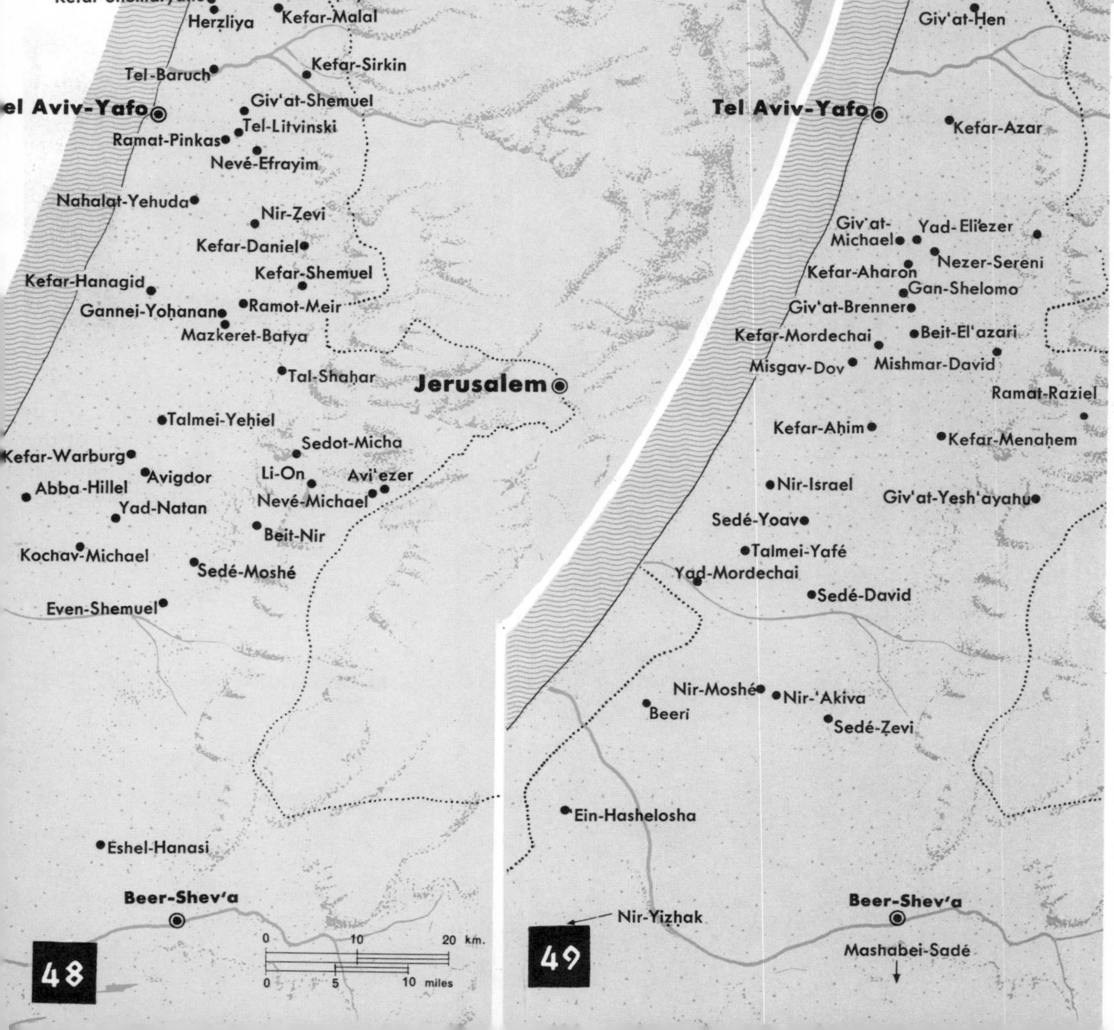
Tel Aviv-Yafo
Kefar-Azar
Giv'at-Michael
Yad-Eliezer
Kefar-Aharon
Nezer-Sereni
Gan-Shelomo
Giv'at-Brenner
Kefar-Mordechai
Beit-El'azari
Misgav-Dov
Mishmar-David
Ramat-Raziel
Kefar-Ahim
Kefar-Menahem
Nir-Israel
Giv'at-Yesh'ayahu
Sedé-Yoav
Talmei-Yafé
Yad-Mordechai
Sedé-David
Nir-Moshé
Nir-'Akiva
Beeri
Sedé-Zevi
Ein-Hashelosha
Nir-Yizhak
Beer-Shev'a
Mashabei-Sadé
49

Many settlements have been named in honor of personalities who earned their fame in the movement of Jewish national rebirth during the past hundred years. First, there were Zionist thinkers and writers who, living in the Diaspora, dreamed of the return to Zion and the ancestral soil and gave expression to their dreams in their writings, in the dawn of Jewry's national reawakening.

Then there were the Zionist leaders who devoted the best years of their lives to the dissemination, among the masses of world Jewry, of the idea of the national rebirth.

Among the immigrants to Palestine were the daring pioneers who helped found the first settlements, then lived and worked in them and shared in the hardships involved in their consolidation.

The following well-known writers had settlements named after them: Zeev Javetz, Haim Nahman Bialik, Yosef Haim Brenner, Alexander Zisskind Rabinowitz (Azar) and Leib Jaffe. There are villages in memory of Eliezer Ben-Yehuda, the man credited with the modern revival of Hebrew speech; Yosef Vitkin, one of the first to teach in Hebrew; Dr. Hillel Jaffe, one of the early pioneer doctors; Rabbi Meir Bar-Ilan, outstanding leader in the Religious-Zionist movement, and others.

SPORT

VARIOUS sports associations are active in Israel, the oldest of which is *Maccabi*. The members of *Hapoel* (the Worker) are recruited from the ranks of the Histadrut (General Federation of Labor). Religious youth is represented in *Elizur*.

Cities, towns and rural areas throughout the country are provided with numerous stadia and sports grounds. The most popular sports are football and basketball. Among the favorite participation-sports are the regular marches held at various times of the year, and swimming races in pools, lakes and the sea.

The major event, among the marches, is the 'four-day march' to Jerusalem, traditionally held a few days before Passover. The best-known of the races are the cross-country run around Mount Tabor and the relay-race at Hannukah, in which a torch is carried from the graves of the Maccabees at Modi'im to the President's Residence in Jerusalem.

The two big swimming events of the year are the crossing of Lake Kinneret (Sea of Galilee) from Tiberias to 'Ein-Gev and the 'Crossing of the Red Sea' in the Gulf of Eilat.

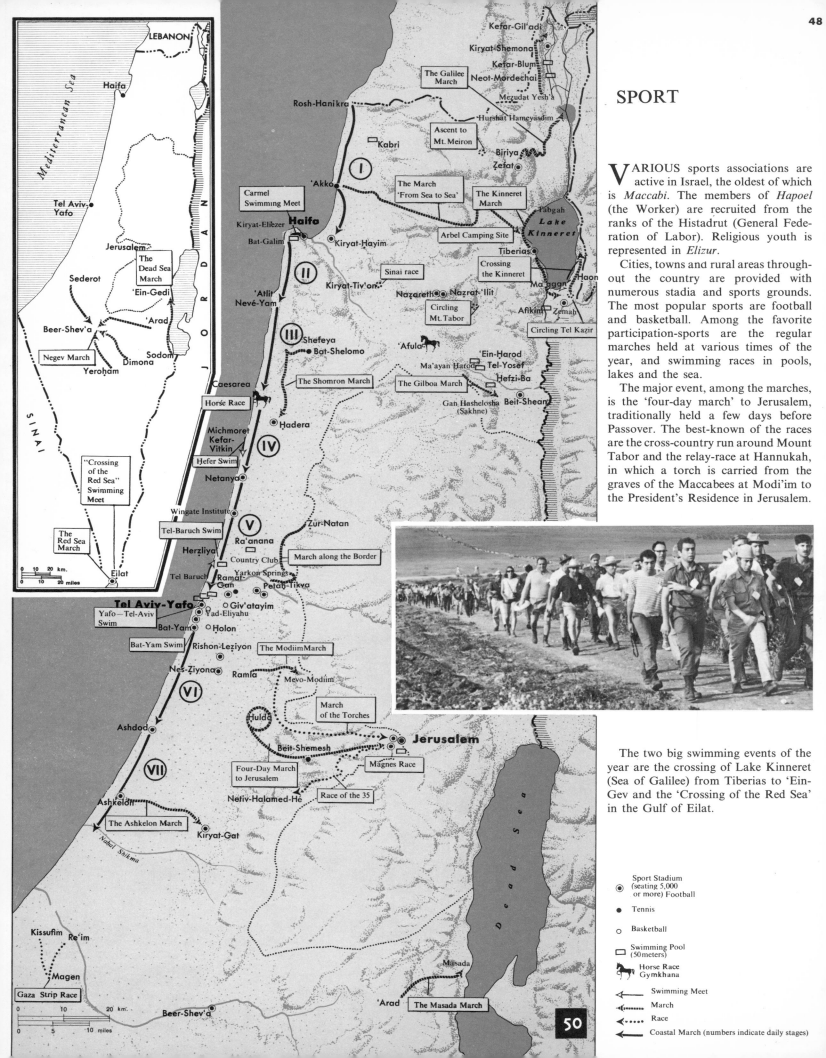

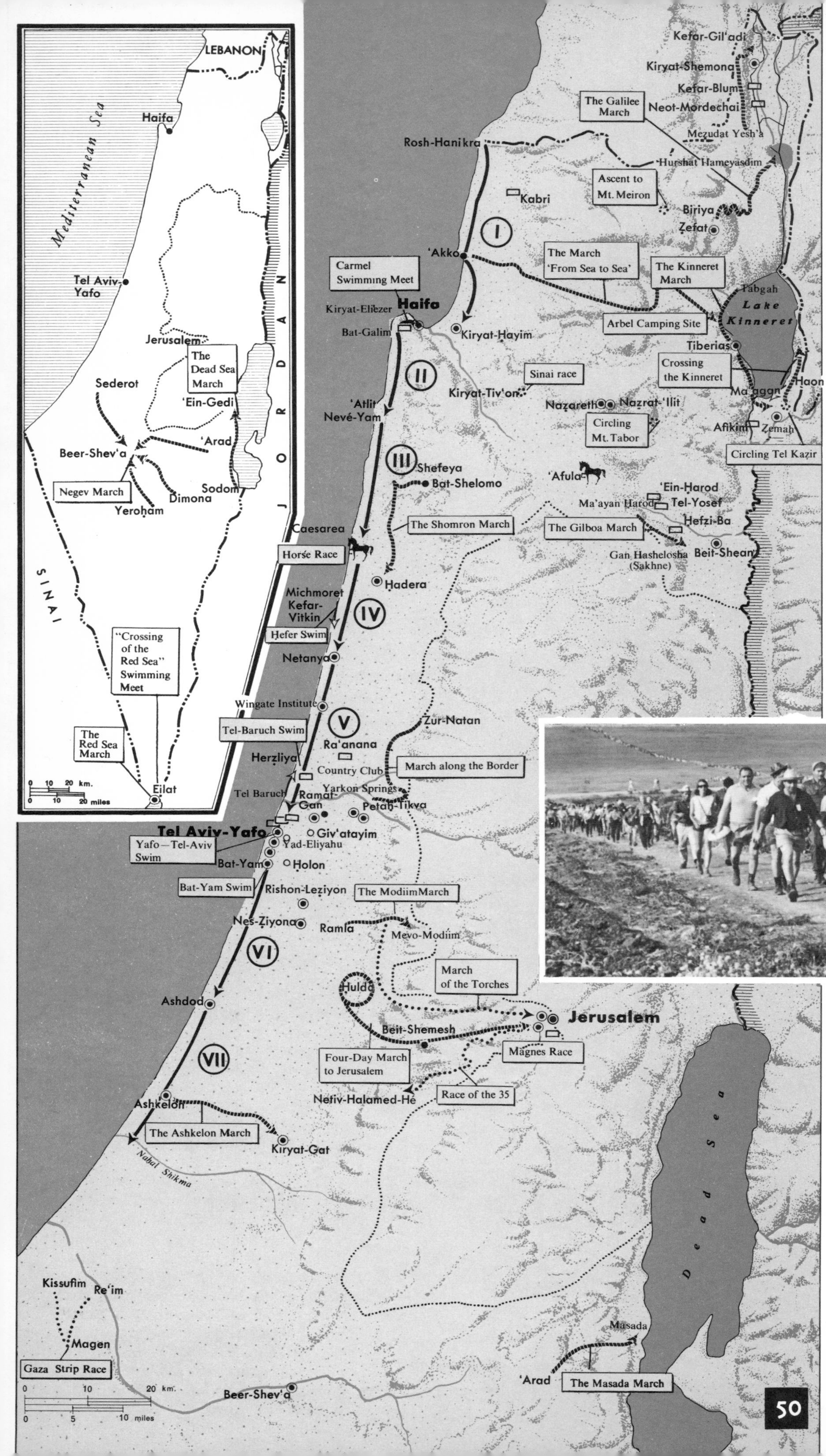
LEBANON
Mediterranean Sea
Haifa
Tel Aviv-Yafo
Jerusalem
The Dead Sea March
Sederot
'Ein-Gedi
'Arad
Beer-Shev'a
Negev March
Sodom
Dimona
Yeroham
JORDAN
SINAI
"Crossing of the Red Sea" Swimming Meet
The Red Sea March
Eilat
0 10 20 km.
0 10 20 miles
Kefar-Gil'adi
Kiryat-Shemona
Kefar-Blum
The Galilee March
Neot-Mordechai
Mezudat Yesh'a
Rosh-Hanikra
Hurshat Hameyasdim
Ascent to Mt. Meiron
Kabri
Bjiriya
Zefat
I
'Akko
The March 'From Sea to Sea'
The Kinneret March
Carmel Swimming Meet
Tabgah
Lake Kinneret
Kiryat-Eliezer
Haifa
Arbel Camping Site
Bat-Galim
Kiryat-Hayim
Tiberias
II
Sinai race
Crossing the Kinneret
Kiryat-Tiv'on
Ma'agan
Haon
'Atlit
Neve-Yam
Nazareth
Nazrat-'Ilit
Circling Mt. Tabor
Afikim
Zemah
Circling Tel Kazir
III
Shefeya
Bat-Shelomo
'Afula
'Ein-Harod
Ma'ayan Harod
Tel-Yosef
The Shomron March
The Gilboa March
Hefzi-Ba
Caesarea
Horse Race
Gan Hashelosha (Sakhne)
Beit-Shean
Hadera
Michmoret
Kefar-Vitkin
IV
Hefer Swim
Netanya
Wingate Institute
V
Zur-Natan
Tel-Baruch Swim
Ra'anana
Herzliya
Country Club
March along the Border
Yarkon Springs
Tel Baruch
Ramat-Gan
Petah-Tikva
Tel Aviv-Yafo
Giv'atayim
Yafo—Tel-Aviv Swim
Yad-Eliyahu
Bat-Yam
Holon
Bat-Yam Swim
Rishon-Leziyon
The Modiim March
Nes-Ziyona
Ramla
Mevo-Modiim
VI
March of the Torches
Hulda
Ashdod
Jerusalem
Beit-Shemesh
Magnes Race
VII
Four-Day March to Jerusalem
Race of the 35
Ashkelon
Netiv-Halamed-He
The Ashkelon March
Kiryat-Gat
Nahal Shikma
Dead Sea
Kissufim
Re'im
Magen
Gaza Strip Race
Masada
'Arad
The Masada March
Beer-Shev'a
0 10 20 km.
0 5 10 miles
50
Sport Stadium (seating 5,000 or more) Football
Tennis
Basketball
Swimming Pool (50 meters)
Horse Race Gymkhana
Swimming Meet
March
Race
Coastal March (numbers indicate daily stages)

69-58

Kravitz Memorial Library
of Park Synagogue

TOURISM

THE TOURIST trade is a major factor in Israel's economy. Recent years have witnessed a considerable expansion and improvement of the facilities necessary for its development: top-grade hotels, suitable transportation services and a cadre of trained and authorized guides.

Officially graded hotels are to be found in all the towns and cities, and most of the larger cities have a choice of several which are Grade A by international standards. A unique feature is the well-kept guest houses at several of Israel's kibbutzim, which provide tourists with the opportunity to gain a first-hand acquaintance with life on a kibbutz. Scattered across the country is a network of reasonably-priced youth hostels.

Though many of Israel's visitors are Jews coming to observe the growth and development of the young Jewish State, a growing proportion in recent years have been Christians. Of particular interest to them is Israel as the Land of the Bible and as the scene of places connected with the birth and development of Christianity—in addition to the modern drama of a nation reborn in its ancient homeland.

Israel abounds not only in sites of special religious and historical interest; it also offers a wide and colorful array of people, of forms of agricultural settlement, of modern industrial enterprises and of scientific, educational and cultural institutions. It is, besides, a land characterized by remarkable contrasts in climate and terrain, and by scenes of great natural beauty and grandeur. The rugged mountainscape of the Negev; the Dead Sea, lowest spot on the earth's surface, with the gaunt rock-fortress of Masada and the lush oasis of 'Ein-Gedi on its western shore; the austere majesty of Jerusalem and the Judean Hills; the tranquility and mirror-like surface of the Sea of Galilee; and the green valleys and wooded hills of Western Galilee—these are but a few examples.

On Mount Carmel and in the hills of Galilee there are caves once used by Prehistoric Man. Across the length and breadth of the land there are sites of important events dating to the Biblical period, and at many of these sites archaeological excavations have unearthed potsherds, foundations of ancient buildings, mosaics and other remnants of the past. Among the finds are the remains of the earliest synagogues in the world.

Places relating to events connected with the life of Jesus and his disciples are to be found in various parts of the country. Archaeologists have uncovered traces of some of the oldest churches in the world, as well as vestiges of castles and monasteries from Crusader times and remnants of structures of Moslem and Turkish origin.

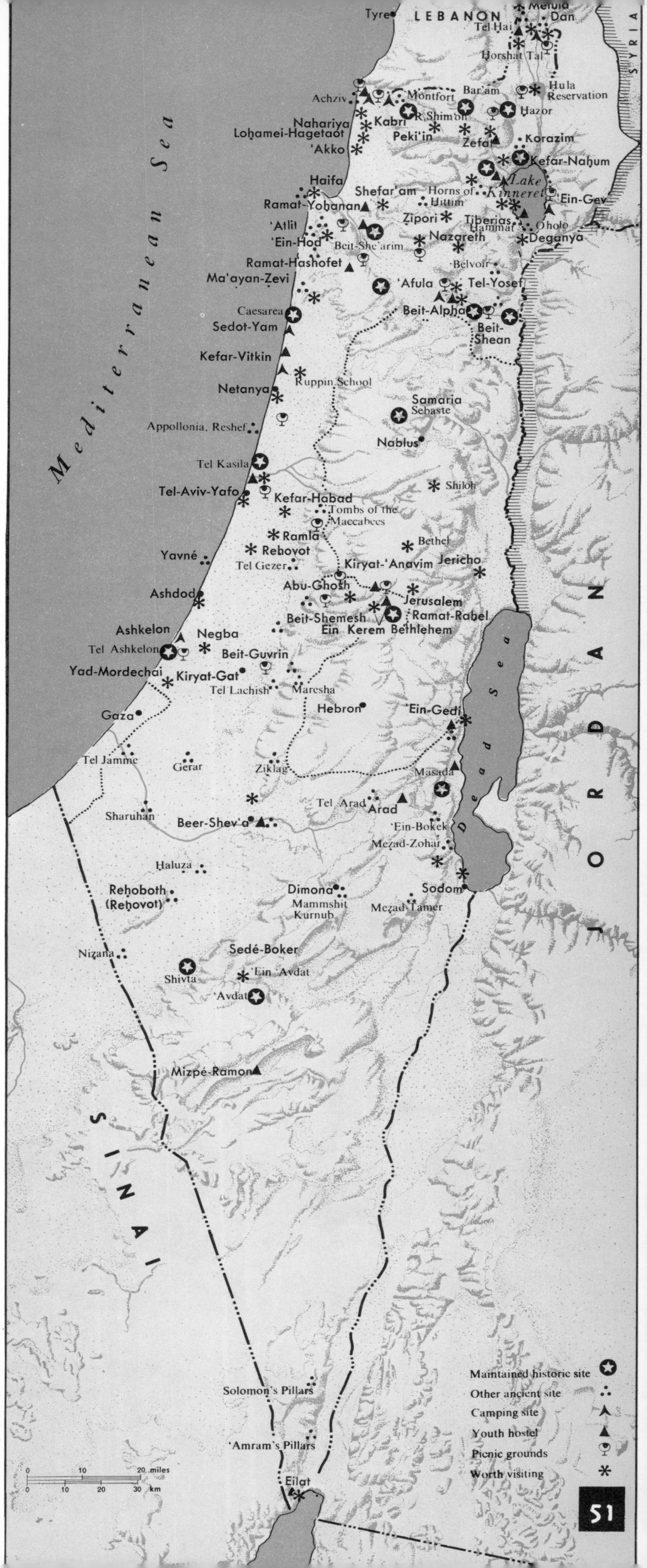

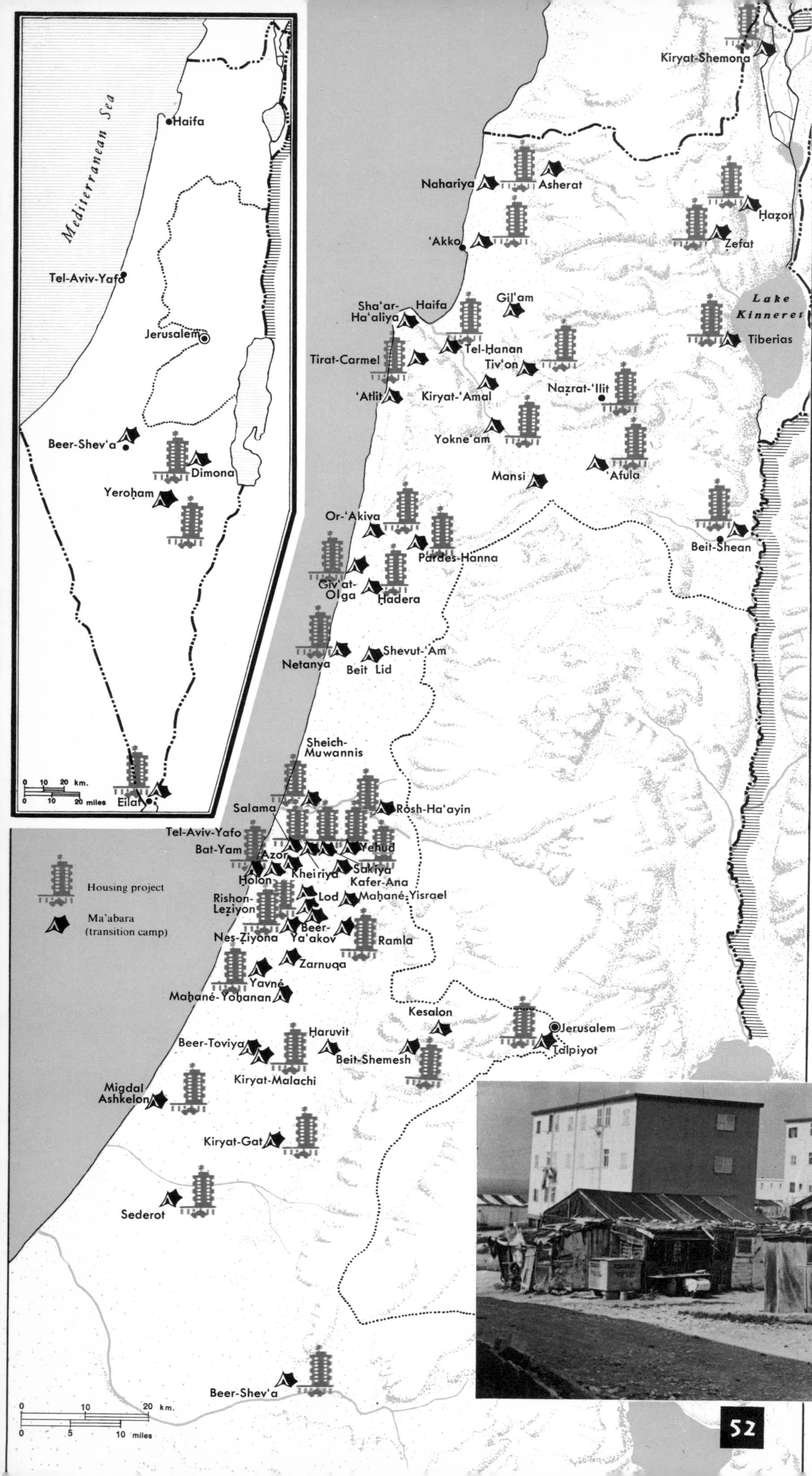
Mediterranean Sea
Haifa
Tel-Aviv-Yafo
Jerusalem
Beer-Shev'a
Dimona
Yeroham
Eilat
0 10 20 km.
0 10 20 miles
Kiryat-Shemona
Nahariya
Asherat
Hazor
'Akko
Zefat
Lake Kinneret
Gil'am
Sha'ar-Ha'aliya
Haifa
Tiberias
Tel-Hanan
Tiv'on
Tirat-Carmel
Nazrat-'Ilit
'Atlit
Kiryat-'Amal
Yokne'am
'Afula
Mansi
Or-'Akiva
Beit-Shean
Pardes-Hanna
Giv'at-Olga
Hadera
Netanya
Shevut-'Am
Beit Lid
Sheich-Muwannis
Salama
Rosh-Ha'ayin
Tel-Aviv-Yafo
Bat-Yam
Azor
Yehud
Holon
Kheiriya
Sakiya
Kafer-Ana
Rishon-Leziyon
Lod
Mahané-Yisrael
Nes-Ziyona
Beer-Ya'akov
Ramla
Zarnuqa
Yavné
Mahané-Yohanan
Kesalon
Jerusalem
Haruvit
Talpiyot
Beer-Toviya
Beit-Shemesh
Kiryat-Malachi
Migdal Ashkelon
Kiryat-Gat
Sederot
Beer-Shev'a
0 10 20 km.
0 5 10 miles
Housing project
Ma'abara (transition camp)

FROM TENT
TO HOUSE

WITH THE establishment of the State
1948 came the mass immigration: ref
gees from the rubble of Europe and masses
Jews from Moslem countries in Asia a
Africa. They streamed, through wide-op
gates, into the infant State before it had h
a chance to recover from the Arab onslaugh
Since the newcomers came to Israel penniles
the burden of their settlement and integratio
rested on the Zionist Organization and i
settlement arm, working with the genero
financial assistance of world Jewry.

Many of the immigrants settled in the tow
and cities and in townships and villag
abandoned during the fighting by their form
Arab inhabitants. *Ma'abarot* — tempora
camps of tents or huts—were hastily erecte
near towns and cities in various parts of t
country to put up the waves upon waves
newcomers, pending the construction of pe
manent housing quarters. Other immigran
were housed in former British army barrack
Conditions in these places were primitive, an
the inhabitants of the ma'abarot suffered muc
hardship. Meanwhile, the Government an
the Jewish Agency began building housin
developments—either as suburbs of existin
cities or in new localities, often around th
nucleus of a ma'abara. These came to be know
as development towns. With the help and en
couragement of the Government, industria
enterprises were set up in these towns i
order to provide basic employment oppor
tunities. Thus, gradually, the ma'abara popu
lation was transferred to permanent housin
projects.

Many of the ma'abarot dwellers moved t
existing agricultural villages; others founde
settlements of their own.

·AḤAL SETTLEMENTS

N AḤAL—brief form of *No'ar Ḥaluẓi Loḥem* (Fighting Pioneer Youth) is a ›ecial branch of the Israel Defence Forces. is a unique system of combined agricultur- ! and military training that simultaneously ›rves two purposes: (1) it gives youngsters ›e opportunity to perform their military ›rvice in a social atmosphere of their own ›oosing; (2) it creates new agricultural ›ttlements of special strategic value.

Naḥal members are graduates of youth ›ovements who declare themselves ready to ›ndertake pioneering work. As a first step, ›e volunteers are assigned to an existing ›ttlement where they are put to work on ›e farm and, at the same time, are given reg- ›ar training. Later, they are sent to a new, › yet uncultivated spot, usually near the ›order, and are given the task of founding new settlement. Naḥal's twin function is ›mbolized in its official emblem: sickle ›d sword.

The first Naḥal settlement was Naḥal- ›z, founded in 1951 near the border of the ›aza Strip. Others followed, some of them ›ing transformed in time into independent ›rmanent settlements within the kibbutz › moshav movement. Among the Naḥal ›ttlements are Yotvata, Gerofit, 'Ein- ›ahav and Ḥaẓeva—all in the 'Arava, near ›e Jordanian border; Mevo-Modi'im, near ›e birthplace of the Maccabees; Magal ›d Ẓur-Natan, in the Sharon Plain; Mei- ›mi and Ma'alé-Hagilbo'a, formerly at ›e northern Jordanian border; Tel-Kaẓir ›d Haon, on the eastern shore of Lake ›inneret and at the foot of the Golan ›ountains; Almagor, looking down on the ›iver Jordan's entry into the Kinneret; ›d Gonen, on the very edge of the Ḥula ›alley.

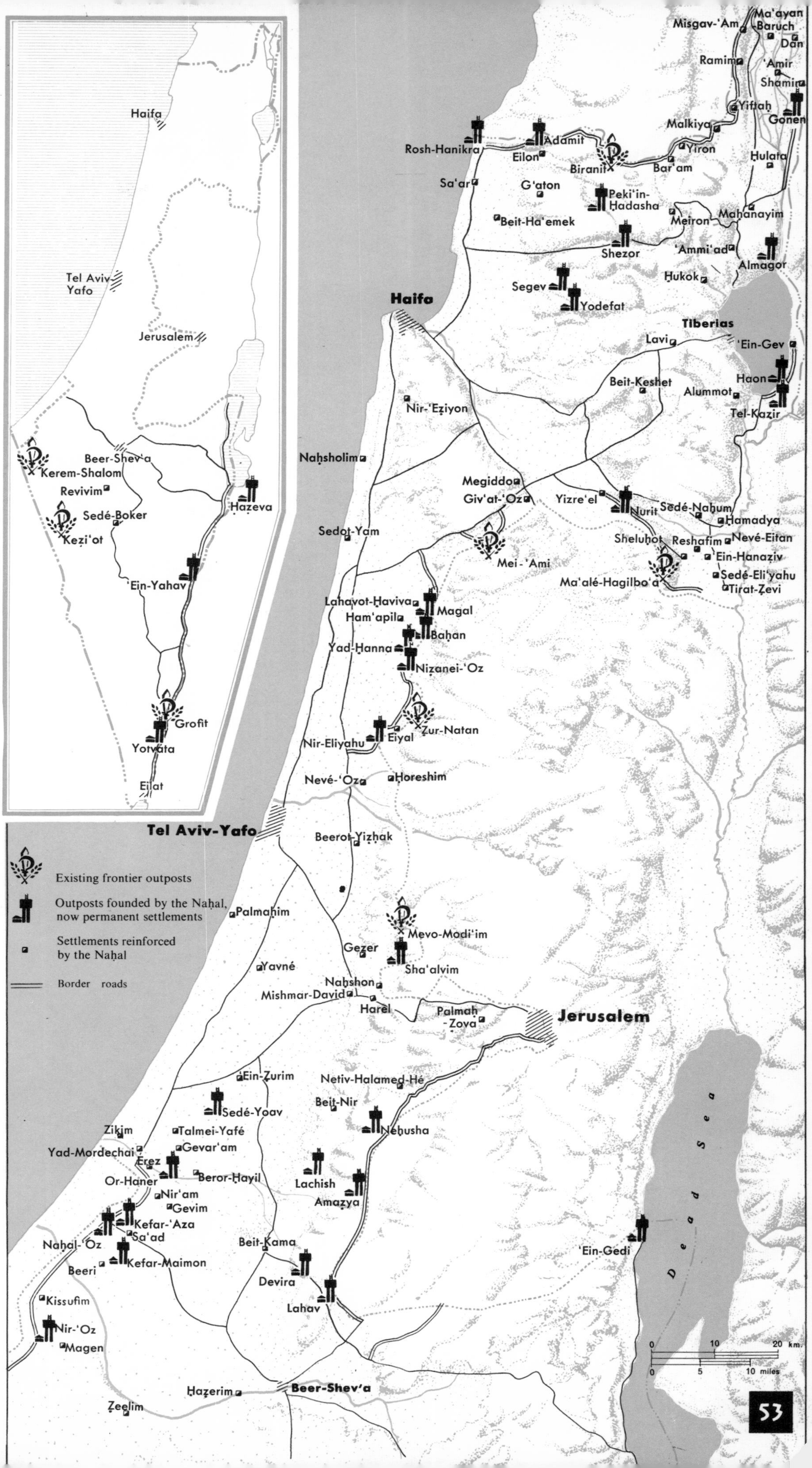

ISRAEL IN 1948

1948—Jerusalem

IN MAY 1948, before the proclamation of Israel's independence, the country, then known as Palestine, was ruled by Britain under a League of Nations mandate issued in 1922. Of Palestine's total population of 1,850,000, about 650,000 were Jews and 1,200,000 were Arabs—most of them Moslems, the rest Christians and Druzes (20,000).

The country was in a state of utter chaos. Armed Arab bands were running amok in the towns, attacking farming settlements and ambushing road traffic across the length and breadth of the country. The Jewish defenders, organized for the most part in the *Haganah* (meaning "defense"), doggedly stood their ground and held off the attackers, at some points even registering gains, though not without paying a high price in human lives. Their task was greatly complicated by the one-sided attitude of the British authorities in Palestine, who went out of their way to undermine the economic and security position of the Jewish community. They imposed curfews, conducted frequent arms searches, carried out mass arrests and exiled Jewish leaders to distant lands, and at the same time encouraged and even assisted the Arab forces in their aggressive designs.

Impatient with the policy of restraint and the strictly defensive attitude adopted by the Haganah, the members of the two Jewish underground organizations—*Irgun Ẓevai Leumi*—National Military Corps, and *Loḥamei Ḥerut Israel*—Freedom Fighters of Israel, went over to the attack, expressing their protest against British rule and pro-Arab policy by carrying out attacks on British army installations and personnel.

Jewish military victories in such towns as Tiberias, Haifa and Yafo, coupled with enticements from Arab leaders abroad, caused many of the Arab inhabitants of these towns to flee to the neighboring countries. Their expectation was to await there the departure of the British and the invasion of the Arab armies that would surely crush the Jewish state-in-the-making, and then to return and pick up the spoils. But their hopes were shattered by Jewish resistance and ultimate victory over the invading Arab armies.

Palmach unit being briefed for action

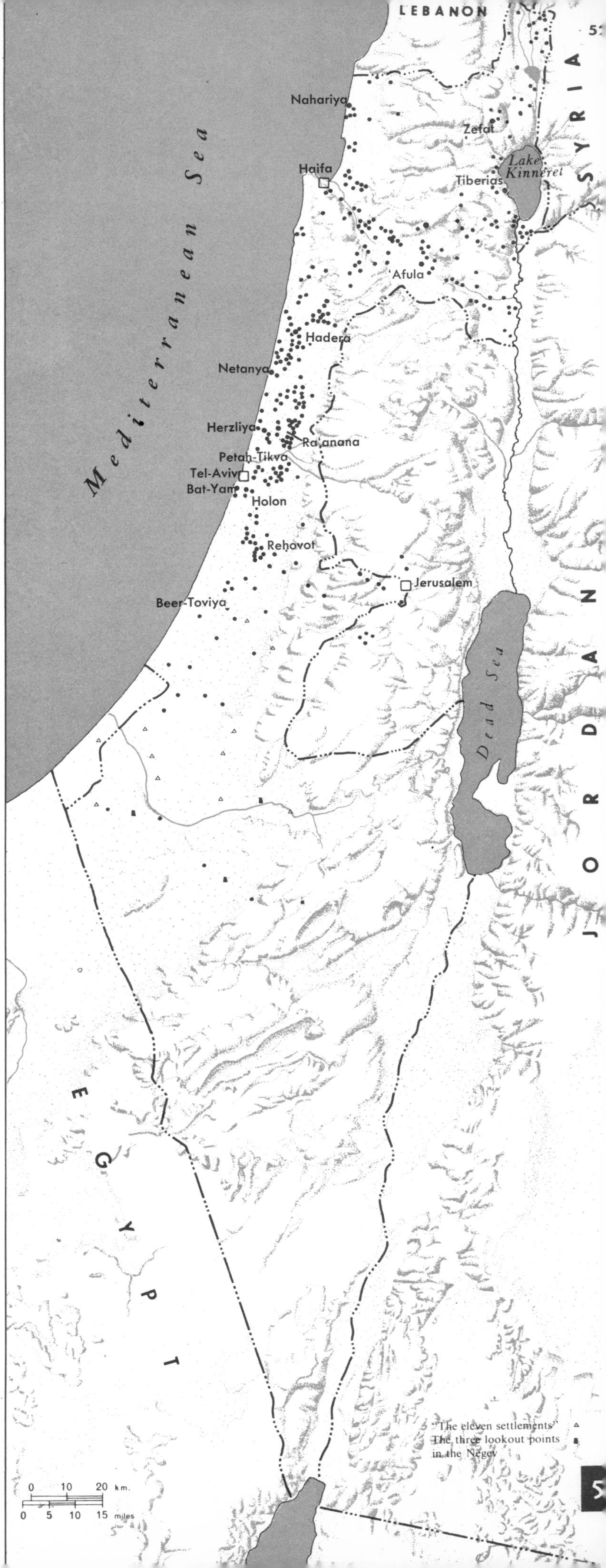

ISRAEL IN 1960

THE STATE is twelve years old and has 2,150,400 inhabitants. Of these, 1,911,300 are Jews, while 239,100 are non-Jews: 166,300 Moslems, 49,600 Christians, 23,100 Druzes and 200 Bahais.

Thanks to large-scale immigration, the cities have expanded, and settlements have turned into towns; ramshackle *ma'abarot*—transit camps, have disappeared or grown into burgeoning development towns or *moshavim* (smallholders' settlements). Industrial enterprises have increased in number and have expanded and been modernized; the areas under cultivation have multiplied and their crops have been improved and diversified—thanks, in part, to the major water projects put into operation in various parts of the country. The products of Israel agriculture and industry have begun to capture a place on world markets—an increasingly important factor in the national economy.

The masses of immigrants, hailing from many different lands, have begun to participate actively in the great nation-molding process, the major unifying elements being a common national consciousness; a common historical-spiritual heritage; the Hebrew language; and—with particular reference to the new generation—compulsory education and military service.

After Israel's victory in the Sinai Campaign in 1956 and the stationing of a United Nations force in Sinai, the Egypt-Israel frontier has become quiet. Arab terrorist activities continue, however, across the borders with Syria and Jordan, taking a growing toll in lives and damage to property. The Israel Defence Forces are constantly on the alert. Moreover, the country's border security is buttressed, from time to time, with the establishment of additional border farming settlements.

Housing for immigrants

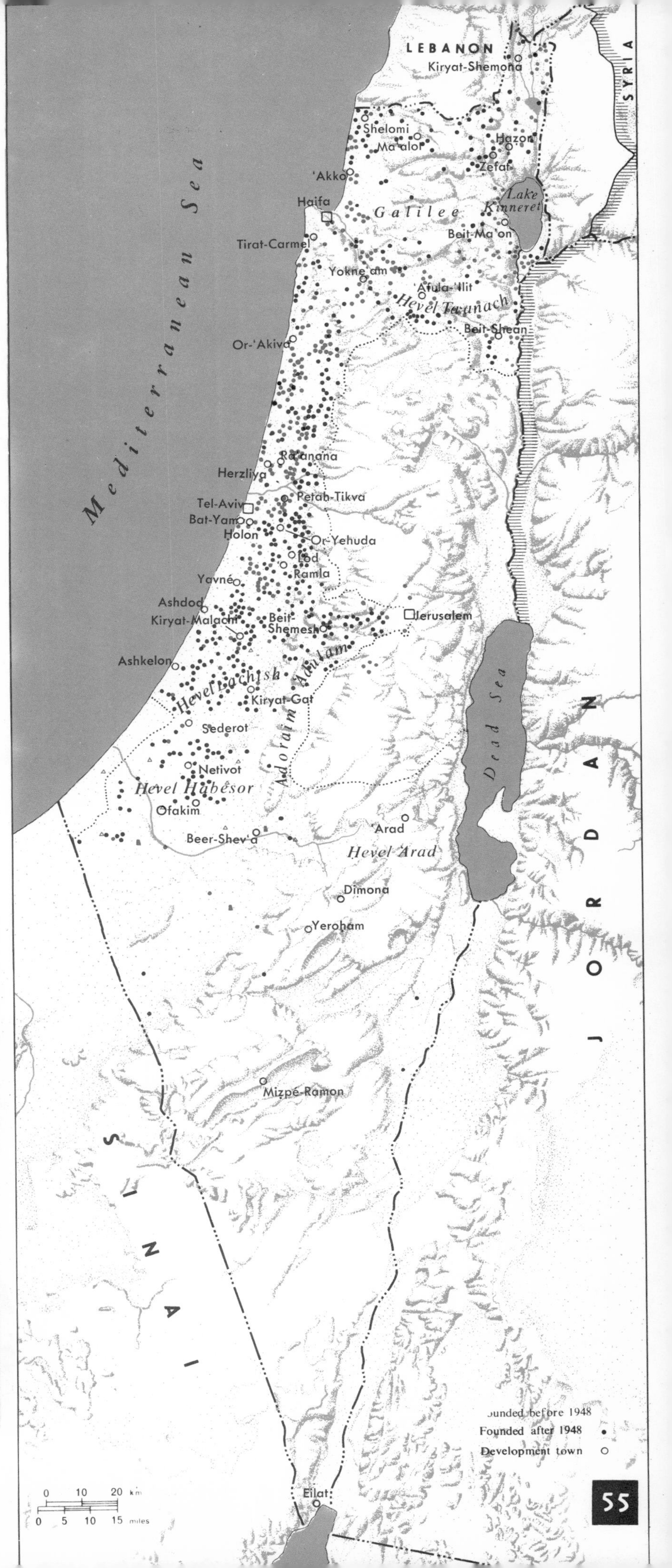

THE TWENTIETH YEAR. . .

IN THE course of two decades of independence, Israel registered gains in all fields of endeavor: in the expansion of areas of urban and rural settlement, the fructification of barren areas, the development of industrial enterprises and of institutions of learning, the advancement of the country's security establishment and the growth of its population by nearly two million souls, from 77,5000 in 1948 to 2,700,000 in 1968.

During these twenty years, Israel has had to do battle three times with the armies of her Arab neighbors, who have not abandoned their design to destroy Israel by force of arms. The first time, in 1948, Israel had to repel the joint assault of the surrounding Arab countries on the very day of her birth. In open defiance, however, of the armistice agreements they subsequently signed with Israel, the Arab States continued their campaign. The second full-scale encounter came in the autumn of 1956, when the Israel Defence Forces routed the Egyptian Army in the Gaza Strip and the Sinai Desert and put an end to the terrorist raids which had had their origin in these areas.

The Arabs utilized the years that followed to prepare their third full-scale attempt at annihilation. It came in May and June of 1967, with Egypt, Jordan and Syria joining in the onslaught. In the "Six-Day War" (June 5-10), the Israel Defence Forces succeeded in routing the armies of these three countries and in destroying or capturing huge quantities of armaments. The Israel Army captured the entire Sinai peninsula, advancing to the Suez Canal in the west and to the Strait of Tiran at the southern tip of the peninsula. On the central front, Israel took the territory formerly under Jordanian control up to the Jordan River, including the eastern sector of Jerusalem and the historic cities of Hebron, Bethlehem and Shechem (Nablus). And, in repulsing the Syrian attack in the North, the Israelis captured the Golan mountain range, from whose commanding heights the Syrian Army had, for twenty years, kept the nearby Israel villages in the valley below under constant bombardment or threat of bombardment.

As a result, Israel expanded her harassed frontiers and added a new and hitherto unknown dimension of security to her towns and settlements, East Jerusalem, including the Old City, steeped in Jewish history and tradition, was reunited with the rest of Jerusalem, and the capital of Israel was no longer a divided city. For the first time since Israel regained her sovereignty, it became possible for the country's inhabitants and for people from all over the world to visit all the places sanctified by Jewish tradition, and the holy places of Islam and Christianity.

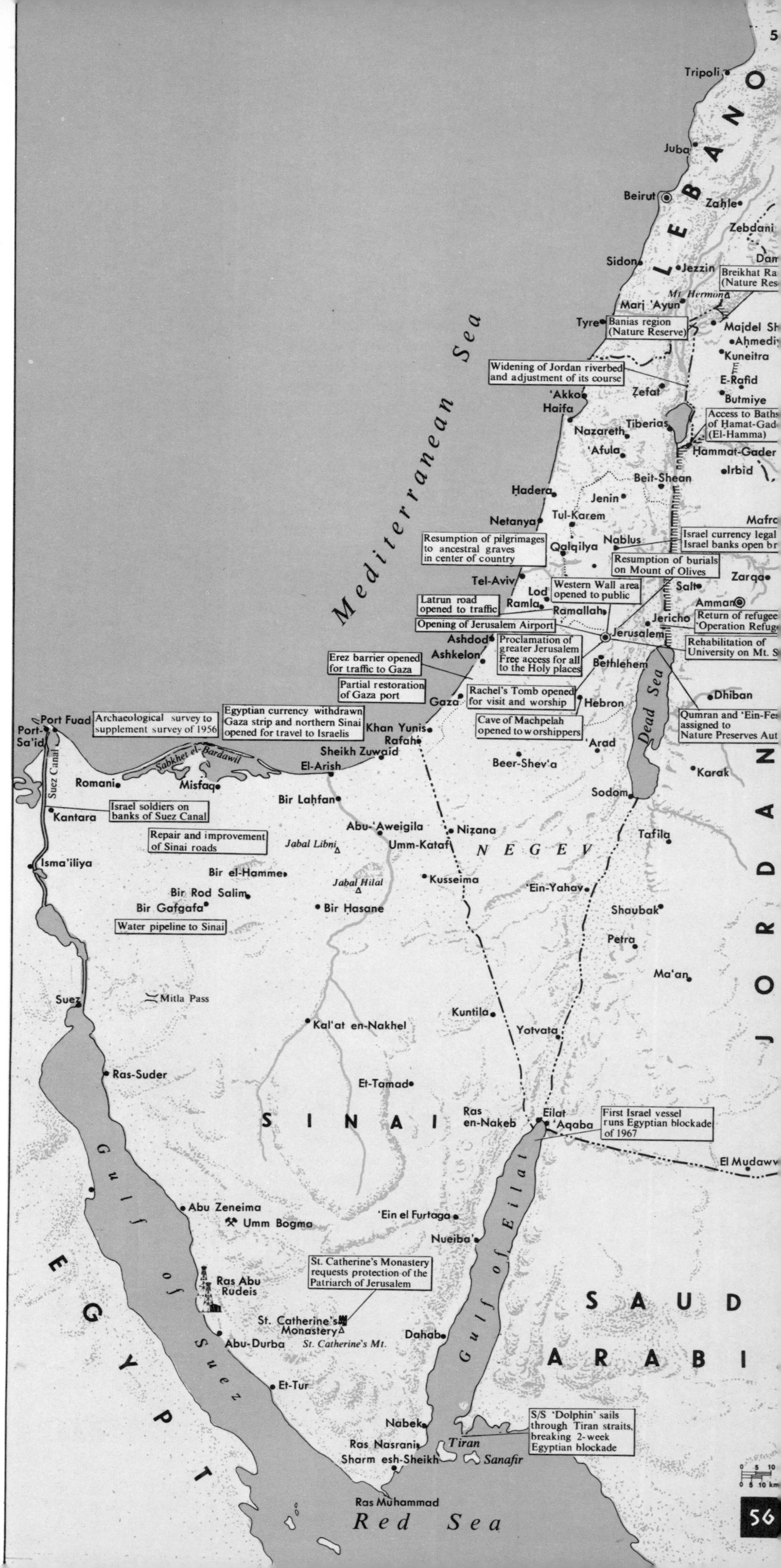

the struggle for independence

THE NATION RETURNS TO ITS LAND

Theodor Herzl (1860-1904), father of Zionism and visionary of the Jewish State

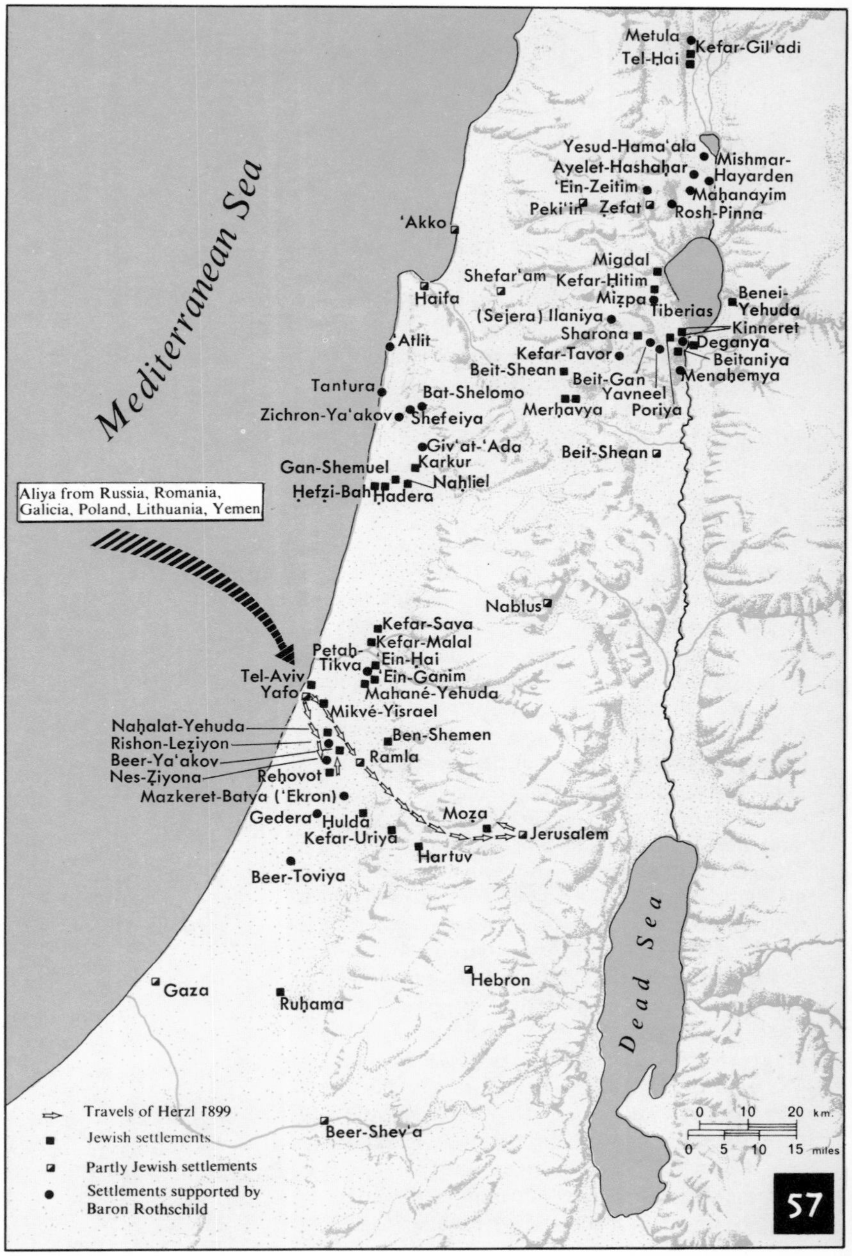

IN THE year 1880 the only Jewish settlement in Palestine was Petaḥ-Tikva; with the beginnings of the national awakening in the Jewish world, we witness the First Pioneering Aliya (wave of immigration to Israel). The first comers were mainly from Russia, Poland and Romania, and it is they who laid the foundations of Rishon-Leẓiyon, in the southern coastal area, of Zichron-Ya'akov, at the foot of Mount Carmel, and of Rosh-Pinna, in Upper Galilee. Members of the Bilu movement, a group of religious pioneers, founded Gedera, in the south.

The generosity of Baron Benjamin (Edmond) de Rothschild, of Paris, was a major factor in the acquisition of lands in the Palestine of that day, as well as in the expansion and consolidation of the Jewish farming community there. Land was purchased in Transjordan as well.

In the years that followed, the stream of immigrants swelled, the urban communities grew, and new rural settlements were added, many of them on lands purchased by the Jewish National Fund. In 1909 a group of Jews of Yafo founded a suburb of that ancient Palestinian port and called it Tel-Aviv (Hill of Spring). Today Tel-Aviv is a teeming metropolis—Israel's commercial and industrial center and largest city.

World War I (1914-1918) brought much suffering to the country in general and to its Jewish community in particular. However, despite restrictions and persecution on the part of the Turkish authorities, settlements were founded, even in those hard times, in the far north.

In 1917 the British army, moving up from the Sinai Desert, captured the southern part of Palestine from the Turks; by the following year, the entire country was in British hands. The conquering army included two Jewish battalions—one from Britain, the other from the United States; after the conquest of Palestine, they were joined by a third battalion—from Palestine itself.

Britain's conquest of Palestine opened a new era in the history of the land—and of the Jewish people.

Rishon Leẓiyon, 1882

ATTACKS ON JEWISH SETTLEMENTS (1920, 1929, 1936-38)

THE FIRST anti-Jewish riots in Palestine took place after the military rule that had followed in the wake of the British conquest had ended. Herbert Samuel was the first British High Commissioner of Palestine, and it was during his term of office that the extremist-nationalist rabble-rouser, Haj Amin el-Ḥusseini, succeeded, by subterfuge and terror, to suppress his more moderate opponents among the Palestinian Arab leadership and to rise to the important influential position of Grand Mufti of Jerusalem.

In May 1921, riots broke out mainly in Jerusalem and Jaffa, and many Jews were killed. The Jews soon realized that they could not depend on the British authorities to protect life and property. Gradually, self-defense units were formed in the Jewish towns and settlements which subsequently united in the community-wide defense organization called *Haganah*. As the Jewish community grew, the ranks of the Haganah were swelled by additional volunteers, who were to acquit themselves nobly in the defense of their land and homes.

Again in 1929, Arab bands went on a rampage, taking an even heavier toll of life, particularly in the ancient town of Hebron, where virtually the entire Jewish community was wiped out. Thanks to the Haganah, however, the Jews this time were able to repulse the attackers in several places. Seven years later, the attacks were renewed with yet greater force, and for three years the country was in turmoil and near-chaos. But the Jews held their ground—and more: despite the danger and the losses they had suffered, young men and women, aided by Haganah forces, went out and laid the foundations for new farming settlements in various parts of the country, even in the most dangerous spots.

A key role in training the Haganah was played by Major Charles Orde Wingate, a British officer with strong Zionist sympathies.

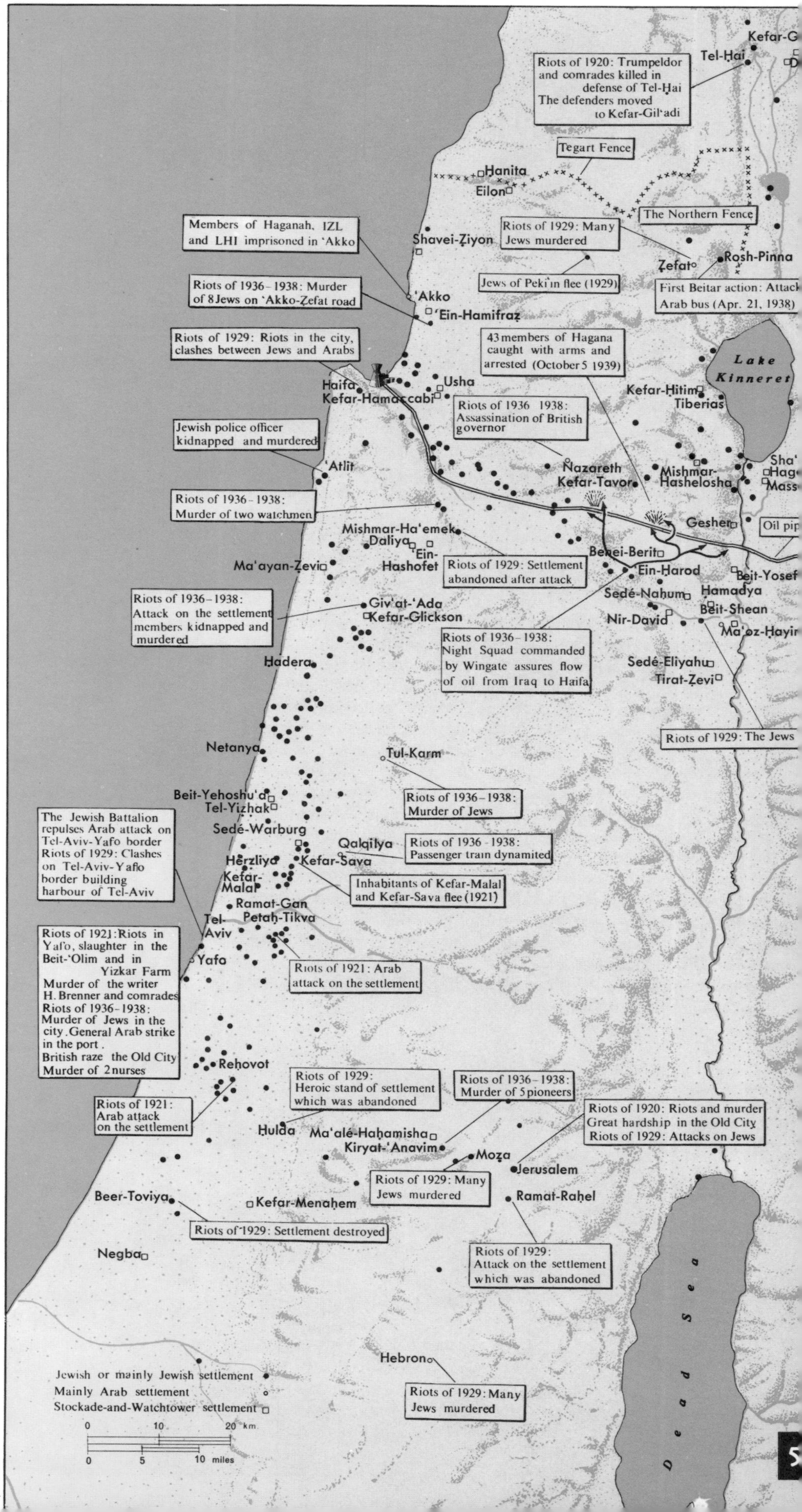

Riots of 1920: Trumpeldor and comrades killed in defense of Tel-Ḥai The defenders moved to Kefar-Gil'adi
Tel-Ḥai
Kefar-G
Tegart Fence
Ḥanita
Eilon
The Northern Fence
Members of Haganah, IZL and LHI imprisoned in 'Akko
Shavei-Ẓiyon
Riots of 1929: Many Jews murdered
Ẓefat
Rosh-Pinna
Jews of Peki'in flee (1929)
First Beitar action: Attack Arab bus (Apr. 21, 1938)
Riots of 1936-1938: Murder of 8 Jews on 'Akko-Ẓefat road
'Akko
'Ein-Hamifraẓ
Riots of 1929: Riots in the city, clashes between Jews and Arabs
43 members of Hagana caught with arms and arrested (October 5 1939)
Lake Kinneret
Haifa
Kefar-Hamaccabi
Usha
Riots of 1936 1938: Assassination of British governor
Kefar-Ḥitim
Tiberias
Jewish police officer kidnapped and murdered
'Atlit
Nazareth
Kefar-Tavor
Mishmar-Hasheloshа
Riots of 1936-1938: Murder of two watchmen
Mishmar-Ha'emek
Daliya
'Ein-Hashofet
Gesher
Oil pip
Riots of 1929: Settlement abandoned after attack
Benei-Berit
'Ein-Ḥarod
Beit-Yosef
Ma'ayan-Ẓevi
Riots of 1936-1938: Attack on the settlement members kidnapped and murdered
Giv'at-'Ada
Kefar-Glickson
Sedé-Naḥum
Ḥamadya
Nir-David
Beit-Shean
Ma'oz-Ḥayim
Riots of 1936-1938: Night Squad commanded by Wingate assures flow of oil from Iraq to Haifa
Ḥadera
Sedé-Eliyahu
Tirat-Ẓevi
Riots of 1929: The Jews
Netanya
Tul-Karm
Riots of 1936-1938: Murder of Jews
Beit-Yehoshu'a
Tel-Yiẓhak
Sedé-Warburg
The Jewish Battalion repulses Arab attack on Tel-Aviv-Yafo border Riots of 1929: Clashes on Tel-Aviv-Yafo border building harbour of Tel-Aviv
Qalqilya
Riots of 1936-1938: Passenger train dynamited
Herzliya
Kefar-Sava
Kefar-Malal
Inhabitants of Kefar-Malal and Kefar-Sava flee (1921)
Ramat-Gan
Petaḥ-Tikva
Tel-Aviv
Yafo
Riots of 1921: Riots in Yafo, slaughter in the Beit-'Olim and in Yizkar Farm Murder of the writer H. Brenner and comrades Riots of 1936-1938: Murder of Jews in the city. General Arab strike in the port. British raze the Old City Murder of 2 nurses
Riots of 1921: Arab attack on the settlement
Reḥovot
Riots of 1929: Heroic stand of settlement which was abandoned
Riots of 1936-1938: Murder of 5 pioneers
Riots of 1920: Riots and murder Great hardship in the Old City Riots of 1929: Attacks on Jews
Riots of 1921: Arab attack on the settlement
Ḥulda
Ma'alé-Haḥamisha
Kiryat-'Anavim
Moẓa
Jerusalem
Riots of 1929: Many Jews murdered
Beer-Toviya
Kefar-Menaḥem
Ramat-Raḥel
Riots of 1929: Settlement destroyed
Negba
Riots of 1929: Attack on the settlement which was abandoned
Dead Sea
Hebron
Riots of 1929: Many Jews murdered
Jewish or mainly Jewish settlement
Mainly Arab settlement
Stockade-and-Watchtower settlement
0 10 20 km
0 5 10 miles

Arab Marauders

THE STRUGGLE AGAINST RESTRICTIONS (1939-1945)

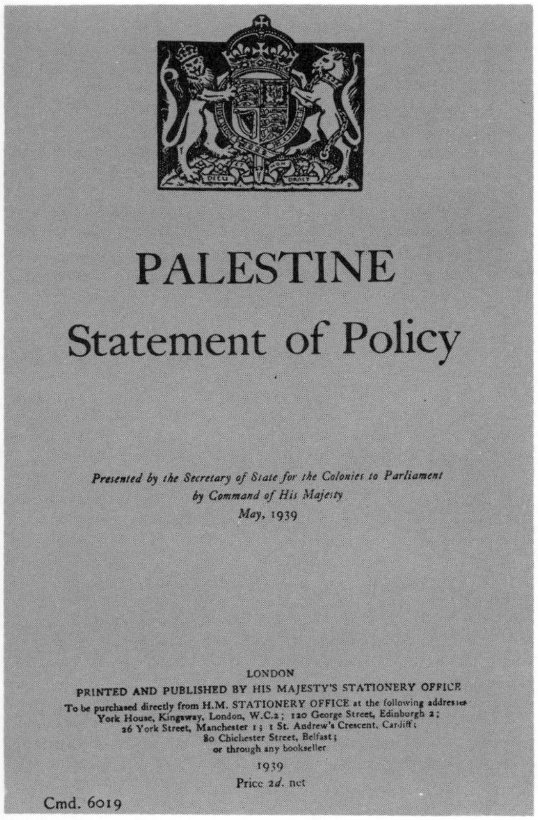

PALESTINE

Statement of Policy

Presented by the Secretary of State for the Colonies to Parliament by Command of His Majesty
May, 1939

LONDON
PRINTED AND PUBLISHED BY HIS MAJESTY'S STATIONERY OFFICE
To be purchased directly from H.M. STATIONERY OFFICE at the following addresses: York House, Kingsway, London, W.C.2; 120 George Street, Edinburgh 2; 26 York Street, Manchester 1; 1 St. Andrew's Crescent, Cardiff; 80 Chichester Street, Belfast; or through any bookseller
1939
Price 2*d.* net
Cmd. 6019

Front cover of "White Paper" curtailing Jewish immigration and land purchases

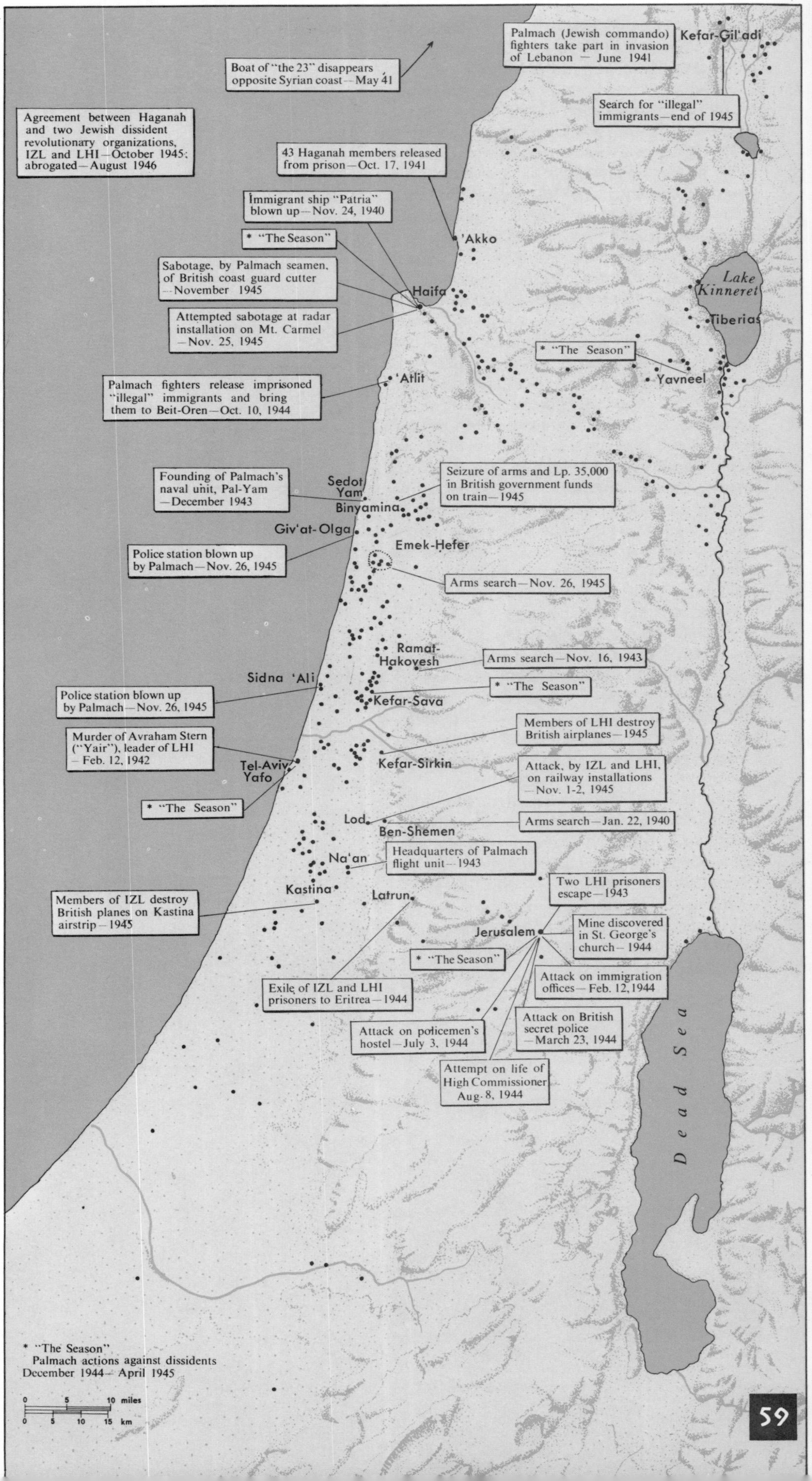

Palmach (Jewish commando) fighters take part in invasion of Lebanon — June 1941
Kefar-Gil'adi
Boat of "the 23" disappears opposite Syrian coast—May 41
Search for "illegal" immigrants—end of 1945
Agreement between Haganah and two Jewish dissident revolutionary organizations, IZL and LHI—October 1945; abrogated—August 1946
43 Haganah members released from prison—Oct. 17, 1941
Immigrant ship "Patria" blown up—Nov. 24, 1940
* "The Season"
'Akko
Sabotage, by Palmach seamen, of British coast guard cutter—November 1945
Haifa
Lake Kinneret
Attempted sabotage at radar installation on Mt. Carmel—Nov. 25, 1945
Tiberias
* "The Season"
Yavneel
Palmach fighters release imprisoned "illegal" immigrants and bring them to Beit-Oren—Oct. 10, 1944
'Atlit
Founding of Palmach's naval unit, Pal-Yam—December 1943
Sedot Yam
Seizure of arms and Lp. 35,000 in British government funds on train—1945
Binyamina
Giv'at-Olga
Emek-Hefer
Police station blown up by Palmach—Nov. 26, 1945
Arms search—Nov. 26, 1945
Ramat-Hakovesh
Arms search—Nov. 16, 1943
Sidna 'Ali
* "The Season"
Police station blown up by Palmach—Nov. 26, 1945
Kefar-Sava
Members of LHI destroy British airplanes—1945
Murder of Avraham Stern ("Yair"), leader of LHI—Feb. 12, 1942
Tel-Aviv Yafo
Kefar-Sirkin
Attack, by IZL and LHI, on railway installations—Nov. 1-2, 1945
* "The Season"
Lod
Ben-Shemen
Arms search—Jan. 22, 1940
Headquarters of Palmach flight unit—1943
Na'an
Kastina
Latrun
Two LHI prisoners escape—1943
Members of IZL destroy British planes on Kastina airstrip—1945
Jerusalem
Mine discovered in St. George's church—1944
* "The Season"
Attack on immigration offices—Feb. 12, 1944
Exile of IZL and LHI prisoners to Eritrea—1944
Attack on policemen's hostel—July 3, 1944
Attack on British secret police—March 23, 1944
Attempt on life of High Commissioner Aug. 8, 1944
Dead Sea
* "The Season" Palmach actions against dissidents December 1944—April 1945
0 5 10 miles
0 5 10 15 km

WITH THE outbreak of the Second World War, Palestine became an armed camp manned by British forces, menaced on two flanks by Britain's enemies: in North Africa by the armies of Germany and Italy, and in Syria and Lebanon by the forces of Vichy France. Throughout the neighboring Arab countries, the prevailing mood was sympathy for the Axis powers and the hope that Britain and her allies would be defeated.

Notwithstanding the strained relations between the Jewish Agency and the British authorities because of the latter's anti-Jewish policies in Palestine, the Jewish leadership decided to mobilize its youth for the British forces and to lend whatever assistance it could to the war effort against Nazi Germany. Thousands of young Jewish men and women volunteered for service in the ranks of the British Army. After a long struggle, the British Government also agreed to the formation of a Jewish Brigade composed of Palestinian volunteers.

In this period, too, the *Palmach (Pelugot Maḥaẓ*—"striking forces") was born. This force was composed of youth drawn mainly from the communal settlements and formed the striking arm or commando corps of the Haganah.

The dissident movements—*Irgun Ẓevai Leumi* (IZL) and *Loḥamei Ḥerut Israel* (LHI)—began independent actions against the mandatory authorities.

THE STRUGGLE AGAINST BRITISH POLICY (1945–1948)

THE ALLIED victory in World War II gave rise to hopes, in the Jewish community in Palestine, that the British authorities would now open the gates of the homeland to the streams of suffering humanity, refugees from Hitler's concentration camps, survivors of the great holocaust of European Jewry, who were desperately knocking on those gates.

The British Government, however, reverted to its former policy of hostility to Palestine's Jewish community and its aspirations and, instead of expanding Jewish immigration, actually restricted it still further. Reacting instantaneously and forcefully to this official callousness, the Jews organized a movement of "illegal" immigration to Palestine. In defiance of coastguards and land patrols, they succeeded in bringing in thousands of Jewish refugees, by land and by sea.

The British continued, even after World War II, their policy of seeking to appease Arab leadership by hampering Jewish growth and development at every step and particularly by restricting Jewish immigration. But curfews, arrests, arms searches and various other forms of discrimination and suppression merely served to galvanize Palestine Jewry into action, to unite the community and to heighten its determination to attain full political independence.

Units of the Jewish underground movements—Haganah (including the Palmach), IZL and LHI—took a growing toll of British lives and continued their sabotage activities against military installations. Forces of the Haganah and Palmach, shunning terrorist activities, concentrated on strictly military objectives, blowing up bridges and freeing illegal immigrants imprisoned by the authorities.

Over the years, a number of international commissions came to Palestine to study the Jewish-Arab conflict and seek a solution. The last of these was the United Nations Special Committee on Palestine (UNSCOP), which conducted a long and thorough investigation and, in the autumn of 1947, recommended the partition of the country into independent Jewish and Arab States.

A train derailed near Lod

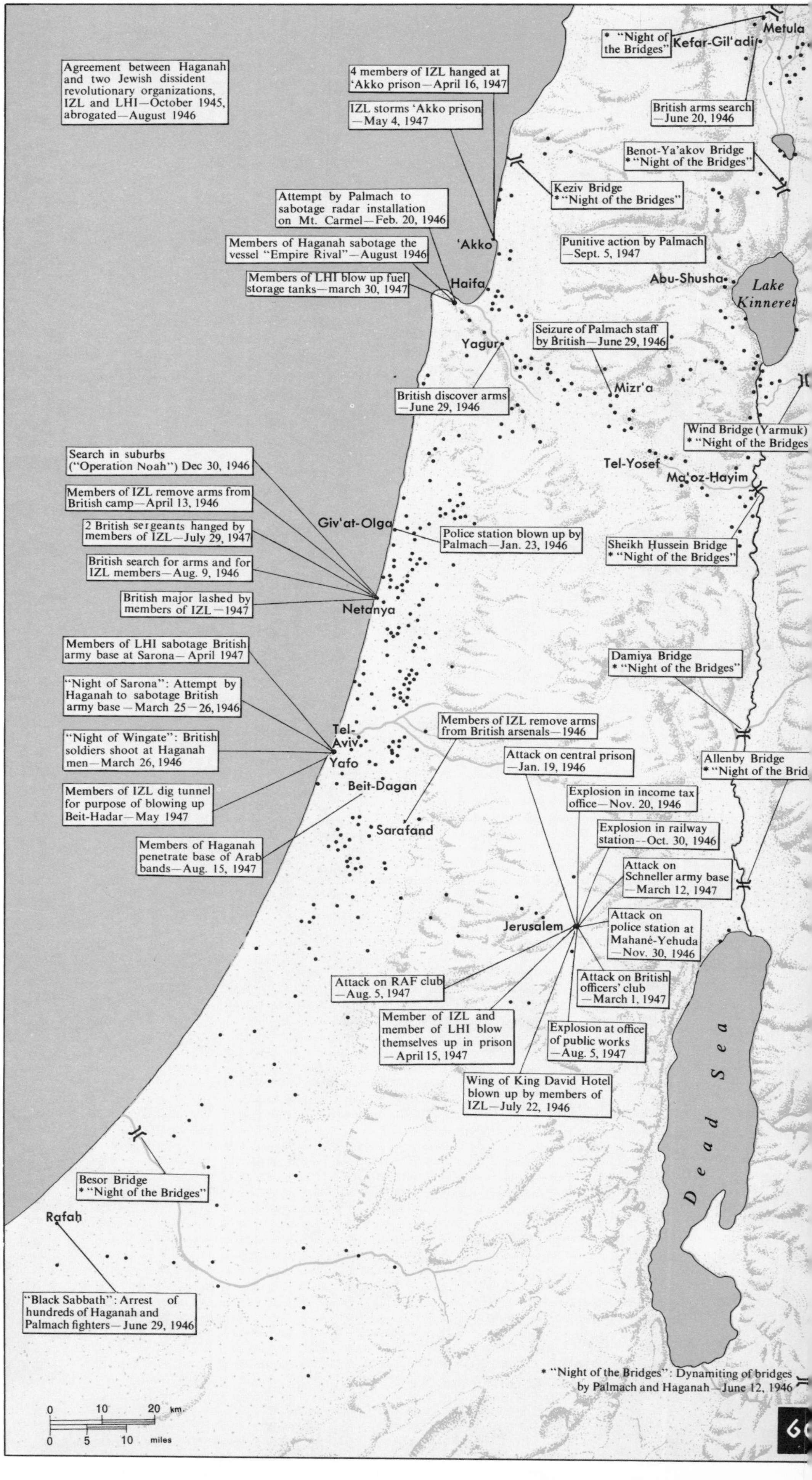
Metula
* "Night of the Bridges"
Kefar-Gil'adi
Agreement between Haganah and two Jewish dissident revolutionary organizations, IZL and LHI—October 1945, abrogated—August 1946
4 members of IZL hanged at 'Akko prison—April 16, 1947
IZL storms 'Akko prison—May 4, 1947
British arms search—June 20, 1946
Benot-Ya'akov Bridge * "Night of the Bridges"
Keziv Bridge * "Night of the Bridges"
Attempt by Palmach to sabotage radar installation on Mt. Carmel—Feb. 20, 1946
'Akko
Punitive action by Palmach—Sept. 5, 1947
Members of Haganah sabotage the vessel "Empire Rival"—August 1946
Members of LHI blow up fuel storage tanks—march 30, 1947
Haifa
Abu-Shusha
Lake Kinneret
Yagur
Seizure of Palmach staff by British—June 29, 1946
Mizr'a
British discover arms—June 29, 1946
Wind Bridge (Yarmuk) * "Night of the Bridges"
Search in suburbs ("Operation Noah") Dec 30, 1946
Tel-Yosef
Ma'oz-Hayim
Members of IZL remove arms from British camp—April 13, 1946
2 British sergeants hanged by members of IZL—July 29, 1947
Giv'at-Olga
Police station blown up by Palmach—Jan. 23, 1946
Sheikh Hussein Bridge * "Night of the Bridges"
British search for arms and for IZL members—Aug. 9, 1946
British major lashed by members of IZL—1947
Netanya
Members of LHI sabotage British army base at Sarona—April 1947
Damiya Bridge * "Night of the Bridges"
"Night of Sarona": Attempt by Haganah to sabotage British army base—March 25–26, 1946
Members of IZL remove arms from British arsenals—1946
Tel-Aviv
Yafo
"Night of Wingate": British soldiers shoot at Haganah men—March 26, 1946
Attack on central prison—Jan. 19, 1946
Allenby Bridge * "Night of the Brid
Beit-Dagan
Members of IZL dig tunnel for purpose of blowing up Beit-Hadar—May 1947
Explosion in income tax office—Nov. 20, 1946
Sarafand
Explosion in railway station—Oct. 30, 1946
Members of Haganah penetrate base of Arab bands—Aug. 15, 1947
Attack on Schneller army base—March 12, 1947
Jerusalem
Attack on police station at Mahané-Yehuda—Nov. 30, 1946
Attack on RAF club—Aug. 5, 1947
Attack on British officers' club—March 1, 1947
Member of IZL and member of LHI blow themselves up in prison—April 15, 1947
Explosion at office of public works—Aug. 5, 1947
Wing of King David Hotel blown up by members of IZL—July 22, 1946
Dead Sea
Besor Bridge * "Night of the Bridges"
Rafah
"Black Sabbath": Arrest of hundreds of Haganah and Palmach fighters—June 29, 1946
* "Night of the Bridges": Dynamiting of bridges by Palmach and Haganah—June 12, 1946
0 10 20 km.
0 5 10 miles

THE VOTE AT THE UNITED NATIONS

THE PARTITION proposal of the United Nations Special Committee on Palestine (UNSCOP) was submitted in the autumn of 1947 to the plenary session of the General Assembly. The discussion in the Assembly was accompanied by a concerted effort by representatives of Palestinian Jewry to present the Jewish case before the various delegations. On November 29, 1947, the Assembly voted, by more than a two-thirds majority, for the establishment in Palestine of independent Jewish and Arab States. Some six months later, on May 14, 1948 (5 Iyar, 5708), the Jewish State was officially proclaimed, and not long thereafter Jerusalem became its capital.

Thus the dream of generations, the yearning for redemption and the prayers intoned by millions upon millions of Jews, their faces and their hearts turned to the land of their fathers and the site of their ancient Temple, were realized and became a living fact. In the Land of the Patriarchs, the land that, since its devastation at Roman hands, has undergone so many violent changes, the State of Israel had arisen.

One year after the proclamation of its independence, on May 16, 1949, Israel was accepted as a member of the United Nations, and took its place alongside all the free peoples of the earth.

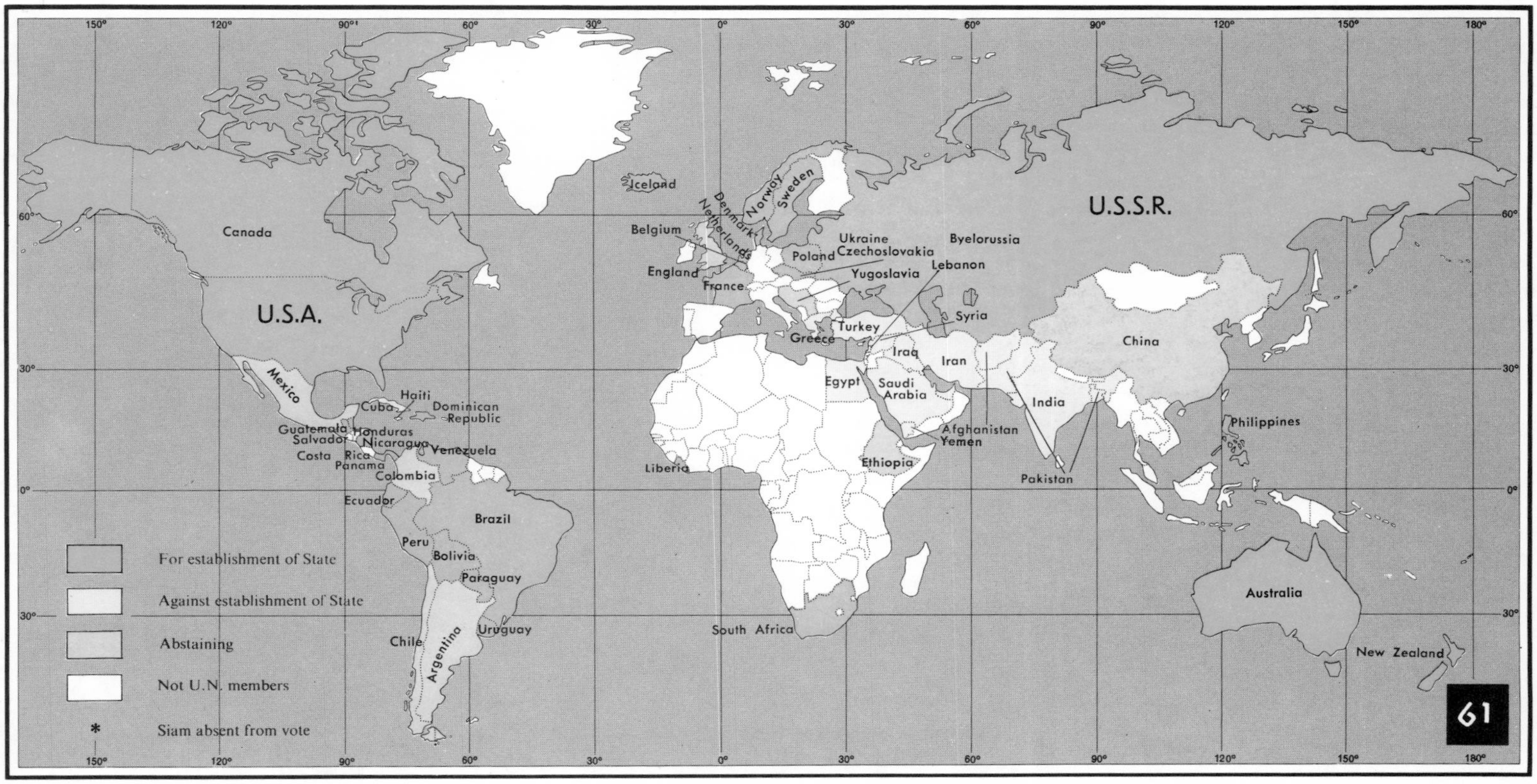

U.N. session voting on the establishment of the State Nov. 29, 1947

INVASION BY ARAB ARMIES

MAY 14, 1948 (the 5th of Iyar, 5708) marked two crucial events: the completion of the British withdrawal from Palestine, and the proclamation of the independent State of Israel. On the morning of the following day the new State was invaded by the armies of the four neighboring states: Egypt, Jordan, Syria, Lebanon, and of Iraq, joined by contingents from two more: Saudi Arabia and Yemen.

The *Egyptians* advanced from the Suez Canal along the northern Sinai coast into the Gaza Strip. Continuing northward, one column penetrated by way of the Arab townships of Majdal (Niẓanim) and Ashdod as far as the 'Ad Halom Bridge. The second column moved through Faluja to the western approaches of Jerusalem. Another column moving through Niẓana and Beer-Shev'a to Beit–Leḥem (Bethlehem) attacked Jerusalem from the south.

The *Jordanians*—their fighting force made up of soldiers of the Arab Legion and their British officers—crossed the Allenby Bridge over the southern part of the Jordan River and advanced to Jerusalem, Lod and Ramla. They were joined by Jordanian units that had been stationed in the western part of Palestine during the last days of the British Mandate. Yet another Jordanian force attempted to penetrate into the country by way of the Naharayim Bridge just south of the Kinneret, but this force was repulsed.

The *Syrians* tried to enter Israel in two main columns. One descended from the heights of the Golan Mountains into the Jordan Valley and to the shore of Lake Kinneret (Sea of Galilee), penetrating as far as Degania, where it was halted and pushed back. Another Syrian column reached the Benot Ya'akov Bridge on the upper Jordan River and threatened the settlement of Mishmar-Hayarden.

The *Iraqis* moved along the road running parallel to the oil pipeline to Haifa. They crossed the Jordan River, using the Damiya Bridge, traversed the Samarian highlands and reached the town of Jenin, at the entrance to the Jezreel valley, Tul-Karm opposite Netanya, and Migdal-Afek opposite Petaḥ-Tikva.

The *Lebanese* first of all gained control of Rosh-Hanikra, on the Mediterranean coast. One column drove deep into Galilee, heading for the central part of that region, but was driven back by the Jewish forces. Towards the end of the war, the Israel Army succeeded in capturing a large area of Lebanese territory. After the armistice talks, this area was returned to Lebanon, while Lebanon returned Rosh-Hanikra to Israel.

Yad-Mordechai after Egyptian bombardment

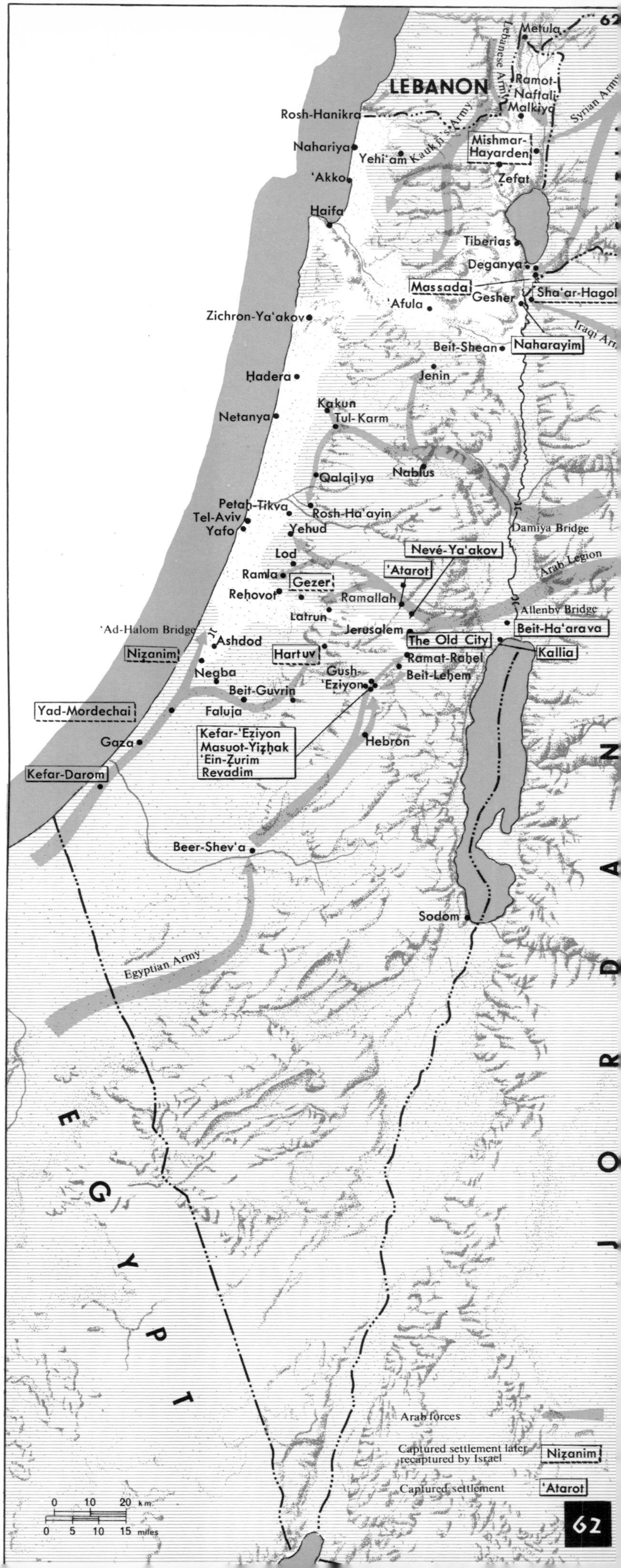

THE WAR OF INDEPENDENCE

TO ALL intents and purposes, the war began on the morrow of the UN General Assembly's decision of November 28, 1947, concerning the establishment of a Jewish State in the western part of Palestine. Its early stages were marked by attacks by armed Arab bands on Jewish settlements and ambushes of Jewish vehicles on the roads. Young fighters, though small in numbers and poor in equipment, fought back with courage and determination. The Arabs succeeded, however, in gaining control over several main roads, as a result of which a number of Jewish settlements were all but cut off, and only armed convoys were able to maintain contact between them. The Arabs of Palestine were reinforced by para-military units from the neighboring lands. In the battle for Mishmar Ha'emek, near Haifa, on April 10, 1948, a combined force of local and neighboring Arab irregulars was defeated.

The *Syrian* forces attacked from the Golan heights in the northeast. Their immediate objective was the Jordan Valley and Galilee.

On the Mediterranean coast, at Israel's northern border, Rosh-Hanikra fell to *Lebanese* troops, which then sought to penetrate, with the aid of local Arab forces, to the heart of Upper Galilee.

Meanwhile, with the proclamation of the State of Israel (on 14 May), the Jewish fighting groups had abandoned their underground status and pledged their allegiance to the fledgling Israel Defence Forces—Ẓahal. Heavy fighting broke out on a long, winding front, as Jewish fighters, few in number and poorly armed, doggedly stood their ground against the organized armed might of five invading armies. At the cost of many young lives, the Jewish defenders finally succeeded in halting the Arab advance, gradually driving the invaders out of the areas they had captured.

House to house fighting

Ramat-Raḥel after the battle

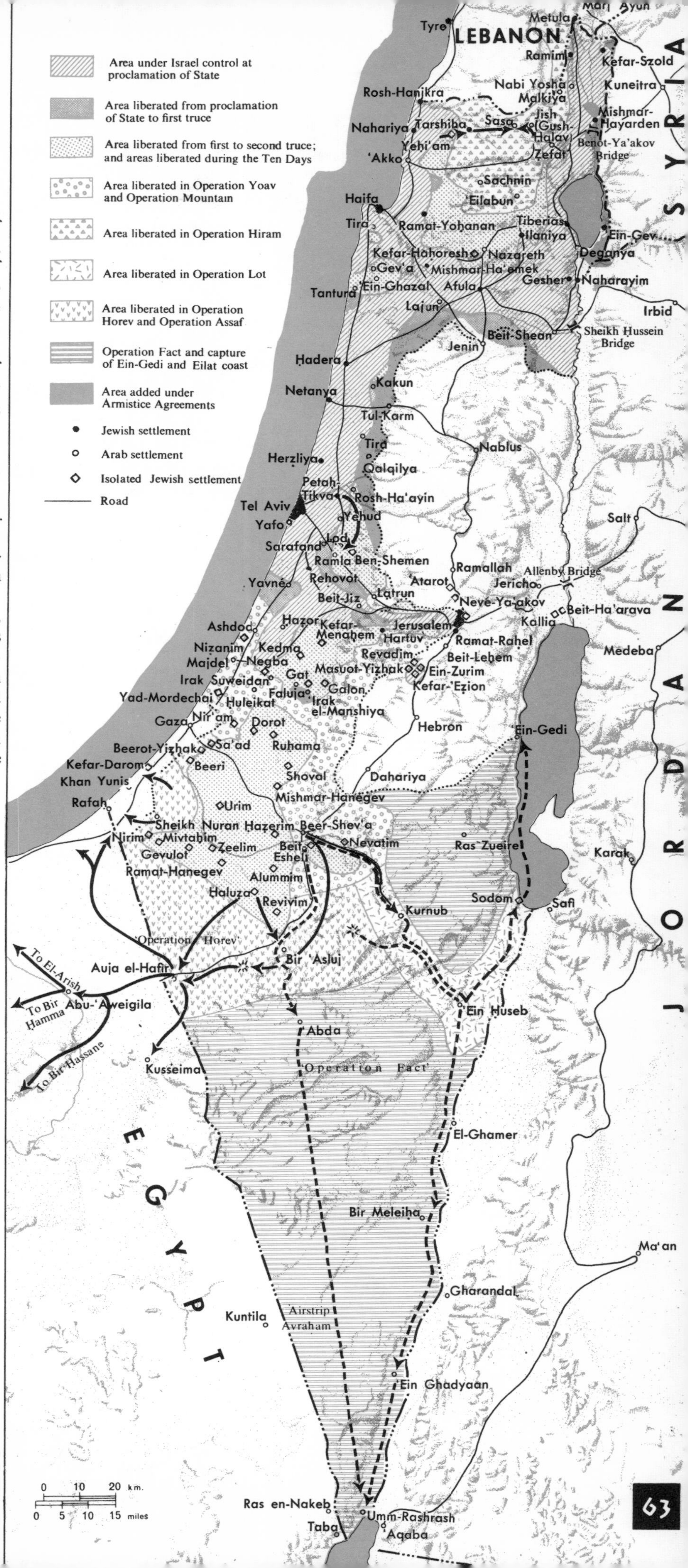

BATTLES IN THE WAR OF INDEPENDENCE: NORTH

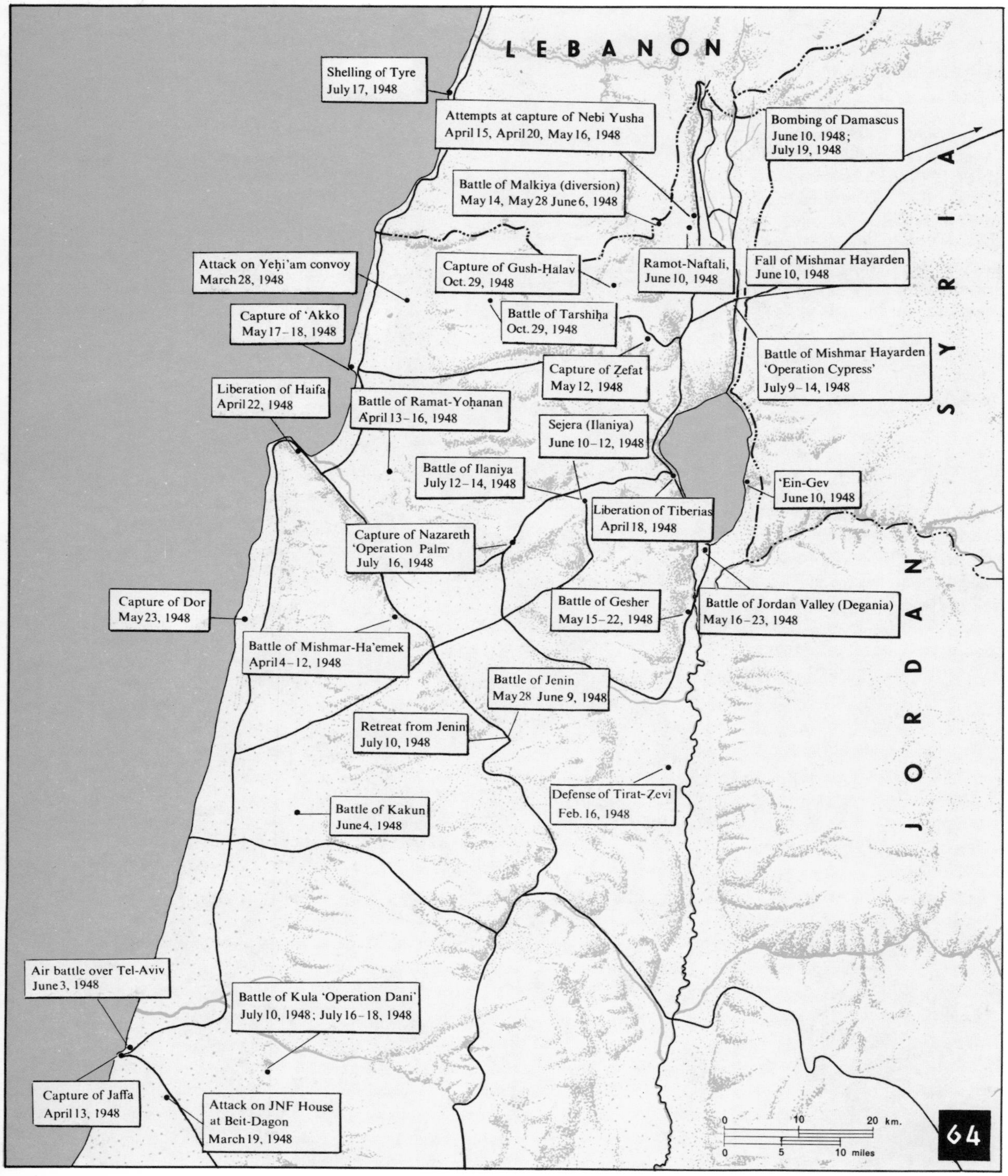
LEBANON
SYRIA
JORDAN
Shelling of Tyre
July 17, 1948
Attempts at capture of Nebi Yusha
April 15, April 20, May 16, 1948
Bombing of Damascus
June 10, 1948;
July 19, 1948
Battle of Malkiya (diversion)
May 14, May 28 June 6, 1948
Attack on Yeḥi'am convoy
March 28, 1948
Capture of Gush-Ḥalav
Oct. 29, 1948
Ramot-Naftali,
June 10, 1948
Fall of Mishmar Hayarden
June 10, 1948
Capture of 'Akko
May 17–18, 1948
Battle of Tarshiḥa
Oct. 29, 1948
Battle of Mishmar Hayarden
'Operation Cypress'
July 9–14, 1948
Capture of Ẓefat
May 12, 1948
Liberation of Haifa
April 22, 1948
Battle of Ramat-Yoḥanan
April 13–16, 1948
Sejera (Ilaniya)
June 10–12, 1948
Battle of Ilaniya
July 12–14, 1948
'Ein-Gev
June 10, 1948
Liberation of Tiberias
April 18, 1948
Capture of Nazareth
'Operation Palm'
July 16, 1948
Capture of Dor
May 23, 1948
Battle of Gesher
May 15–22, 1948
Battle of Jordan Valley (Degania)
May 16–23, 1948
Battle of Mishmar-Ha'emek
April 4–12, 1948
Battle of Jenin
May 28 June 9, 1948
Retreat from Jenin
July 10, 1948
Defense of Tirat-Ẓevi
Feb. 16, 1948
Battle of Kakun
June 4, 1948
Air battle over Tel-Aviv
June 3, 1948
Battle of Kula 'Operation Dani'
July 10, 1948; July 16–18, 1948
Capture of Jaffa
April 13, 1948
Attack on JNF House
at Beit-Dagon
March 19, 1948
0 10 20 km.
0 5 10 miles
64

Israel Defence Forces

Air Force

Navy

Palmach

STAGES IN THE W

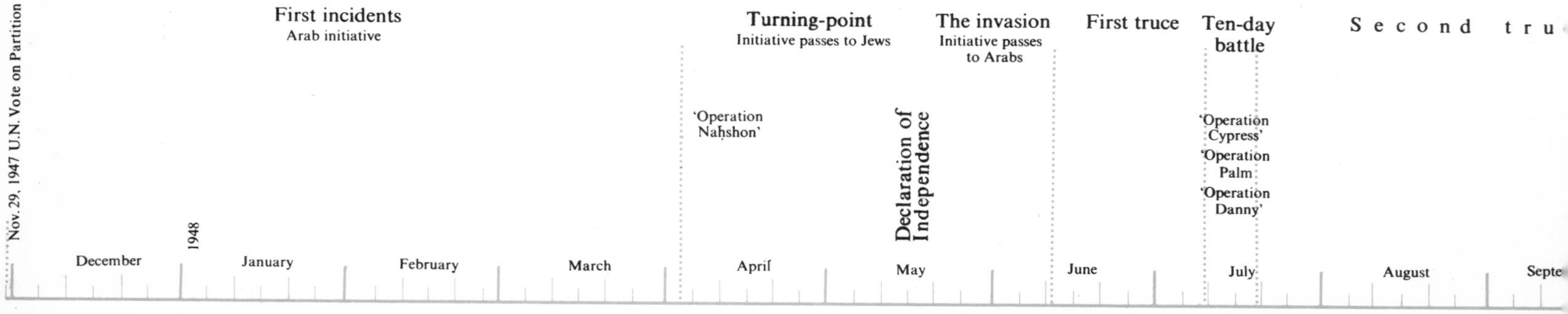
Nov. 29, 1947 U.N. Vote on Partition
First incidents
Arab initiative
Turning-point
Initiative passes to Jews
The invasion
Initiative passes
to Arabs
First truce
Ten-day
battle
S e c o n d t r u
'Operation
Naḥshon'
Declaration of
Independence
'Operation
Cypress'
'Operation
Palm
'Operation
Danny'
1948
December
January
February
March
April
May
June
July
August
Septe

BATTLES IN THE WAR OF INDEPENDENCE: SOUTH

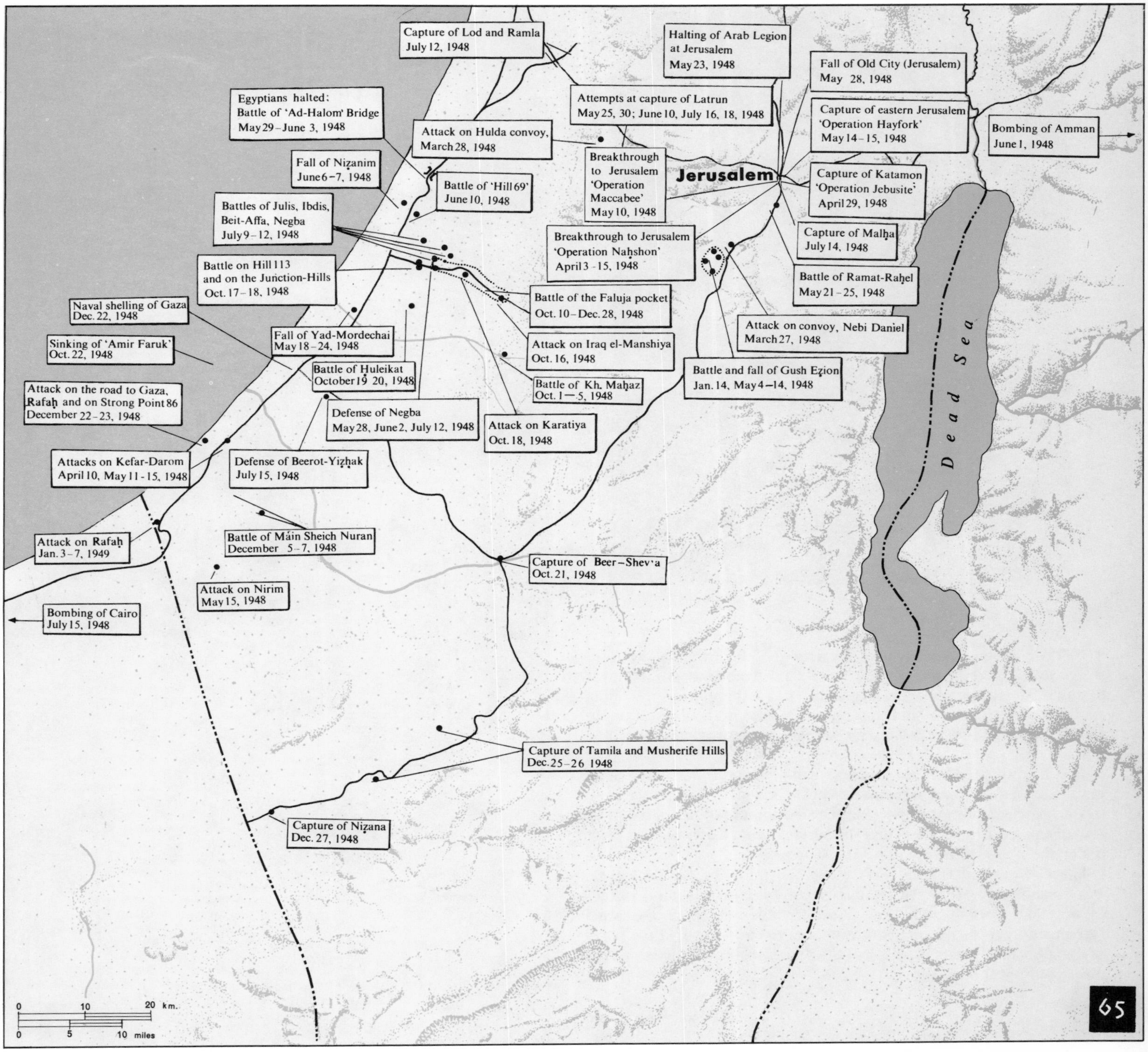
Capture of Lod and Ramla
July 12, 1948
Halting of Arab Legion at Jerusalem
May 23, 1948
Fall of Old City (Jerusalem)
May 28, 1948
Egyptians halted:
Battle of 'Ad-Halom' Bridge
May 29 - June 3, 1948
Attempts at capture of Latrun
May 25, 30; June 10, July 16, 18, 1948
Capture of eastern Jerusalem
'Operation Hayfork'
May 14-15, 1948
Bombing of Amman
June 1, 1948
Attack on Hulda convoy,
March 28, 1948
Fall of Nizanim
June 6-7, 1948
Breakthrough to Jerusalem
'Operation Maccabee'
May 10, 1948
Jerusalem
Capture of Katamon
'Operation Jebusite'
April 29, 1948
Battle of 'Hill 69'
June 10, 1948
Battles of Julis, Ibdis, Beit-Affa, Negba
July 9-12, 1948
Breakthrough to Jerusalem
'Operation Nahshon'
April 3-15, 1948
Capture of Malha
July 14, 1948
Battle on Hill 113 and on the Junction-Hills
Oct. 17-18, 1948
Battle of Ramat-Rahel
May 21-25, 1948
Battle of the Faluja pocket
Oct. 10-Dec. 28, 1948
Naval shelling of Gaza
Dec. 22, 1948
Attack on convoy, Nebi Daniel
March 27, 1948
Fall of Yad-Mordechai
May 18-24, 1948
Attack on Iraq el-Manshiya
Oct. 16, 1948
Sinking of 'Amir Faruk'
Oct. 22, 1948
Battle of Huleikat
October 19 20, 1948
Battle and fall of Gush Ezion
Jan. 14, May 4-14, 1948
Battle of Kh. Mahaz
Oct. 1-5, 1948
Attack on the road to Gaza, Rafah and on Strong Point 86
December 22-23, 1948
Defense of Negba
May 28, June 2, July 12, 1948
Attack on Karatiya
Oct. 18, 1948
Dead Sea
Attacks on Kefar-Darom
April 10, May 11-15, 1948
Defense of Beerot-Yizhak
July 15, 1948
Battle of Main Sheich Nuran
December 5-7, 1948
Attack on Rafah
Jan. 3-7, 1949
Capture of Beer-Shev'a
Oct. 21, 1948
Attack on Nirim
May 15, 1948
Bombing of Cairo
July 15, 1948
Capture of Tamila and Musherife Hills
Dec. 25-26 1948
Capture of Nizana
Dec. 27, 1948
0 10 20 km.
0 5 10 miles
65

vember 29, 1947 - July 20, 1949

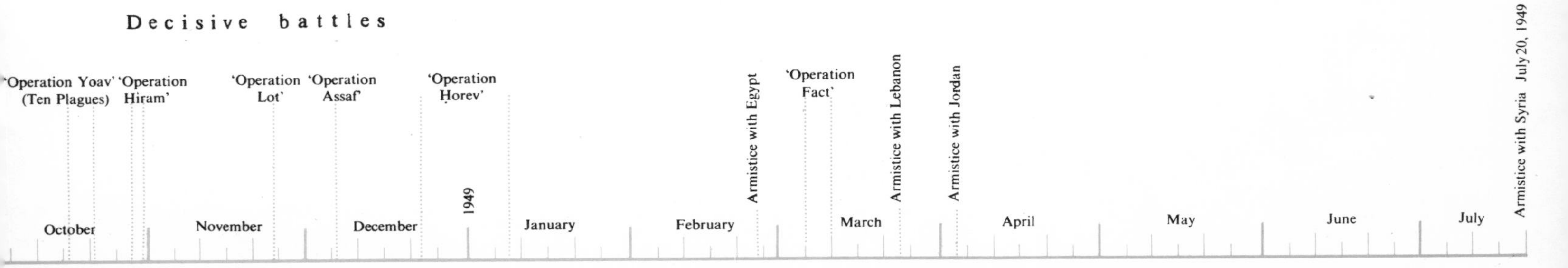
Decisive battles
'Operation Yoav' (Ten Plagues)
'Operation Hiram'
'Operation Lot'
'Operation Assaf'
'Operation Horev'
Armistice with Egypt
'Operation Fact'
Armistice with Lebanon
Armistice with Jordan
Armistice with Syria July 20, 1949
1949
October
November
December
January
February
March
April
May
June
July

TROUBLED BORDERS

On night guard

IN THE wake of the defeat of the armies of the neighboring Arab countries in their war against Israel, the Arab leaders attempted to sow fear and panic in the hearts of Israel's populace by sending specially trained armed bands across the border in the dark of night, to kill people and to blow up their homes and destroy what they had built.

The Egyptians organized units of saboteur-infiltrators who were given the Arabic name *fedayun*—"suicide squads." The Jordanians, too, despatched infiltrators who perpetrated acts of sabotage in farming settlements near the border; and the Syrians activated gangs that went under the name of *El-Fataḥ*—"The Conquest".

Israel responded in two ways. A special unit, the Border Police, was established within the regular police force to maintain border security and prevent infiltration. And, from time to time, the Israel Defence Forces would carry out retaliatory actions against the bases of the saboteurs, which usually had the desired effect of quieting things down, at least for a while.

Border police on patrol

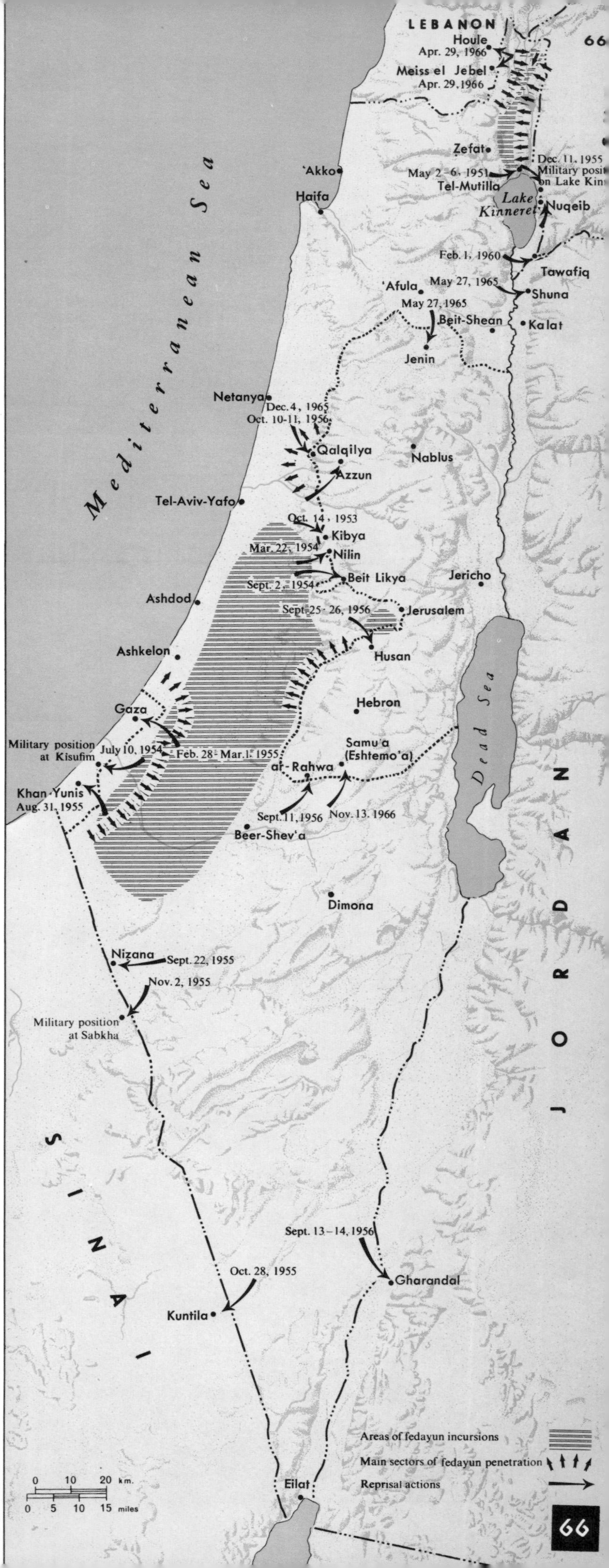

THE 1956 SINAI CAMPAIGN

St. Catherine's Monastery, Sinai

ALTHOUGH the Armistice Agreement between Israel and Egypt (like that between Israel and the other neighboring Arab countries) called for a cessation of all belligerent activities and was intended, by its terms, to serve as a transition from war to peace, the Egyptian Government paid no heed to these central provisions; on the contrary, it openly declared that it still considered itself to be in "a state of war" with Israel. Using this doctrine of belligerency as their pretext, the Egyptians closed the Suez Canal to Israeli shipping, halting not only Israel ships but all vessels carrying cargo destined for or coming from an Israel port, and confiscating their cargoes. They also harassed vessels plying the Red Sea-Gulf of Eilat route to or from Israel's southern port of Eilat, at the Strait of Tiran.

In addition, Egypt began training bands of fedayun who carried out regular forays into Israel for purposes of murder, arson, sabotage and pillage. Their bases were located in northern Sinai and the Gaza Strip.

After enduring untold suffering and hundreds of casualties, Israel struck back on 29 October 1956, in a quick thrust into the Gaza Strip and the Sinai Desert that came to be known as the Sinai Campaign, or "Operation *Kadesh*"—after Kadesh-Barnea, the name of the Sinai Desert oasis that served as the main camping site of the tribes of Israel during their Exodus from ancient Egypt.

One column of the Israel Defence Forces moved into the heart of the Sinai peninsula, while Israeli paratroopers landed behind the Egyptian lines, on the direct route to the Suez Canal. Meanwhile, other columns were advancing into other parts of the peninsula and yet another captured the Gaza Strip. By 4 November, the Egyptian Army had been routed and the Israel forces had reached positions near the east bank of the Suez Canal and at the southernmost tip of the peninsula, where until then Egyptian gun batteries had been blocking Israel-bound maritime traffic through the Strait of Tiran.

Under pressure from the United Nations, which undertook to ensure freedom of navigation through the Strait of Tiran at the entrance of the Gulf of Eilat, Israel withdrew its forces from the positions they had occupied in Sinai and the Gaza Strip. In their place came troops of the UN Emergency Force. For the next decade, there was relative tranquillity on the Egypt-Israel border.

Also, thanks to the Sinai Campaign, the shipping lanes to Eilat were opened once more, leading to an era of growth and expansion that has turned this port into Israel's gateway to East Africa and the Far East.

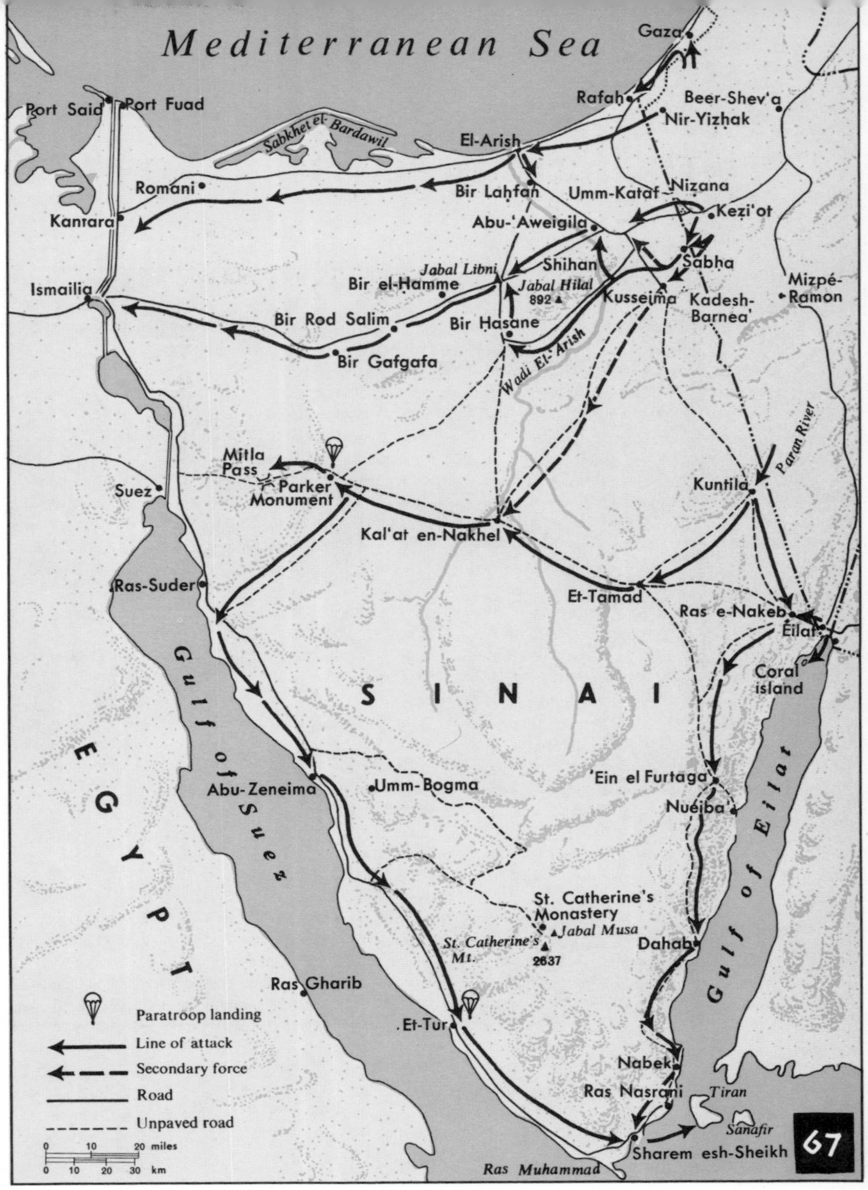

Spiked Egyptian gun at Sharem esh-Sheikh

THE ARAB DEPLOYMENT FOR ATTACK—1967

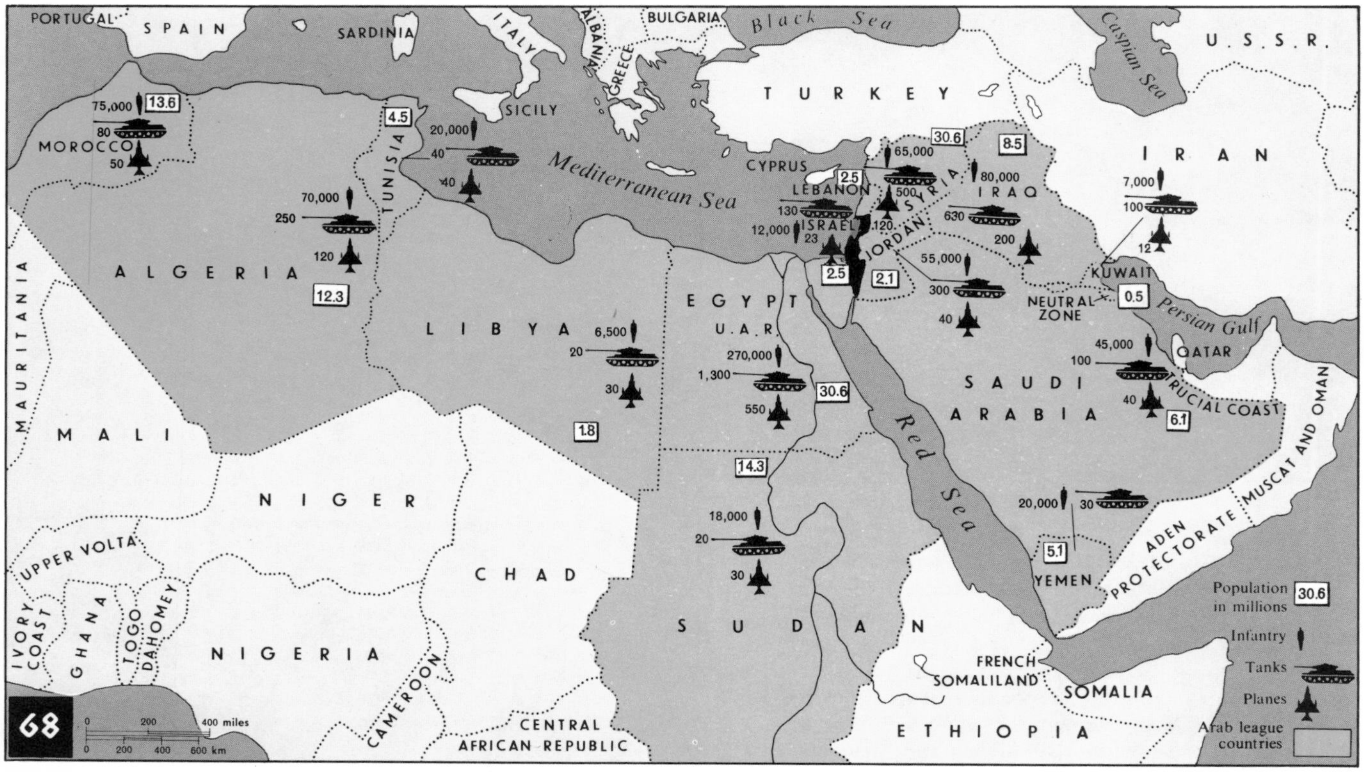

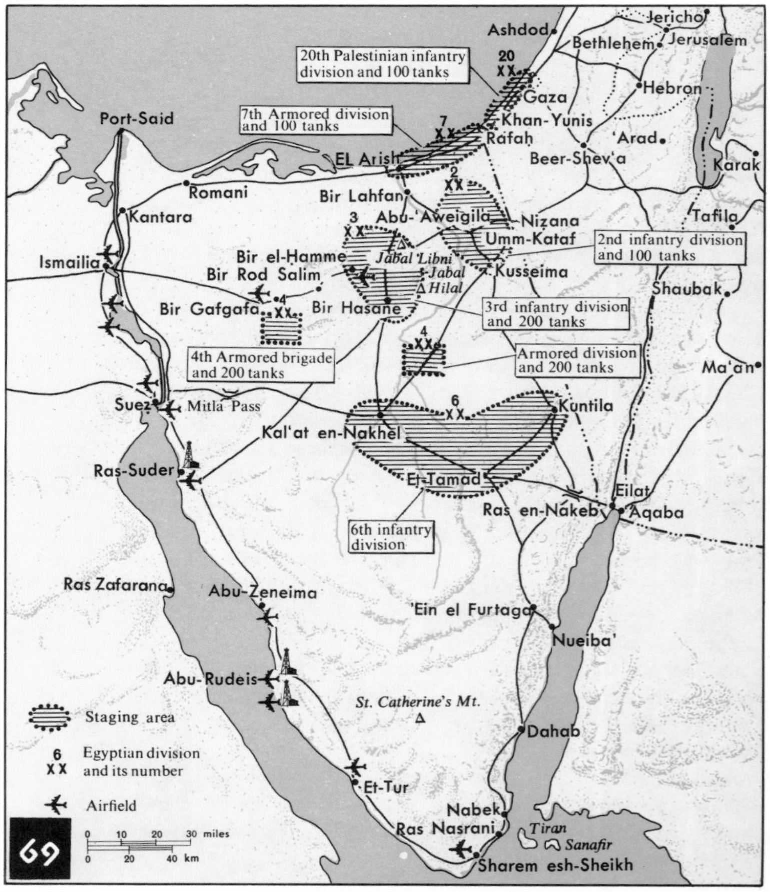

EGYPTIAN PREPARATIONS FOR BATTLE

During the last ten years, the neighboring countries—particularly Egypt in the South and Syria in the North sank their energies and resources in an all-out effort to build up their arsenals, fortify their military positions and train their fighting men, with the aid of foreign powers and their experts. They declared openly that their aim was the annihilation of the State of Israel.

Egypt took upon itself the central role in the implementation of this plan. Its ally, Syria, depended heavily on its topographical advantage vis-à-vis Israel, the mountain range on its border with Israel commanding a whole row of Jewish settlements in the valley below. As the date of the projected Egyptian-Syrian assault approached, the Kingdom of Jordan joined the line-up.

Then, in six successive days of fighting, the Israel Defence Forces succeeded in destroying the enemy armies, capturing large areas that had been used until then to threaten and harass Israel, and thereby buttressed the security of the State.

THE SIX DAY WAR: SINAI

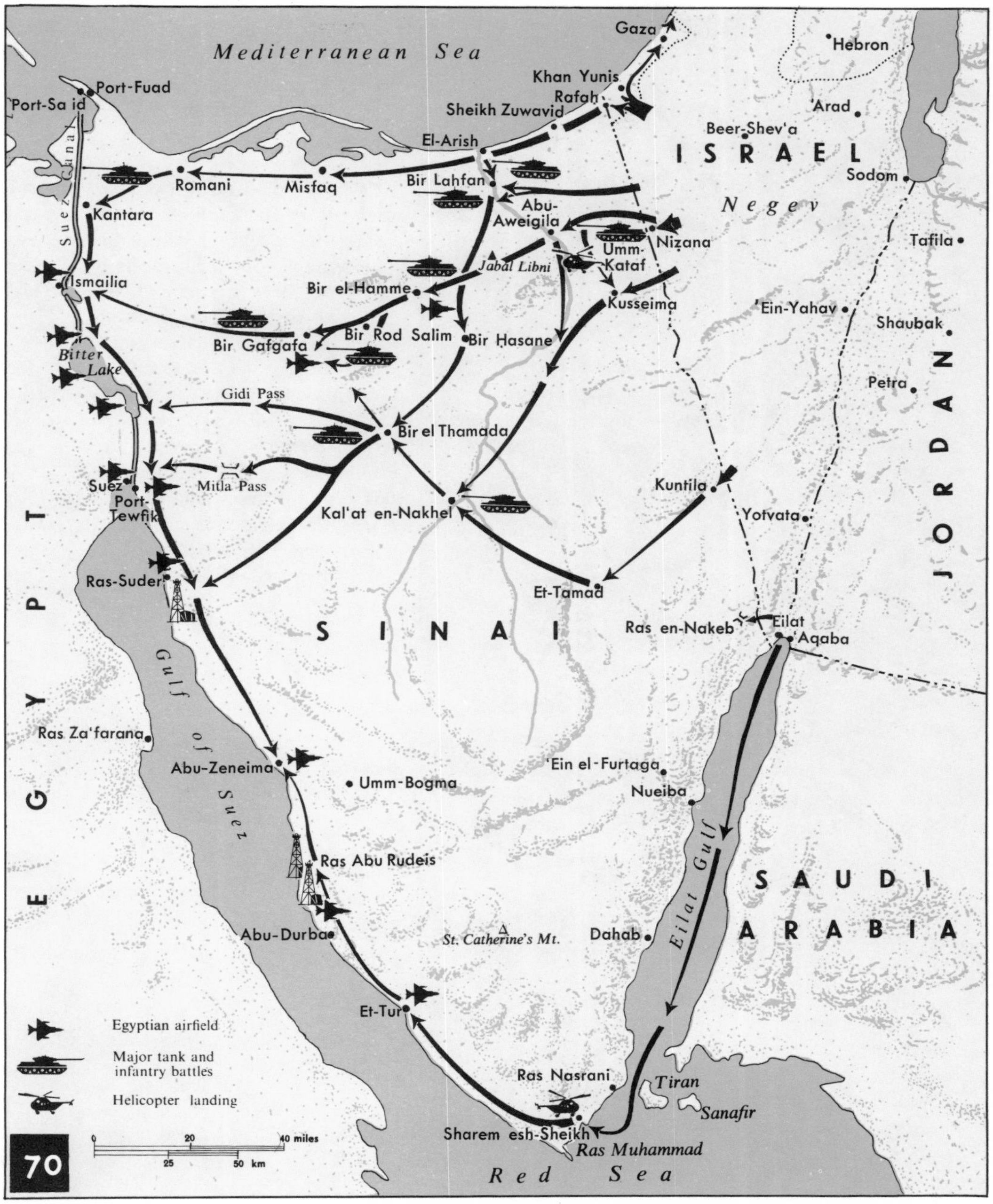
Mediterranean Sea
Gaza
Hebron
Khan Yunis
Rafah
Port-Fuad
Port-Sa id
Sheikh Zuwavid
'Arad
El-Arish
Beer-Shev'a
ISRAEL
Sodom
Romani
Misfaq
Bir Lahfan
Suez Canal
Kantara
Abu-Aweigila
Negev
Nizana
Tafila
Umm-Kataf
Jabal Libni
Ismailia
Bir el-Hamme
Kusseima
'Ein-Yahav
Shaubak
Bir Gafgafa
Bir Rod Salim
Bir Hasane
Bitter Lake
Petra
Gidi Pass
Bir el Thamada
JORDAN
Kuntila
Suez
Mitla Pass
Port-Tewfik
Kal'at en-Nakhel
Yotvata
EGYPT
Ras-Suder
Et-Tamad
SINAI
Ras en-Nakeb
Eilat
'Aqaba
Gulf of Suez
Ras Za'farana
Abu-Zeneima
'Ein el-Furtaga
Umm-Bogma
Nueiba
Ras Abu Rudeis
Eilat Gulf
SAUDI ARABIA
Abu-Durba
St. Catherine's Mt.
Dahab
Et-Tur
Egyptian airfield
Major tank and infantry battles
Helicopter landing
Ras Nasrani
Tiran
Sanafir
Sharem esh-Sheikh
Ras Muhammad
0
20
40 miles
25
50 km
70
Red Sea

IN THE first phase of the campaign on the Egyptian front, the Israel Air Force struck at Egyptian airfields in various parts of the Sinai peninsula and took a heavy toll of Egyptian warplanes, thus disrupting the enemy's war machine from the very start. As Israel troops continued their advance into the Gaza Strip, El 'Arish, the capital of Northern Sinai, and the rest of the Sinai peninsula, Egyptian resistance collapsed.

Israel troops reached the Strait of Tiran, at the southern tip of the Sinai peninsula, and, at its western end, the eastern bank of the Suez Canal.

Vicinity of Rafaḥ

THE SIX DAY WAR: THE WEST BANK

THE BATTLE for the West Bank region began, after the Jordanian attack on Jerusalem, on the southern and northern borders of Samaria. Israel forces moving out from what was formerly the Jerusalem Corridor stormed the Jordanian positions and, following their capture, began to penetrate the hills of Ramallah. Meanwhile, at the northern end of the area, Israel troops advanced from the Megiddo district to the town of Jenin and thence southward through Samaria and the Jordan Valley rapidly advancing to the Damyia, Allenby and Abdallah Bridges across the Jordan River.

Other units of the Israel Defence Forces meanwhile moved against the Jordanian positions that had attacked Jerusalem from the south and pushed back the enemy forces, capturing Bethlehem and Hebron, in the southern Judean Hills, and cleared the area of Jordanian forces.

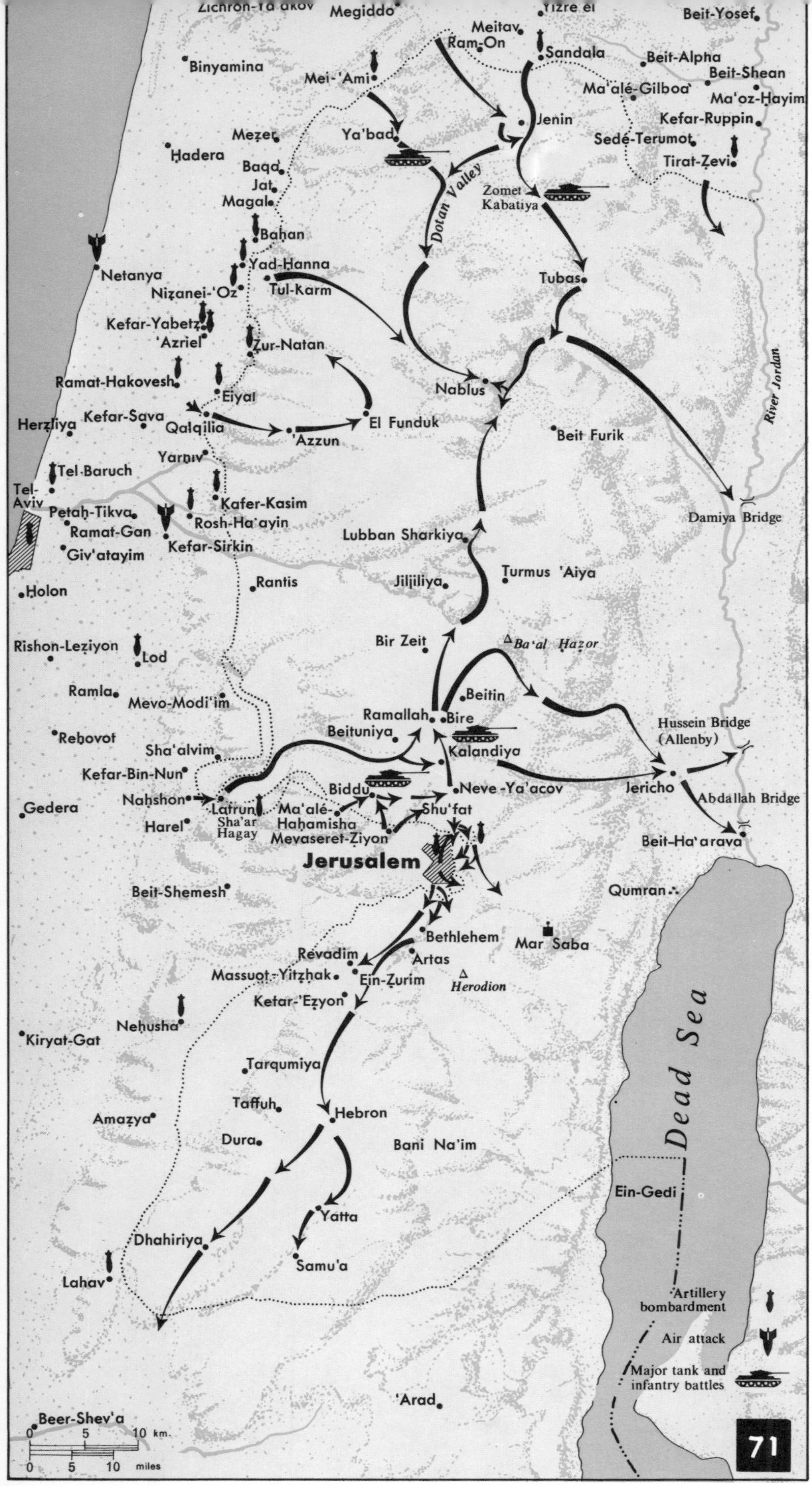

THE SIX DAY WAR: GOLAN HEIGHTS

FROM THEIR bases in eastern Upper Galilee, the Israel forces, moving in several columns, stormed up the slopes of the Golan Mountain range, along which the Syrians were entrenched. It was an extremely difficult operation, considering the Syrians' topographical situation, their heavily fortified positions and the steep approaches to these positions, covered as they were with huge basalt boulders.

After several bloody battles, the Israel forces managed to reach the top of the mountain range and routed the Syrians, who fled eastward. With the capture of Kuneitra, the largest and most important of the cities on the Golan Heights—located at a road junction and also on the main road to Damascus—the operation came to an end, and the entire area came under the control of the Israel Defence Forces.

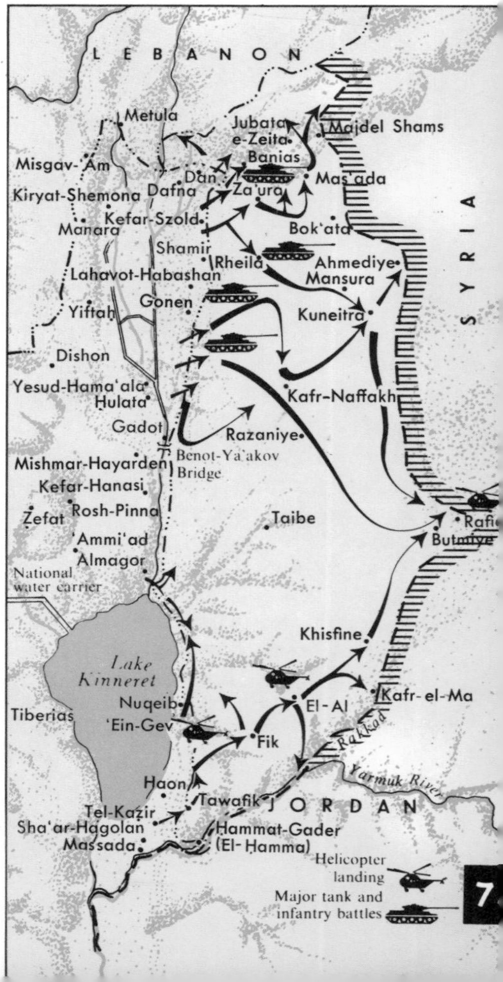

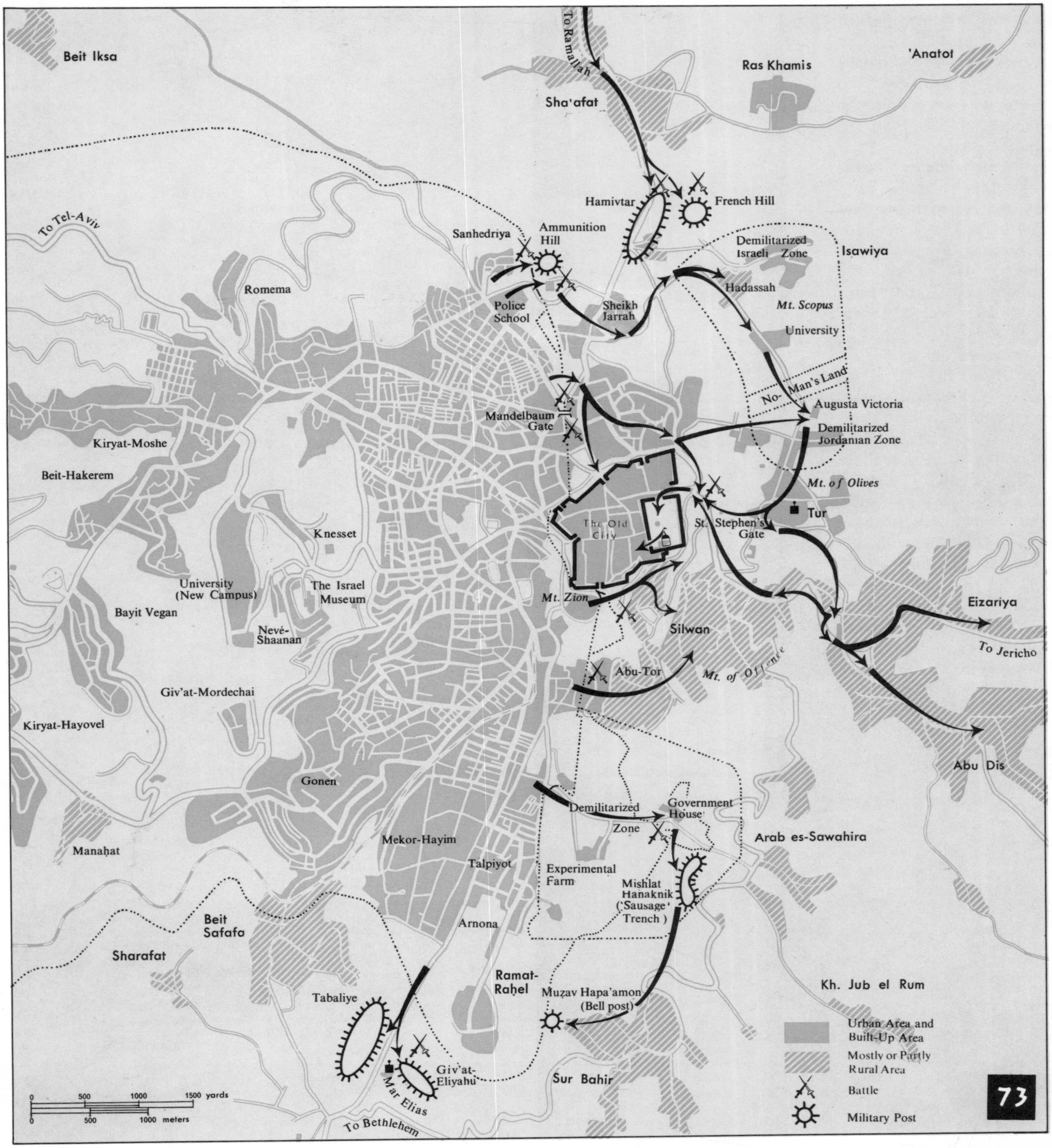
To Ramallah
Beit Iksa
Ras Khamis
'Anatot
Sha'afat
Hamivtar
French Hill
To Tel-Aviv
Sanhedriya
Ammunition Hill
Demilitarized Israeli Zone
Isawiya
Romema
Police School
Sheikh Jarrah
Hadassah
Mt. Scopus
University
No-Man's Land
Augusta Victoria
Mandelbaum Gate
Demilitarized Jordanian Zone
Kiryat-Moshe
Beit-Hakerem
Mt. of Olives
Tur
The Old City
St. Stephen's Gate
Knesset
University (New Campus)
The Israel Museum
Bayit Vegan
Mt. Zion
Eizariya
Nevé-Shaanan
Silwan
To Jericho
Abu-Tor
Mt. of Offence
Giv'at-Mordechai
Kiryat-Hayovel
Abu Dis
Gonen
Demilitarized Zone
Government House
Arab es-Sawahira
Manahat
Mekor-Hayim
Talpiyot
Experimental Farm
Mishlat Hanaknik ('Sausage' Trench)
Beit Safafa
Arnona
Sharafat
Ramat-Rahel
Kh. Jub el Rum
Tabaliye
Muzav Hapa'amon (Bell post)
Urban Area and Built-Up Area
Mostly or Partly Rural Area
Giv'at-Eliyahu
Sur Bahir
Battle
Mar Elias
Military Post
To Bethlehem
500 1000 1500 yards
500 1000 meters
73

THE SIX DAY WAR: THE BATTLE FOR JERUSALEM

AFTER THE Jordanian Army had opened a murderous artillery bombardment of the Israel sector of Jerusalem, and its troops had seized Government House, headquarters of the United Nations observers, the Israel Defence Forces launched their counterattack against the Jordanian positions in East Jerusalem. In fierce fighting, Government House at the southern end of the Jerusalem front was recaptured by Israel troops, while a unit of paratroopers stormed the Police School in the north, penetrated into the Arab sector of the city and made their way up the Mount of Olives, which commands the eastern part of Jerusalem. From there, the paratroopers broke into the walled Old City through St. Stephen's Gate. The date: June 7, 1967. The young warriors' emotion-charged encounter with the Western Wall, most revered of Jewry's holy places, marked the end of the battle for Jerusalem.

WAR MEMORIALS

THE SOIL of Israel is strewn with hundreds of graves of young heroes who gave their lives on the battlefield and were denied the privilege of witnessing the emergence of the State of Israel.

At the wayside, on mountain heights, in parks and public squares in towns and settlements, monuments have been erected in memory of fighting units, of military operations and of those who fell in Israel's War of Liberation in 1948.

On many of the memorials are engraved the names of the fallen and suitable verses from Scripture, such as: "Thy glory, O Israel, is slain upon thy high places: how are the mighty fallen!"[1] "They were swifter than eagles, they were stronger than lions."[2] "For the builders, everyone had his sword girded by his side and so builded."[3] "And they were among the mighty men, helpers of the war."[4] "Refrain thy voice from weeping, and thine eyes from tears, for thy work shall be rewarded."[5] "And I will get them praise and fame. . ."[6]

[1] II Sam. 1:19 [2] II Sam. 1:23
[3] Nehemiah 4:12
[4] I Chron. 12:1
[5] Jer. 31:16 [6] Zeph. 3:19

Memorial at 'Ein-Gev

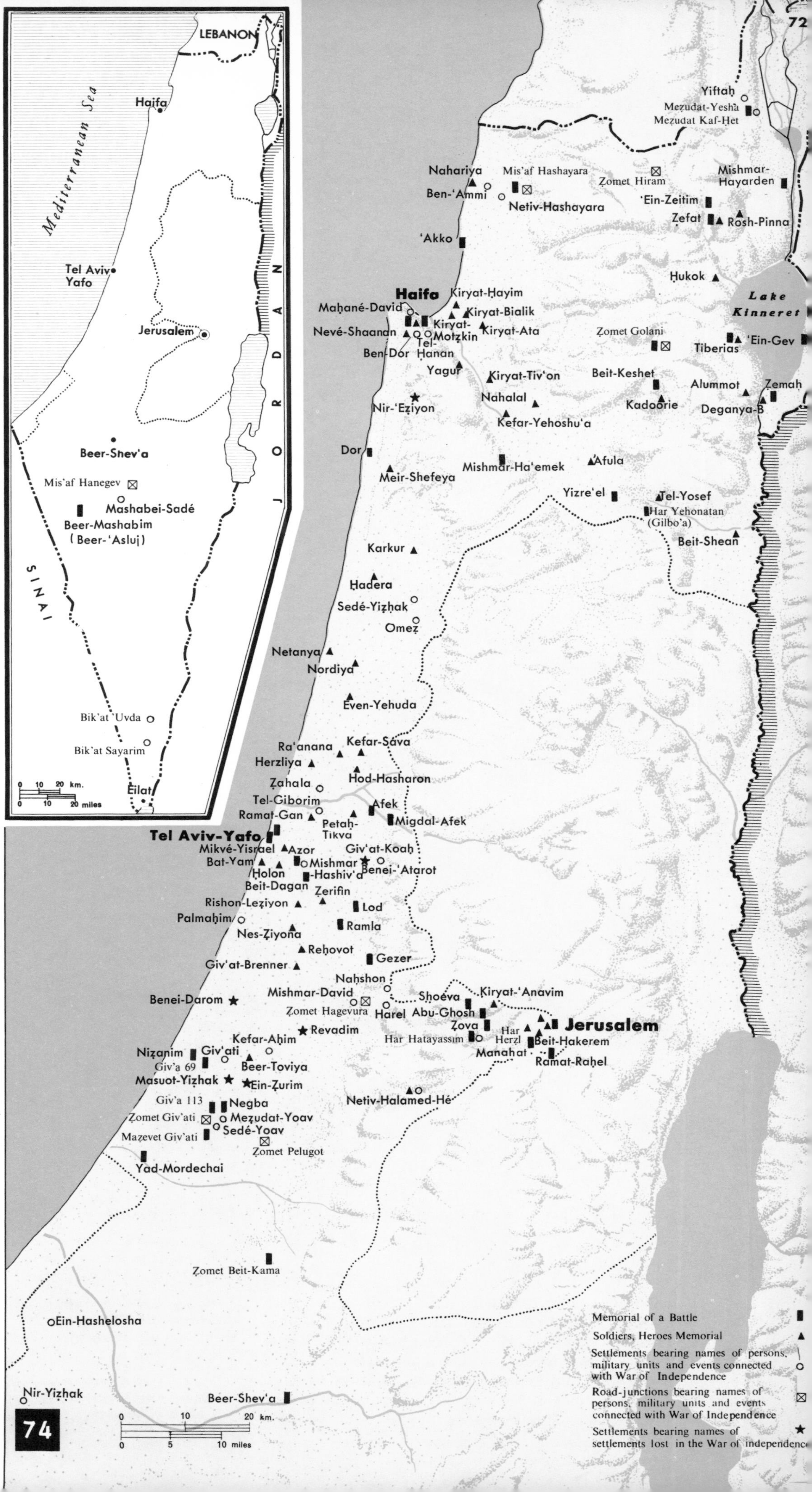

roots in the past

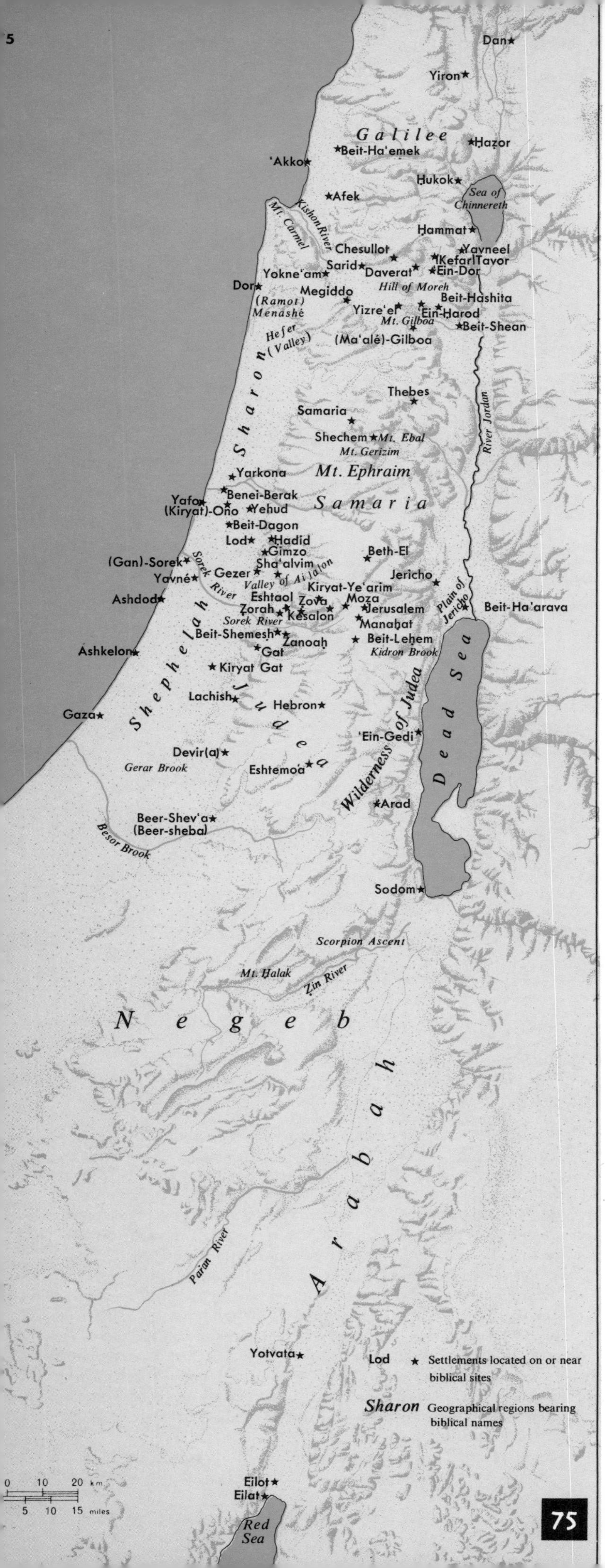
Dan
Yiron
Galilee
Beit-Ha'emek
Hazor
'Akko
Hukok
Sea of Chinnereth
Afek
Mt. Carmel
Kishon River
Hammat
Chesullot
Yavneel
Kefar Tavor
Sarid
Daverat
Ein-Dor
Yokne'am
Dor
Megiddo
Hill of Moreh
Beit-Hashita
(Ramot) Menashé
Yizre'el
Ein-Harod
Mt. Gilboa
Beit-Shean
Hefer (Valley)
(Ma'alé)-Gilboa
Sharon
Thebes
Samaria
Shechem
Mt. Ebal
Mt. Gerizim
River Jordan
Yarkona
Mt. Ephraim
Yafo
Benei-Berak
Samaria
(Kiryat)-Ono
Yehud
Beit-Dagon
Lod
Hadid
Gimzo
Beth-El
(Gan)-Sorek
Sha'alvim
Sorek River
Valley of Ai Jalon
Yavné
Gezer
Jericho
Kiryat-Ye'arim
Ashdod
Eshtaol
Zova
Moza
Jerusalem
Plain of Jericho
Beit-Ha'arava
Zorah
Kesalon
Sorek River
Manahat
Beit-Shemesh
Zanoah
Beit-Lehem
Ashkelon
Gat
Kidron Brook
Kiryat Gat
Shephelah
Judea
Dead Sea
Lachish
Hebron
Gaza
Wilderness of Judea
'Ein-Gedi
Devir(a)
Gerar Brook
Eshtemoa
Arad
Beer-Shev'a
(Beer-sheba)
Besor Brook
Sodom
Scorpion Ascent
Mt. Halak
Zin River
Negeb
Arabah
Paran River
Yotvata
Lod ★ Settlements located on or near biblical sites
Sharon Geographical regions bearing biblical names
Eilot
Eilat
Red Sea
0 10 20 km
5 10 15 miles

NEW SETTLEMENTS—BIBLICAL NAMES

Jerusalem on 2nd century coin

RIGHT FROM the start, the founders of towns and settlements in the Land of Israel tried to use Biblical names for these places, as a sign and symbol of their bond with the heritage of their ancestral past in this land and of their deep affection for the Book of Books. Many of the new settlements were built on or near the sites of ancient habitations and, quite naturally, were called by the same names: Yafo, Ashkelon, Ashdod, Beer-Shev'a, Yizre'el, Beit-Shean, 'Ein-Dor, Beit-Hashita, Kesalon, Ẓorah, Eshtaol, Beit-Shemesh, Sha'alvim, Yehud, Ẓova, Nahalal and numerous others.

Other places were given Biblical names even though their historical antecedents were in another part of the country.

As the early pioneers went up to settle the land, the Bible was their trusted and constant companion. They saw in the national rebirth of the Jewish people the fulfillment of the vision of the ancient Hebrew Prophets. The words of the Prophets and the Psalmist aroused their spirits and gave succour and comfort in times of trial and planted in their hearts the faith in their ultimate success. Many of the early settlements, therefore, were named after Biblical phrases designed to symbolize the mood and spirit of their founders.

The first suburb to be built outside the walls of Old Jerusalem was called Mishkenot-Shaananim ("Dwellings of Serenity"), based on a verse in Isaiah;[1] Other Biblical passages have provided the inspiration for Mikvé-Israel ("Hope of Israel");[2] Petaḥ-Tikva ("Door of Hope");[3] Rishon-Leẓiyon ("First to Zion");[4] Nes-Ẓiona ("A Banner to Zion");[5] Rosh-Pinna ("Cornerstone");[6] Merḥavia ("Large place. . . of the Lord").[7]

[1] Isa. 32:18 [2] Jer. 14:8 [3] Hos. 2:17 [4] Isa. 41:27 [5] Jer. 4:6 [6] Psalms 118:22 [7] *ibid.* 118:5

Seal from Gezer

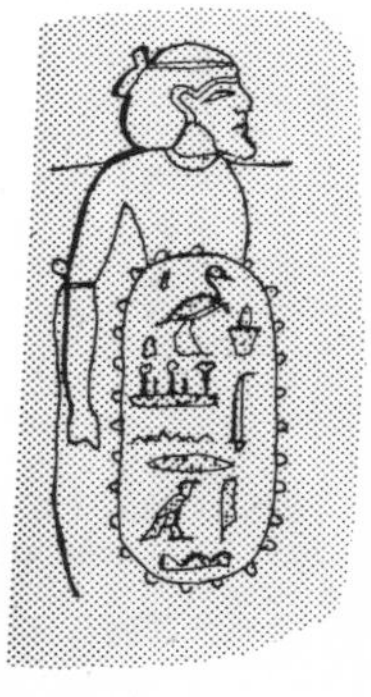

Beit-Shean in hieroglyphic script

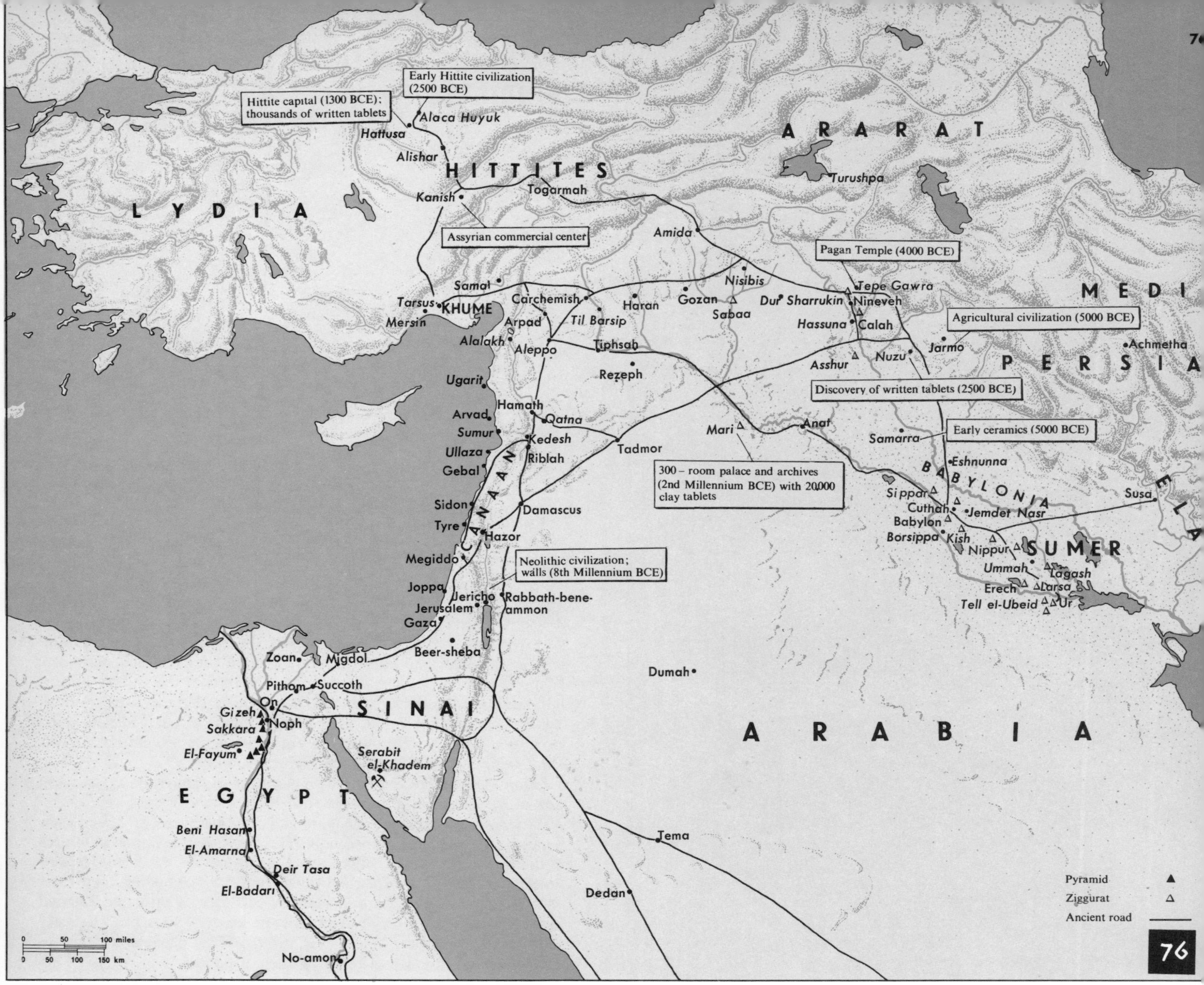
Early Hittite civilization (2500 BCE)
Hittite capital (1300 BCE); thousands of written tablets
Alaca Huyuk
Hattusa
Alishar
HITTITES
Kanish
Togarmah
LYDIA
ARARAT
Turushpa
Assyrian commercial center
Amida
Pagan Temple (4000 BCE)
Nisibis
Tepe Gawra
MEDI
Samal
Tarsus
KHUME
Mersin
Carchemish
Haran
Gozan
Sabaa
Dur Sharrukin
Nineveh
Arpad
Til Barsip
Hassuna
Calah
Agricultural civilization (5000 BCE)
Alalakh
Aleppo
Tiphsah
Asshur
Nuzu
Jarmo
Achmetha
PERSIA
Ugarit
Rezeph
Discovery of written tablets (2500 BCE)
Hamath
Arvad
Qatna
Sumur
Kedesh
Mari
Anat
Samarra
Early ceramics (5000 BCE)
Ullaza
Riblah
Tadmor
Eshnunna
Gebal
CANAAN
300 – room palace and archives (2nd Millennium BCE) with 20,000 clay tablets
BABYLONIA
Sidon
Damascus
Sippar
Cuthah
Jemdet Nasr
Susa
ELA
Tyre
Hazor
Babylon
Borsippa
Kish
Nippur
SUMER
Megiddo
Neolithic civilization; walls (8th Millennium BCE)
Ummah
Lagash
Joppa
Jericho
Rabbath-bene-ammon
Erech
Larsa
Jerusalem
Tell el-Ubeid
Ur
Gaza
Beer-sheba
Zoan
Migdol
Dumah
Pithom
Succoth
On
Gizeh
Noph
SINAI
Sakkara
El-Fayum
ARABIA
Serabit el-Khadem
EGYPT
Beni Hasan
El-Amarna
Tema
Deir Tasa
El-Badari
Dedan
Pyramid
Ziggurat
Ancient road
0 50 100 miles
0 50 100 150 km
No-amon
76

Winged Sphinx,
Mesopotamia, 9th century BCE

THE ANCIENT EAST

THE ANCIENT Near East comprised the Land of Israel and its neighbors, Aram and Assyria, in Asia, as well as Egypt in Africa. Israel served as a land-bridge between the two great powers of the day, Egypt and Assyria, and therein lay its paramount geopolitical importance. Along its coastal plain ran the famed Coastal Route, traversed in peacetime by commercial caravans and in wartime by the marching columns of warriors. From time to time, the country was the site of battles between these powers; these wars left their imprint on the historical image of the ancient Near East, and of the Land of Israel in particular, for many generations.

On other occasions, the Assyrians would sweep into Israel in order to establish a bridgehead against Egypt. In one of these campaigns, Assyria put an end to the Kingdom of Israel. Its sister kingdom, Judea, survived for another 135 years, only to be overrun by the forces of Babylonia, which had supplanted Assyria as the major power of the north.

Babylonia, too, perished in turn and on its ruins rose the Persian Kingdom, a mighty empire whose domain included the Land of Israel.

Every place that the sole of your foot shall tread upon, that have I given unto you, as I said unto Moses. From the wilderness and this Lebanon even unto the great river, the river Euphrates, all the land of the Hittites, and unto the great sea toward the going down of the sun, shall be your coast.

Joshua 1:3–4

JOSHUA'S CONQUEST

AFTER THE conquest of the country under Joshua, the tribes of Israel began to settle on the land. Each tribe received its inheritance according to its size, as is related in the Bible: "To these shall the land be apportioned as an inheritance. . . to the numerous shalt thou give a larger portion, and to the small in number—a smaller portion: each (tribe) is to be given its portion according to its population. . . According to the lot shall the possession thereof be divided between the many and the few."[1]

Our sages relate that the lottery was conducted in the presence of the High Priest: "How was it done? El'azar (the priest) was attired in the *Urim* and *Thummim*, as Joshua and all Israel stood before him. An urn containing the names of the tribes was placed before him, and another, containing the names of the regions (to be inherited). And he was directed by the Spirit of God. . ."[2] ". . . And two young priests attended. Each raised a name (from each of the two urns)—and thus the apportionment was made."[3]

The type of crops planted depended on the terrain: in the valleys were grown the grains and other field crops, while the hilly regions were reserved for orchards and vineyards. There were towns and villages, the latter being divided into "mother-villages" and "daughter-villages" grouped around them. The farmers of the mother-village would move to one of the daughter-villages in the vicinity during the sowing and harvest seasons, perform the work that had to be performed in the fields and then return to their homes in the mother-village.

Around the town or village were pasture-lands for the grazing of cattle and sheep. The villages skirting the desert were generally provided with enclosures housing the shepherds and their flocks.

[1] Num. 26:53-56 [2] Talmud (Babylonian), Baba-Batra 122a
[3] Talmud (Jerusalem), Yuma, 4, 1.

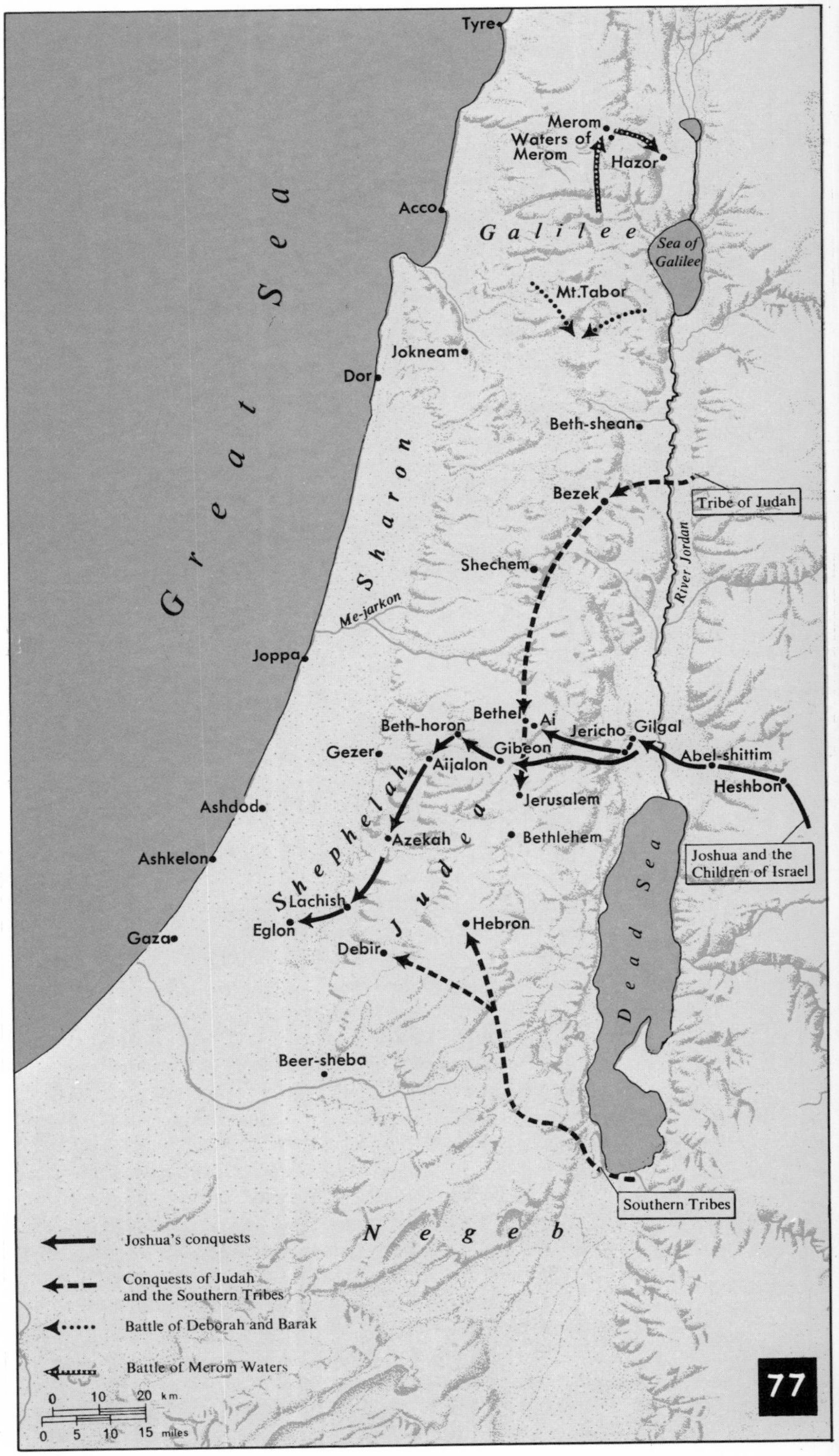

"ISRAEL" in hieroglyphic script

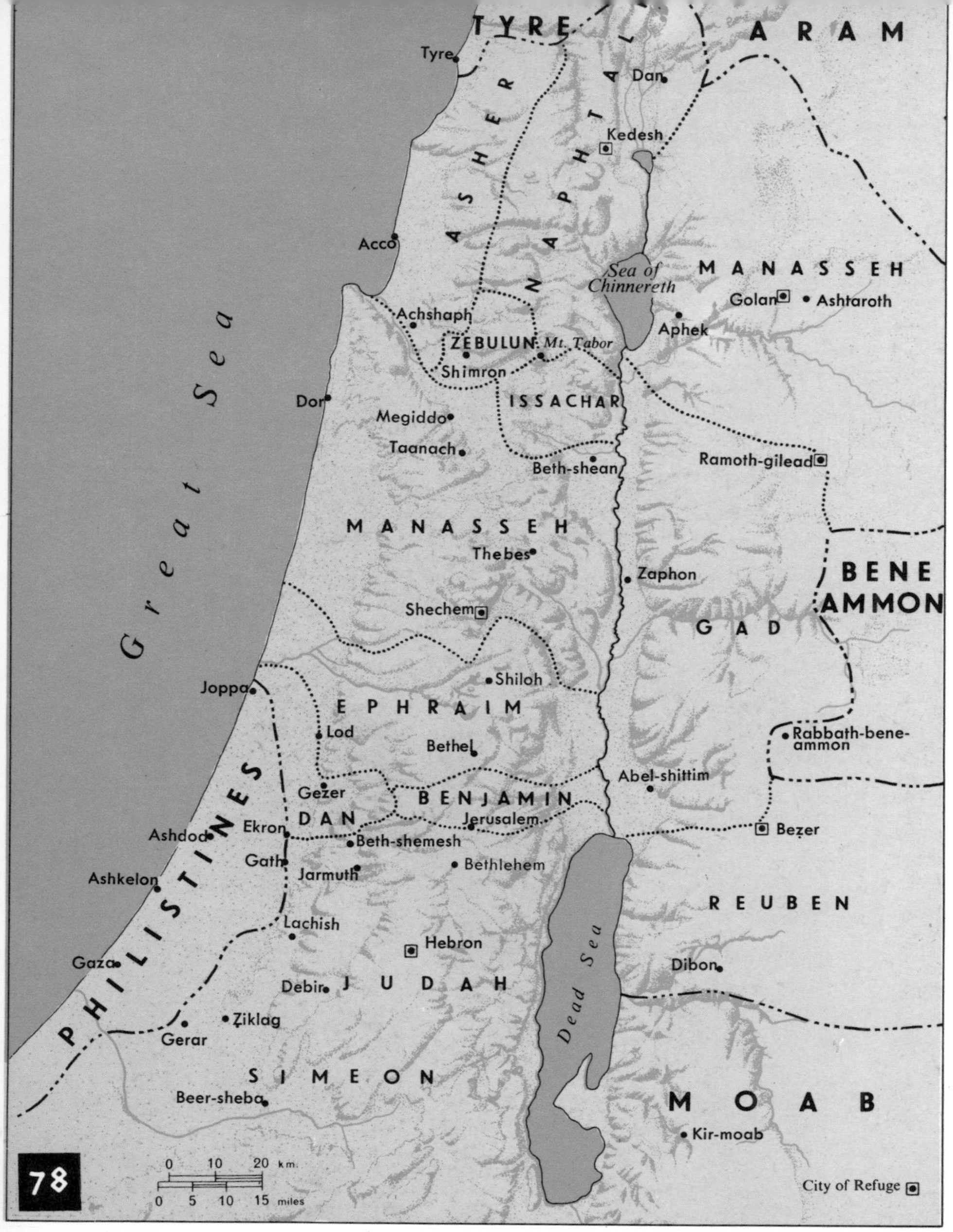

THE TRIBES OF ISRAEL

THE FIRST to settle down were the two and one-half tribes that chose to remain in the area east of the River Jordan. Of them, the Bible tells us: "The sons of Reuben, and the Gadites, and half the tribe of Manasseh were men of valor, able to wear buckler and sword, and to shoot with bow, and skillful in war. . ."[1]

The southern part of the west bank of the Jordan River was assigned to the tribe of Judah. To Simeon went the deep south, the Negev; for support and protection, the Simeonites looked to their more powerful neighbors, the sons of Judah.[2]

The tribe of Dan settled in the foothills of the Judean Mountains and part of the adjacent coastal plain. They were harassed by hostile neighbors,[3] a situation which eventually caused some of the families of the tribe to migrate northward and to found there the city (Dan) that was to gain Biblical fame as the northernmost town in Israel.

To the north of Judah settled the sons of Benjamin, the territories of the two tribes meeting at Jerusalem. The Samarian hill country went to the sons of Joseph: Ephraim in the southern portion, Manasseh in the northern. Though large in area, much of this territory was woodland and thus offered little room for cultivation—a fact of which the sons of Joseph had occasion to complain to Joshua.[4]

Further north, in the area stretching from the fertile Jezreel Valley westward to the Mediterranean coast, the tribes of Issachar and Zebulun made their home. Western Galilee was settled by Asher, Eastern Galilee by Naphtali, whose territory included Lake Kinneret (Sea of Galilee) and its shores on all sides.

[1] I Chron. 5:18 [2] Josh. 19:2
[3] Judg. 1:34 [4] Josh. 17:14-15

SAUL'S KINGDOM

KING SAUL, Israel's first monarch, was a member of the tribe of Benjamin. His first task was the molding of the separate tribes into a single nation,[1] a task considerably facilitated for him by the presence, on all sides of the new kingdom, of hostile nations whose armies were a constant threat: in the coastal plain—the Philistines; in the south—Amalek; to the east—Moabites, Ammonites and Edomites; and to the north—Arameans.

Saul's first specific concern was the mobilization of a strong, effective permanent army.[2] He took the field against Israel's foes and succeeded in inflicting one defeat after another upon them. First he routed the Ammonites, in Transjordan, who had been harassing Israelite settlements on the west bank of the Jordan.[3] In another encounter, he defeated the Philistines, who had invaded his own tribe of Benjamin with a force of "thirty thousand chariots and six thousand horsemen and people as the sand which is on the seashore in multitude."[4] Saul also hurled back his enemies in the south.[5]

At the end of his reign, Saul became involved in another bitter struggle with the Philistines, who had once again invaded the kingdom in force. The decisive battle took place on the slopes of Mount Gilbo'a, where Saul and three of his sons were killed in the heavy fighting. In a deeply moving elegy, David (whose best friend had been Saul's son Jonathan) mourns the fallen heroes, ending his lament with the words: "How are the mighty fallen and the weapons of war perished!"[6]

[1] I Sam. 14:47 [2] *ibid.* 52 [3] *ibid.* 11:11
[4] *ibid.* 13:5 [5] *ibid.* 14:48 [6] II Sam. 1:27

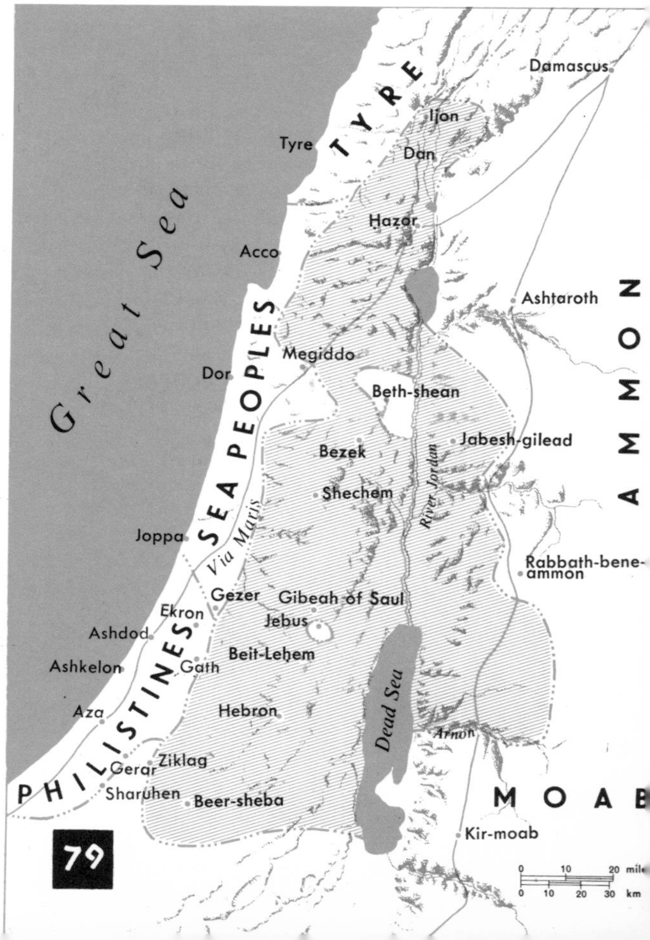

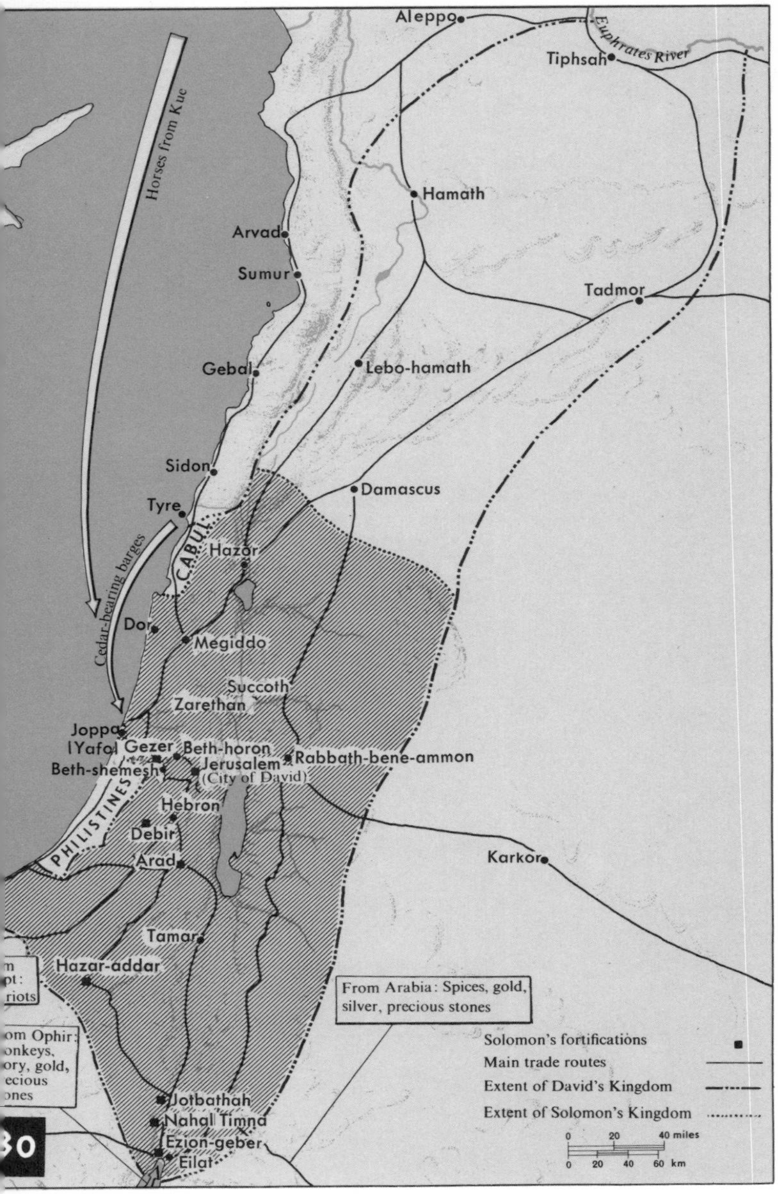

And Judah and Israel dwelt safely, every man under his vine and under his fig tree, from Dan even to Beer-sheba, all the days of Solomon.

I Kings 4:25

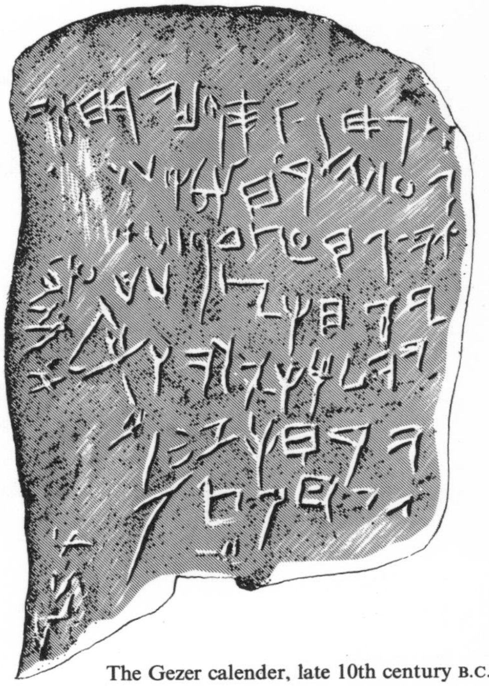

The Gezer calender, late 10th century B.C.E

DAVID AND SOLOMON

ISRAEL'S Golden Era in Biblical times were the years of David's and Solomon's reigns. It was in their days that the divine promise to Abraham, the father of the Hebrew nation, was fulfilled: "Unto thy seed have I given this land from the river of Egypt unto the great river, the river Euphrates."[1]

David ascended the throne in the city of Hebron. Seven years later he captured the mountain stronghold of Jerusalem, named it the City of David and made it his capital. He consolidated his position, and that of his new capital, by defeating the Philistines in the nearby Valley of Rephaim. In the years that followed, David piled victory on victory, routed Israel's foes, and greatly expanded the territory of the kingdom. Towards the end of his days, he readied a plot of land on Mount Moriah, in Jerusalem, for the erection of a Temple to the Lord—a plan that was to be implemented later by David's son, Solomon.

Under King Solomon, the people of Israel were able to enjoy the fruits of David's extensive military victories: ". . . And he had peace on all sides round about him, and Judah and Israel dwelt safely, every man under his vine and under his fig-tree. . . "[2]

Solomon built the Temple in all its glory, and he erected royal citadels, where he stationed large detachments of horsemen and chariots, at strategic points throughout the land: at Gezer in Judah, Megiddo at the entrance to the Jezreel Valley, and Ḥaẓor in Upper Galilee. He divided the country into twelve districts, for each of which he appointed a governor who was responsible for keeping the Royal House supplied during one month in the year.

He maintained a powerful army that included tens of thousands of horses, riders and chariots.[3] King Solomon signed treaties with the neighboring kingdoms, and foreign potentates visited him in Jerusalem, to see the splendor of the Temple, to hear the words of wisdom from the king's lips and to participate in the general prosperity. "And God gave Solomon wisdom," the Bible relates, "and understanding exceeding much, and largeness of heart. . . and his fame was in all the nations round about."[4]

Solomon's reign lasted forty years.

[1] Gen. 15:18 [2] I Kings 4:25 [3] *ibid.* 5:6 [4] *ibid.* 5:9,11

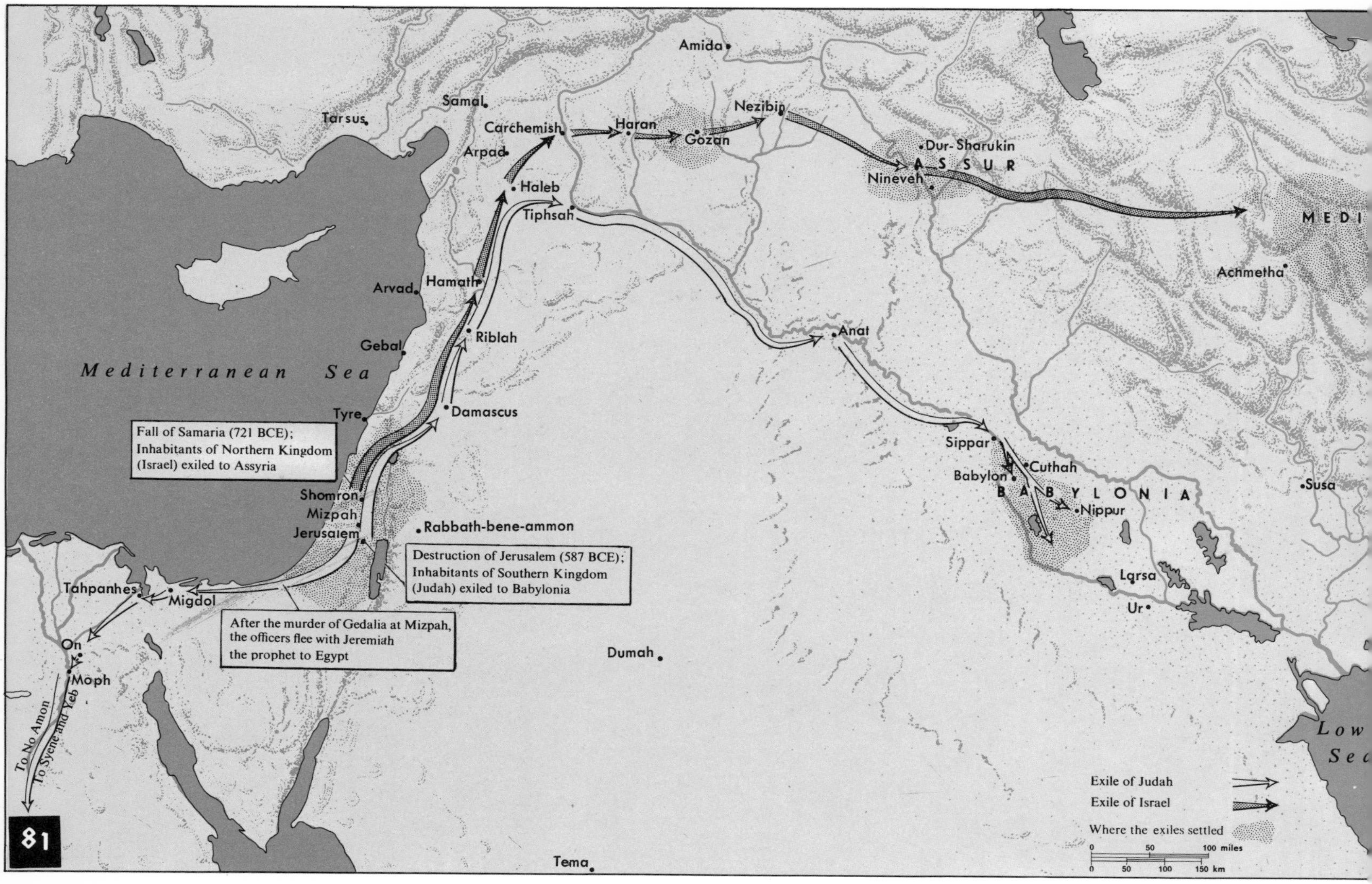

DESTRUCTION AND EXILE

THE INVASION of the Assyrian army, under Shalmaneser V, and the capture of Samaria brought to an end the Kingdom of Israel in the year 722 BCE. A part of the population was exiled to distant lands,[1] and in their place came tribes from various parts of the Assyrian Kingdom and from the land of Cutha. These migrants were assimilated among the remaining population of Samaria, and from them sprang the Samaritans, also known as Cuthites.

The Kingdom of Judah continued its existence until it was invaded by Nebuchadnezzar (Nebuchadrezzar), at the head of the Babylonian army. Nebuchadnezzar took Jerusalem and burned down the Temple on the 9th of Av, in the year 587 BCE, thus putting an end to the southern Kingdom—135 years after the demise of its northern sister-monarchy. Many of Judah's sons were exiled to Babylonia: none was left behind, relates the Book of Kings, but "the poorest sort of the people of the land."[2] The exiles remembered Zion from afar and prayed for an opportunity to return to it and rebuild it. "By the rivers of Babylon, there we sat down, yea, we wept, when we remembered Zion. . . How shall we sing the song of the Lord in a strange land?. . . If I forget thee, O Jerusalem, let my right hand forget her cunning. Let my tongue cleave to the roof of my mouth if I do not remember thee, if I prefer not Jerusalem above my chief joy."[3]

[1] II Kings 17:22 [2] *ibid.* 24:14 [3] Psalms 137:1-6

Jehu, King of Israel offering tribute to Assyrian king

81

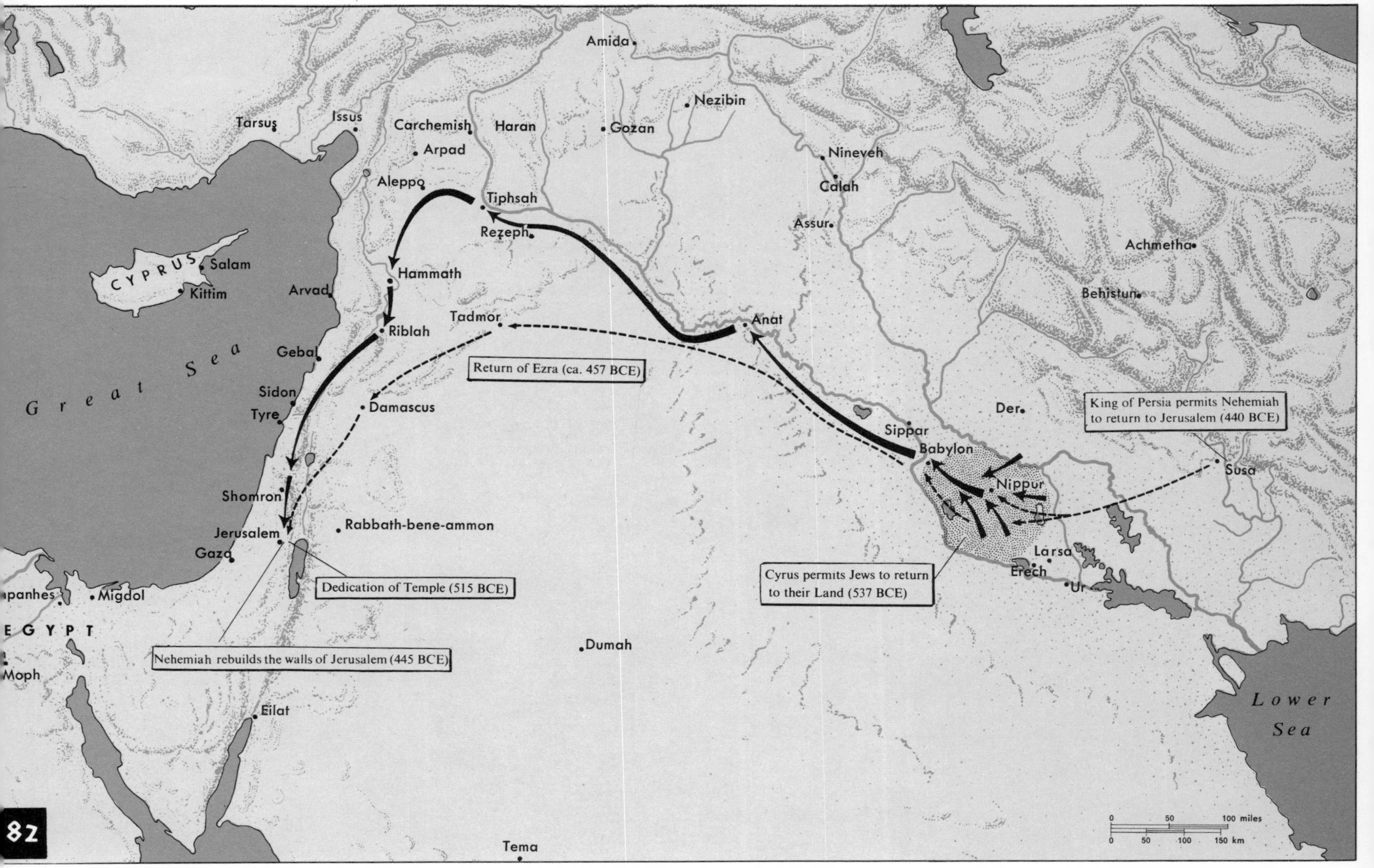

RETURN TO ZION

THE EXILES' hope of returning to Zion was realized a generation later. Babylonia was conquered by Persia, whose king, Cyrus, permitted the Jews to return to the land of their fathers. The first wave of returning exiles, headed by Sheshbazzar, of the Royal House of Judah, reached Jerusalem in the year 537 BCE. Sixteen years later came the second wave, under the leadership of Zerubabel, who was appointed Governor of Judah. He rebuilt the Temple, which was dedicated in 515: "And all the people shouted with a great shout in praise of the Lord upon the founding of the House of the Lord. But many of the older priests and Levites and heads of families who had seen the First House, when the foundation of this House was laid before their eyes, wept with a loud voice, and many (others) shouted aloud for joy. So that the people could not discern the noise of the shout of joy from the noise of the weeping of the people. . . and the sound was heard afar off."[1]

The dedication of the Temple served as a stimulus for a third wave of returnees, headed by Ezra the Scribe. After him came Nehemiah, who in 445 BCE rebuilt and refortified the walls of Jerusalem, despite continuous threats and interference from hostile elements, among them a man described as "Geshem the Arabian." By arming his builders and keeping them in a state of constant alert—"with one hand he did the work and, with the other, held the weapon"—Nehemiah managed to complete his task in 52 days.[2]

[1] Ezra 3:11-13 [2] Nehemiah 4:11-17

The Persians were defeated by Alexander the Great at the Battle of Issus in 333 BCE, and Greek rule replaced that of the Persians in Palestine. After the death of Alexander the Great, disputes broke out among his generals, the country eventually falling into the hands of Seleucus, founder of the Seleucid Empire. The Seleucid rulers were fervent admirers of Greek culture and one of them, Antiochus Epiphanes, embarked on an extensive program of Hellenization. This process led to a royal edict forbidding practice of the Jewish religion and the Temple in Jerusalem was defiled and converted into a temple to Jupiter.

Jewish coin from Persian period

THE HASMONAEAN KINGDOM 167–142 BCE

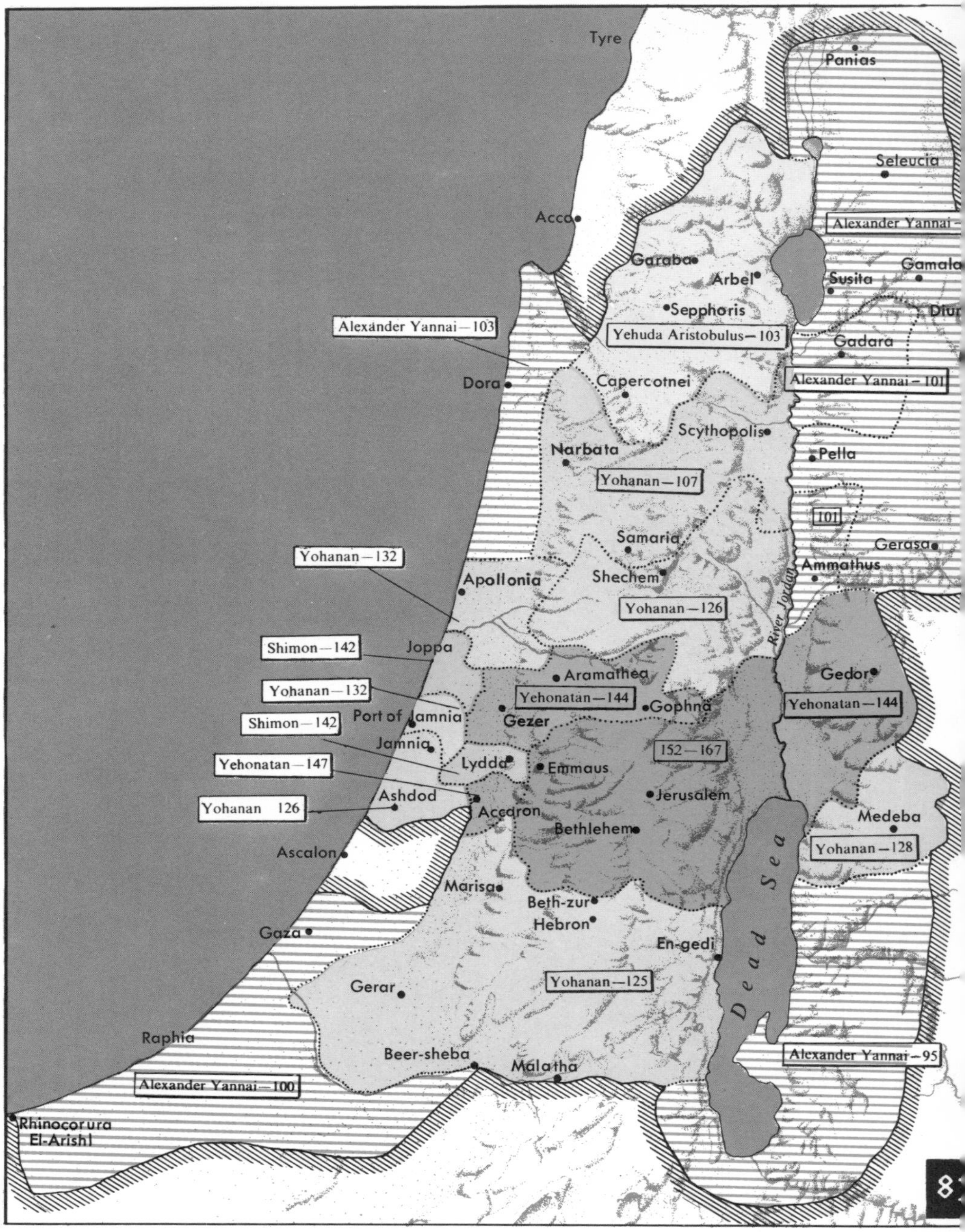

Conqueror and Date of Conquest — Yohanan 126

Province of Judah

Yehonatan

Shimon

Yohanan

Yehuda Aristobulus

Alexander Yannai

IN THE small village of Modi'im, tucked away in the foothills of the Judean Mountains, the banner of the Hasmonaean revolt was first raised, in 167 BCE, by a family of farmer-priests known as the Maccabees. In the early stages, the rebels operated in small bands in the vicinity of Modi'im. Using guerrilla tactics, they would strike at the Greek conquerors from ambush, then scatter and conceal themselves in creek-beds and mountain caves. Gradually, the insurgents gathered strength and raised their sights: their ultimate objective now was the liberation of Jerusalem and the Temple.

The Greeks' attempts to put down the revolt did not succeed. The Maccabees, going over to open warfare, won their first major victory over the Greeks at Beit-Horon, an important strategic point on the main route to the capital, still being held by the enemy. Continuing their advance towards Jerusalem, the Maccabees, under the leadership of Judah, captured Mizpa, a commanding height north of Jerusalem and traditional site of the Prophet Samuel's grave (its Arabic name today is Nebi Samuil). There Judah deployed his forces in regular military formation, massing for the final assault on Jerusalem.

Their hearts filled with awe and reverence, Judah's hardy warriors entered the Holy Temple, purified it and rededicated it in 165 BCE.

But the war was not yet won. More battles had to be fought in the Jerusalem area and further north, and in one of these Judah Maccabee was slain. His brothers took his place, brought the war to a successful conclusion, consolidated the Jews' newly-won independence and founded what came to be known as the Hasmonaean dynasty.

Temple—Gold glass from 4th century C.E

83

HASMONAEAN CAMPAIGNS
142–76 BCE

WHEN THE Maccabees captured Jerusalem, the remnant of the Greek defenders of the city took refuge in the Acra (Hacra), a strongly fortified citadel near the Temple. After Judah's death, his brother Simon (Shimon) captured this last enemy stronghold in Jerusalem. He also captured Jaffa and turned it into a major port and trading center. On the family grave at Modi'im, Shimon erected a grand monument adorned with representations of weapons, in memory of his fallen brothers, and of vessels of the sea—symbol of the Maccabees' nautical ambitions.

Following Simon's death, his son Yohanan Hyrcanus continued to expand the realm, capturing two additional seaports: Apollonia, north of Yafo, and Yavne-on-sea, to the south. Turning eastward, Yohanan crossed the Jordan and captured Meidaba and much of the surrounding area. Other conquests were carried out in the Samarian highlands to the north of Jerusalem and in the Land of Judea, to the south, where the cities of Maresha, Hebron, Adoraim and Beersheba fell to his forces. Eventually, the Hasmonaean army took possession of the entire south known as Edom (or Idumaea), compelling its inhabitants to adopt the Jewish faith. This act of "political conversion" some years later produced the emergence and rise to power of Herod the Great, a descendant of an Idumaean family.

Yohanan completed his string of conquests by adding the fertile Jezreel Valley to his domain, thus creating a direct geographical link with the Jewish-populated Galilee region in the extreme north of the country.

The monarchy continued to expand under Yohanan's son and successor, Alexander Yannai, who completed the conquest of the coastal plain along the Mediterranean and went on to capture part of the Sinai peninsula. In Transjordan, he extended his father's conquests in the highlands of Moab and Gilead, as far north as Mount Hermon. At the end of his reign, the Hasmonaean Kingdom comprised all of the Land of Israel, on both sides of the River Jordan.

Prow of warship, Hasmonaean period

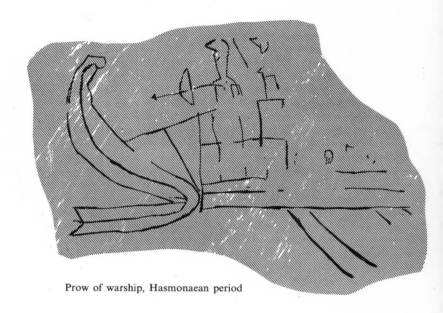

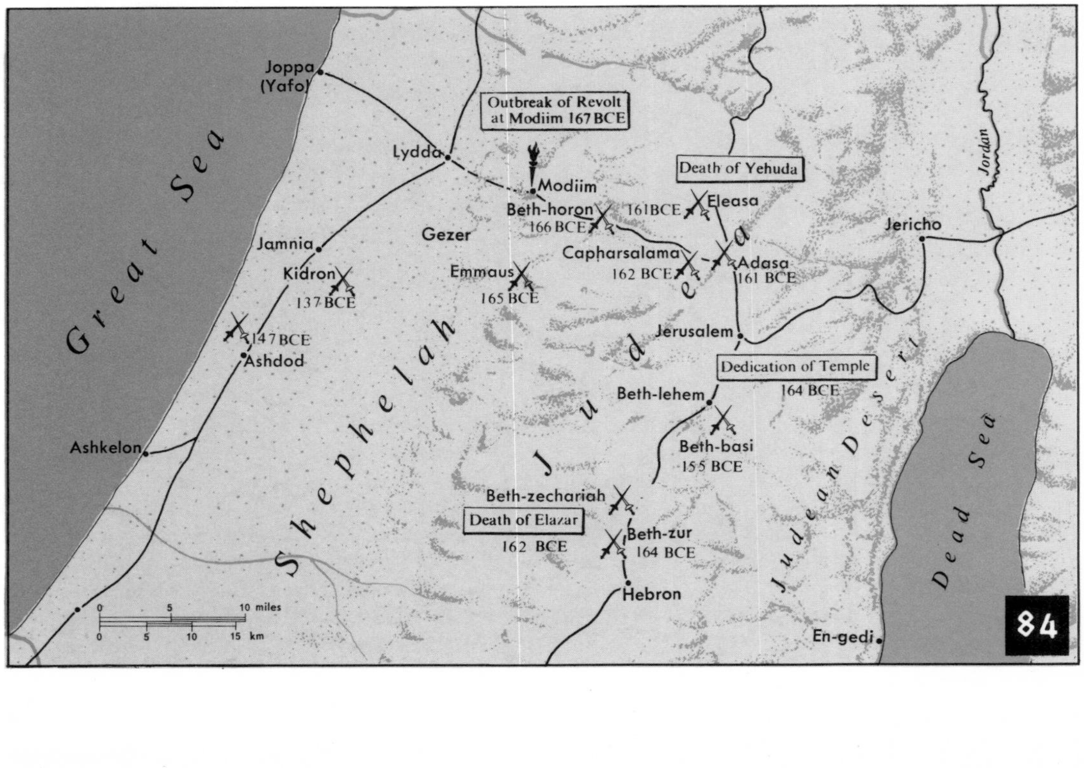

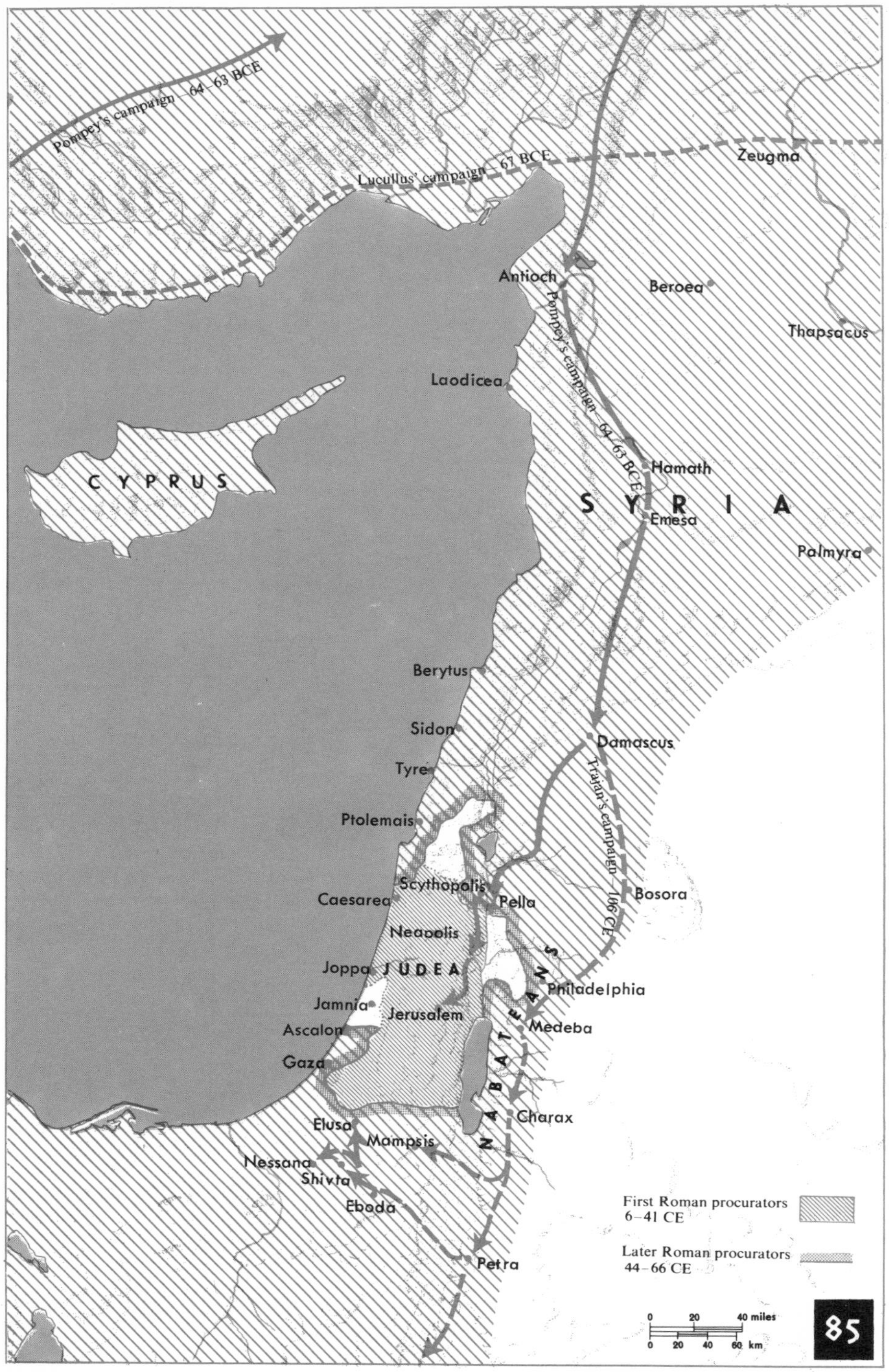

HEROD'S KINGDOM 37-4 BCE

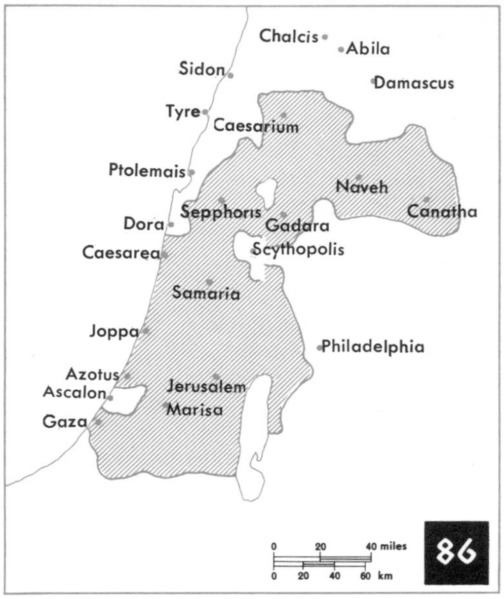
Chalcis
Abila
Sidon
Damascus
Tyre
Caesarium
Ptolemais
Naveh
Dora
Sepphoris
Gadara
Canatha
Caesarea
Scythopolis
Samaria
Joppa
Philadelphia
Azotus
Ascalon
Jerusalem
Marisa
Gaza
0 20 40 miles
0 20 40 60 km
86

KINGDOM OF AGRIPPA I 41-44 CE

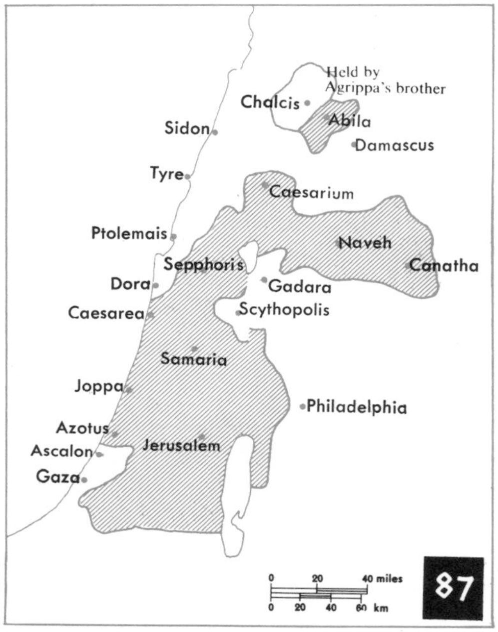
Held by Agrippa's brother
Chalcis
Abila
Sidon
Damascus
Tyre
Caesarium
Ptolemais
Naveh
Sepphoris
Canatha
Dora
Gadara
Caesarea
Scythopolis
Samaria
Joppa
Philadelphia
Azotus
Ascalon
Jerusalem
Gaza
0 20 40 miles
0 20 40 60 km
87

ROMAN RULE

THE ROMAN military conquest of Judea took place in the year 63 BCE, when Pompey entered the country at the head of his armies. Pompey made his move from Damascus, advancing through the lands of Bashan and Gilead, crossed the Jordan and marched south along the Jordan Valley to Jericho, where he turned westward for the assault on Jerusalem. After taking the capital, he made himself master of the country.

Even after these Roman victories, however, Jewish resistance continued, especially at Hyrcania, a fort in the Judean Desert, at Alexandrion, in the Jordan Valley, and at Machor (Machaerus), in Transjordan.

The Romans appointed as Governor of Judah, Antipater, the son of an Edomite chieftain who had been converted to Judaism. He was a master of politics and intrigue who had managed to ingratiate himself with the Roman authorities. He, in turn, placed his older son, Phasael, in charge of Jerusalem and his second, Herod, in charge of the northern province of Galilee.

With the help of the Romans, Herod steadily enhanced his position in the years that followed, finally becoming king of all Judea. His reign (37-4 BCE) was marked by numerous frontier wars, by ruthless suppression of all opposition to his rule and policies within the realm, and by notable achievements in the sphere of monumental architecture, particularly in Jerusalem the capital, the port city of Caesarea, and the mountain city of Samaria. After his death, the kingdom was divided among his sons. In the year 6 CE, the Romans appointed the first Procurator of Judea.

The birth, ministry and death of Jesus took place during the administration of the Roman Procurator Pontius Pilate.

The last stronghold of the Jews—Masada

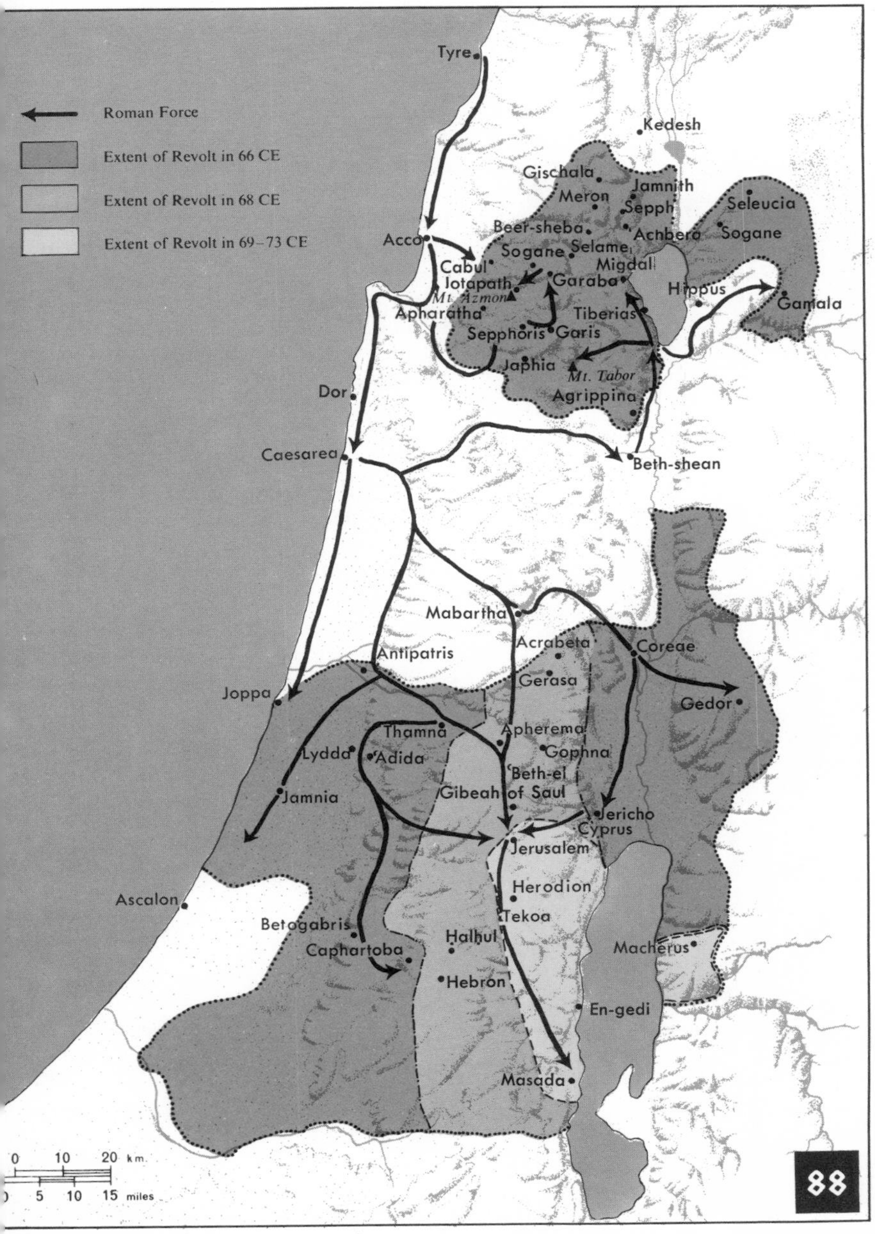
Roman Force
Extent of Revolt in 66 CE
Extent of Revolt in 68 CE
Extent of Revolt in 69–73 CE
Tyre
Kedesh
Gischala
Jamnith
Meron
Seleucia
Acco
Beer-sheba
Sogane
Sogane
Selame
Achbera
Cabul
Migdal
Jotapath
Garaba
Hippus
Mt. Azmon
Gamala
Apharatha
Tiberias
Sepphoris
Garis
Japhia
Mt. Tabor
Dor
Agrippina
Caesarea
Beth-shean
Mabartha
Acrabeta
Coreae
Antipatris
Gerasa
Joppa
Gedor
Thamna
Apherema
Lydda
Adida
Gophna
Beth-el
Gibeah of Saul
Jamnia
Jericho
Cyprus
Jerusalem
Herodion
Ascalon
Tekoa
Betogabris
Halhul
Caphartoba
Macherus
Hebron
En-gedi
Masada
0 10 20 km
5 10 15 miles
88

THE FIRST JEWISH REVOLT

THE JEWISH inhabitants of Judea, who had never acquiesced in the Roman conquest of their land, were aroused to a new pitch of anger and resentment by the Romans' restrictive decrees against them, by their contempt for and desecration of Jewish sacred sites and buildings, and by the erection of Roman idols in public places throughout the land. A dispute centered on the synagogue of Caesarea lit the fuse of the rebellion against the Roman oppressor that quickly spread throughout the country.

The Romans, unable to cope with the uprising with the troops stationed in Judea at the time, brought the best of their legions, which moved against the focal points of the revolt in Judea, Galilee and Transjordan. After a fierce battle, the key Galilean stronghold of Jotapath fell to the Romans. Other battles raged on the heights of Mount Tabor, on the shores of Lake Kinneret (Sea of Galilee) and in the hills surrounding the lake.

The best of the Roman troops, led by Vespasian, laid siege to Jerusalem, which managed to hold out for nearly a year. During this time, Vespasian was recalled to Rome and made Emperor, eventually to be succeeded by Titus. Finally, the walls of the Holy City succumbed to the mechanized might of Rome, and Titus' legions stormed into the starving city, killing and looting, and burning the Temple to the ground. That was on the 9th of Av, in the year 70 CE; less than a month later, the end of all resistance in the city spelled the end of Jewish Jerusalem.

But resistance continued elsewhere—at Herodion, near Bethlehem, at Machor, in Transjordan and atop the fortified mountain of Masada (Maẓada), on the western shore of the Dead Sea. Masada was the last Jewish stronghold to fall. But when the Romans finally broke into the fortified positions on top, they found not a living soul: the Jewish defenders had all taken their own lives, rather than fall into Roman hands—and slavery.

With the fall of Masada—on 17 Iyar 3833 (73 CE)—the end came to a thousand years of almost continuous Jewish self-rule in the Land of Israel.

THE SECOND JEWISH REVOLT

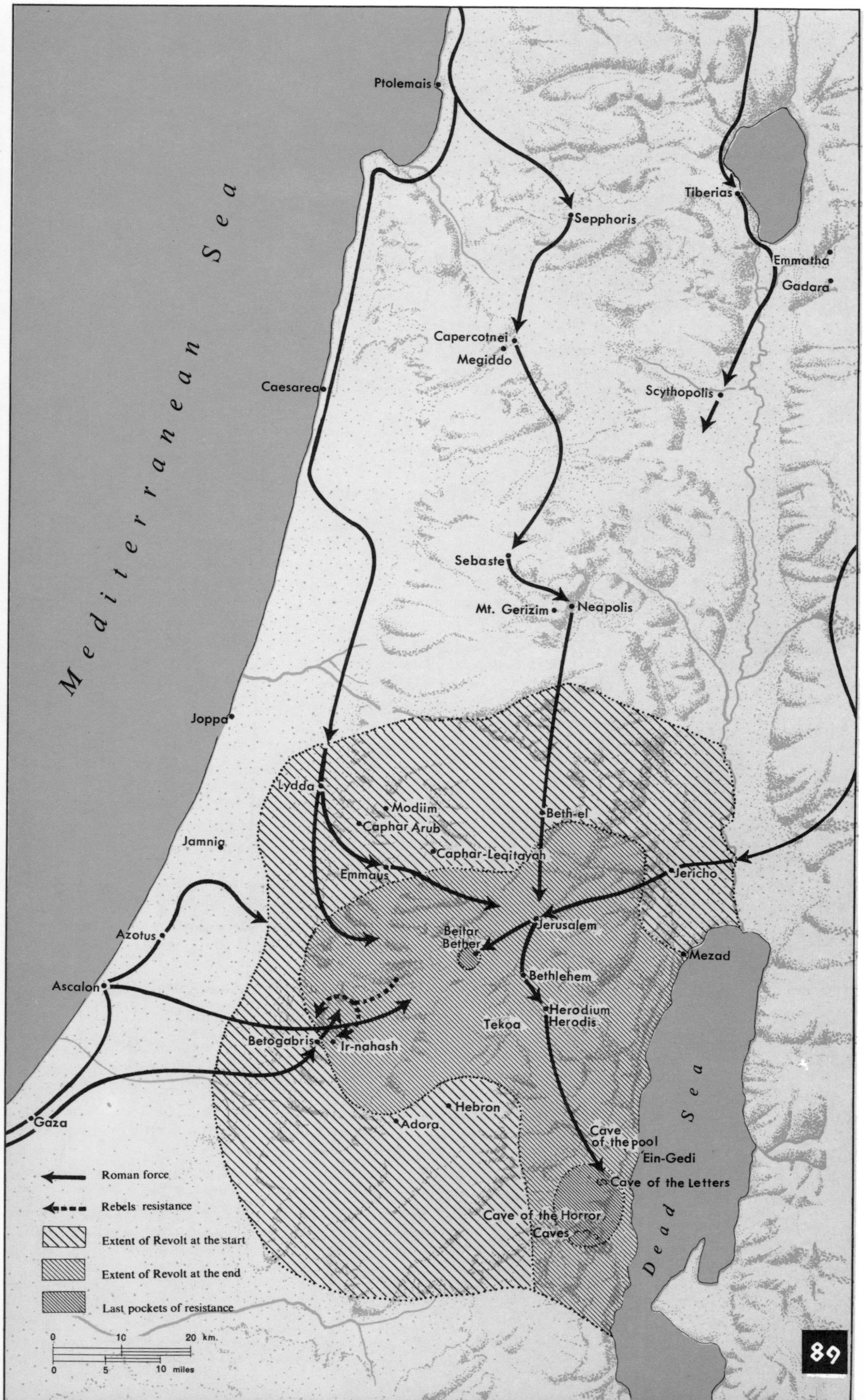
Mediterranean Sea
Ptolemais
Tiberias
Sepphoris
Emmatha
Gadara
Capercotnei
Megiddo
Caesarea
Scythopolis
Sebaste
Mt. Gerizim
Neapolis
Joppa
Lydda
Modiim
Caphar Arub
Beth-el
Jamnia
Caphar-Leqitayah
Emmaus
Jericho
Azotus
Beitar
Bether
Jerusalem
Mezad
Ascalon
Bethlehem
Herodium
Herodis
Tekoa
Betogabris
Ir-nahash
Hebron
Gaza
Adora
Cave of the pool
Ein-Gedi
Cave of the Letters
Cave of the Horror
Caves
Dead Sea
Roman force
Rebels resistance
Extent of Revolt at the start
Extent of Revolt at the end
Last pockets of resistance
0 10 20 km.
0 5 10 miles
89

THE FAILURE of the first Jewish revolt, against Roman tyranny, the destruction of their Temple, their fortifications and their dwelling places, and the wave of restrictive decrees that followed did not dampen their ardent desire to renew their national independence on the ancestral soil. Some sixty-two years after the suppression of the first revolt, another uprising took place against the Roman rulers, headed by Shim'on Bar-Kochba. The focal point of the revolt was at the town of Beitar, near Jerusalem, whence it quickly spread to the rest of the country. A series of surprising successes in the early phases of the fighting earned the Jewish rebels a brief respite from Roman overlordship; but they were not to enjoy it very long. Determined to crush Bar-Kochba and his followers and to punish this flagrant breach of Roman imperial discipline, Emperor Hadrian poured the best of his legions into Palestine, and in the year 135, after several heavy and brutal battles, the Romans routed the Jewish forces and put an end to this heroic but short-lived attempt to revive Jewish sovereignty in the Land of Israel. The population, especially of the land of Judea, was decimated, and many Jewish towns and villages, including Beitar, were destroyed. Remnants of Bar-Kochba's citadel may be seen today in the Arab village of Battir; the Arabs call the citadel Khirbet el-Yahud—Ruins of the Jews.

Very little was known about the life and times of Bar-Kochba or about the details of the revolt he led, until a few years ago archaeologists discovered numerous relics of the period—including utensils, remains of food, pieces of garments, skeletons and letters written by Bar-Kochba himself and by some of his men—in several caves near the western shore of the Dead Sea, in the Wilderness of Judea.

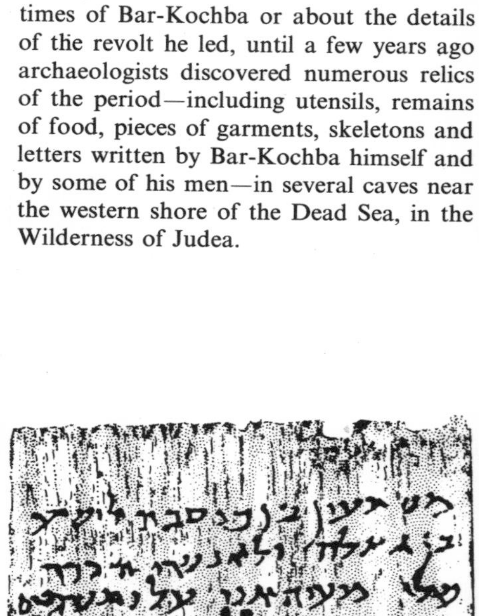
Bar-Kochba letter

Mosaic pavement, Beit-Alpha, 6th century

THE PERIOD OF THE MISHNA AND THE TALMUD

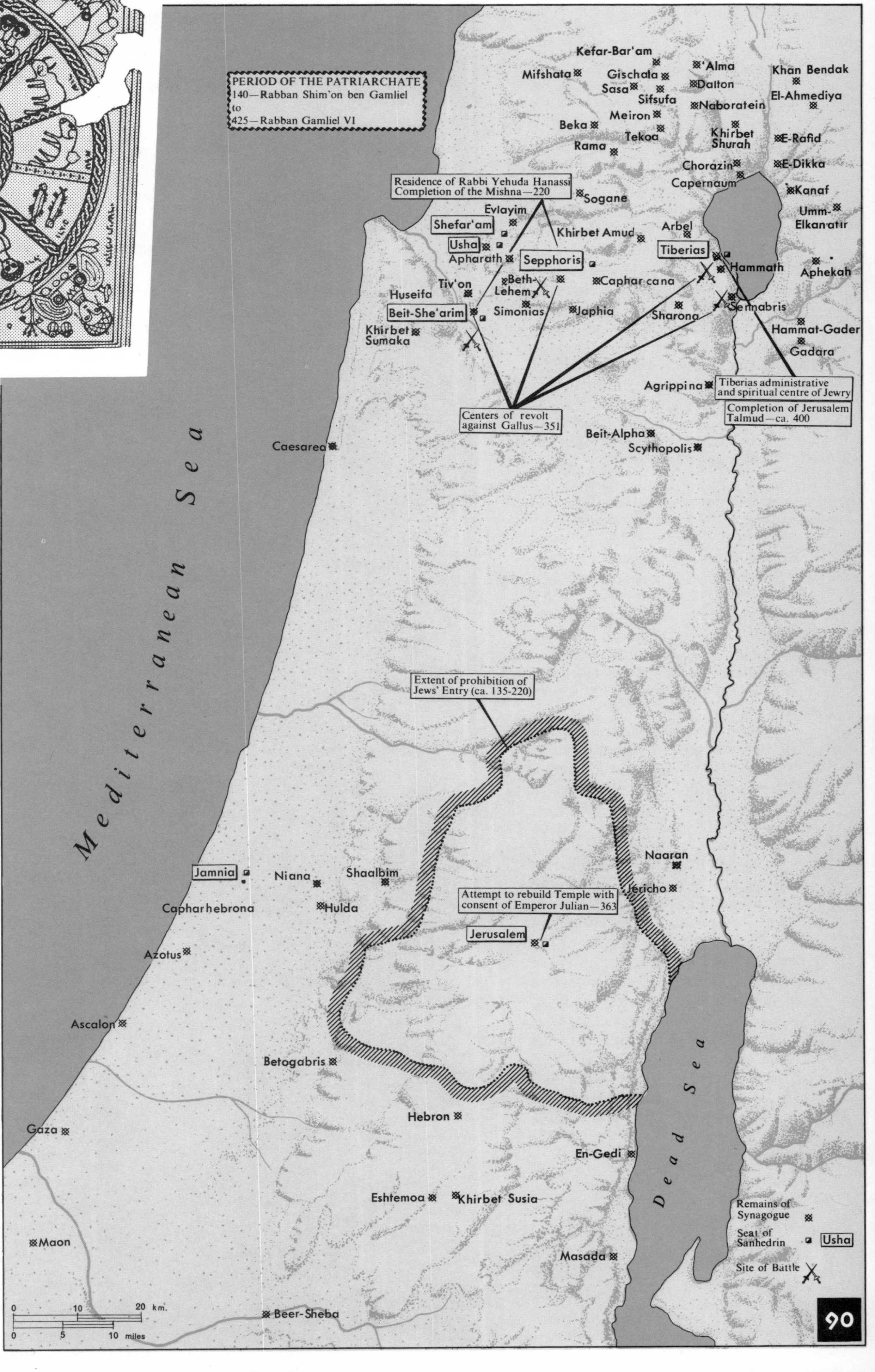
PERIOD OF THE PATRIARCHATE
140—Rabban Shim'on ben Gamliel
to
425—Rabban Gamliel VI
Kefar-Bar'am
Mifshata
Gischala
'Alma
Khan Bendak
Sasa
Dalton
El-Ahmediya
Sifsufa
Naboratein
Meiron
Beka
Tekoa
Khirbet Shurah
E-Rafid
Rama
Chorazin
E-Dikka
Residence of Rabbi Yehuda Hanassi
Completion of the Mishna—220
Capernaum
Kanaf
Sogane
Evlayim
Umm-Elkanatir
Shefar'am
Arbel
Khirbet Amud
Usha
Tiberias
Apharath
Sepphoris
Hammath
Aphekah
Tiv'on
Beth-Lehem
Caphar cana
Huseifa
Sennabris
Beit-She'arim
Simonias
Japhia
Sharona
Khirbet Sumaka
Hammat-Gader
Gadara
Agrippina
Tiberias administrative and spiritual centre of Jewry
Completion of Jerusalem Talmud—ca. 400
Centers of revolt against Gallus—351
Caesarea
Beit-Alpha
Scythopolis
Mediterranean Sea
Extent of prohibition of Jews' Entry (ca. 135-220)
Naaran
Jamnia
Niana
Shaalbim
Jericho
Attempt to rebuild Temple with consent of Emperor Julian—363
Capharhebrona
Hulda
Jerusalem
Azotus
Ascalon
Betogabris
Dead Sea
Hebron
Gaza
En-Gedi
Eshtemoa
Khirbet Susia
Remains of Synagogue
Seat of Sanhedrin
Usha
Maon
Masada
Site of Battle
0 10 20 km.
0 5 10 miles
Beer-Sheba
90

After the destruction of Jerusalem, its spiritual functions passed to the town of Yavne, in the coastal plain, which became both the center of learning and the seat of the Sanhedrin—the supreme judicial-legislative body in Israel. Other settlements in the southern part of the country—among them Benei-Berak, Lod (Lydda) and Ono—also grew, during this period, into populous towns and centers of learning. Galilee, on the other hand, came to be known as the scene of prosperous farms. The ancients had a saying: "If you would acquire wisdom," they said, "go south; if it is wealth that you seek—go north."

It was the sages of Yavne and vicinity who laid the groundwork for the Oral Law (later to be written down)—the Mishna. Roman persecution caused a migratory movement to the North; among those who made the move were many of the rabbis of the Mishna. The Sanhedrin, too, transferred its seat to Galilee and there also did not settle down in one place but kept on the move. Tiberias became a new center for the study of Torah, as did Ẓippori (Sepphoris) and other Galilean towns. Rabbi Yehuda Hanassi achieved greatness both as a scholar and sage and as the leader of his people. It was in Galilee, towards the end of the second century, that Rabbi Yehuda Hanassi edited and codified the Mishna. In its six volumes are reflected the way of life, the needs and the problems of the Jewish people in its land during the days of Roman rule.

THE BYZANTINE PERIOD

At THE end of the period of Roman rule, Palestine passed into the hands of Byzantium, becoming a tiny fragment in a widespread empire whose capital was Constantinople—the Istanbul of today. The city was named after its founder, Emperor Constantine the Great, whose mother, Helen, came to Palestine and there laid the foundations of the earliest Christian shrines.

The Byzantines gave Greek names to many of the places in Palestine, some of which dated back to the Roman era while others were founded by the Byzantines themselves. Jerusalem was known both as Ierosolyma or Hierusalem, (a corruption of the Hebrew *Yerushalayim*) and by the Roman appellation, Aelia.

Administratively, the whole country was divided into three districts:

Palaestina Prima, the first district, covered the entire coastal plain, from the district of Phoenicia, in Lebanon, to Jerusalem and its vicinity down to the approaches of the Negev and the Sinai Desert; its capital was Caesarea on the sea.

Palaestina Secunda, the second of the districts, extended from Eastern Galilee, through the Jezreel Valley and the middle Jordan Valley, eastward to the mountains of Golan and northern Gilead, beyond Lake Kinneret; its capital was Beit-Shean in the Jordan Valley.

Palaestina Tertia, the third district, comprised the Negev, the 'Arava and Mount Edom in southern Transjordan; its capital was Petra in the Mountains of Edom.

During this period there lived in Palestine several Christian theologians and historians (Eusebius, Jerome, Procopius, Cyrillus Scythopolitanus), who are considered to have been the Fathers of the Church; two of them (Epiphanius and Sozomenus) were of Jewish extraction. Their writings serve as an important source of information on the Byzantine era in Palestine.

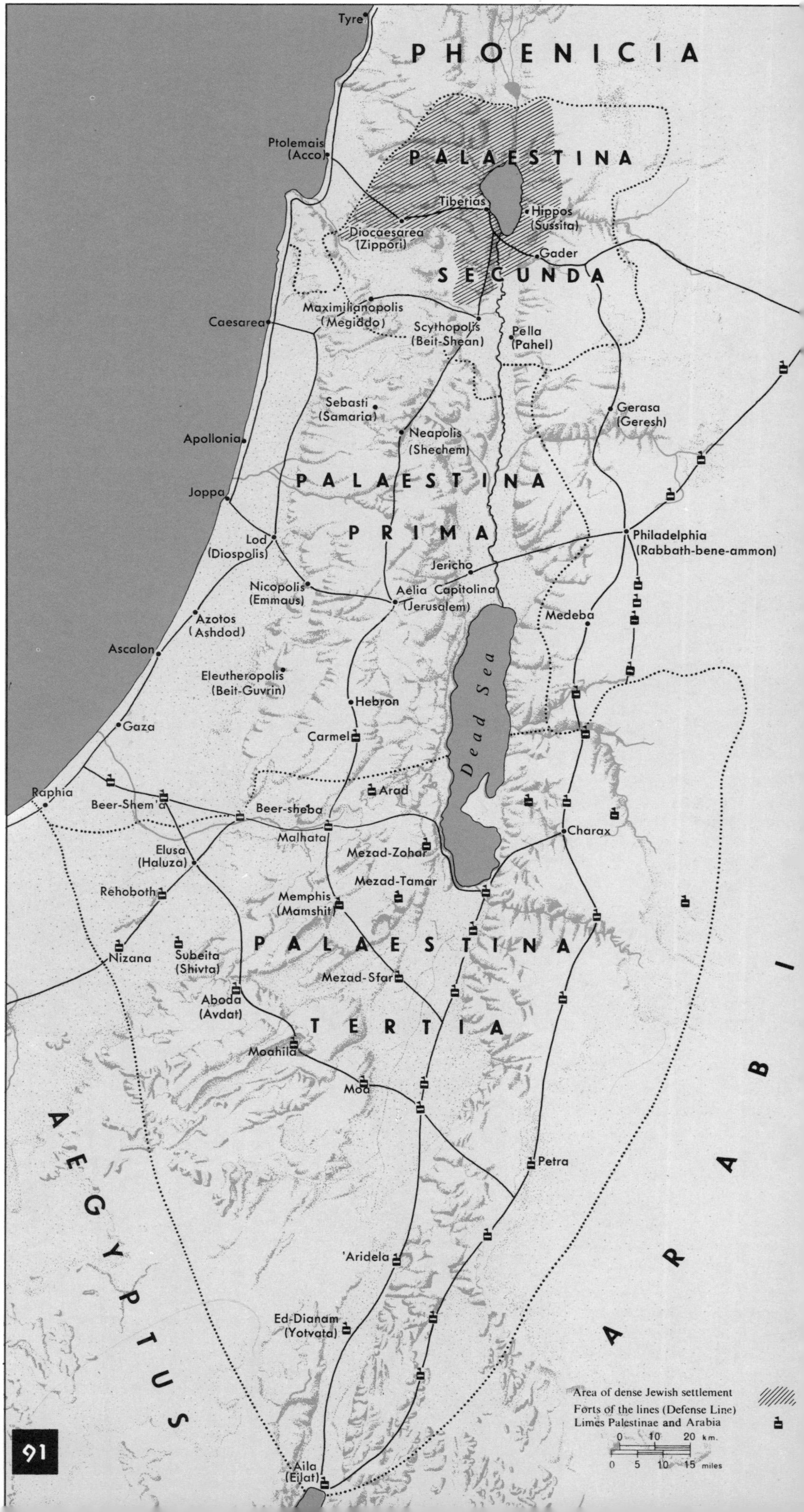

Shapur—king of Persia

THE PERSIAN CONQUEST

IN THE early part of the seventh century, the Persian Army invaded Palestine, which was then under Christian-Byzantine rule, and conquered it. The country's Jews, who had been oppressed and persecuted by their Christian overlords, assisted the Persians who, under King Chosroes II, were favorably inclined to them.

The conquerors, for their part, encouraged the Jews, arousing in them hopes for redemption and the rebuilding of the Temple. Had not the sages said that "When you see a Persian horse tethered in the Land of Israel, you may expect the advent of the Messiah"?

However, neither Persian suzerainty nor the Jews' joy that came in its wake lasted very long. Twenty-two years after the Persian conquest, the Byzantines, under their king, Heraclius, succeeded in driving out the Persians and reestablishing their rule in the country. Once more, it was the Jews who bore the brunt of their vengeance.

But the Byzantines' rule, this time, was even more short-lived. A new force, the Moslem Arabs, stormed out of the Arabian peninsula, routed the Byzantine forces and made themselves masters of the land, ushering in a new era in its long and stormy history.

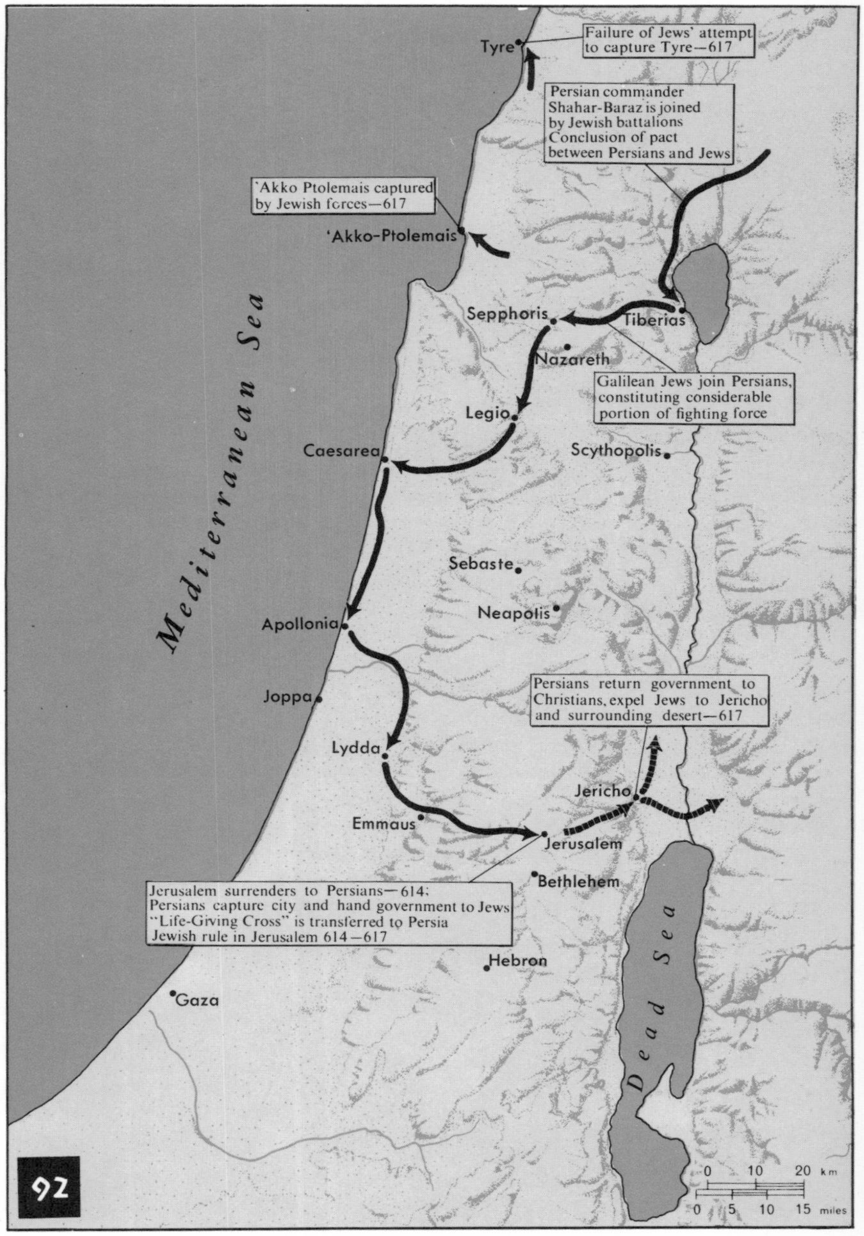
Failure of Jews' attempt to capture Tyre—617
Persian commander Shahar-Baraz is joined by Jewish battalions Conclusion of pact between Persians and Jews
'Akko Ptolemais captured by Jewish forces—617
Galilean Jews join Persians, constituting considerable portion of fighting force
Persians return government to Christians, expel Jews to Jericho and surrounding desert—617
Jerusalem surrenders to Persians—614; Persians capture city and hand government to Jews "Life-Giving Cross" is transferred to Persia Jewish rule in Jerusalem 614—617
Tyre
'Akko-Ptolemais
Sepphoris
Tiberias
Nazareth
Legio
Scythopolis
Caesarea
Mediterranean Sea
Sebaste
Neapolis
Apollonia
Joppa
Lydda
Jericho
Emmaus
Jerusalem
Bethlehem
Hebron
Gaza
Dead Sea
0 10 20 km
0 5 10 15 miles
92

Byzantine Shivta

THE ARAB-MOSLEM CONQUEST

WITHIN the lifetime of Mohammed, the Prophet of Islam, his Moslem-Arab followers began to carry out sporadic raids into Palestine, which was in the hands of the Christian Byzantines. It was not until after his death, however, that the large-scale invasion began. The attack, led by Caliph 'Omar Ibn Ḥattab was made through Transjordan, one column also moving up along the 'Arava and the Negev into the heartland of Judea. The decisive battle took place at 'Ajnadein, near the foothills of Jerusalem, where the Byzantine forces were routed. Meanwhile the main Arab force advanced northward on the east bank of the Jordan and prepared to cross into Palestine by way of the Yarmuk and Beit-Shean Valleys. The plan was eventually successful, but only after bitter fighting between the rival forces at that point. Jerusalem was besieged, and surrendered to the Arab armies in 637. The Moslem conquest of Palestine was completed at Caesarea in 640.

The empire, of which Palestine formed a progressively smaller and smaller part as the Moslem conquests were extended, was ruled, in the early years of its existence, by caliphs of the Omayyad dynasty.

Hisham Palace near Jericho

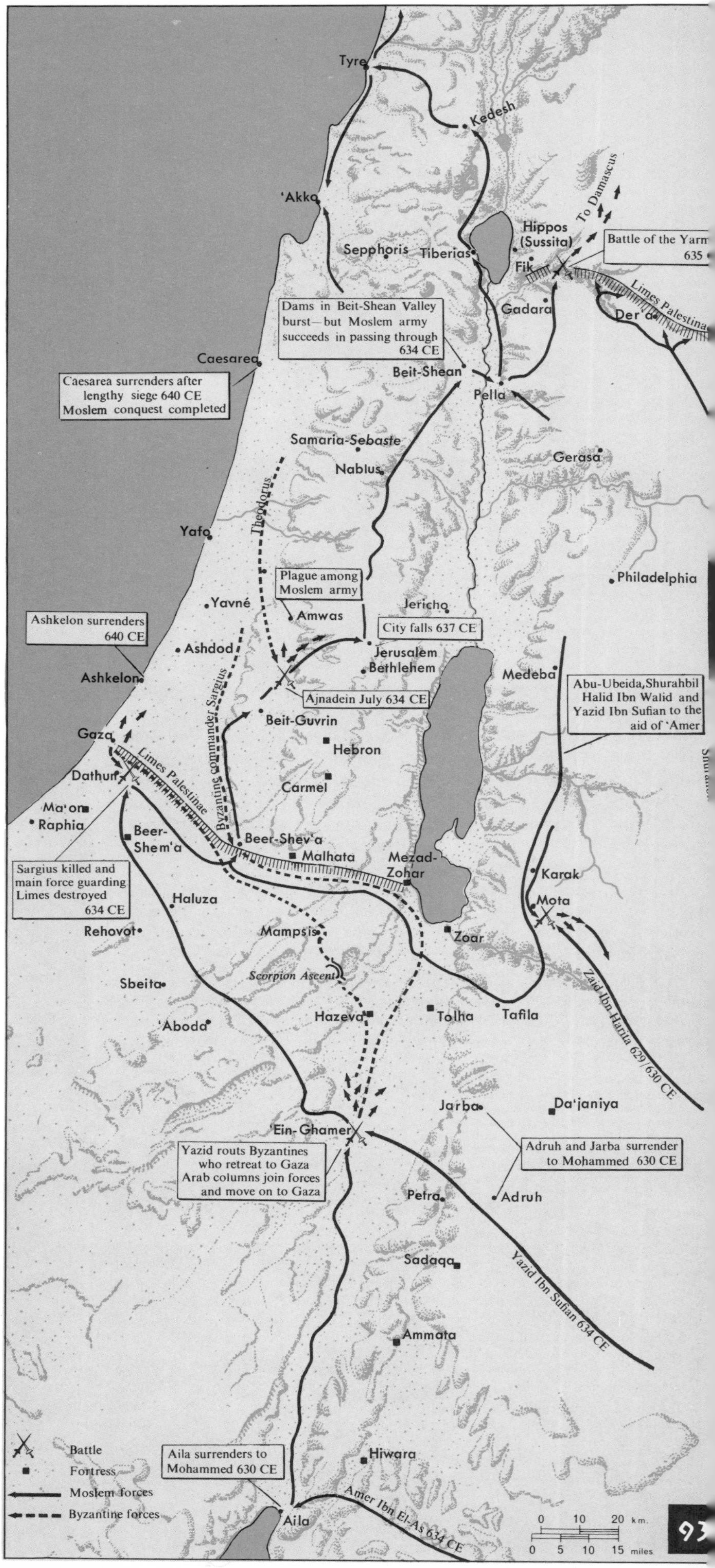
Tyre
Kedesh
To Damascus
'Akko
Hippos (Sussita)
Battle of the Yarm
635
Sepphoris
Tiberias
Fik
Limes Palestinae
Gadara
Der'a
Dams in Beit-Shean Valley burst—but Moslem army succeeds in passing through 634 CE
Caesarea
Beit-Shean
Pella
Caesarea surrenders after lengthy siege 640 CE Moslem conquest completed
Samaria-Sebaste
Nablus
Gerasa
Theodorus
Yafo
Plague among Moslem army
Philadelphia
Yavné
Amwas
Jericho
Ashkelon surrenders 640 CE
City falls 637 CE
Ashdod
Jerusalem
Bethlehem
Ashkelon
Ajnadein July 634 CE
Medeba
Byzantine commander Sargius
Abu-Ubeida, Shurahbil Halid Ibn Walid and Yazid Ibn Sufian to the aid of 'Amer
Gaza
Beit-Guvrin
Hebron
Dathur
Limes Palestinae
Carmel
Ma'on
Raphia
Beer-Shem'a
Beer-Shev'a
Malhata
Mezad-Zohar
Sargius killed and main force guarding Limes destroyed 634 CE
Karak
Haluza
Mota
Rehovot
Mampsis
Zoar
Scorpion Ascent
Sbeita
Zaid Ibn Harita 629/630 CE
'Aboda
Hazeva
Tolha
Tafila
Jarba
Da'janiya
Ein-Ghamer
Yazid routs Byzantines who retreat to Gaza Arab columns join forces and move on to Gaza
Adruh and Jarba surrender to Mohammed 630 CE
Petra
Adruh
Sadaqa
Yazid Ibn Sufian 634 CE
Ammata
Battle
Fortress
Moslem forces
Byzantine forces
Aila surrenders to Mohammed 630 CE
Hiwara
Aila
Amer Ibn El-As 634 CE
0 10 20 km.
0 5 10 15 miles
93

JEWS UNDER ARAB-MOSLEM RULE

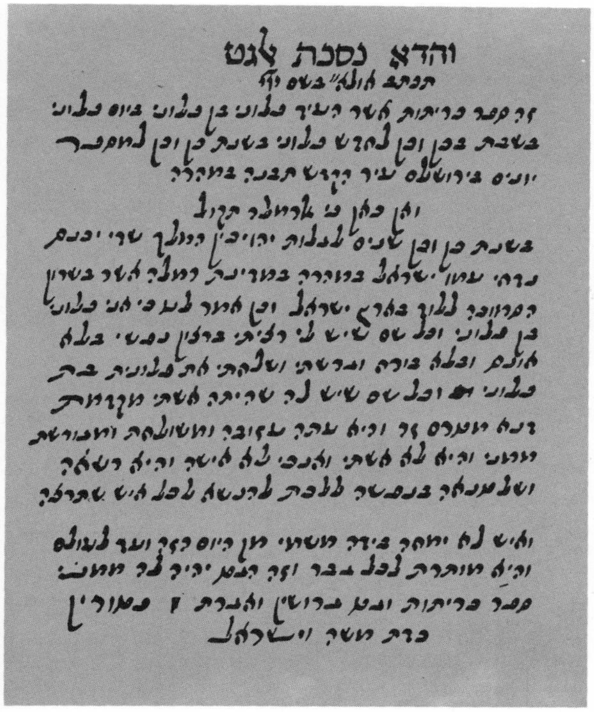
והדא נסכת אלגט

בשבת בכך וכך לחדש פלוני בשנת כך וכך למספר
יונים בירושלם עיר הקדש תבנה במהרה

Document from the Cairo Genizah

THE ARAB wave of conquest in the seventh century that eventually encompassed a vast area stretching from Baghdad in the east to the Atlantic coast of Africa and Spain in the west also swept through Palestine. Between the years 636 and 640 the Mohammedans gained control of all of Palestine, which had been under Byzantine rule. They found a few scattered Jewish communities, mostly in an impoverished state, as a result of the restrictions and persecutions of the previous generations. Their sources of livelihood were limited. In the towns they earned their bread as merchants and artisans; in the villages, as peasants. There was little in the way of literary creation. The head of the community bore the title of Gaon, and he maintained close contact with the Jewish community in Egypt, which acted as a kind of guardian or custodian to the Palestinian community in spiritual matters. In the course of time, the Jews of Palestine adopted many of the ways of their new Arab neighbors, including their language, and were known as *Mustarabim* —"like Arabs". Compared to the ruthless oppression of previous rulers, the Arab conquerors of Palestine treated their Jewish subjects with considerable tolerance and even sympathy.

Historical material on this period is sparse. One important source is a collection of manuscripts found in the archives (Genizah) of an Egyptian synagogue, containing portions of letters, official notices and other documents pertaining to this period and written partly in Hebrew and partly in Arabic rendered in Hebrew characters. Fragmentary reports on the Jews of Palestine may be found also in Moslem geographical-historical literature of the medieval period.

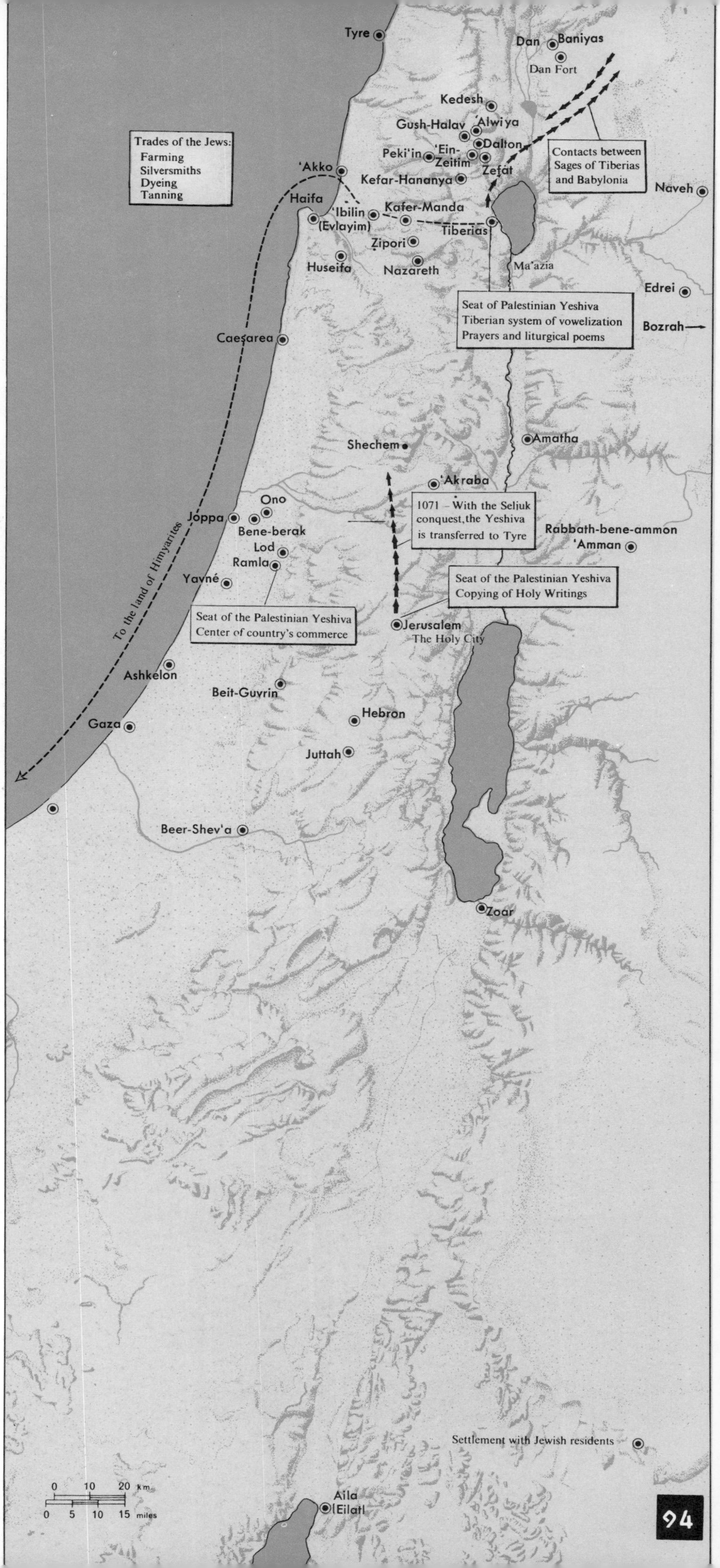

THE CRUSADER KINGDOM
1099-1291

WITH "the liberation of the Holy Land and the places sacred to Christianity from the Moslem infidels" as their declared aim and slogan, the Bearers of the Cross, hailing from various European lands, made their way eastward, amassing a huge following as they went, and, after a long march through Asia Minor and Syria-Lebanon, stormed Palestine from the north, at Rosh-Hanikra. They advanced along the coastal plain, then headed for their sacred destination: Jerusalem. After bitter fighting, they succeeded in breaching the city's massive fortifications, penetrated the town and captured it in a terrible bloodbath in which most of Jerusalem's Jews were slaughtered.

The Crusaders made the Holy City their capital and named their new State, in its honor, the Kingdom of Jerusalem.

Eighty years later, the Crusaders' arch-foe, Saladin (Salaḥ ed-Din), having consolidated and strengthened his forces, challenged the Christians' domination of the country and, in a violent battle at the Horns of Hittin, in Lower Galilee, routed the Crusader forces and recaptured Jerusalem. As a result of Saladin's victories, Crusader rule was confined mainly to the coastal plain and Galilee; Saint Jean d'Acre became their new capital. In a long series of battles over the years, the Mameluke Sultans made constant inroads on the areas under Crusader control until finally, in 1291, they also took Acre, thus putting an end, after 200 years, to Christian rule in the Holy Land.

Isle de Graye, an island off Eilat

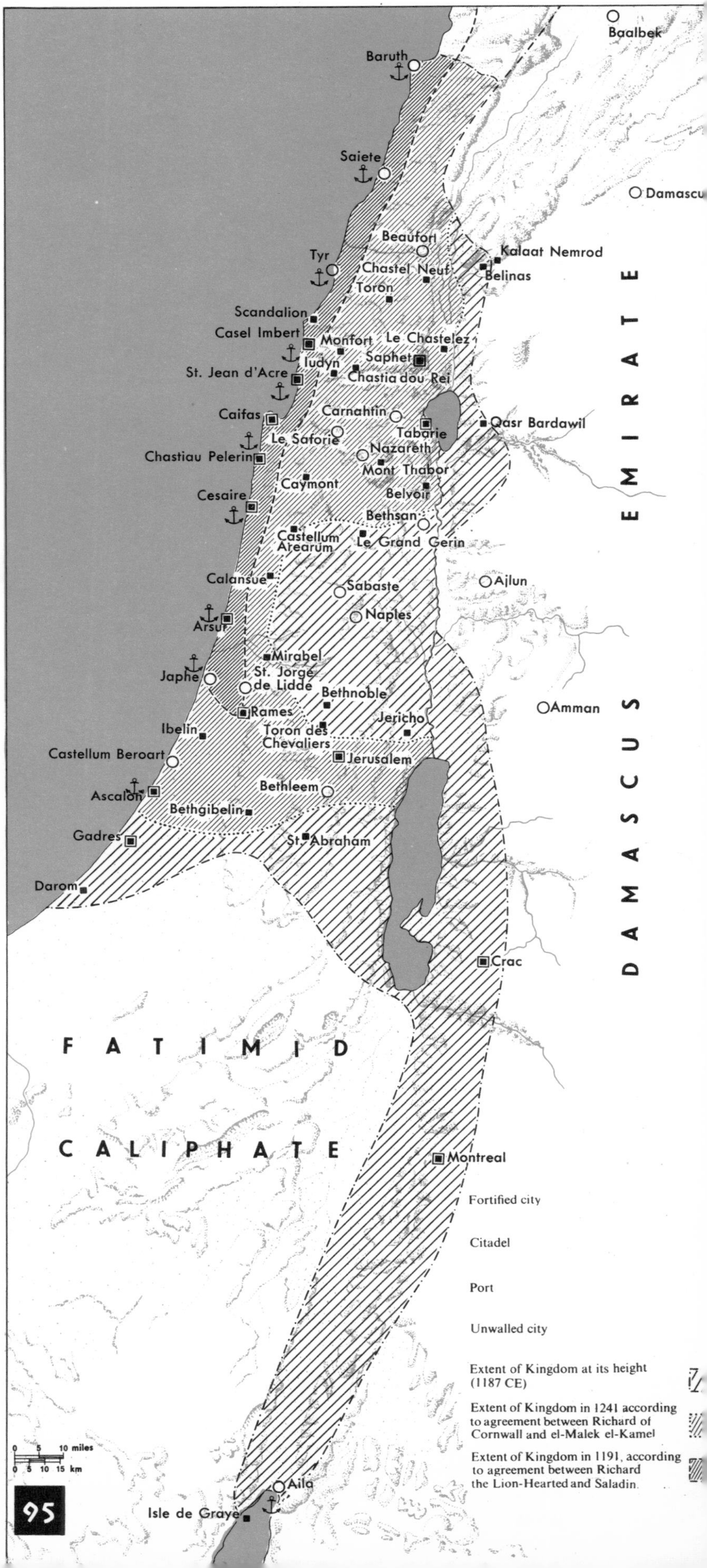

THE CRUSADER CAMPAIGNS

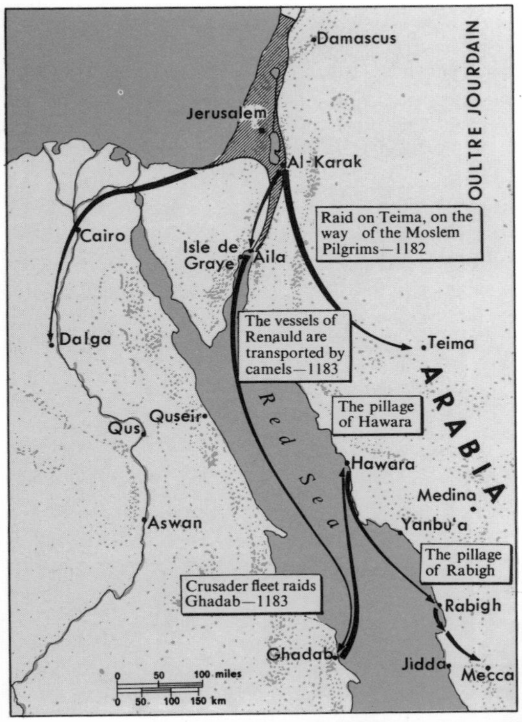

Damascus
OULTRE JOURDAIN
Jerusalem
Al-Karak
Raid on Teima, on the way of the Moslem Pilgrims—1182
Cairo
Isle de Graye
Aila
The vessels of Renauld are transported by camels—1183
Teima
Dalga
ARABIA
Red Sea
The pillage of Hawara
Quseir
Qus
Hawara
Medina
Aswan
Yanbu'a
The pillage of Rabigh
Crusader fleet raids Ghadab—1183
Rabigh
Ghadab
Jidda
Mecca
0 50 100 miles
0 50 100 150 km

DURING the period of Crusader rule in Palestine in the twelfth century, the Crusader forces from time to time carried out raids into Moslem territory—in Syria, Transjordan, Arabia and Egypt—with the aim of sowing chaos and confusion in Moslem ranks, plundering their goods, decimating their forces and deterring them from making forays into areas under Crusader control. The Crusaders also set ambushes for caravans of Moslem pilgrims on their way to Mecca and Medina, Islam's holy cities in Arabia. (Every Moslem who performed the commandment of the pilgrimage to Mecca received the honored title of "Haj"; this is the custom in Moslem society to this day.)

One of the pilgrims' routes, the Darb el-Haj (in Arabic), passed along the border of the Crusader Kingdom, from Egypt through the Sinai peninsula to Arabia. Another route used by the pilgrims began in Damascus and moved southward along Transjordan and the edge of the desert.

A Crusader leader who gained notoriety for his daring raids was the Frenchman, Renauld de Châtillon, who ruled over an extensive region in southern Transjordan. In one such raid, he struck deep into Arabian territory, moving south along the Red Sea coast.

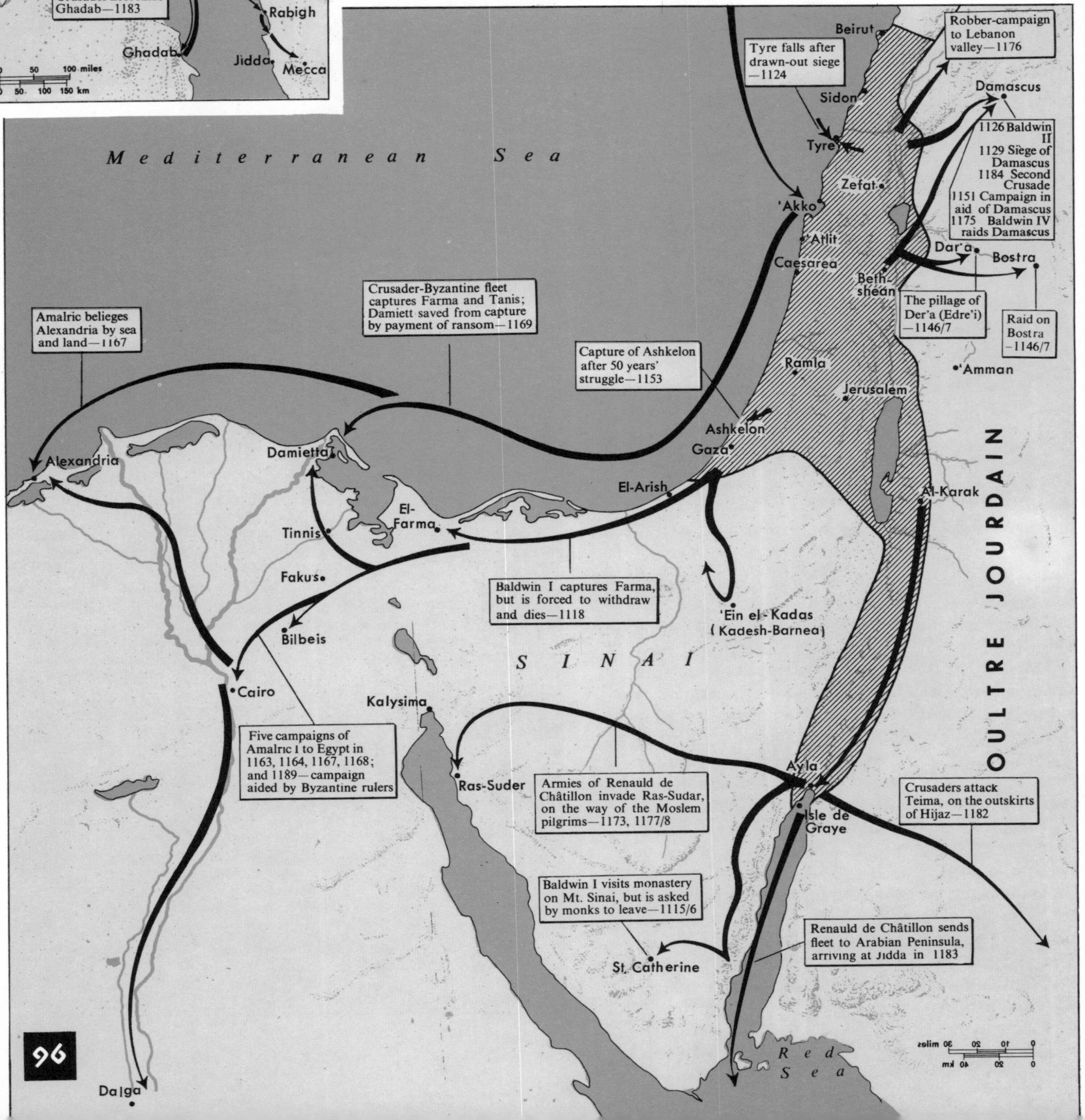

Beirut
Robber-campaign to Lebanon valley—1176
Tyre falls after drawn-out siege—1124
Sidon
Damascus
Mediterranean Sea
Tyre
1126 Baldwin II
1129 Siege of Damascus
1184 Second Crusade
1151 Campaign in aid of Damascus
1175 Baldwin IV raids Damascus
Zefat
'Akko
'Atlit
Caesarea
Dar'a
Bostra
Beth-shean
The pillage of Der'a (Edre'i)—1146/7
Raid on Bostra—1146/7
Crusader-Byzantine fleet captures Farma and Tanis; Damiett saved from capture by payment of ransom—1169
Amalric belieges Alexandria by sea and land—1167
Capture of Ashkelon after 50 years' struggle—1153
Ramla
'Amman
Jerusalem
Ashkelon
Gaza
Alexandria
Damietta
El-Arish
Al-Karak
El-Farma
Tinnis
Fakus
Baldwin I captures Farma, but is forced to withdraw and dies—1118
'Ein el-Kadas (Kadesh-Barnea)
Bilbeis
SINAI
OULTRE JOURDAIN
Cairo
Kalysima
Five campaigns of Amalric I to Egypt in 1163, 1164, 1167, 1168; and 1189—campaign aided by Byzantine rulers
Ras-Suder
Armies of Renauld de Châtillon invade Ras-Sudar, on the way of the Moslem pilgrims—1173, 1177/8
Ayla
Isle de Graye
Crusaders attack Teima, on the outskirts of Hijaz—1182
Baldwin I visits monastery on Mt. Sinai, but is asked by monks to leave—1115/6
Renauld de Châtillon sends fleet to Arabian Peninsula, arriving at Jidda in 1183
St. Catherine
96
Red Sea
Dalga

JEWS UNDER CRUSADERS AND MAMELUKES

A. Under the Crusaders 1099-1291

WHEN THE Crusaders arrived in Palestine, they found there Jewish communities dating back generations. In Jerusalem and Haifa, the Jews joined forces with their Arab neighbors in the defense of their cities against the Crusaders. Once the Christians had gained the upper hand, they conducted a merciless slaughter among the Jews.

The great Jewish scholar and philosopher, Maimonides, came to Palestine in 1165 but, because of the unrest plaguing the land at that time, went to Egypt, where he spent the better part of his creative life. Rabbi Benjamin, from the Spanish town of Tudela, toured the Holy Land in about 1175 as did, some ten years later, Rabbi Petaḥia of Regensburg, Germany. Another visitor in this period was the poet Yehuda Alḥarizi, who came in 1218. These travelers provide a rich source of information on the land and, in particular, its Jewish community.

Notwithstanding Christian rule and unsettled conditions, the Crusader period witnessed the immigration of Jews to Palestine. The most notable of these migratory moves was that of three hundred rabbis from France and England in 1211.

In a long series of wars, the Moslems gradually advanced to the north until, with the fall of the last Christian stronghold at Acre in 1291, the Crusader Kingdom in the Holy Land came to an end.

White tower—Ramla, from the Mameluke period

B. Under the Mamelukes 1269-1516

It was the Mameluke Moslems, centered in neighboring Egypt, who finally ousted the Crusaders and substituted their own rule in Palestine for the next 256 years, until replaced by the Ottoman Turks. The Mamelukes were sympathetic to the Jews, and in their time the Jewish community in Palestine prospered. The noted Bible commentator, Nahmanides, arrived in the country in 1267 and helped restore the Jewish community of Jerusalem. Another immigrant of this period was Rabbi Eshtori Haparhi, who completed there his work *Kaftor va-Feraḥ*, the first Hebrew book about the Land of Israel. Rabbi ‘Ovadia of Bartenora, who wrote the famous commentary on the Mishna, came in 1488.

Under the Mamelukes, peace and tranquillity prevailed in the land, and there was a large and uninterrupted stream of Christian and Jewish pilgrims, some of whom committed their impressions of the country to writing. These travel diaries serve as important historical sources on medieval Palestine and the Jewish community

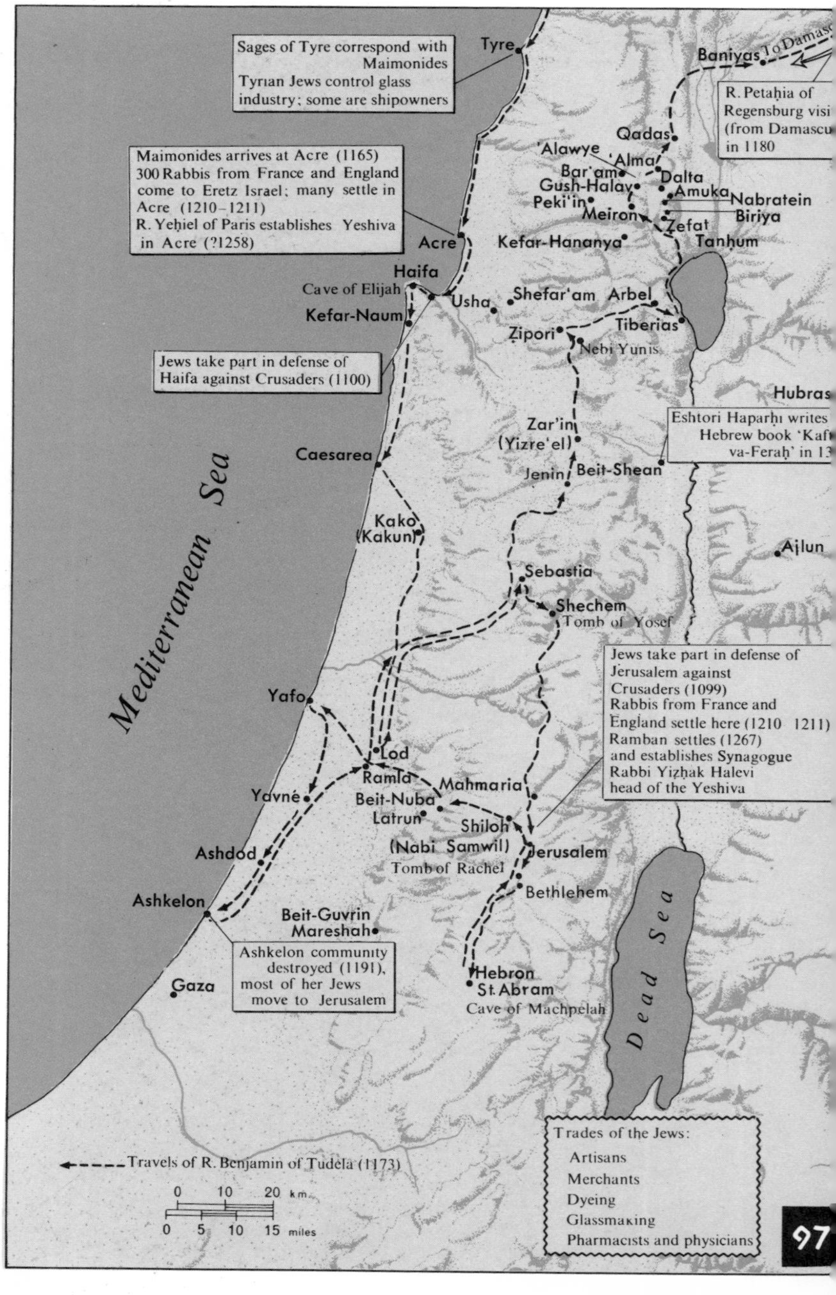
Sages of Tyre correspond with Maimonides
Tyrian Jews control glass industry; some are shipowners
Tyre
Baniyas
To Damasc
R. Petaḥia of Regensburg visi (from Damascu in 1180
Maimonides arrives at Acre (1165)
300 Rabbis from France and England come to Eretz Israel; many settle in Acre (1210–1211)
R. Yeḥiel of Paris establishes Yeshiva in Acre (?1258)
Qadas
'Alawye
'Alma
Bar'am
Dalta
Gush-Halav
Amuka
Nabratein
Peki'in
Meiron
Biriya
Zefat
Acre
Kefar-Hananya
Tanḥum
Haifa
Cave of Elijah
Usha
Shefar'am
Arbel
Kefar-Naum
Tiberias
Zipori
Nebi Yunis
Jews take part in defense of Haifa against Crusaders (1100)
Hubras
Eshtori Haparḥi writes Hebrew book 'Kaf va-Feraḥ' in 13
Zar'in (Yizre'el)
Caesarea
Jenin
Beit-Shean
Mediterranean Sea
Kako (Kakun)
Ajlun
Sebastia
Shechem
Tomb of Yosef
Jews take part in defense of Jerusalem against Crusaders (1099)
Rabbis from France and England settle here (1210 1211)
Ramban settles (1267) and establishes Synagogue
Rabbi Yiẓḥak Halevi head of the Yeshiva
Yafo
Lod
Ramla
Mahmaria
Yavné
Beit-Nuba
Latrun
Shiloh
Ashdod
(Nabi Samwil)
Jerusalem
Tomb of Rachel
Bethlehem
Ashkelon
Beit-Guvrin
Mareshah
Ashkelon community destroyed (1191), most of her Jews move to Jerusalem
Gaza
Hebron
St. Abram
Cave of Machpelah
Dead Sea
Trades of the Jews:
Artisans
Merchants
Dyeing
Glassmaking
Pharmacists and physicians
Travels of R. Benjamin of Tudela (1173)
0 10 20 km
0 5 10 15 miles

TURKISH RULE IN THE MIDDLE EAST

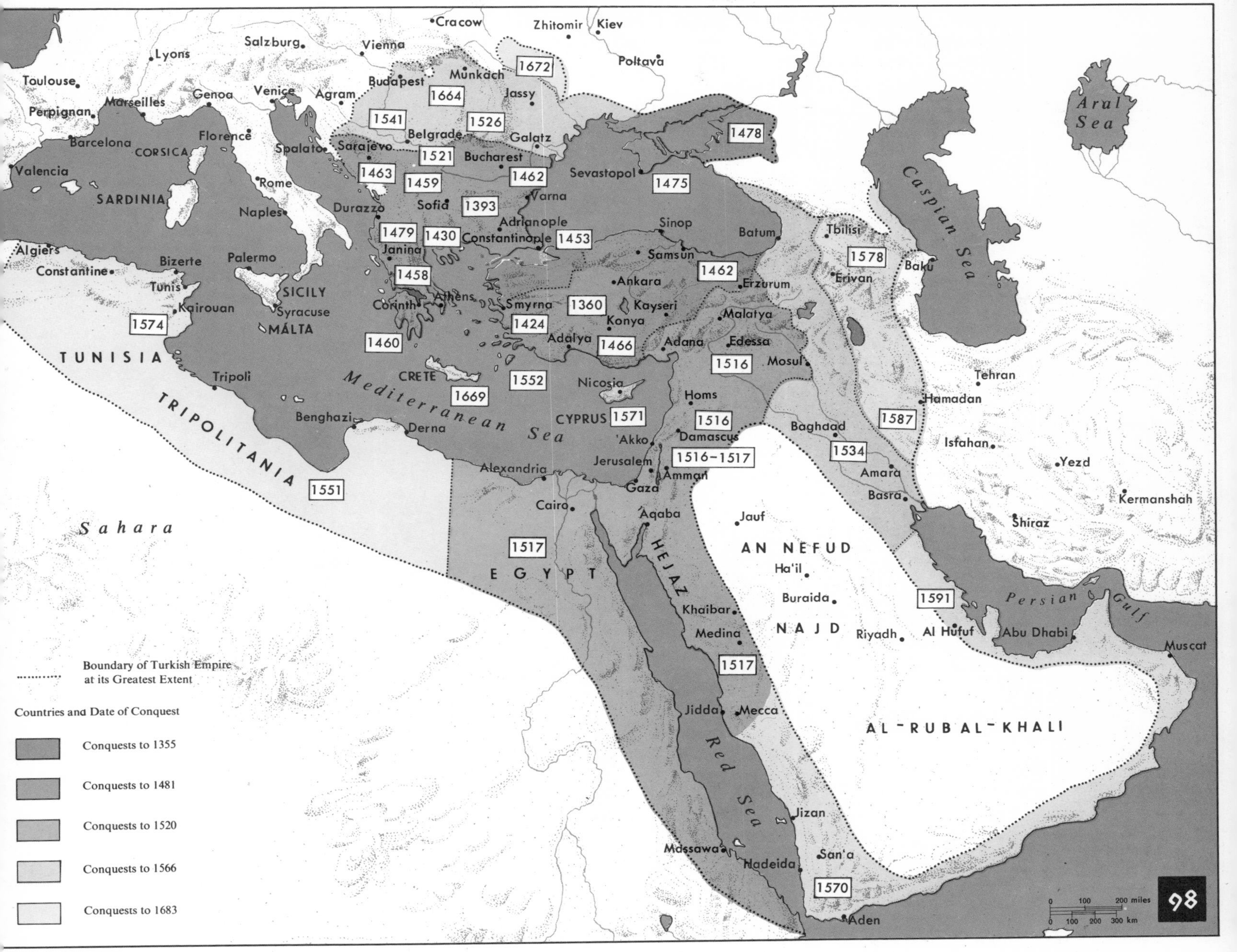

Turkish *Laissez-Passer* from the Sixteenth Century

In THE fourteenth century began the Turkish conquest of Asia Minor, which spread, in the succeeding two centuries, to neighboring lands in Asia and Europe. In 1516–17, in the reign of Sultan Salim I, the Turkish army captured Palestine from the Mamelukes, penetrating into the Mamelukes' home territory, Egypt. Further to the east, the Turks advanced into the Hejaz, in the Arabian peninsula, seizing Mecca and Medina, Islam's holiest cities. By virtue of the Turkish Sultan's rule over the homeland of Islam and over most of the Moslem world, he earned for himself the title of Caliph, head of the believers in the Islamic religion. Turkey's conquests, in this its golden era, came to include also territories in North Africa and the larger islands of the eastern Mediterranean Sea.

Palestine, a small segment of this extensive empire, served—as so often in the past—as a bridge between the continents and a vital junction of the roads and trade routes that crossed the empire. This situation continued for several centuries, until Palestine fell to the British in World War I.

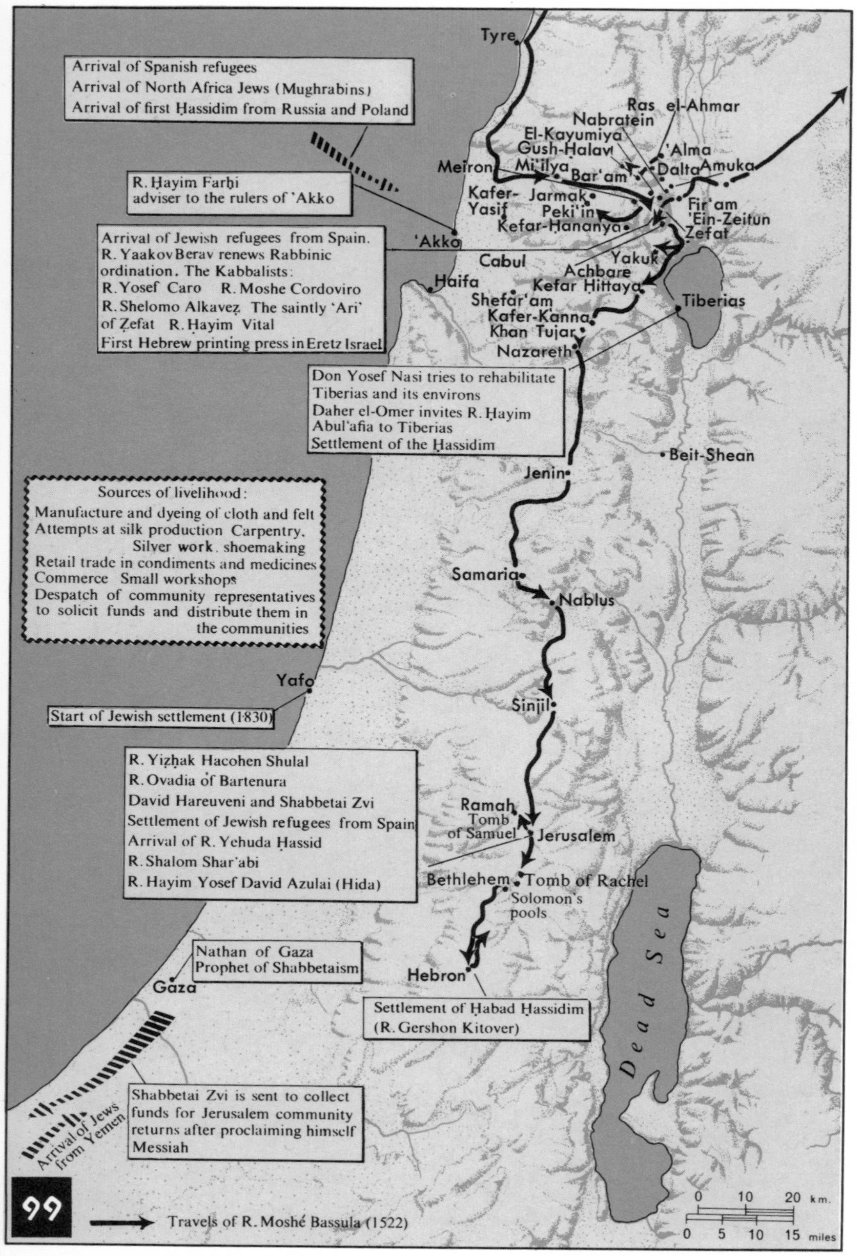
Arrival of Spanish refugees
Arrival of North Africa Jews (Mughrabins)
Arrival of first Ḥassidim from Russia and Poland
R. Ḥayim Farḥi adviser to the rulers of 'Akko
Arrival of Jewish refugees from Spain. R. Yaakov Berav renews Rabbinic ordination. The Kabbalists: R. Yosef Caro R. Moshe Cordoviro R. Shelomo Alkavez. The saintly 'Ari' of Zefat R. Ḥayim Vital
First Hebrew printing press in Eretz Israel
Don Yosef Nasi tries to rehabilitate Tiberias and its environs
Daher el-Omer invites R. Ḥayim Abul'afia to Tiberias
Settlement of the Ḥassidim
Sources of livelihood:
Manufacture and dyeing of cloth and felt
Attempts at silk production Carpentry.
Silver work. shoemaking
Retail trade in condiments and medicines
Commerce Small workshops
Despatch of community representatives to solicit funds and distribute them in the communities
Start of Jewish settlement (1830)
R. Yizḥak Hacohen Shulal
R. Ovadia of Bartenura
David Hareuveni and Shabbetai Zvi
Settlement of Jewish refugees from Spain
Arrival of R. Yehuda Ḥassid
R. Shalom Shar'abi
R. Hayim Yosef David Azulai (Hida)
Nathan of Gaza Prophet of Shabbetaism
Settlement of Ḥabad Ḥassidim (R. Gershon Kitover)
Shabbetai Zvi is sent to collect funds for Jerusalem community returns after proclaiming himself Messiah
Arrival of Jews from Yemen
Tyre
Ras el-Ahmar
Nabratein
El-Kayumiya
Gush-Ḥalav
'Alma
Meiron
Mi'ilya
Bar'am
Dalta
Amuka
Kafer-Yasif
Jarmak
Peki'in
Fir'am
'Ein-Zeitun
Kefar-Ḥananya
Zefat
'Akko
Cabul
Yakuk
Achbare
Haifa
Kefar Ḥittaya
Shefar'am
Tiberias
Kafer-Kanna
Khan Tujar
Nazareth
Beit-Shean
Jenin
Samaria
Nablus
Yafo
Sinjil
Ramah
Tomb of Samuel
Jerusalem
Bethlehem
Tomb of Rachel
Solomon's pools
Hebron
Gaza
Dead Sea
99
Travels of R. Moshé Bassula (1522)
0 10 20 km.
0 5 10 15 miles

THE JEWS OF PALESTINE UNDER THE OTTOMAN TURKS 1517-1840

Medal in honor of Gracia Mendesia Nasi, 1510-1569, prominent Jewish leader and philanthropist

THE MOSLEM Turks captured the country from the Moslem Mamelukes in 1517. During their rule, the Jewish community continued to grow. In Jerusalem there was a sizable Jewish population, and Sultan Suleiman the Great, who rebuilt the walls of Jerusalem, opened Tiberias and several villages in its vicinity to Jewish settlement. In the wake of this edict, the Jews came, rebuilt and repopulated Tiberias and built a wall around it; in the generations that followed, the Jewish community of Tiberias continued to grow.

Ẓefat (Safed), home of the Cabbalists, also had a large Jewish community. There, too, was opened the first Hebrew printing press in 1578, one of the earliest printing presses anywhere, and the first on the Asian continent. There were Jews also in 'Akko (Acre) and in several villages in Upper Galilee. In the sixteenth century Ashkenazi Jews from eastern Europe began immigrating to Palestine, a movement that developed and expanded in the generations that followed.

In the eighteenth century a Beduin sheikh named Daher el-'Omar mounted a successful rebellion in Galilee and made Tiberias his first capital. He invited Rabbi Ḥayim Abul'afia to settle there, and the latter was instrumental in further consolidating the Jewish community in that city. The Turkish Army eventually unseated the Beduin sheikh and restored Turkish rule throughout the land; the capital was established at 'Akko.

One of the better known of the Turkish Governors of Palestine was Aḥmed Jazzar Pasha, whose Finance Minister and top adviser was Ḥayim Farḥi, a Jew from Syria.

In 1831 the country was invaded by an Egyptian army commanded by Ibrahim Pasha, son of Mohammed 'Ali. Under his rule, the urban Jewish population in Palestine flourished, and with his permission and assistance a small village called Jermak was founded in the heights of Upper Galilee.

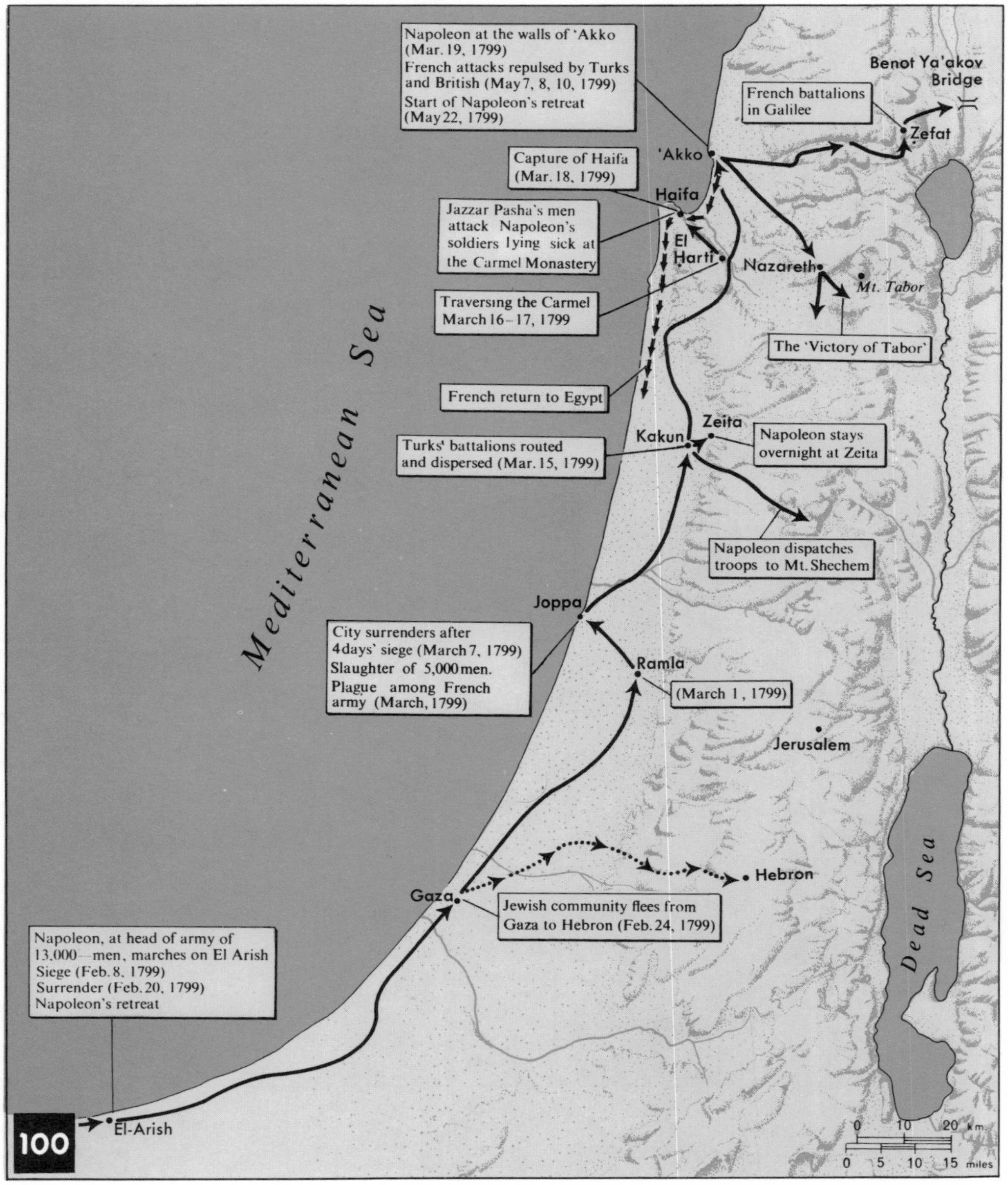
Napoleon at the walls of 'Akko (Mar. 19, 1799)
French attacks repulsed by Turks and British (May 7, 8, 10, 1799)
Start of Napoleon's retreat (May 22, 1799)
Benot Ya'akov Bridge
French battalions in Galilee
Zefat
'Akko
Capture of Haifa (Mar. 18, 1799)
Haifa
Jazzar Pasha's men attack Napoleon's soldiers lying sick at the Carmel Monastery
El Harti
Nazareth
Mt. Tabor
Traversing the Carmel March 16–17, 1799
The 'Victory of Tabor'
Mediterranean Sea
French return to Egypt
Zeita
Kakun
Napoleon stays overnight at Zeita
Turks' battalions routed and dispersed (Mar. 15, 1799)
Napoleon dispatches troops to Mt. Shechem
Joppa
City surrenders after 4 days' siege (March 7, 1799)
Slaughter of 5,000 men.
Plague among French army (March, 1799)
Ramla
(March 1, 1799)
Jerusalem
Hebron
Gaza
Jewish community flees from Gaza to Hebron (Feb. 24, 1799)
Dead Sea
Napoleon, at head of army of 13,000—men, marches on El Arish
Siege (Feb. 8, 1799)
Surrender (Feb. 20, 1799)
Napoleon's retreat
100
El-Arish
0 10 20 km
0 5 10 15 miles

NAPOLEON'S CAMPAIGN (1799)

The Siege of 'Akko, 1799

IT HAD always been Napoleon's dream to establish French rule in the Near East and thereby to thwart the imperial ambitions of his British rivals. Having conquered Egypt, Napoleon set out at the head of his forces, by way of the Sinai Desert, for Palestine. The French army, using the ancient coastal route, advanced into the Holy Land, capturing El-Arish, Gaza, Ramla, and Joppa. Northward along the Sharon Plain, Napoleon's army headed for its main objective—Acre ('Akko), capital of the Turkish rulers of Palestine.

During the siege of Acre, Napoleon despatched several units of his army to Zefat and to the Benot Ya'akov Bridge, on the upper Jordan River, with the aim of cutting off any reinforcements the Turks might be sending in from Damascus. When the French learned that Turkish forces had, nevertheless, succeeded in crossing the Jordan at another point and had penetrated into the Jezreel Valley, a number of French battalions went out to meet them, and, in the valley opposite Mount Tabor, of Biblical fame, the French won their big victory over the Turks.

The siege of Acre, however, proved a failure. Eventually, Napoleon was compelled to retreat, returning to Egypt along the same route by which he had come. Some time later, he had to depart from Egypt too; that was the bitter end of his ambitions in the Near East.

THE JEWS OF PALESTINE UNDER THE OTTOMAN TURKS (1840–1917)

An Arab market at the Sultan's pool

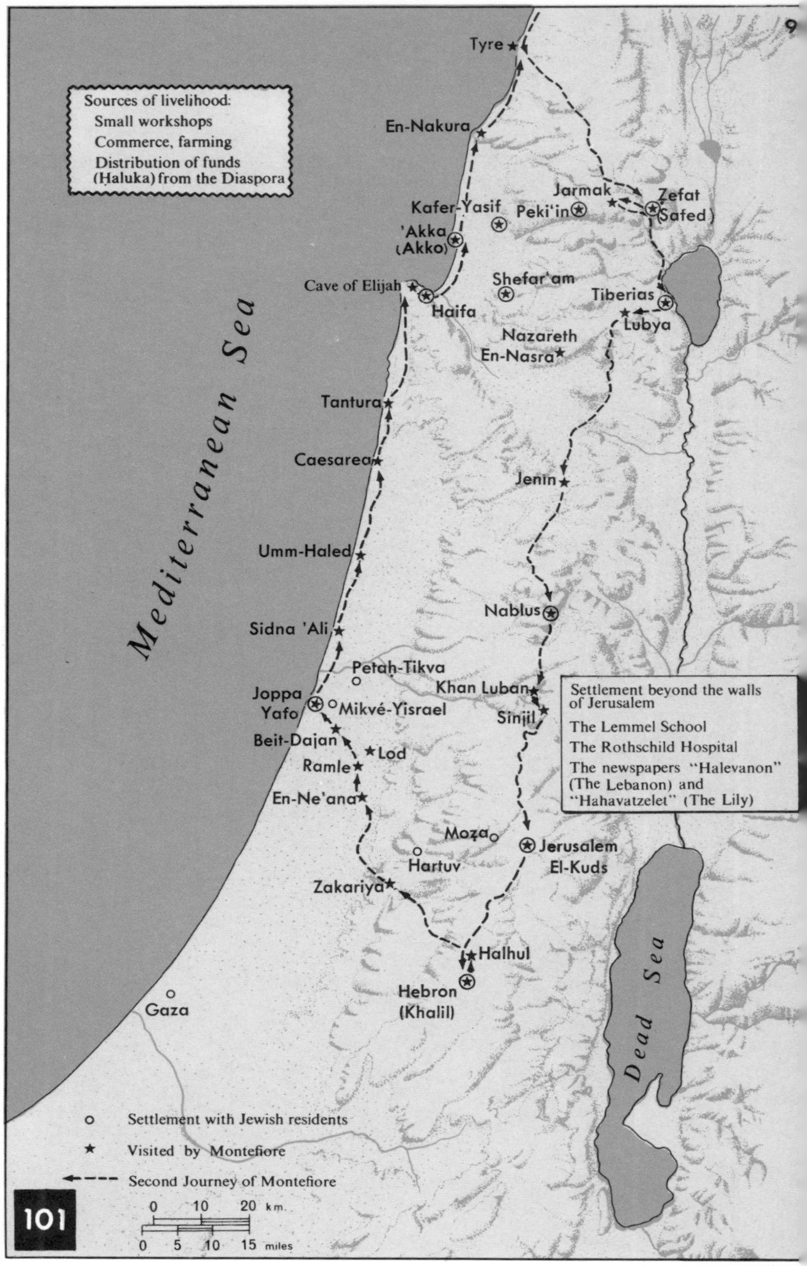

FOLLOWING the expulsion of Ibrahim Pasha, the country came once more under Turkish rule. In the ensuing four decades, there was a marked rise in immigration from eastern Europe, with a resulting reinforcement of the Ashkenazi communities, especially in the four Holy Cities (Jerusalem, Hebron, Tiberias, Ẓefat). Earlier in the century, North African Jews had founded communities in Yafo and Haifa, where up to that time virtually none had existed.

During the second half of the nineteenth century, the Jewish community in Palestine awakened to the need and the possibility of consolidation and expansion in the urban areas where it had its roots, and of striking new roots, as farmers, in the rural parts of the country. In 1860, for the first time in its history, Jerusalem expanded beyond the city walls, with the founding of Mishkenot-Shaananim: this was the birth of the New City that has grown into the modern capital city of Jerusalem of our day. Mikve-Israel was established near Yafo in 1870. Here arose the country's first agricultural school, on land donated by the Turkish Government. In 1878, a group of Jews from Jerusalem went down to the coastal plain to lay the foundations of Petaḥ-Tikva, "the mother of colonies." Located in an area of unpromising and disease-ridden swampland, the project spelled much hardship and suffering for the pioneers who engaged in it, but in their boundless devotion they overcame every obstacle and, with the help of their children, managed in the end to transform Petaḥ-Tikva into one of Israel's major cities.

An English Jew of Italian origin, Sir Moses Montefiore, together with his wife, Lady Judith Montefiore, made seven visits to the Holy Land; he interceded several times with the Turkish authorities on behalf of the Jewish community, particularly of Jerusalem, and was instrumental in founding the first Jewish suburb outside the walls of the Old City, named in his honor, the Montefiore Quarter.

Turks surrender Jerusalem

BRITISH CAMPAIGN (OCTOBER 1917-SEPTEMBER 1918)

DURING World War I, Egypt and the Suez Canal were under British rule. The British kept a large number of troops there, in preparation for the conquest of Palestine, then in the hands of the Turks and their allies, the Germans. With the help of the Germans, the Turkish army tried to gain control of the Suez Canal, the "lifeline" of the British Empire. The British forces managed to repulse these attacks and, after receiving reinforcements, drove the enemy back across the Sinai desert, capturing El-'Arish and Rafah.

After two costly and unsuccessful attempts to storm the heavily fortified town of Gaza, the commander of the British forces was replaced by General Allenby, who led his forces eastward, taking Beer-Shev'a on October 31, 1917. He then turned back to Gaza, stormed and captured it and moved on to Ramla. One column marched on Yafo, while the main force moved on Jerusalem, taking it on 9 December.

The British army now re-formed its lines in two main concentrations: in the Samarian Mountains, some distance north of Jerusalem, and in the coastal plain, north of Tel-Aviv. However, only nine months later did the British break through the Turkish-German front and launch the final push north that was to spell the end of the Ottoman Empire in the Middle East. Moving along the coastal plain and the 'Iron and Jezreel Valleys, the British captured Haifa, Nazareth and Tiberias. Advancing northward through Eastern Galilee, they reached the Benot Ya'akov Bridge, on the upper Jordan River, crossed over into Syria and took Damascus on September 30, 1918. From there, the British forces raced across Syria. When, in October 1918, they neared Asia Minor, Turkey sued for peace.

In more recent times, with the expansion of the British Empire, necessitating as it did assured communications between the many lands under British rule, the value of the Suez Canal as the gateway to distant sea routes gained increased significance. Because the Canal had enhanced the strategic importance of Palestine due to its proximity to this vital lifeline of the British empire, the country became a battlefield during the First World War between Turkey and Germany on the one hand and Britain and her allies on the other. By capturing Palestine from the Turks, she secured for herself greater control over the territories of her vast empire and over the lines of communication between her far-flung possessions. Having undertaken to establish a national home in Palestine for the Jewish people, Britain was given the mandate over the country and ruled it for some thirty years until the creation of the State of Israel.

The British declaration of occupation at the Citadel of David, Jerusalem

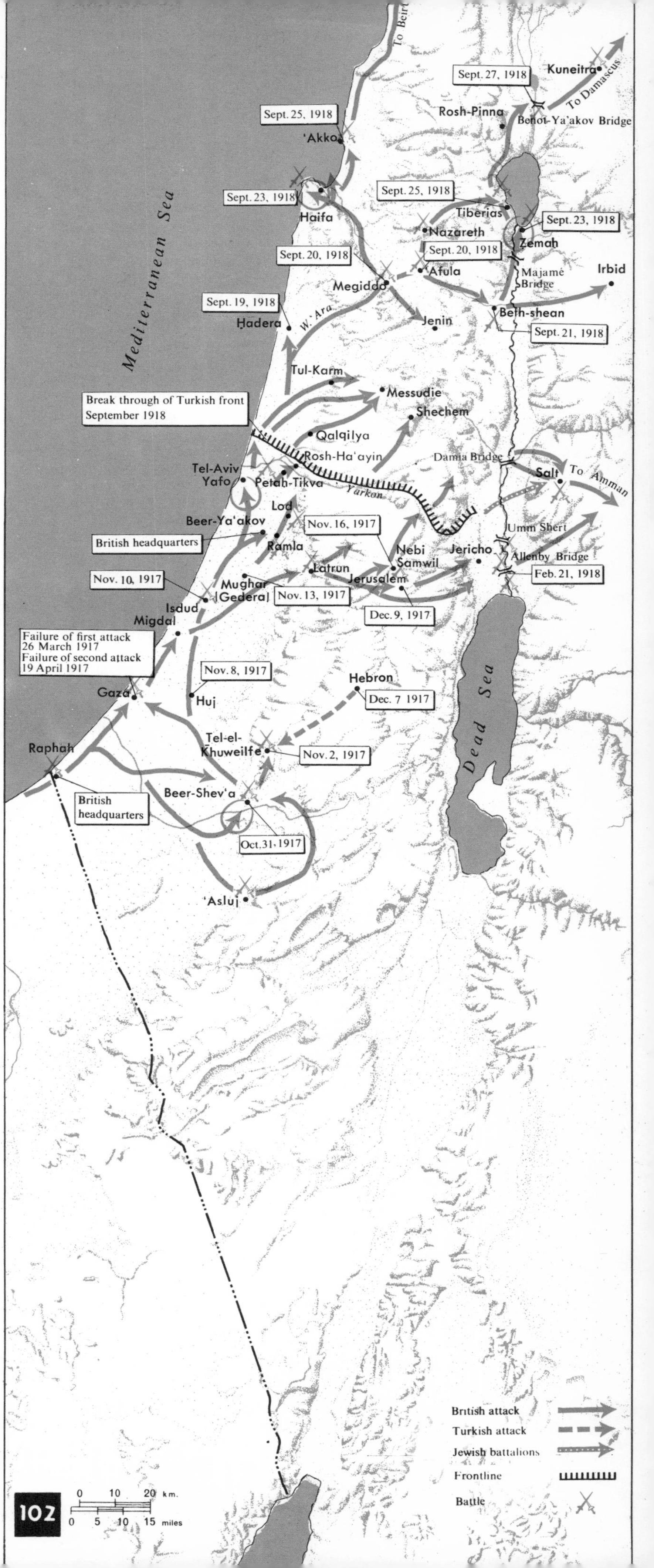

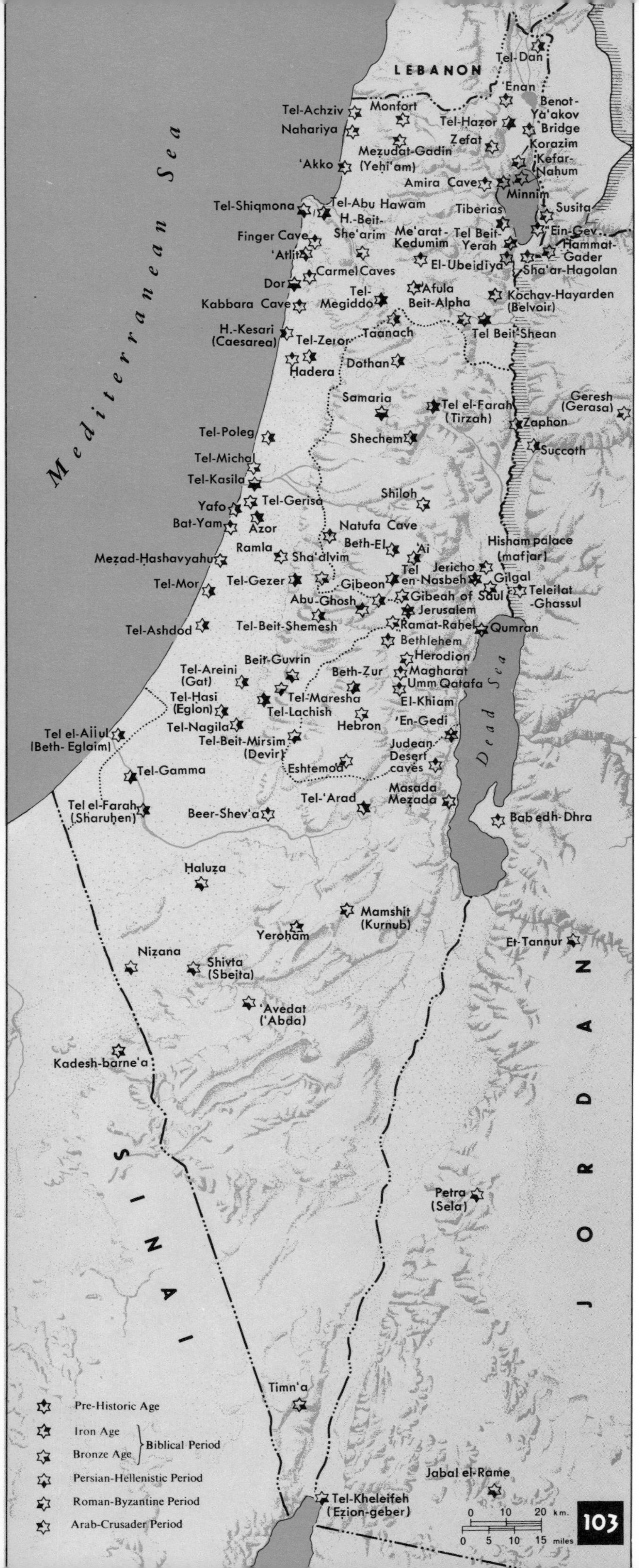
LEBANON
Mediterranean Sea
Tel-Dan
'Enan
Benot-Ya'akov Bridge
Tel-Achziv
Monfort
Tel-Hazor
Nahariya
Zefat
Korazim
Mezudat-Gadin (Yehi'am)
'Akko
Kefar-Nahum
Amira Cave
Minnim
Tel-Shiqmona
Tel-Abu Hawam
Tiberias
Susita
H.-Beit-She'arim
Finger Cave
Me'arat-Kedumim
Tel Beit-Yerah
Ein-Gev
'Atlit
Hammat-Gader
El-Ubeidiya
Sha'ar-Hagolan
Carmel Caves
Dor
Tel-Megiddo
Afula
Beit-Alpha
Kochav-Hayarden (Belvoir)
Kabbara Cave
H.-Kesari (Caesarea)
Tel-Zeror
Taanach
Tel Beit-Shean
Hadera
Dothan
Samaria
Tel el-Farah (Tirzah)
Geresh (Gerasa)
Zaphon
Tel-Poleg
Shechem
Succoth
Tel-Michal
Tel-Kasila
Shiloh
Yafo
Tel-Gerisa
Bat-Yam
Azor
Natufa Cave
Beth-El
Hisham palace (mafjar)
Ramla
'Ai
Mezad-Hashavyahu
Sha'alvim
Jericho
Tel en-Nasbeh
Gilgal
Tel-Mor
Tel-Gezer
Gibeon
Teleilat-Ghassul
Abu-Ghosh
Gibeah of Saul
Jerusalem
Tel-Ashdod
Tel-Beit-Shemesh
Ramat-Rahel
Qumran
Bethlehem
Herodion
Beit-Guvrin
Tel-Areini (Gat)
Beth-Zur
Magharat Umm Qatafa
Tel-Hasi (Eglon)
Tel-Maresha
El-Khiam
Tel-Lachish
Hebron
'En-Gedi
Dead Sea
Tel el-Ajjul (Beth-Eglaim)
Tel-Nagila
Tel-Beit-Mirsim (Devir)
Judean Desert caves
Eshtemoa
Tel-Gamma
Masada Mezada
Tel-'Arad
Tel el-Farah (Sharuhen)
Beer-Shev'a
Bab edh-Dhra
Haluza
Mamshit (Kurnub)
Yeroham
Et-Tannur
Nizana
Shivta (Sbeita)
'Avedat ('Abda)
Kadesh-barne'a
SINAI
JORDAN
Petra (Sela)
Timn'a
Jabal el-Rame
Tel-Kheleifeh (Ezion-geber)
Pre-Historic Age
Iron Age
Bronze Age
Biblical Period
Persian-Hellenistic Period
Roman-Byzantine Period
Arab-Crusader Period
0 10 20 km.
0 5 10 15 miles
103

ARCHAEOLOGICAL EXCAVATIONS

SCIENTIFIC excavations intended to uncover traces of past civilizations are carried out at famous historical sites. The first excavations in Palestine were made in the middle of the nineteenth century in the Old City of Jerusalem. In 1892, a dig was held at Tel-Ḥasi in the South, possibly the site of the ancient Eglon mentioned in the Book of Joshua. Other digs have been made at such well-known Biblical places as Gezer, Beit-Shemesh, Lachish and Devir, all in the territory of the Tribe of Judah, and at the Negev mounds of Tel-Gamma and Tel el-Farah (ancient Sharuḥen). Excavations further north have unearthed treasues at Gibeah of Saul (Giv'at Shaul), Mizpé, Beth-El, 'Ai, Shiloḥ, Shomron (Samaria), Megiddo, Taanach, Beit-Shean, Ḥaẓor, and elsewhere.

The work has been planned and carried out by scientific expeditions from Europe and the United States, and in recent years by Israeli archaeologists.

The first expedition was made by the Palestine Exploration Fund, of Great Britain. The first American one was at Shomron, by a team from Harvard financed by the Jewish millionaire, Jacob Schiff. Many digs have been carried out by such institutions as the American School for Oriental Research, the British School of Archaeology and the Dominicans and Franciscans in Jerusalem.

Among local Jewish groups engaging in archaeology, the leading institution has been the Israel Exploration Society; its first project, in 1920, involved the ancient site of Ḥamata, near Tiberias.

This extensive work of scientific excavation and the unearthing of antiquities in many places throughout the country have shed a great deal of new light on the history of the Holy Land and on the life and customs of its ancient inhabitants in various periods, and have led to a more profound understanding of the Scriptures.

The synagogue at Capernaum

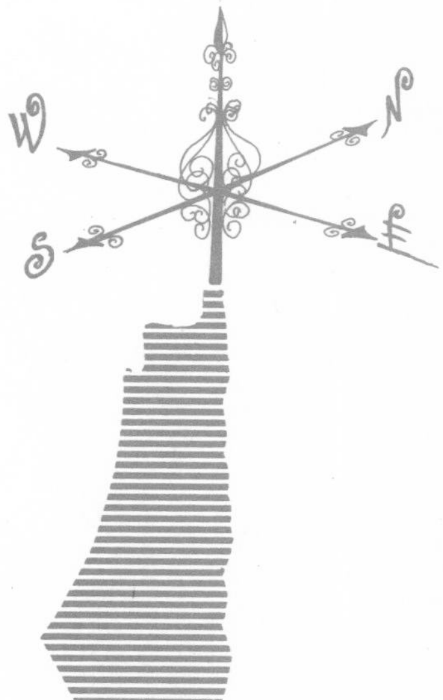

proposals for a jewish state

PROPOSALS FOR A JEWISH STATE

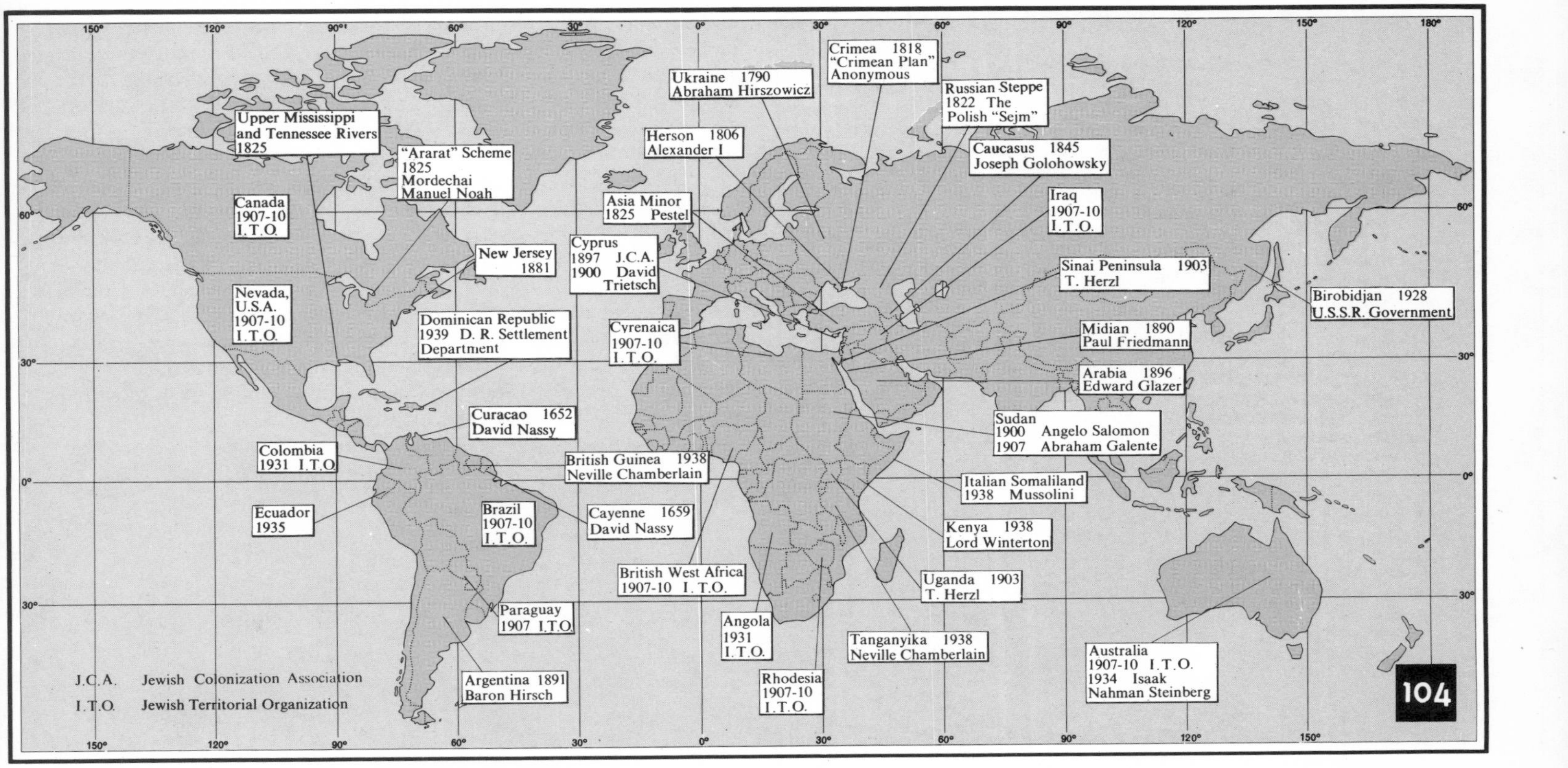

SIR LAWRENCE OLIPHANT'S PROPOSAL (1880)

SIR LAWRENCE Oliphant, a Scotsman by extraction, was born in Capetown, South Africa, and spent a number of years in the Druze village of Dalia, on Mount Carmel. He devoted years of his life to a study of the land, dreaming of the establishment of a Jewish State in the district of Gilead in Transjordan. In a book entitled "The Land of Gilead," published in 1880, he describes his travels in this region, tells of its natural resources and climate, its history and its antiquities. In this book, he also details his proposals: Jewish settlement in Gilead, the founding of towns and villages, and the laying of a railway line.

Although his program was not implemented in Gilead, he is well remembered for the substantial material and moral assistance he extended to the first Jewish settlers in Galilee and Mount Carmel.

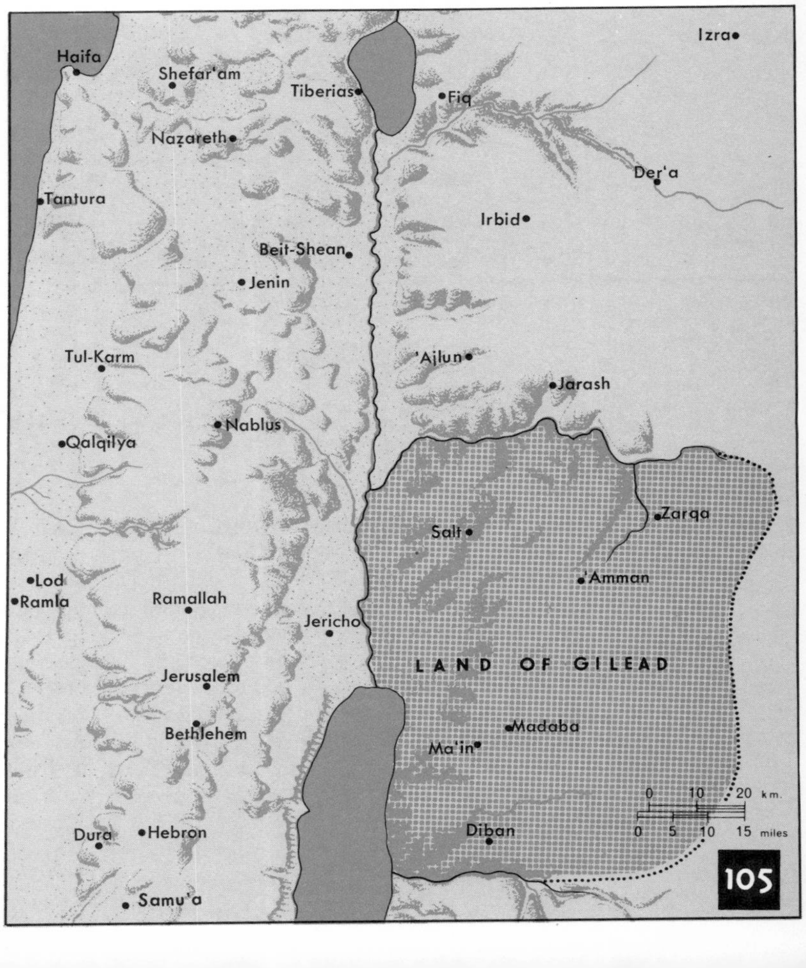

SYKES-PICOT AGREEMENT (1915)

SIR MARK Sykes and George Picot were liaison officers in the First World War. Sykes was a British expert on Middle East affairs, Picot a French consul. At the start of the war, in 1915 before the Entente Powers, Britain and France, had defeated the Turks and broken up the Ottoman Empire, these two officers met in the names of their respective Governments, and signed the agreement that bears their names, concerning the future division of the conquered lands between them: Palestine was to go to Great Britain, Lebanon and Syria to France. The border was to follow a line running westward from Kinneret, in the upper Jordan Valley, to a point north of 'Akko, on the Mediterranean coast.

After the British had captured the countries of the Near East from the Turks, the agreed border was established and, as a result, three Jewish settlements in the northeastern corner of the country—Metulla, Kefar-Gil'adi and Tel-Ḥai—were to come under French rule. An Arab attack on the three villages forced the Jews to evacuate them and retreat, but two years later, when civil rule was restored, this area was added to the British Mandate in Palestine, and the settlers were able to return to their abandoned villages, rebuild them and build several new settlements in the vicinity.

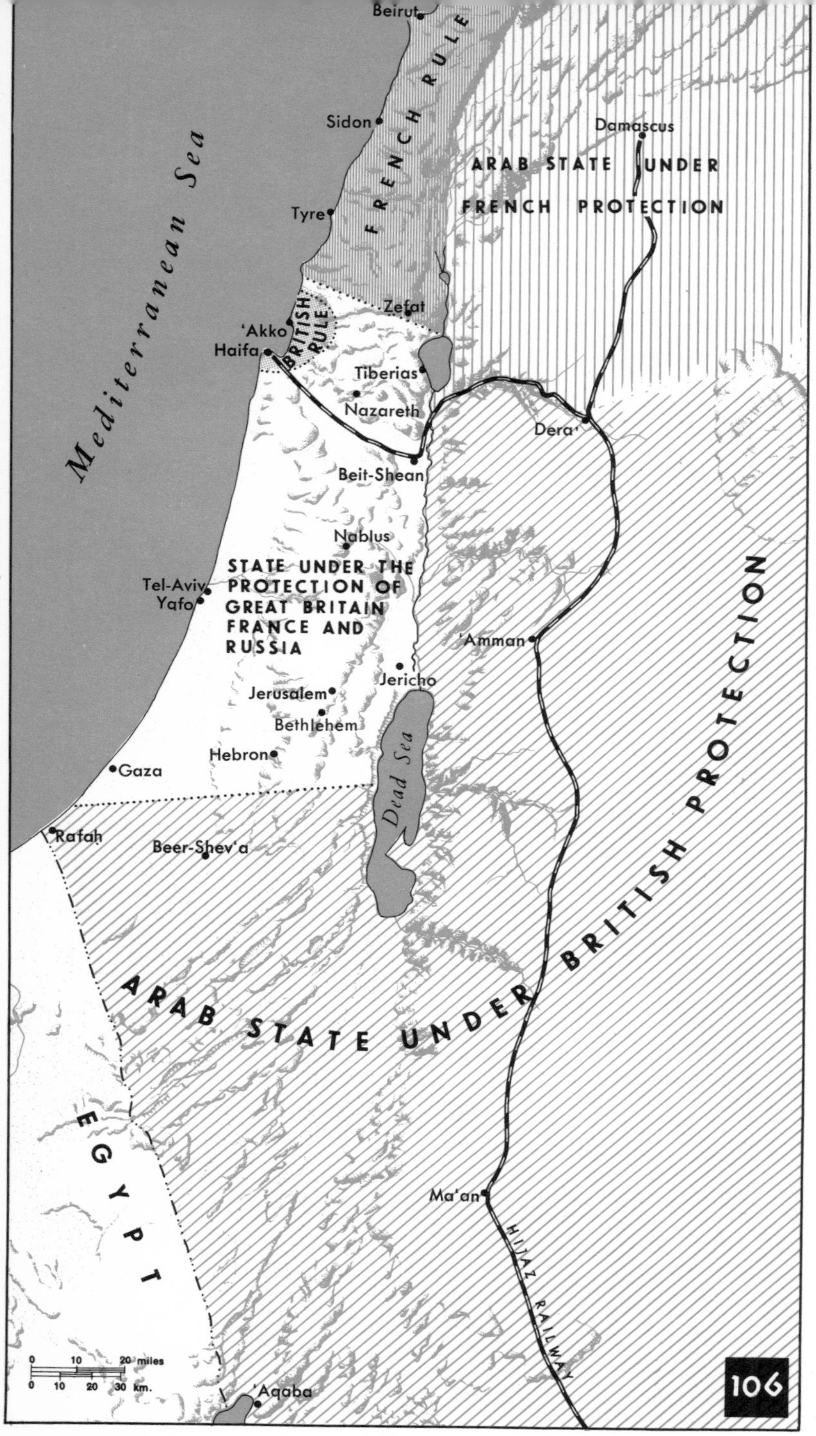

ZIONIST ORGANIZATION'S PROPOSAL

AT THE League of Nations Peace Conference held in Versailles, France, in 1919, the World Zionist Organization presented a map outlining the extent of the territory which it proposed should be set aside for Jewish settlement. The boundary lines on this map were fixed in accordance with the history of ancient Israel and of Jewish settlement in these areas, as attested by historical scholarship and the archaeological remnants that have been found there.

The territory included all the land between the Mediterranean Sea and the Jordan River, from the Litani River in the north to the Sinai Desert in the south, as well as Transjordan, eastward to the edge of the desert, northward to Mount Hermon and southward to the Gulf of Eilat ('Aqaba).

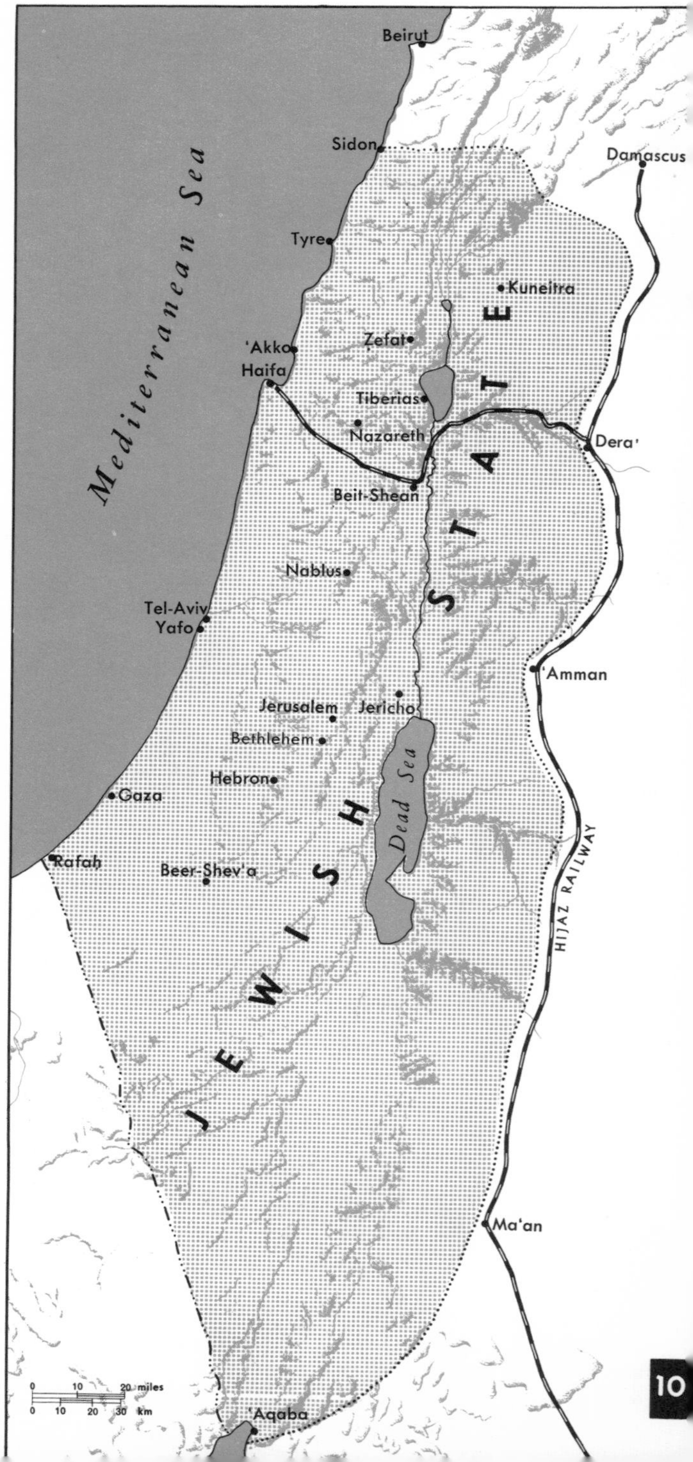

THE BRITISH MANDATE

AFTER World War I, the League of Nations decided to assign Palestine as a mandated territory to Great Britain, with the stated purpose of helping to implement the Balfour Declaration: the establishment in Palestine of a Jewish National Home.

With the arrival of the first British High Commissioner, Sir Herbert Samuel, in 1920, military rule in Palestine was replaced by civilian rule. Britain's first act was to sever Transjordan from the historical territory of Palestine and to hand it to the Arabs: Abdullah the son of Hussein was brought over from his home in Hejaz to become the first ruler of Transjordan. Britain, as the Mandatory Power, continued to hold sway over both parts of Palestine, east and west, but the former was excluded from the terms of reference of the Balfour Declaration.

Nationalist extremists quickly gained control of the Arab leadership in Palestine and launched a campaign of violent opposition to the fulfillment of Jewish national aspirations (though these had been recognized in 1919 in the Feisal-Weizmann agreement) and to any move—such as Jewish immigration—that was likely to advance those aspirations. The British Administration followed a policy of appeasement, which served only to whet the Arabs' appetite. Nevertheless, Jewish immigration continued and even grew in volume. New settlements were established; arid, rocky and swampy soil in various parts of the country was reclaimed for agriculture; and the groundwork was laid for industrial enterprises that would expand the economy and provide a source of livelihood for additional newcomers.

The Arabs' threats and acts of violence gave birth to the Jewish underground defense organization, the *Haganah*, which guarded the Jewish community and helped in its expansion and consolidation. In the wake of growing Arab opposition to Jewish immigration and pressure on the British Government from other Arab States, the British authorities began to proclaim a series of restrictive measures against Palestine Jewry, curtailing purchases and settlement of land and limiting Jewish immigration. However, the Jews still found ways of fulfilling their national tasks and of "bringing up" into the country those Jews who wanted to come, even when this had to be done "illegally."

The bloody riots that sporadically threw Palestine into a state of near-chaos and the constant and worsening friction between Jews and Arabs set the British authorities on the search for a solution to the impasse. Various commissions were brought to Palestine to study the problem and make their recommendations, and generally they proposed dividing the country into Jewish and Arab sectors, under the British Mandate, or some variation on this general theme. All these proposals failed because they were not acceptable to the parties themselves.

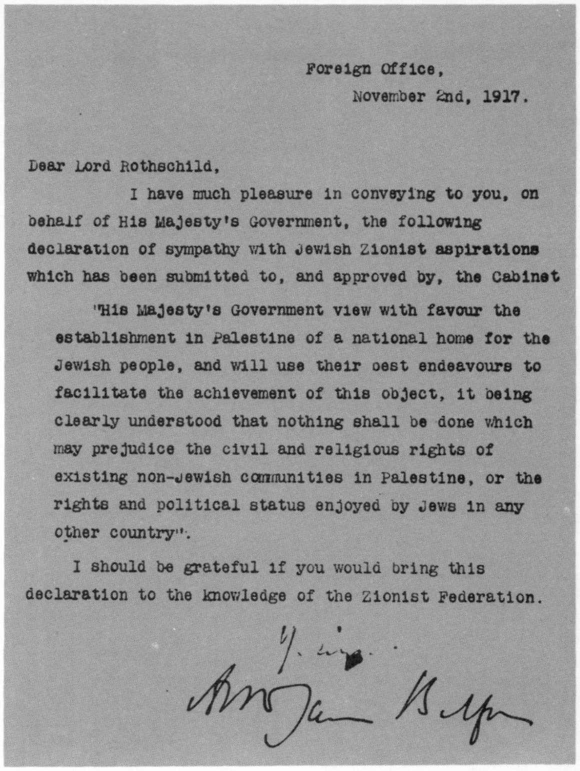

Foreign Office,
November 2nd, 1917.

Dear Lord Rothschild,

I have much pleasure in conveying to you, on behalf of His Majesty's Government, the following declaration of sympathy with Jewish Zionist aspirations which has been submitted to, and approved by, the Cabinet

"His Majesty's Government view with favour the establishment in Palestine of a national home for the Jewish people, and will use their best endeavours to facilitate the achievement of this object, it being clearly understood that nothing shall be done which may prejudice the civil and religious rights of existing non-Jewish communities in Palestine, or the rights and political status enjoyed by Jews in any other country".

I should be grateful if you would bring this declaration to the knowledge of the Zionist Federation.

The Balfour Declaration

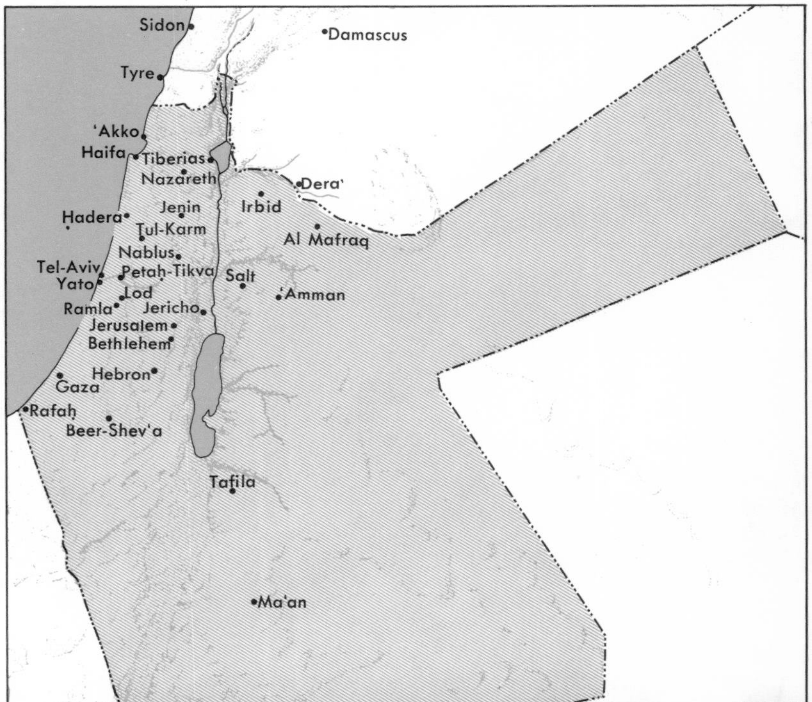

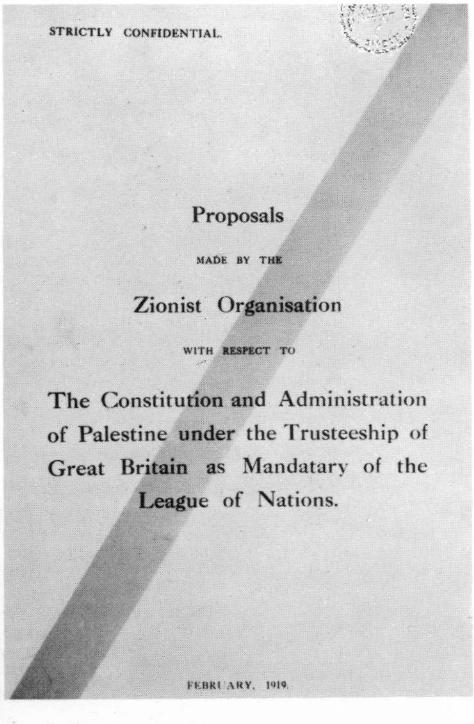

STRICTLY CONFIDENTIAL.

Proposals

MADE BY THE

Zionist Organisation

WITH RESPECT TO

The Constitution and Administration of Palestine under the Trusteeship of Great Britain as Mandatary of the League of Nations.

FEBRUARY, 1919.

Winston Churchill and Herbert Samuel in Jerusalem

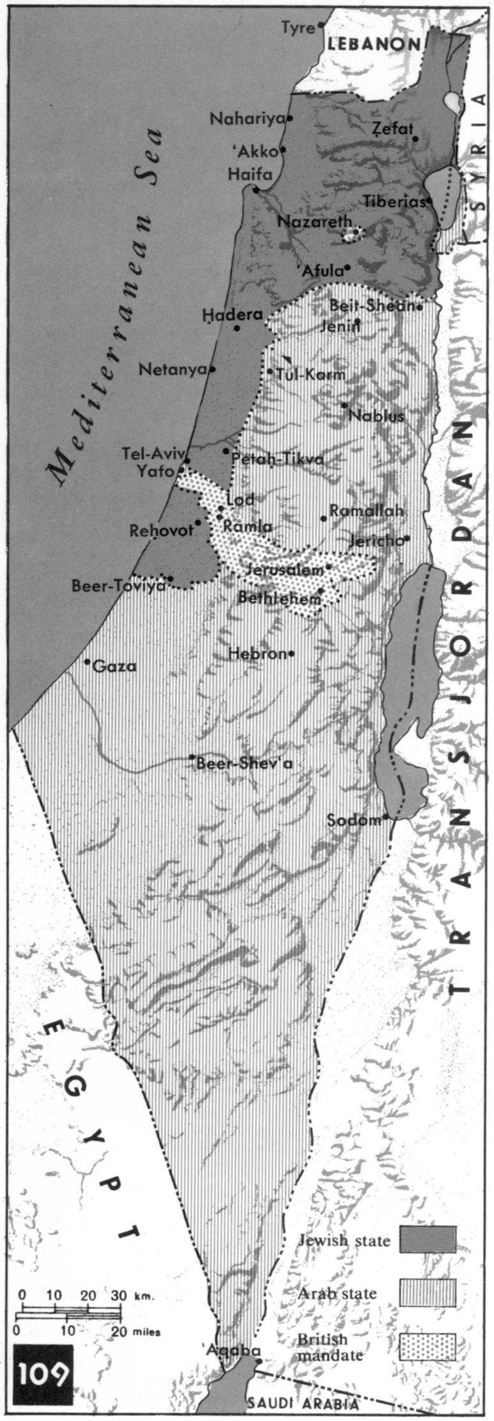

THE PEEL PARTITION PLAN

THE ARAB riots that began in 1936 (and were to continue intermittently for three years) caused the British Government to appoint a Royal Commission of Inquiry headed by the statesman, Lord Peel. After prolonged investigation, the Commission proposed the partition of the country into two states: Jewish and Arab. Under this plan, the Jewish State was to comprise all of Galilee (up to and including the Jezreel Valley in the south), the Haifa district, the Sharon Plain, Tel Aviv and vicinity.

The Arab State was to be made up of the districts of Samaria, Judea and the Negev. Jerusalem, Bethlehem and a strip of land extending westward to the coastal plain were to remain under the British Mandate, which would also be responsible for supervision of all the holy places in Palestine.

Dr. Chaim Weizmann before the Peel Commission

PARTITION PROPOSALS

THE PARTITION Commission was appointed in Febru 1938 by the British Government; it was headed by Sir J Woodhead. Its partition proposals were roughly the same as tha the Peel Commission, except that Western Galilee was to ren under the British Mandate, and Yafo (Jaffa) was to be an Arab clave in the Jewish State.

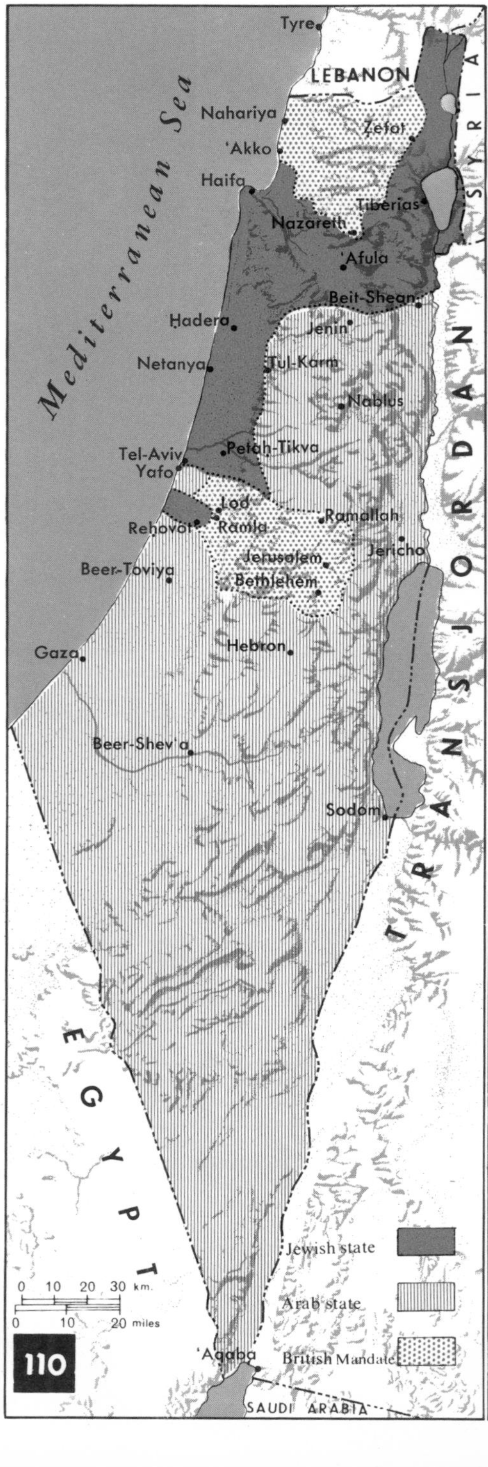

THE ANGLO-AMERICAN COMMISSION'S PROPOSAL

The Anglo-American Commission, 1946

THE ANGLO-AMERICAN Commission was appointed in December 1945 and proposed the partition of Palestine into autonomous Jewish and Arab areas, under the supreme authority of the British High Commissioner, and a strip of land under the British Mandate. The lines were to be drawn in much the same way as in the Peel Plan.

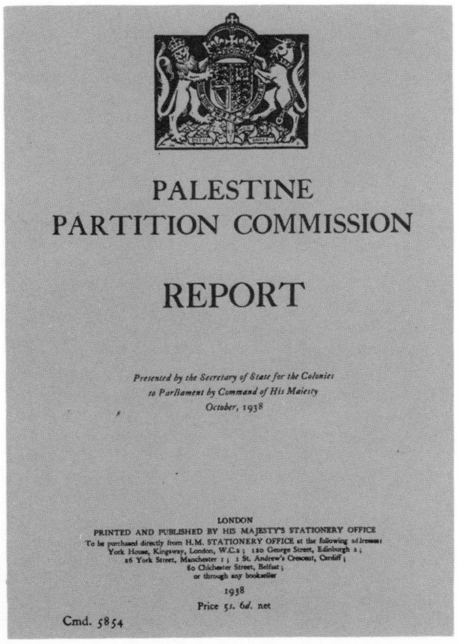

PALESTINE
PARTITION COMMISSION

REPORT

Presented by the Secretary of State for the Colonies to Parliament by Command of His Majesty
October, 1938

LONDON
PRINTED AND PUBLISHED BY HIS MAJESTY'S STATIONERY OFFICE
To be purchased directly from H.M. STATIONERY OFFICE at the following addresses:
York House, Kingsway, London, W.C.2; 120 George Street, Edinburgh 2;
26 York Street, Manchester 1; 1 St. Andrew's Crescent, Cardiff;
80 Chichester Street, Belfast;
or through any bookseller

1938

Price 5*s*. 6*d*. net

Cmd. 5854

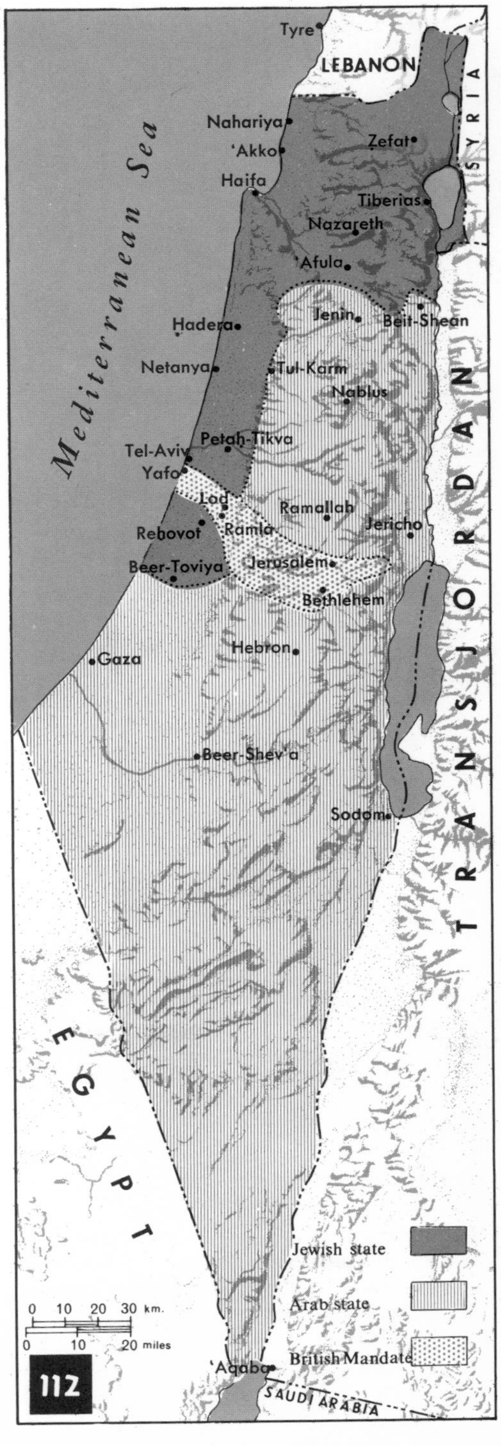

THE JEWISH AGENCY'S PROPOSAL

AFTER studying the Anglo-American plan, the Jewish Agency submitted a partition proposal of its own, under which the Jewish state would cover all of Galilee and the Jezreel Valley, the entire coastal plain except for Jaffa, which would be an Arab enclave, all of the south and the Negev, the wilderness of Judea up to Jericho and the western shore of the Dead Sea. The Samarian highlands and the Judean Hills were to be in the Arab region, while Jerusalem was to be under international control.

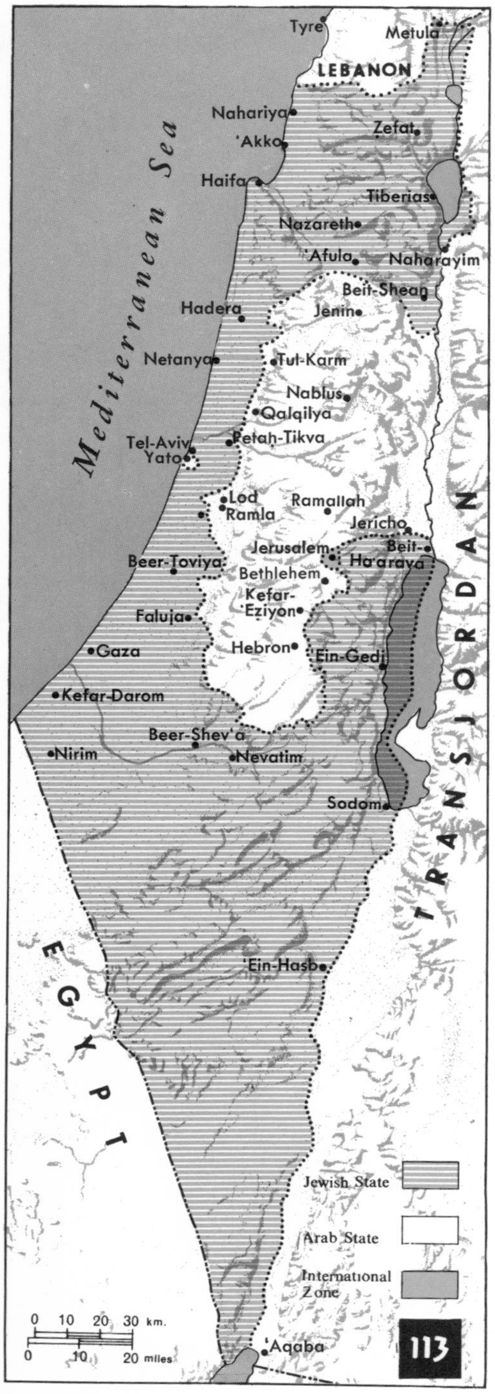

THE GENERAL Assembly of the United Nations on November 29, 1947 decided upon the establishment of the State of Israel and fixed its borders. Within these borders were to be Eastern Galilee, Haifa and Mount Carmel, the entire Sharon Plain, Tel Aviv and vicinity (except Yafo) and a narrow passage to the Negev. Beer-Shev'a and the Niẓana district, down to Eilat, were not included in this domain.

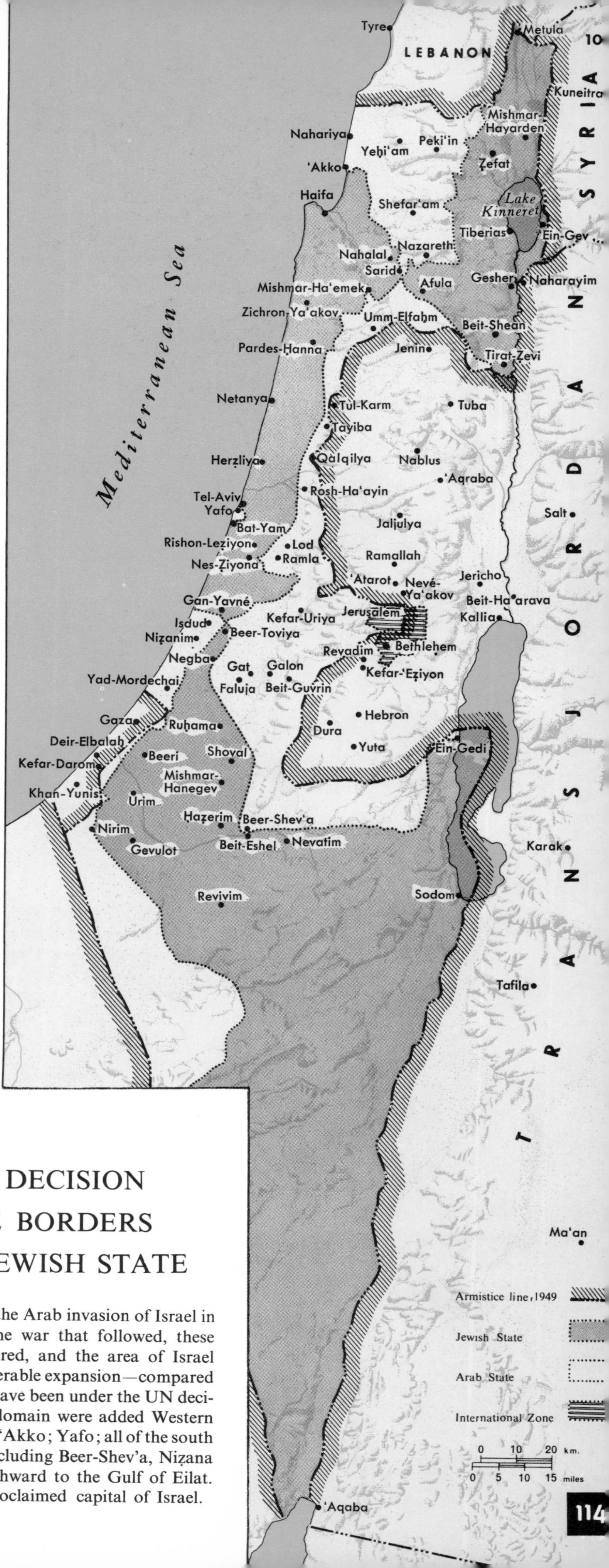

THE U.N. DECISION AND THE BORDERS OF THE JEWISH STATE

In the wake of the Arab invasion of Israel in May 1948 and the war that followed, these borders were altered, and the area of Israel underwent considerable expansion—compared to what it was to have been under the UN decision. To Israel's domain were added Western Galilee, including 'Akko; Yafo; all of the south and the Negev, including Beer-Shev'a, Niẓana and the area southward to the Gulf of Eilat. Jerusalem was proclaimed capital of Israel.

GAZETTEER OF TOWNS AND VILLAGES

ABBA-HILLEL agricultural school near Ashkelon, 1951
ABU-AGWEILA road junction in northern Sinai Desert
ABU-GHOSH Moslem village west of Jerusalem
ABU-SINAN Druze village in Western Galilee
ABU-ZUNEIME point on track between Suez and St. Catherine's Monastery
ACRE the English name of 'Akko. See: 'Akko
ADAMIT kibbutz in Western Galilee, 1958
'ADANIM moshav in Sharon, 1950
ADERET moshav in Judean Mountains, 1961
ADIRIM moshav in Jezreel Valley, 1956
AFEK kibbutz in Zevulun Valley east of Haifa, 1939
AFIKIM kibbutz in Jordan Valley, 1932
'AFULA central town of Jezreel Valley, 1925
'AGUR moshav in Judah, near Beit-Shemesh, 1950
AḤI'EZER moshav north of Lod, 1950
AḤIHUD moshav in Western Galilee, 1950
AḤISAMACH moshav east of Ramla, 1950
AḤITUV moshav in northern Sharon, 1951
AḤUZAM moshav in the South, 1950
'AKBARA Moslem village in Upper Galilee
AKKADA Moslem village in Samaria
'AKKO (ACRE) town on Mediterranean coast
ALMA moshav in Upper Galilee, 1949
ALMAGOR moshav in Upper Galilee, 1961
ALONEI-ABA moshav in Lower Galilee, 1948
ALONEI-YIẒḤAK children's village in Sharon, 1949
ALONIM kibbutz in Jezreel Valley, 1948
'ALUMIM kibbutz near Gaza Strip, 1966
ALUMOT kibbutz in Lower Galilee, 1947
AMAẒIA settlement in the South, 1955
'AMIR kibbutz in the Ḥula Valley, 1939
AMIRIM moshav in Upper Galilee, 1950
'AMKA moshav in Western Galilee, 1949
'AMMI'AD kibbutz in Upper Galilee, 1946
'AMMIKAM moshav in the Menashé Hills, 1950
'AMMINADAV moshav in Judean Mountains, 1950
'AMMI'OZ moshav in the Negev, 1957
'AMMISHAV suburb of Petaḥ-Tikva, 1948
'ARA Moslem village in 'Iron Valley
'ARABA Moslem village in Lower Galilee
'ARAD new town east of Beersheba, 1961
'AR'ARA Moslem village in 'Iron Valley
ARBEL moshav in Galilee near Tiberias, 1949
'ARUGOT moshav in the South, 1948
ARZA sanatorium west of Jerusalem, 1928
'ASERET settlement in the South near Gedera, 1954
ASHDOD new town on Mediterranean coast, 1957
ASHDOD-YA'AKOV kibbutz in Jordan Valley, 1922
ASHKELON new town on Mediterranean coast, 1948
ASHMURA settlement in the Ḥula Valley, 1949
'ATLIT new village on Mediterranean Coast, 1903
'AVDON moshav in Western Galilee, 1952
AVIEL moshav in the Menashé Hills, 1949
AVI'EZER moshav in the Judean Mountains, 1958
AVIGDOR moshav in the South, 1949
AVIḤAYIL moshav in Ḥefer Valley
AVITAL moshav in the Jezreel Valley, 1953
AVIVIM moshav in Upper Galilee, 1960
AVUKA farm in Beit-Shean Valley, 1941
'AYANOT school on Tel-Aviv-Ashkelon highway, 1930
AYELET-HASHAḤAR kibbutz in Upper Galilee, 1917
'AZARYA moshav near Ramla, 1950
AZOR townlet near Tel-Aviv-Yafo, 1949
'AZRIEL moshav in the Sharon Valley, 1951
'AZRIKAM moshav in the South, 1950
'AZZUN Arab village in western Samaria

BAHAN kibbutz in Sharon east of Netanya, 1954
BAKA ELGHARBIYA Moslem village east of Ḥadera
BALFOURIYA moshav in Jezreel Valley, 1922
BANIAS (1) source of Jordan at foot of Mount Hermon and Golan Heights
BANIAS (2) Arab village at foot of Mount Hermon and Golan Heights
BAPTISTS' VILLAGE near Petaḥ Tikva, 1960
BARAK moshav in Jezreel Valley, 1956
BAR'AM kibbutz in Upper Galilee, near Ẓefat, 1949
BAREKET moshav east of Lod, 1953
BAR-GIYORA moshav in Judean Mountains, 1950
BAR-ILAN University near Tel-Aviv, 1956
BARKAI kibbutz in Sharon-Samaria, 1949
BARTA'A Moslem village in Samaria
BATIR Moslem village near Jerusalem
BAT-SHELOMO village near Zikhron-Ya'akov, 1889
BAT-YAM town south of Tel-Aviv-Yafo, 1926
BAYADF Moslem village south of Megiddo
BEERI kibbutz in Negev near Gaza Strip, 1946
BEER-ORA youth village near Eilat, 1950
BEEROTAYIM moshav in Sharon Valley, 1949
BEEROT-YIZHAK kibbutz east of Tel-Aviv, 1943, 1950
BEER-SHEV'A (BEERSHEBA) town in the Negev, 1949
BEER-TOVIYA moshav in the South near Ashkelon, 1887
BEER-YA'AKOV village west of Ramla, 1907
BEIT-ALPHA kibbutz in Jezreel Valley, 1922
BEIT-'ARIF moshav east of Lod, 1949
BEIT-BERL cultural center in Sharon Valley, 1947
BEIT-DAGAN settlement near Tel-Aviv, 1948
BEIT-EL'AZARI moshav near Reḥovot, 1948
BEIT-'EZRA moshav near Ashkelon, 1950
BEIT-GAMALIEL moshav near Reḥovot, 1949
BEIT-GAN village in Galilee, near Yavneel, 1903
BEIT-GUVRIN kibbutz in the South, 1949
BEIT-HA'EMEK kibbutz in Western Galilee, 1949
BEIT-HAGADI moshav in the Negev near Gaza, 1949
BEIT-HALEVI moshav in the Sharon Valley, 1945
BEIT-ḤANAN moshav on Tel-Aviv-Ashkelon highway, 1930
BEIT-ḤANANYA moshav near Binyamina, 1950
BEIT-HASHITA kibbutz in Beit-Shean Valley, 1935
BEIT-ḤERUT moshav in Sharon near Netanya, 1933
BEIT-ḤEVER previous name of Kefar-Daniel, 1950
BEIT-ḤILKIYA moshav on Jerusalem-Beersheba highway, 1953
BEIT-HILLEL moshav in Ḥula Valley, 1940
BEIT-JALA Christian Arab town adjacent to Bethlehem
BEIT-JAN Druze village in Upper Galilee
BEIT-JIMAL monastery in Judean Mountains, 1881
BEIT-KAMA kibbutz in the South, 1949
BEIT-KAẒIR kibbutz in the Jordan Valley, 1949
BEIT-KESHET kibbutz in Lower Galilee, 1948
BEIT-LEḤEM moshav in Lower Galilee, 1948
BEIT-MEIR moshav west of Jerusalem, 1950
BEIT-NEḤEMYA moshav east of Lod airport, 1950
BEIT-NEKOFA moshav west of Jerusalem, 1949
BEIT-NIR kibbutz near Kiryat-Gat, 1955
BEIT-OREN kibbutz on Mount Carmel, 1939
BEIT-'OVED moshav on Tel-Aviv-Ashkelon highway, 1933
BEIT-RABBAN children's village, See: Givat-Washington, 1946
BEIT-RÉIM kibbutz in Negev, See: Re'im, 1949
BEIT-SAFAFA Moslem village south of Jerusalem
BEIT-SHEAN new town in Jordan Valley, 1949
BEIT-SHE'ARIM moshav in Jezreel Valley, 1936
BEIT-SHEMESH town west of Jerusalem, 1950
BEIT-SHEMUEL village near Tel-Aviv-Lod highway, 1960
BEIT-SHIKMA moshav near Ashkelon, 1950
BEIT-'UZIEL moshav south of Ramla, 1957
BEIT-YANNAI moshav on the Netanya-Haifa highway, 1933
BEIT-YEHOSHU'A moshav in Sharon, near Netanya, 1938
BEIT-YERAḤ agricultural school near Lake Kinneret, 1952
BEIT-YIẒḤAK moshav in Sharon near Netanya, 1940
BEIT-YOSEF moshav in Jordan Valley, 1937
BEIT-ZAYIT moshav west of Jerusalem, 1949
BEIT-ZER'A kibbutz in Jordan Valley, 1937
BEIT-ẒEVI agricultural school on Haifa-Ḥadera highway, 1952
BEKO'A moshav in the Judean Mountains, 1952
BEN-'AMMI moshav in Galilee near Nahariya, 1949
BANAYA moshav in the South near Ashkelon, 1949
BEN-DOR urban settlement near Haifa, 1949
BENEI-'ATAROT moshav east of Lod airport, 1948
BNEI-'AYISH moshav in the south near Gedera, 1958
BENEI-BERAK new town near Tel-Aviv, 1924
BENEI-BERIT (MOLEDET) moshav in Lower Galilee, 1937
BENEI-DAROM kibbutz in the South near Ashdod, 1949
BENEI-DEROR moshav in the Sharon Valley, 1946
BENEI-REEM moshav in the South near Gedera, 1949
BENEI-ẒIYON moshav in Sharon Valley, 1947
BENI-NA'IM Arab village near Hebron
BEN-SHEMEN (1) children's village east of Lod, 1921
BEN-SHEMEN (2) moshav east of Lod, 1922, 1952
BEN-ZAKAI moshav on Tel-Aviv-Ashkelon highway, 1950
BERECHYA moshav in the South near Ashkelon, 1950
BEROR-ḤAYIL kibbutz in the South near Ashkelon, 1948
BEROSH moshav on Gaza-Beersheba highway, 1952
BERURIM farm in the South near Gedera, 1950
BETHLEHEM Christian Arab town south of Jerusalem
BEZET moshav in Galilee east of Nahariya, 1949
BIAR Moslem village in 'Iron Valley
BIDDU Arab village north of Jerusalem
B'INA Moslem village in Upper Galilee
BINYAMINA village on Ḥadera-Haifa highway, 1922
BIRANIT settlement in Upper Galilee, 1964
BIREH 71 Arab town adjacent to Ramallah
BIR-ELMAKSUR Beduin village in Lower Galilee
BIR-ESSIKKA Moslem village in Sharon Valley
BIRIYA moshav in Upper Galilee near Ẓefat, 1945
BITAN-AHARON moshav in Sharon near Netanya, 1936
BITḤA moshav on Beersheba-Gaza highway, 1950
BIẒARON moshav in the south near Gedera, 1935
BOẒRA moshav in Sharon near Raanana, 1946
BU'EINA Moslem village in Galilee near Nazareth
BUKEIA Arabic name of Peki'in See: Peki'in
BURGETA moshav in Sharon near Netanya, 1949
BUSTAN-HAGILIL moshav on 'Akko-Nahariya highway, 1948

CAESAREA on Mediterranean coast
CANA Arab village See: Kefar-Kanna
CAPERNAUM ruins on Lake Kinneret
CARMIEL townlet on the 'Akko-Ẓefat highway, 1965
CASTEL west of Jerusalem. See: Ma'oz-Ẓiyon

DABURIYA Moslem village at foot of Mount Tabor
DAFNA kibbutz in Ḥula Valley, 1939
DAHARIYE Arab village on Hebron-Beersheba highway
DAHI Moslem village east of 'Afula
DALIYA kibbutz in Hills of Menashé, 1939
DALIYAT ELKARMEL Druze village on Mt. Carmel
DALTON moshav in Upper Galilee, 1953
DAMUN prison on Mount Carmel
DAN kibbutz in northern Ḥula Valley, 1939
DANUN Moslem village in Western Galilee
DAVERAT kibbutz in Jezreel Valley, 1947
DEGANIA ALEF kibbutz in Jordan Valley, 1909
DEGANIA BET kibbutz in Jordan Valley, 1920
DEIR-ELASAD Moslem village in Galilee
DEIR-HANNA Christian village in Galilee
DEVIRA kibbutz in the South, 1951
DEVORA moshav in Jezreel Valley, 1956
DIMONA town in Negev near Beersheba, 1955
DISHON moshav in Upper Galilee, 1953
DOR moshav on Mediterranean coast, 1949
DOROT kibbutz in the south near Gaza, 1941
DOSHEN farm in Jordan Valley, 1955
DOVEV moshav in Galilee north of Ẓefat, 1963
DURA Arab village in Hebron Hills

EF'AL settlement near Tel-Aviv, 1946
'EILABUN Christian village in Galilee, near Tiberias
EILAT southernmost town in Israel, 1950
EILON kibbutz in Western Galilee, 1938
EILOT kibbutz near Eilat on Beersheba highway, 1962
'EINAT kibbutz east of Petaḥ-Tikva, 1953
'EIN-AYALA moshav on Haifa-Ḥadera highway, 1950
'EIN-BOKEK hostel on the Dead Sea, 1958
'EIN-CARMEL kibbutz on Carmel coast, 1947
'EIN-DOR kibbutz in Jezreel Valley, 1948
'EIN-ELASAD Druze village in Upper Galilee
'EIN-ESSAHLA Moslem village in 'Iron Valley
'EIN-GEDI kibbutz on shore of the Dead Sea, 1952
'EIN-GEV kibbutz on the shore of Kinneret, 1937
'EIN-HA'EMEK moshav in Hills of Menashé, 1944
'EIN-HAḤORESH kibbutz in Ḥefer Valley, 1931
'EIN-HAMIFRAẒ kibbutz in Zevulun Valley, 1938
'EIN-HANAẒIV kibbutz in Beit-Shean Valley, 1946
'EIN-ḤAROD kibbutz in Jezreel Valley, 1921
'EIN-HASHELOSHA kibbutz in Negev near Gaza Strip, 1950
'EIN-HASHOFET kibbutz in Hills of Menashé, 1937
'EIN-HATEKHLET moshav north of Netanya, 1939
'EIN-HOD artists' village on Carmel, 1953
'EIN-IBRAHIM Moslem village in 'Iron Valley
'EIN-'IRON moshav east of Ḥadera, 1934
'EIN-KAREM urban suburb west of Jerusalem, 1948
'EIN-MAHIL Moslem village in Lower Galilee
'EIN-RAFA Moslem village west of Jerusalem
'EIN-SARID moshav in Sharon near Tel-Mond, 1952
'EIN-SHEMER kibbutz in Sharon east of Ḥadera, 1933
'EIN-VERED moshav in Sharon Valley, 1930
'EIN-YA'AKOV moshav in Western Galilee, 1950
'EIN-YAHAV moshav on Sodom-Eilat highway, 1950
'EIN-ZEITIM settlement in Upper Galilee, 1891, 1932
'EIN-ẒURIM kibbutz in the South near Ashkelon, 1949
EITAN moshav in the South near Kiryat-Gat, 1955
EITANIM sanatorium in Judean Mountains, 1952
EIYAL kibbutz in Sharon east of Kefar-Sava, 1949
'EKRON village in the South near Reḥovot, 1949
EL'AL Arab village on Golan Heights
EL-'ARISH Arab town and capital of Sinai
ELIFELET moshav in Galilee near Rosh-Pinna, 1949
ELISHAM'A moshav in the Sharon Valley, 1951
ELKOSH moshav in Upper Galilee, 1949

ELYAKHIN moshav in Ḥefer Valley, 1950
ELYAKIM moshav in Samaria near Yokneam, 1949
ELYASHIV moshav in Ḥefer Valley, 1933
EMUNIM moshav in the South near Ashdod, 1950
EREZ kibbutz in the South near Gaza Strip, 1949
ESHBOL moshav in the South, 1954
ESHEL-HANASI agricultural school in Negev, 1952
ESHKOLOT farm in the South near Ashkelon, 1951
ESHTAOL moshav in Judean Mountains, 1949
ET-TUR point in Sinai desert
EVEN-MENAḤEM moshav in Upper Galilee, 1960
EVEN-SAPIR moshav west of Jerusalem, 1950
EVEN-SHEMUEL settlement in the South, 1956
EVEN-YEHUDA village in the Sharon, 1932
EVEN-YIẒḤAK kibbutz in Hills of Menashé, 1945
'EVRON kibbutz in Western Galilee, 1945

FASUTA Christian village in Galilee
FIK Arab village on Golan Heights
FUREIDIS Moslem village on Haifa-Ḥadera highway

GA'ASH kibbutz on Tel-Aviv-Netanya highway, 1951
GADISH moshav in Jezreel Valley near 'Afula, 1956
GADOT kibbutz in Upper Galilee, 1949
GAL'ED kibbutz in the Hills of Menashé, 1945
GALLIM agricultural school near Haifa, 1952
GALON kibbutz in the South near Kiryat-Gat, 1946
GAN-HADAROM moshav near Ashdod, 1951
GAN-ḤAYIM moshav in Sharon Valley, 1935
GANNE'AM suburb of Hod-Hasharon, 1934
GANNEI-TIKVA moshav east of Tel-Aviv, 1953
GANNEI-YEHUDA moshav east of Tel-Aviv, 1950
GANNEI-YOḤANAN moshav near Reḥovot, 1949
GANNEI-YONA See: Gannei Yoḥanan
GANNEI-ẒEVI suburb of Hod-Hasharon, 1956
GANNOT moshav near Tel-Aviv, 1950
GANNOT-HADAR moshav east of Netanya, 1954
GAN-SHELOMO kibbutz near Reḥovot, 1927
GAN-SHEMUEL kibbutz in Sharon near Ḥadera, 1896
GAN-SHOMRON moshav in northern Sharon, 1934
GAN-SOREK moshav near Rishon-Lezion, 1950
GAN-YAVNÉ village in the South near Ashdod, 1931
GAN-YOSHIYA moshav in northern Sharon, 1949
GAT kibbutz in the South near Kiryat-Gat, 1942
GAT-RIMON suburb of Petaḥ-Tikva, 1926
GATON kibbutz in Galilee east of Nahariya, 1948
GAZA Arab town on the Mediterranean coast (the Gaza Strip)
GAZIT kibbutz in Lower Galilee, 1948
GEA moshav in the South near Ashkelon, 1949
GEALIYA moshav west of Reḥovot near Yavné, 1948
GEDERA settlement in the South, 1884
GEFEN moshav in the South near Beit-Shemesh, 1955
GELIL-YAM kibbutz in Sharon near Herẓliya, 1943
GEROFIT settlement in the 'Arava near Eilat, 1963
GESHER kibbutz in Jordan Valley, 1939
GESHER-HAZIV kibbutz near Nahariya, 1949
GEULEI-TEIMAN moshav in Ḥefer Valley, 1947
GEULIM moshav in Sharon near Netanya, 1936
GEV'A kibbutz in Jezreel Valley, 1921
GEV'A-CARMEL moshav on Carmel coast, 1949
GEVAR'AM kibbutz in the South near Ashkelon, 1942
GEVAT kibbutz in Jezreel Valley, 1926
GEVIM kibbutz in the South near Gaza, 1947
GEVULOT kibbutz in western Negev, 1943
GEZER kibbutz in Judean Mountains near Ramla, 1945
GIBETON moshav in the South near Reḥovot, 1933
GID'ONA moshav in Jezreel Valley, 1949
GIL'AM suburb of Kiryat-Ata, 1950
GIL-'AMAL suburb of Magdiel in Sharon, 1950
GILAT moshav in the Negev near Beersheba, 1949
GIMZO moshav east of Lod, 1950
GINNATON moshav east of Lod, 1949
GINNEGAR kibbutz in Jezreel Valley, 1922
GINNOSAR kibbutz in Galilee on Lake Kinneret, 1937
GIV'AT-'ADA village in Samaria, 1903
GIV'AT-BRENNER kibbutz near Reḥovot, 1928
GIV'AT-HASHELOSHA kibbutz near Petaḥ-Tikva, 1925
GIVAT-ḤAVIVA educational center near Ḥadera, 1949
GIV'AT-ḤAYIM kibbutz in Ḥefer Valley, 1932
GIV'AT-ḤEN moshav in Sharon near Raanana, 1933
GIV'AT-KOAḤ moshav east of Lod, 1950
GIV'AT-MIKHAEL suburb of Nes-Ẓiyona, 1935
GIV'AT-NILI moshav in the Hills of Menashé, 1953
GIV'AT-'OZ kibbutz in Jezreel Valley, 1949
GIV'AT-RAMBAM suburb of Giv'atayim, 1935
GIV'AT-SHAPIRA moshav in Ḥefer Valley, 1958
GIV'AT-SHEMUEL townlet east of Tel-Aviv, 1945
GIV'AT WASHINGTON children's village near Yavné, 1950
GIV'AT YE'ARIM moshav west of Jerusalem, 1950
GIV'AT YESH'AYAHU moshav south of Beit-Shemesh, 1958
GIV'ATAYIM town east of Tel-Aviv, 1922
GIV'ATI moshav in the South near Ashkelon, 1950
GIV'OLIM moshav in Negev on Beersheba-Gaza highway, 1952
GIV'OT ZAID suburb of Kiryat-Tivon, 1943
GONEN kibbutz in Ḥula Valley, 1951
GOREN moshav in western Galilee, 1950
GUSH-ḤALAV (JISH) Christian village in northern Galilee

HABONIM moshav on Carmel coast, 1949
HADARIYA farm in the South near Ashkelon, 1950
HADAR-'AM moshav in Ḥefer Valley, 1933
HADAR-RAMATAYIM settlement. See: Hod-Hasharon, 1925
HADASSIM agricultural school near Netanya, 1947
ḤADERA town on Tel-Aviv-Haifa highway, 1890
ḤADID moshav east of Lod, 1949
ḤAFEẒ-ḤAYIM kibbutz in the South near Gedera, 1944
ḤAGOR moshav east of Rosh-Ha'ayin, 1959
HAGOSHERIM kibbutz in Ḥula Valley, 1948
HAḤOTERIM kibbutz on Carmel coast, 1948
HAIFA biggest town in north on the Mediterranean
HAKHLIL moshav in the Judean Mountains
HAM'APIL kibbutz in Ḥefer Valley, 1945
ḤAMADYA kibbutz in Beit-Shean Valley, 1942
ḤANITA kibbutz in Western Galilee, 1938
ḤANNIEL moshav in Sharon near Netanya, 1950
HA'OGEN kibbutz in Ḥefer Valley, 1947
HAON kibbutz on Lake Kinneret, 1949
HAREL kibbutz in Judean Mountains, 1948
HARTUV settlement in Judean Mountains, 1895
ḤARUẒIM moshav in southern Sharon, 1951
HASOLELIM kibbutz in Galilee near Nazareth, 1949
ḤAVAT-HASHOMER children's village in Galilee, 1956
ḤAVAẒELET suburb of Reḥovot on Gedera highway, 1939
ḤAVAẒELET-HASHARON north of Netanya, 1934
HAYOGEV moshav in Jezreel Valley, 1949
ḤAẒAV moshav in the South near Gedera, 1949
ḤAẒERIM kibbutz in the Negev near Beersheba, 1946
ḤAẒEVA moshav in the 'Arava near the Dead Sea, 1965
ḤAẒOR settlement in Galilee near Rosh-Pinna, 1953
ḤAẒOR-ASHDOD kibbutz in the South near Ashdod, 1946
HAZORE'A kibbutz in Jezreel Valley, 1936
HAZOR'IM moshav in Lower Galilee, 1939
HEBRON Arab town in Hebron Hills
ḤEFẒI-BAH (1) kibbutz in Jezreel Valley, 1922
ḤEFẒI-BAH (2) suburb of Ḥadera in Sharon, 1910
ḤELEẒ moshav in the South near Ashkelon, 1950
ḤEMED moshav in the vicinity of Tel-Aviv, 1950
ḤEREV-LAET moshav south of Ḥadera, 1947
ḤERUT moshav in Sharon near Tel-Mond, 1930
HERẒLIYA town in Sharon, 1924
ḤIBAT-ẒIYON moshav in Ḥefer Valley, 1934
HODAYOT school near Nazareth, 1952
HOD-HASHARON town in southern Sharon, 1945
HODIYA moshav in the South, 1949
ḤOFIT settlement Netanya-Ḥadera highway, 1955
ḤOGLA moshav in Ḥefer Valley, 1933
ḤOLON town near Tel-Aviv-Yafo, 1933
ḤORESHIM kibbutz east of Rosh-Ha'ayin, 1955
ḤOSSEN moshav in Upper Galilee, 1949
ḤOTER suburb of Beer-Ya'akov, near Ramla, 1949
ḤUKOK kibbutz in Galilee near Tiberias, 1945
ḤULATA kibbutz south of Ḥula Valley, 1936
ḤULDA kibbutz east of Reḥovot, 1907
HURFEISH Druze village in Upper Galilee

'IBILIN Moslem village in western Galilee
IBIM farm in the South, 1953
IBTIN Moslem hamlet in Samarian Hills
IKSAL Moslem village in Jezreel Valley
ILANIYA settlement in Lower Galilee, 1902
ILANOT forest nursery in Sharon, 1948
'ILUT Moslem village in Galilee near Nazareth
'ISFIYA Druze-Christian village on Mt. Carmel
ISMAILIA town on Suez Canal

JAFFA English version of the Hebrew Yafo
JALJULYA Moslem village near Kefar-Sava
JAT (1) Moslem village in Sharon
JAT (2) Druze village in Galilee
JENIN Arab town on border of Jezreel Valley and Samaria
JERICO Arab town in southern Jordan Valley
JERUSALEM in the Judean Mountains, capital of Israel
JISH See: Gush Ḥalav
JISR EZZARKA Moslem village near Binyamina
JUDEIDA Moslem village in Galilee
JULIS Druze village in Western Galilee
JURDEIH Moslem village in Upper Galilee

KABABIR Moslem (Ahmadiya) village in Haifa
KABRI kibbutz in Western Galilee near Nahariya, 1949
KABUL Moslem village in Galilee near 'Akko
KADIMA townlet in Sharon near Netanya, 1933
KADOORIE agricultural school in Galilee, 1933
KAFER-BARA Moslem village east of Petaḥ-Tikva
KAFER-KAMA Moslem (Circassian) village in Galilee, 1880
KAFER-KANNA (CANA) See Kefar Kanna
KAFER-KAR'I Moslem village in Hills of Menashé
KAFER-KASIM Moslem village east of Rosh-Ha'ayin
KAFER-MANDA Moslem village in Galilee near Nazareth
KEFAR-MISR Moslem village in Galilee near 'Afula
KAFER-SUME'I Druze village in Western Galilee
KAFER-YASIF Christian-Druze village in Galilee

KALANDIA Jerusalem airport
KALANSUWA Moslem village in Sharon Valley
KALMANIYA farm in the Sharon Valley, 1927
KANNOT agricultural school near Gedera, 1952
KANTARA town on Suez Canal
KAREI-DESHE farm in Galilee near Tiberias, 1955
KAREI-NA'AMAN farm in Zevulun Valley near 'Akko, 1955
KARKUR village in Sharon near Ḥadera, 1926
KARMIYA kibbutz south of Ashkelon, 1950
KARMON formerly a settlement near Ashkelon, 1952
KAUKAB Moslem village in Lower Galilee
KEDMA kibbutz in the South near Kiryat-Malakhi, 1939
KEFAR-AHARON village on Nes-Ẓioniya highway, 1926
KEFAR-AḤIM moshav near Kiryat-Malakhi, 1949
KEFAR-ATA town near Haifa, 1926
KEFAR-AVIV moshav in the South near Ashdod, 1950
KEFAR-'AZA kibbutz near Gaza Strip, 1951
KEFAR-AZAR moshav east of Tel-Aviv, 1932
KEFAR-BARUCH moshav in Jezreel Valley, 1926
KEFAR-BATYA children's village in Ra'anana, 1949
KEFAR-BIALIK moshav in Zevulun valley, 1934
KEFAR-BILU moshav near Reḥovot, 1932
KEFAR-BIN-NUN moshav east of Ramla, 1952
KEFAR-BLUM kibbutz in Ḥula Valley, 1943
KEFAR-BRANDEIS suburb of Ḥadera, 1928
KEFAR-DANIEL moshav east of Lod, 1949
KEFAR-'EKRON settlement near Reḥovot, 1950
KEFAR-'EẒIYON settlement in the vicinity of Hebron, 1946, 1967
KEFAR GALIM agricultural school near Haifa, 1952
KEFAR-GANNIM village east of Tel-Aviv, 1932
KEFAR-GAVIROL moshav west of Reḥovot, 1950
KEFAR-GID'ON moshav in Jezreel Valley, 1924
KEFAR-GIL'ADI kibbutz in Upper Galilee, 1916
KEFAR-GLICKSON kibbutz in the Hills of Menashé, 1939
KEFAR-ḤABAD moshav in the vicinity of Tel-Aviv, 1949
KEFAR-HABAPTISTIM see: Baptists' village, 1960
KEFAR-HAḤORESH kibbutz in Galilee near Nazareth, 1933
KEFAR-HAMACCABI kibbutz in Zevulun Valley, 1936
KEFAR-MAKABIYA hostel near Tel-Aviv, 1958
KEFAR-HANAGID moshav near Yavné, 1949
KEFAR-HANASI kibbutz in Upper Galilee, 1948
KEFAR-HANO'AR HADATI children's village, 1937
KEFAR-ḤARIF moshav near Kiryat-Malakhi, 1956
KEFAR-HAROE moshav in Ḥefer Valley, 1933
KEFAR-ḤASIDIM moshav near Haifa, 1924
KEFAR-HAYAROK agricultural school near Tel-Aviv, 1950
KEFAR-HAYEOR another name of Kefar-Aviv, 1954
KEFAR-ḤAYIM moshav in Ḥefer Valley, 1933
KEFAR-HESS moshav in the Sharon, 1933
KEFAR-HITTIM moshav near Tiberias, 1914, 1924, 1932
KEFAR-KANNA (CANA) Arab village near Nazareth
KEFAR-KISH moshav in Lower Galilee, 1946
KEFAR-MAIMON moshav in Negev near Gaza, 1958
KEFAR-MALAL moshav in southern Sharon, 1914, 1922
KEFAR-MASARYK kibbutz in Zevulun Valley, 1940
KEFAR-MENAḤEM kibbutz in the South, 1937
KEFAR-MESUBIM moshav east of Tel-Aviv, 1951
KEFAR-MONASH moshav in Ḥefer Valley, 1946
KEFAR-MORDECHAI moshav near Gedera, 1950
KEFAR-NAḤMAN suburb of Ra'anana, 1950
KEFAR-NAHUM (CAPERNAUM) Ruins on Lake Kinneret
KEFAR-NETER moshav in Sharon near Netanya, 1939
KEFAR-PHILADELPHIA children's village near 'Akko, 1960
KEFAR-PINES moshav east of Ḥadera, 1933
KEFAR-RUPPIN kibbutz in Beit-Shean Valley, 1938
KEFAR-ROSH HANIKRA kibbutz near Nahariya, 1949
KEFAR-SAVA town in southern Sharon, 1903
KEFAR-SHAMMAI moshav in Upper Galilee, 1949
KEFAR-SHARET settlement in Ḥula Valley, 1967
KEFAR-SHAUL village in western Jerusalem, 1949
KEFAR-SHEMARYAHU moshav near Herẓliya, 1937
KEFAR-SHEMUEL moshav east of Ramla, 1950
KEFAR-SILVER agricultural school near Ashkelon, 1951
KEFAR-SIRKIN moshav near Petaḥ-Tikva, 1936
KEFAR-SZOLD kibbutz in Ḥula Valley, 1942
KEFAR-TAVOR village in Lower Galilee, 1901
KEFAR-TRUMAN moshav east of Lod airport, 1949
KEFAR-URIYA moshav in Judean Mountains, 1912, 1944
KEFAR-VITKIN moshav in Ḥefer Valley, 1933
KEFAR-WARBERG moshav in the South, 1939
KEFAR-YABETZ moshav in the Sharon, 1932
KEFAR-YEDIDIA moshav in Ḥefer Valley, 1935
KEFAR-YEḤEẒKEL moshav in Jezreel Valley, 1921
KEFAR-YEHOSHU'A moshav in Jezreel Valley, 1927
KEFAR-YOḤANNA youth village in Beer-Ya'akov, 1950
KEFAR-YONA village in Sharon near Netanya, 1932
KEFAR-ZEITIM moshav in Lower Galilee, 1950
KEFAR-ZEKHARYA moshav south of Beit-Shemesh, 1950
KEFAR-ẒEVI youth village near Haifa, 1952
KEFAR-ZIV moshav in Sharon Valley, 1950
KELAHIM moshav in Negev near Beersheba, 1954
KEREM BEN-ZIMRA moshav in Upper Galilee, 1949
KEREM-MAHARAL moshav on Mt. Carmel, 1949
KEREM-SHALOM kibbutz near the Gaza Strip, 1956
KESALON moshav west of Jerusalem, 1950
KEVUẒAT-SHILLER kibbutz near Reḥovot, 1927
KEVUẒAT-YAVNÉ kibbutz in the South, 1942
KEẒIYOT kibbutz in Negev near Niẓana, 1953
KHAN YUNIS Arab town in the Gaza Strip
KHISFIN Arab village on Golan Heights

KIDRON moshav in the South near Gedera, 1949
KINNERET (1) moshav on Lake Kinneret, 1909
KINNERET (2) kibbutz on Lake Kinneret, 1908
KIRYAT-'ANAVIM kibbutz west of Jerusalem, 1920
KIRYAT-ATA townlet near Haifa, 1966
KIRYAT BIALIK suburb in Zevulun Valley, 1934
KIRYAT-GAT town in the South, 1956
KIRYAT-HADASSAH medical center west of Jerusalem, 1960
KIRYAT-ḤAROSHET settlement near Haifa, 1935
KIRYAT-ḤAYIM urban suburb near Haifa, 1933
KIRYAT-MALAKHI townlet in the South, 1951
KIRYAT-MOTZKIN urban suburb near Haifa, 1935
KIRYAT-ONO settlement near Tel-Aviv, 1939
KIRYAT-SHAUL settlement near Tel-Aviv, 1924
KIRYAT-SHEMONA townlet in Upper Galilee, 1949
KIRYAT-TIVON townlet near Haifa, 1937
KIRYAT-YAM urban suburb near Haifa, 1946
KIRYAT YE'ARIM children's village near Jerusalem, 1952
KISRA Druze village in Western Galilee
KISUFIM kibbutz near the Gaza Strip, 1950
KOKHAV moshav in the South, 1950
KOMEMIYUT moshav in the South, 1950
KUNEITRA Arab town on Golan Heights on Damascus highway

LACHISH moshav in Judean Mountains, 1955
LAHAV kibbutz in the South, 1952
LAHAVOT-HABASHAN kibbutz in Ḥula Valley, 1945
LAHAVOT-ḤAVIVA kibbutz in the Sharon, 1949
LAVI kibbutz in Lower Galilee near Tiberias, 1949
LIMAN moshav in Western Galilee, 1949
LI-ON settlement in Adullam region, 1961
LOD (LYDDA) new town near Ramla, 1949
LOD (LYDDA) Israel's international airport, 1942
LOḤAMEI-HAGETAOT kibbutz near Nahariya, 1949
LUBBAN SHARQUIE Arab village on Jerusalem-Shechem highway
LUZIT moshav in the Judean Mountains, 1955

MA'ABAROT kibbutz in Ḥefer Valley, 1933
MA'AGAN kibbutz in Jordan Valley, 1949
MA'AGAN-MICHAEL kibbutz near Haifa, 1949
MA'ALÉ-HAGILBOA settlement near Beit-Shean, 1962
MA'ALÉ-HAḤAMISHA kibbutz near Jerusalem, 1938
MA'ALOT townlet in Western Galilee, 1957
MA'ANIT kibbutz in the Hills of Menashé, 1942
MA'AS moshav near Petaḥ-Tikva, 1934
MA'ASIYA prison between Ramla and Lod, 1954
MA'AYAN-BARUCH kibbutz in Ḥula Valley, 1947
MA'AYAN-ẒEVI kibbutz near Zichron-Ya'akov, 1938
MABU'IM settlement in Negev, 1958
MAGAL kibbutz east of Netanya, 1953
MAGDIEL suburb of Hod-Hasharon, 1924
MAGEN kibbutz near the Gaza Strip, 1949
MAGHAR Druze village in Galilee near Tiberias
MAGSHIMIM moshav near Petaḥ-Tikva, 1949
MAḤANAYIM kibbutz in Upper Galilee, 1898, 1949
MAḤANÉ-ISRAEL formerly immigrant camp near Lod, 1949
MAḤSEYA moshav in Judean Mountains, 1950
MAJDAL-SHAMS Druze village on slopes of Mount Hermon
MAJD ELKURUM Moslem village in Galilee near 'Akko
MAKR Moslem village in Galilee near 'Akko
MAKURA Moslem hamlet on Mount Carmel
MALKIYA kibbutz in Upper Galilee, 1949
MANZURA Circassian village on Golan Heights
MAOR moshav in the Sharon Valley, 1953
MA'OZ-ḤAYIM kibbutz in Beit-Shean Valley, 1937
MA'OZ-ẒIYON settlement near Jerusalem, 1951
MARGALIYOT moshav in Upper Galilee, 1955
MAR'IT farm in the South near Dorot, 1957
MARJA Moslem village east of Netanya
MASHABEI-SADÉ kibbutz in Negev near Beersheba, 1950
MASH-HAD Moslem village in Galilee near Nazareth
MASH'EN moshav in the South near Ashkelon, 1950
MASHMIYA-SHALOM settlement in the South, 1949
MASLUL moshav in the Negev near Beersheba, 1950
MASMIYA Arabic name of Mashmiya-Shalom
MASADA kibbutz in Jordan Valley, 1937
MASSUOT-YIẒḤAK moshav in the South near Ashkelon, 1949
MATTA moshav in Judean Mountains, 1950
MATTE-'OZ settlement in Upper Galilee, 1953, 1967
MAZKERET-BATYA settlement near Reḥovot, 1883
MAẒLIAḤ moshav near Ramla-Jerusalem highway, 1950
MAZOR moshav east of Lod airport, 1949
MAZRA'A Moslem village in Western Galilee near Nahariya
MAẒUVA kibbutz in Western Galilee, 1940
MEFALSIM kibbutz in the South near the Gaza Strip, 1949
MEGADIM moshav on Carmel coast near Haifa, 1949
MEGED suburb of Pardes-Ḥanna
MEGIDDO kibbutz near historical Megiddo, 1949
MEI-'AMI settlement near Ḥadera-'Afula highway, 1963
MEIR-SHEFAYA children's village in Mt. Carmel, 1923
MEIRON moshav in Upper Galilee near Ẓefat, 1949
MEISAR Moslem village east of Baka Elgharbiya
MEISHAR moshav in the South near Gedera, 1950
MEITAV moshav in Jezreel Valley, 1954
MELEA moshav in Jezreel Valley, 1956
MELILOT moshav on Gaza-Beersheba highway, 1953
MENAḤAMIYA village in Jordan Valley, 1902
MENARA kibbutz in Upper Galilee, 1943
MENUḤA moshav in the South, 1953
ME'ONA moshav in Upper Galilee, 1949
MERḤAVYA (1) kibbutz in Jezreel Valley, 1911, 1929
MERḤAVYA (2) moshav in Jezreel Valley, 1912
MESILAT-ẒIYON moshav west of Jerusalem, 1950
MESILOT kibbutz in Beit-Shean Valley, 1938
METULA northernmost settlement, 1896
MEVASERET-YERUSHALAYIM village near Jerusalem, 1951
MEVASERET-ẒIYON village near Jerusalem, 1960
MEVO-BEITAR kibbutz in Judean Mountains, 1950
MEVO-MODI'IM settlement east of Lod, 1965
MEVU'OT-YAM fishery school near Netanya, 1955
MEZER kibbutz in Samarian Hills, 1953
MIDRACH-'OZ moshav in Jezreel Valley, 1952
MIDRASHA RUPPIN agricultural school in Ḥefer Valley, 1948
MIGDA farm in the Negev near Beersheba, 1957
MIGDAL village in Galilee on Lake Kinneret, 1910
MIGDAL-ASHKELON suburb of Ashkelon, 1948
MIGDAL-HA'EMEK town near Nazareth, 1953
MI'ILYA Christian village in Upper Galilee
MICHMORET moshav near Netanya, 1945
MIKVE-YISRAEL agricultural school near Tel-Aviv, 1870
MISGAV-'AM kibbutz in Upper Galilee, 1945
MISGAV-DOV moshav in the South near Gedera, 1950
MISHMAR-AYALON moshav near Ramla, 1949
MISHMAR-DAVID kibbutz on Jerusalem highway, 1948
MISHMAR-HA'EMEK kibbutz in Jezreel Valley, 1926
MISHMAR-HANEGEV kibbutz in the Negev, 1947
MISHMAR-HASHARON kibbutz in Ḥefer Valley, 1933
MISHMAR-HASHELOSHA moshav in Lower Galilee, 1937
MISHMAR-HASHIV'A moshav near Tel-Aviv, 1950
MISHMAR-HAYARDEN moshav in Upper Galilee, 1890, 1949
MISHMAROT kibbutz in northern Sharon, 1933
MISHMERET moshav in Sharon near Tel-Mond, 1947
MIVḤOR farm in the South near Kiryat-Gat, 1955
MIVTAḤIM moshav in Negev near the Gaza Strip, 1950
MIẒPA village in Galilee near Tiberias, 1908
MIẒPAK station on Gaza-Kantara railroad
MIẒPÉ-RAMON settlement on Beersheba-Eilat highway, 1954
MIZR'A kibbutz in Jezreel Valley near Nazareth, 1923
MOLEDET moshav in Lower Galilee, 1937
MOẒA settlement west of Jerusalem, 1859
MOẒA-'ILLIT settlement west of Jerusalem, 1933
MU'AWIYA Moslem village near 'Iron Valley
MUKEIBILA Moslem village in Jezreel Valley
MULLAKA Moslem village in 'Iron Valley
MURTAFI'A Moslem hamlet on 'Afula-Ḥadera highway
MUSMUS Moslem village on 'Afula-Ḥadera highway

NA'AMANIM settlement in the southern Sharon, 1953
NA'AN kibbutz east of Reḥovot, 1930
NABLUS see Shechem
NAHALA moshav in the South, 1953
NAHALAL moshav in Jezreel Valley, 1921
NAḤALAT-JABOTINSKI suburb of Binyamina, 1946
NAḤALAT-YEHUDA moshav near Rishon-Leẓiyon, 1921
NAḤALAYIM moshav near Petaḥ-Tikva, 1948
NAḤAL-'OZ kibbutz near Gaza Strip, 1951
NAḤAM moshav near Jerusalem, 1950
NAHARIYA town on the Mediterranean coast, 1934
NAHF Moslem village in Upper Galilee.
NAḤLAOT farm in Jezreel Valley, 1954
NAḤSHOLIM kibbutz on the Mediterranean coast, 1948
NAḤSHON kibbutz in Judah near Jerusalem, 1950
NAḤSHONIM kibbutz near Petaḥ-Tikva, 1949
NASRA Arabic name of Nazareth
NA'URA Moslem village east of 'Afula
NAZARETH town in Lower Galilee
NEGBA kibbutz in the South near Ashkelon, 1933
NEḤALIM moshav near Petaḥ-Tikva, 1948
NEḤORA settlement near Ashkelon, 1956
NEḤUSHA kibbutz in Judean Mountains, 1955
NEIM (NA'IM) Moslem village in Jezreel Valley
NEOT-HAKIKAR settlement near Sodom, 1961
NEOT-MORDECHAI kibbutz in the Ḥula Valley, 1946
NES-HARIM moshav in the Judean Mountains, 1950
NES-ẒIYONA town on Rishon-Leẓiyon-Reḥovot highway, 1882
NESHER urban settlement near Haifa, 1925
NETA farm in the South, 1955
NETA'IM moshav near Rishon-Leẓiyon, 1932
NETANYA town on Tel-Aviv—Haifa highway, 1929
NETIVA moshav in the South, 1956
NETIV-HALAMED-HÉ kibbutz near Jerusalem, 1949
NETIV-HASHAYARA moshav near Nahariya, 1950
NETIVOT settlement near Gaza Strip, 1956
NEURIM children's village near Netanya, 1953
NEVATIM moshav near Beersheba, 1946
NEVÉ-'AMIEL children's village near Haifa, 1948
NEVE-AVOT old-age home in Pardes-Hanna, 1948
NEVÉ-EFRAIM settlement near Tel-Aviv, 1953
NEVÉ-EITAN kibbutz in Beit-Shean Valley, 1938
NEVÉ-HADASSA children's village near Ra'anana, 1949
NEVÉ-ILAN settlement near Jerusalem, 1947
NEVÉ-MICHAEL settlement in the 'Adullam region, 1958
NEVÉ-MIDBAR road house on Beersheba—Eilat highway, 1960
NEVÉ-MIVTAḤ moshav in the South, near Gedera, 1950
NEVÉ-NEEMAN suburb in Hod-Hasharon, 1950
NEVÉ-TIRẒA women's prison near Netanya, 1950
NEVÉ-UR kibbutz in Jordan Valley, 1949
NEVÉ-YA'AR agricultural station near Haifa, 1954
NEVÉ-YAM kibbutz on the Mediterranean coast, 1939
NEVÉ-YAMIN moshav in Sharon, near Kefar-Sava, 1949
NEVÉ-YAROK moshav in southern Sharon, 1951
NEVÉ-ZOHAR hostel on the Dead Sea, 1962
NEẒER-SERENI kibbutz near Ramla, 1948
NIRA moshav east of Netanya, 1941
NIR-'AKIVA moshav in the Northern Negev, 1953
NIR'AM kibbutz in the South near Gaza, 1943
NIR-BANIM moshav in the South, 1954
NIR-DAVID kibbutz in Beit-Shean Valley, 1936
NIR-ELIYAHU kibbutz in Sharon near Kefar-Sava, 1950
NIR-'EẒIYON kibbutz on Mount Carmel, 1950
NIR-GALIM moshav in the South near Ashdod, 1949
NIR-ḤEN moshav in the South near Ashkelon, 1955
NIRIM kibbutz near the Gaza Strip, 1946
NIR-ISRAEL moshav in the South near Ashkelon, 1949
NIR-MOSHÉ moshav in Negev near Kiryat-Gat, 1953
NIR-'OZ kibbutz near the Gaza Strip, 1955
NIR-YAFE moshav in Jezreel Valley, 1956
NIR-YIẒḤAK kibbutz near the Gaza Strip, 1949
NIR-ẒEVI moshav near Ramla, 1954
NIVA agricultural farm in the South, 1954
NIẒANEI-'OZ moshav east of Netanya, 1951
NIẒANIM (1) kibbutz in the South near Ashkelon, 1943
NIẒANIM (2) children's village near Ashkelon, 1949
NO'AM moshav in the South near Kiryat-Gat, 1955
NOFECH moshav near Lod airport, 1949
NOF-YAM suburb of Herẓliya, 1949
NOGAH moshav in Lachish region near Ashkelon, 1955
NORDIYA moshav in Sharon near Netanya, 1948
NOTERA formerly settlement in the Ḥula Valley, 1958
NURIT settlement on Mount Gilboa, 1950

OFAKIM town in Negev, west of Beersheba, 1955
'OFER moshav on Mount Carmel, 1950
OHALO cultural center on Lake Kinneret, 1951
'OLESH moshav in Sharon east of Netanya, 1949
'OMEN settlement near 'Afula, 1958
'OMER moshav east of Beersheba, 1949
OMEẒ moshav in central Sharon, 1949
ORA moshav west of Jerusalem, 1950
OR-'AKIVA moshav near Caesarea, 1951
ORANIM teachers' training college near Haifa, 1951
OR-HANER kibbutz in the South near Ashkelon, 1957
ORON phosphate plant in Negev, 1952
OROT moshav in the South near Beer-Toviya, 1952
OR-YEHUDA town near Tel-Aviv, 1950
'OZEM moshav in Lachish region, near Ashkelon, 1950

PA'AMEI-TASHAZ moshav near Beersheba, 1953
PALMAḤIM kibbutz on the sea, near Rishon-Leẓiyon, 1949
PARDES-ḤANNA village in Sharon, 1929
PARDESIYA moshav in the Sharon, 1942
PAROD kibbutz in Upper Galilee, 1942
PATISH moshav west of Beersheba, 1950
PEDAYA moshav near Ramla on Jerusalem highway, 1951
PEDUYIM moshav west of Beersheba, 1950
PEKI'IN Druze-Christian-Jewish village in Galilee
PEKI'IN-ḤADASHA moshav in Upper Galilee, 1955
PERAZON moshav in Jezreel Valley, 1953
PETAḤ-TIKVA town east of Tel-Aviv, 1878
PETAḤYA moshav near Ramla on Jerusalem highway, 1951
PORAT moshav in central Sharon, 1950
PORIYA (1) moshav in Lower Galilee, 1950
PORIYA (2) hospital in Lower Galilee, 1960
PORIYA (3) hostel in Lower Galilee near Tiberias, 1958

RA'ANANA town in southern Sharon, 1921
RAFIAḤ Arab town in the Gaza Strip
RAFID Arab village on Golan Heights
RAMA Christian-Druze village in Galilee
RAMALLAH Arab town north of Jerusalem
RAMATAIM suburb of Hod-Hasharon, 1925
RAMAT-DAVID kibbutz in Sorek Valley, 1926
RAMAT-GAN town east of Tel-Aviv, 1922
RAMAT-HADAR village in southern Sharon, 1938
RAMAT-HADASSA children's village near Haifa, 1950
RAMAT-HAKOVESH kibbutz in Sharon near Kefar-Sava, 1932
RAMAT-HASHARON town in southern Sharon, 1923
RAMAT-HASHOFET kibbutz in the Hills of Menashé, 1940
RAMAT-PINKAS settlement near Tel-Aviv, 1952
RAMAT-RAḤEL kibbutz south of Jerusalem, 1926
RAMAT-RAZIEL settlement west of Jerusalem, 1948

RAMAT-TIOMKIN suburb of Netanya, 1942
RAMAT-YISHAI village in Jezreel Valley, 1926
RAMAT-YIẒḤAK suburb of Ramat-Gan, 1950
RAMAT-YOḤANAN kibbutz in Zevulun Valley, 1932
RAMAT-ẒEVI moshav in Lower Galilee, 1942
RAMIM kibbutz in Upper Galilee, 1943
RAMLA town in coastal plain, 716
RAM-ON moshav in Jezreel Valley
RAMOT-HASHAVIM moshav in southern Sharon, 1933
RAMOT-MEIR moshav near Reḥovot, 1949
RAMOT-MENASHÉ kibbutz in the Hills of Menashé, 1948
RAMOT-NAFTALI moshav in Upper Galilee, 1945
RANNEN moshav in Negev, west of Beersheba, 1950
RAS ABU-RUDEIS point in Sinai desert
RAS-NAẒRANI small peninsula on Red Sea coast facing Tiran
RAS-SUDAR point in western Sinai desert
RECHASIM settlement near Haifa, 1951
REGAVIM kibbutz in Hills of Menashé, 1948
REGBA moshav near Nahariya, 1946
REḤAVA moshav in the South near Kiryat-Gat, 1953
REḤOV moshav in Beit-Shean Valley, 1951
REḤOVOT town in the South, 1890
RE'IM kibbutz near Gaza Strip, 1949
REINA Christian village in Lower Galilee near Nazareth,
RESHAFIM kibbutz in Beit-Shean Valley, 1948
RESHEF suburb of Herẓliya, 1949
REVADIM kibbutz in the South, 1949
REVAYA moshav in Beit-Shean Valley, 1943
REVIVIM kibbutz in Negev near Beersheba, 1943
RIḤANIYA Circassian village in Upper Galilee
RINNATYA moshav east of Lod airport, 1949
RISHON-LEẒIYON town south of Tel-Aviv, 1882
RISHPON moshav in the southern Sharon, 1936
ROGELIT moshav in Adullam region, 1958
ROMANI station on Gaza-Kantara highway
ROSH-HA'AYIN settlement east of Petaḥ-Tikva, 1950
ROSH-HANIKRA kibbutz in Western Galilee, 1949
ROSH-PINNA settlement in Upper Galilee, 1882
RUḤAMA kibbutz in the South, 1911, 1944
RUMMANA Moslem village in Galilee near Nazareth

SA'AD kibbutz in Negev near Gaza Strip, 1947
SA'AR kibbutz east of Nahariya, 1948
SACHNIN Moslem village in Lower Galilee
SAFED Arabic name of Ẓefat (see: Ẓefat)
SAJUR Druze village in Upper Galilee
SALIM Moslem village in Jezreel Valley
SAMUA Arab village in southern Hebron Hills
SANAFIR small island at entrance to Bay of Eilat
SANDALA Moslem village in Jezreel Valley
SARID kibbutz in Jezreel Valley, 1926
SASA kibbutz in Upper Galilee, 1949
SAVYON settlement east of Tel-Aviv, 1954
SEDÉ-BOKER settlement in Negev, 1952
SEDÉ-DAVID moshav in the south, 1955
SEDÉ-ELI'EZER moshav in Upper Galilee
SEDÉ-ELIAHU kibbutz in Beit-Shean Valley, 1939
SEDÉ-ḤEMED moshav in Sharon near Kefar-Sava, 1952 —
SEDÉ-ILAN moshav in Lower Galilee, 1949
SEDÉ-MOSHE moshav in the South, 1955
SEDÉ-NAḤUM kibbutz in Jezreel Valley, 1937
SEDÉ-NEḤAMIA kibbutz in Ḥula Valley, 1940
SEDEROT town in the South near Gaza Strip, 1951
SEDÉ-TERUMOT moshav in Beit-Shean Valley, 1951
SEDÉ-UZIYA moshav in the South near Ashkelon, 1950
SEDÉ-WARBURG moshav in Sharon near Kefar-Sava, 1938
SEDÉ-YA'AKOV moshav in Jezreel Valley, 1927
SEDÉ-YIẒḤAK moshav in Sharon near Ḥadera, 1952
SEDÉ-YOAV kibbutz in the South near Ashkelon, 1952
SEDÉ-ẒEVI moshav in the South near Beersheba, 1953
SEDOM Hebrew name of SODOM
SEDOT-MICHA moshav in the South near Beit-Shemesh, 1955
SEDOT-YAM kibbutz near Caesarea on Mediterranean coast, 1940
SEGEV moshav in Upper Galilee, 1953
SEGULA moshav in the South, 1953
SEMADAR moshav in Galilee near Yavneel, 1950
SHA'AB Moslem village in Lower Galilee
SHA'AFAT Arab village on Jerusalem-Ramallah highway
SHA'ALVIM kibbutz east of Ramla, 1949
SHA'ANAN moshav in the South near Kiryat-Gat, 1955
SHA'AR-EFRAIM moshav in Sharon, 1953
SHA'AR-HA'AMAKIM kibbutz near Haifa, 1935
SHA'AR HAGOLAN kibbutz in Jordan Valley, 1937
SHA'AR ḤEFER moshav east of Netanya, 1940
SHA'AR-MENASHÉ village for the aged in Sharon, 1953
SHADMOT-DEVORA moshav in Lower Galilee, 1939
SHAF'AMER Christian-Druze town in Galilee
SHAFIR moshav in the South near Ashkelon, 1949
SHAḤAR moshav in the South near Ashkelon, 1955
SHAḤARIYA formerly a farm near Kiryat-Gat, 1958
SHALVA moshav in the South near Kiryat-Gat, 1952
SHAMIR kibbutz in the Ḥula Valley, 1944
SHARM ESH-SHEIKH bay at southern tip of Sinai
SHARONA moshav in Lower Galilee, 1913, 1938
SHARSHERET moshav in the Negev, 1946
SHAVEI-ẒIYON moshav in Western Galilee, 1938
SHAVIV suburb of Herẓliya, 1950
SHEAR-YASHUV moshav in Ḥula Valley, 1944
SHECHEM (NABLUS) Arab town in Samaria
SHEDEMA moshav in the South near Gedera, 1955
SHEFAYIM kibbutz on the sea near Tel-Aviv, 1935
SHEFAR'AM Druze-Christian town east of Haifa
SHEFAYA children's village near Zikhron-Ya'akov, 1890
SHEFER moshav in Upper Galilee, 1950
SHEIK-DANNUN Moslem village near Nahariya
SHEKHUNAT-BEILINSON suburb of Petaḥ-Tikva, 1938
SHELOMI moshav in Western Galilee, 1950
SHELUḤOT kibbutz in Beit-Shean Valley, 1948
SHETULIM moshav in the South near Ashkelon, 1950
SHEVUT-'AM settlement east of Netanya, 1949
SHEZOR moshav in Galilee, 1953
SHIBOLIM moshav in Negev, 1953
SHIF'A farm in Beit-Shean Valley, 1955
SHOEVA moshav west of Jerusalem, 1950
SHOKEDA moshav in Negev near Gaza Strip, 1957
SHOMERA moshav in Upper Galilee, 1949
SHOMERAT kibbutz in Western Galilee, 1948
SHORESH moshav west of Jerusalem, 1948
SHOSHANAT-HA'AMAKIM village near Netanya, 1956
SHOVAL kibbutz in the South, 1946
SHUNEM Hebrew name of the Moslem village Sulam
SHUVA moshav in Negev near Gaza Strip, 1950
SIFSUFA moshav in Upper Galilee, 1949
SITRIYA moshav south of Ramla, 1949
SODOM 75 m. under Dead Sea, 1934
SULAM Moslem village east of 'Afula

TABGHA Benedictine monastery on Lake Kinneret
TABOR monastery and basilica on Mount Tabor
TALMEI-BILU moshav in Negev near Beersheba, 1953
TALMEI-EL'AZAR moshav in Sharon east of Ḥadera, 1952
TALMEI-MENASHÉ moshav west of Ramla, 1950
TALMEI-YAFÉ kibbutz in the South near Ashkelon, 1950
TALMEI-YEḤIEL moshav in the South, 1949
TAL-OR farm in the western Negev, 1954
TAL-SHAḤAR moshav in Judean Mountains, 1948
TAMRA (1) Moslem village in western Galilee
TAMRA (2) Moslem village in eastern Galilee
TANTURA Arabic name of Dor (See Dor)
TA'OZ moshav in Judean Mountains, 1950
TARSHISHA Christian-Moslem village in western Galilee
TARUM moshav in Judean Mountains, 1950
TAYIBA (1) Moslem village in Sharon near Netanya
TAYIBA (2) Moslem village in eastern Galilee
TEASHUR moshav in Negev, 1953
TEKUMA moshav in northern Negev, 1946
TEL-ADASHIM moshav in Jezreel Valley, 1913
TELAMIM moshav in the South near Ashkelon, 1950
TEL-ASHER settlement in Sharon near Kefar-Sava, 1940
TEL-AVIV—YAFO biggest town in Israel, 1909
TEL-ḤAI youth hostel in Galilee, 1916, 1960
TEL-ḤANAN urban settlement near Haifa, 1948
TEL-HASHOMER hospital near Tel-Aviv, 1934
TEL-KAẒIR kibbutz in the Jordan Valley, 1949
TEL-LETVINSKY urban settlement near Tel-Aviv, 1934
TEL-MILH Beduin settlement near Beersheba
TEL-MOND (1) settlement in southern Sharon, 1929
TEL-MOND (2) prison west of Tel-Mond
TEL-YIẒḤAK kibbutz in central Sharon, 1938
TEL-YOSEF kibbutz in Jezreel Valley, 1921
TEL-ẒUR suburb of Even-Yehuda, 1932
TENUVOT moshav in Sharon, near Netanya, 1952
TERKUMIE Arab village at foot of western Judean Mountains
TEVERIYA Hebrew name of Tiberias
TIBERIAS biggest town in Lower Galilee
TIDHAR moshav in northern Negev, 1953
TIFRAḤ moshav in northern Negev, 1949
TIMN'A copper mine and plant near Eilat, 1955
TIMORIM moshav in the South, 1955
TIMRAT farm in Jezreel Valley near Nahalal, 1955
TIRA Moslem village in southern Sharon
TIRAN small island at entrance to Gulf of Eilat
TIRAT-CARMEL suburb south of Haifa, 1949
TIRAT-SHALOM moshav near Nes-Ẓiyona, 1931
TIRAT-YA'EL farm in Upper Galilee, 1949
TIRAT-YEHUDA moshav near Lod airport, 1949
TIRAT-ẒEVI kibbutz in Beit-Shean Valley, 1937
TIROSH moshav in the South, 1955
TIVON northern part of Kiryat-Tivon, 1935
TOḤELET settlement near Tel-Aviv, 1951
TUBA Moslem-Beduin village in Upper Galilee
TUBAS Arab village in eastern Samaria
TUL-KAREM Arab town on border of Samaria and Sharon
TUR'AN Moslem village in Lower Galilee
TUSHIYA moshav in the Negev near Gaza Strip, 1958

UDIM moshav in Sharon near Netanya, 1948
UM-BOGMA mining area in western Sinai
UMM ELFAHEM Moslem village in 'Iron Valley
UMM ELGHANAM Moslem village on Mt. Tabor
UMM ELKUFUF Moslem village in 'Iron Valley
URIEL suburb of Gedera, 1949
URIM kibbutz in Negev west of Beersheba, 1946
USHA kibbutz in Zevulun Valley near Haifa, 1937
'UZA moshav in the South near Kiryat-Gat, 1950
'UZEIR Moslem village in Lower Galilee, near Nazareth

VERED-HAGALIL farm in Upper Galilee, 1960

WADI-ELHAMAM Moslem village in Galilee near Tiberias
WADI-ELKASSAB Moslem village in 'Iron Valley
WILHELMA previous name of Benei-'Atarot

YA'ABED Arab village in northern Samaria
YA'ARA moshav east of Nahariya, 1950
YA'AROT-HACARMEL farm on Mount Carmel, 1934
YAD-BINYAMIN youth village in the South, 1960
YAD-ḤANNA (1) kibbutz east of Netanya, 1950
YAD-ḤANNA (2) kibbutz east of Netanya, 1954
YAD-MORDECHAI kibbutz near Ashkelon, 1943
YAD-NATAN moshav in the South, Lachish region, 1953
YAD-RAMBAM moshav near Ramla, 1955
YA'EL settlement in Jezreel Valley, 1960
YAFA (1) Arabic name of Yafo. See Yafo
YAFA (2) Arab village in Galilee near Nazareth
YAFO city on Mediterranean Coast
YAGEL moshav near Lod, 1950
YAGUR kibbutz near Haifa, 1922
YAKHINI moshav in the South near Gaza, 1950
YAKUM kibbutz in Sharon near Netanya, 1947
YAMMA Moslem village in Sharon
YANUH Druze village in Galilee
YANUV moshav east of Netanya, 1950
YARDENA moshav in Jordan Valley, 1952
YARḤIV moshav near Kefar-Sava, 1949
YARKONA moshav in southern Sharon, 1932
YASHRESH moshav south of Ramla, 1951
YA'SUR kibbutz in Galilee near 'Akko, 1949
YAVNÉ townlet in the South near Reḥovot, 1949
YAVNEEL village in Lower Galilee, 1901
YAVOR farm in Zevulun Valley, 1952
YAẒIV suburb of Kadima in Sharon, 1952
YAZIZ moshav in the vicinity of Ramla, 1950
YEDIDIA moshav in Ḥefer Valley, 1935
YEḤI'AM kibbutz in Western Galilee, 1946
YEHUD settlement near Lod airport, 1949
YEMIN-ORDE children's village on Mount Carmel, 1950
YEROḤAM town in Negev near Beersheba, 1951
YESH'A moshav in Negev near Gaza Strip, 1957
YESODOT kibbutz in Judean Mountains, 1948
YESUD-HAMA'ALA village in Upper Galilee, 1883
YEVULA farm in Negev near Beersheba, 1956
YIF'AT kibbutz in Jezreel Valley, 1952
YIFTAH kibbutz in Upper Galilee, 1948
YIKKON moshav in central Sharon, 1950
YINNON moshav in the South, 1952
YIRKA Druze village in western Galilee
YIRON kibbutz in Upper Galilee, 1949
YISH'I moshav near Beit-Shemesh, 1950
YIZRE'AM farm on Gaza—Beersheba highway, 1953
YIZRE'EL kibbutz in Jezreel Valley, 1949
YOKNE'AM settlement in Jezreel Valley, 1936
YOSHIVYA moshav in the northern Negev, 1950
YOTVATA kibbutz in 'Arava, north of Eilat, 1951
YUVAL moshav in Ḥula Valley, 1952

ẒAFRIRIM moshav near Beit-Shemesh, 1958
ẒAFRIYA moshav near Tel-Aviv, 1949
ẒAHAL previous name of Liman, 1949
ẒAHALA suburb of Tel-Aviv in Sharon, 1952
ZALAFA Moslem village near Megiddo
ZANOAH moshav in Judean Mountains, 1950
ZAR'IT moshav in Upper Galilee, 1967
ZARNUKA western suburb of Reḥovot, 1949
ZAVDIEL moshav in the South near Kiryat-Gat, 1950
ẒEFAT biggest town in Upper Galilee
ZEḤELIM kibbutz in the Negev, 1947
ZEKHARYA moshav south of Beit-Shemesh, 1950
ZEKHER-DOV previous name of Misgav-Dov, 1950
ẒELAFON moshav in Judean Mountains, 1950
ẒEMAKH police station on Lake Kinneret
ZEMUROT moshav in the South near Ashkelon, 1955
ZERAḤYA moshav in the South, 1950
ẒERIFIN camp near Tel-Aviv, 1917
ZERU'A moshav in the northern Negev, 1953
ẒERUFA moshav on Carmel coast, 1949
ZIKHRON-YA'AKOV settlement on Mount Carmel, 1882
ZIKIM kibbutz in the South near Gaza Strip, 1949
ZIMRAT moshav in the northern Negev, 1957
ẒIPORI moshav in Lower Galilee, 1949
ẒOFIT moshav in southern Sharon, 1933
ZOHAR moshav in the South near Ashkelon, 1956
ẒOR'A kibbutz in Judean Mountains, 1949
ẒOVA kibbutz west of Jerusalem, 1948
ẒUR-HADASSA settlement south of Jerusalem, 1960
ẒURIEL moshav in Upper Galilee, 1950
ẒUR-MOSHÉ moshav in Sharon near Netanya, 1938
ẒUR-NATAN settlement in eastern Sharon, 1966
ẒUR-SHALOM settlement in Zevulun Valley, 1935